Shojo Beat

ORESAMA TEACHER

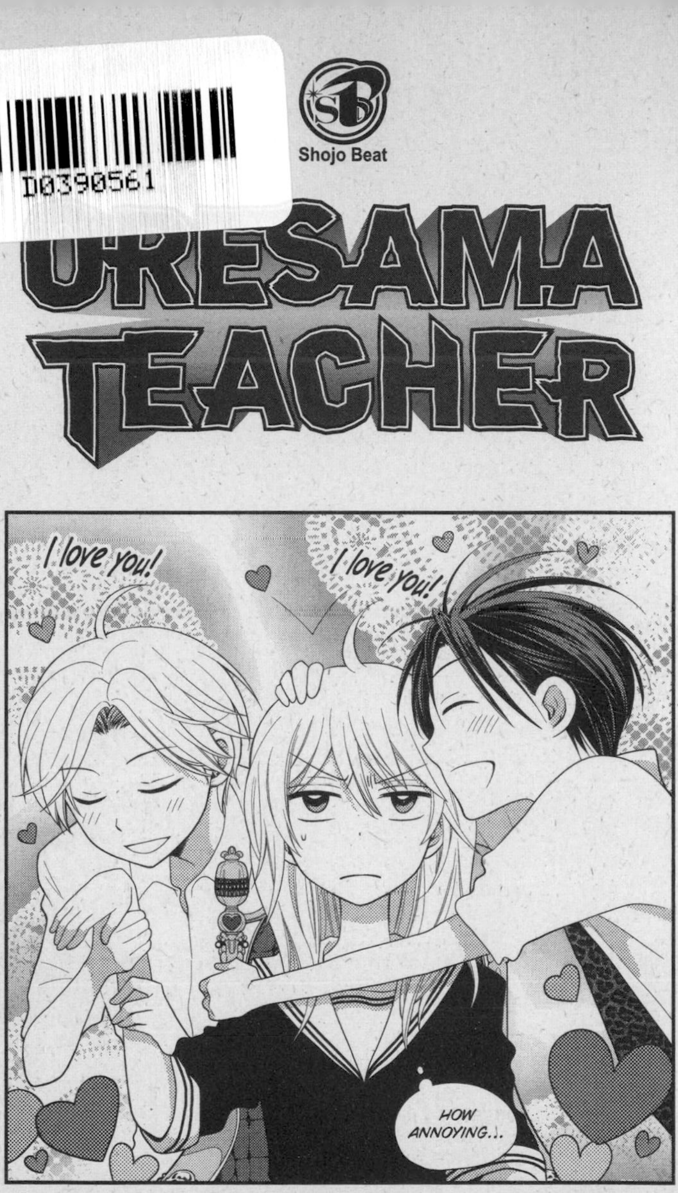
I love you!
I love you!
HOW ANNOYING...

Vol. 5

Story & Art by

Izumi Tsubaki

little free library

NORTHERN LIGHTS LIBRARY SYSTEM

Scan me

ORESAMA TEACHER

Story & Characters

Mafuyu Kurosaki was the successful leader of a high school gang who united Saitama Prefecture under her flag. But she got too active in her role and was caught by the police. When her angry mother "suggested" she transfer to the remote Midorigaoka Academy, Mafuyu saw it as her chance for a sparkling new start.

Unfortunately, her childhood friend Takaomi Saeki is her new homeroom teacher—the very person who set her on the path to delinquency! With Takaomi around, Mafuyu's high school life once again starts to stray from the straight and narrow.

Mafuyu fights to save her first new friend, Hayasaka, from his troubles. But in order to hide her identity, she wears a rabbit mask and becomes **Super Bun**...

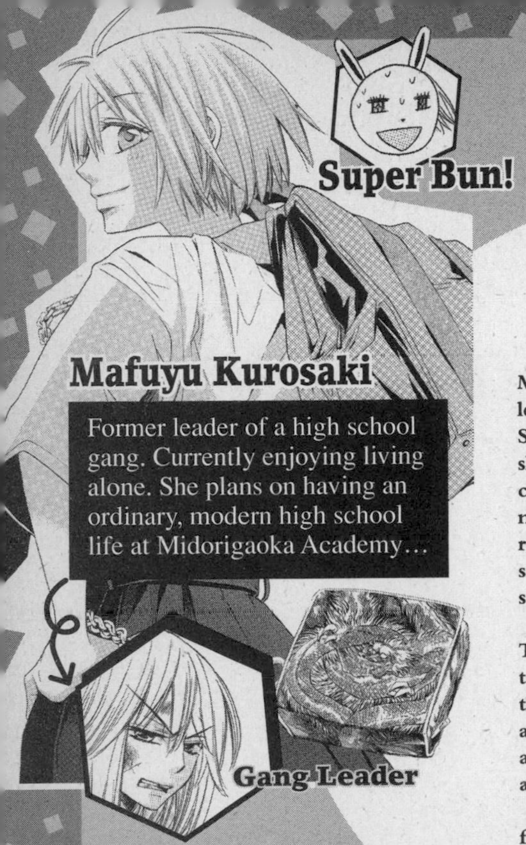
Super Bun!
Gang Leader

Mafuyu Kurosaki

Former leader of a high school gang. Currently enjoying living alone. She plans on having an ordinary, modern high school life at Midorigaoka Academy...

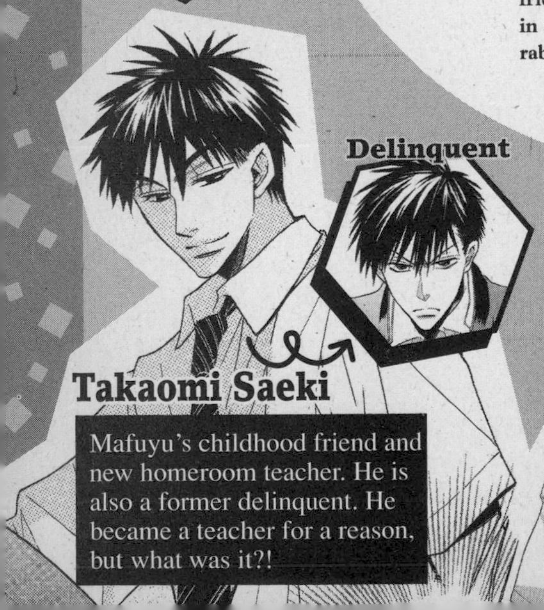
Delinquent

Takaomi Saeki

Mafuyu's childhood friend and new homeroom teacher. He is also a former delinquent. He became a teacher for a reason, but what was it?!

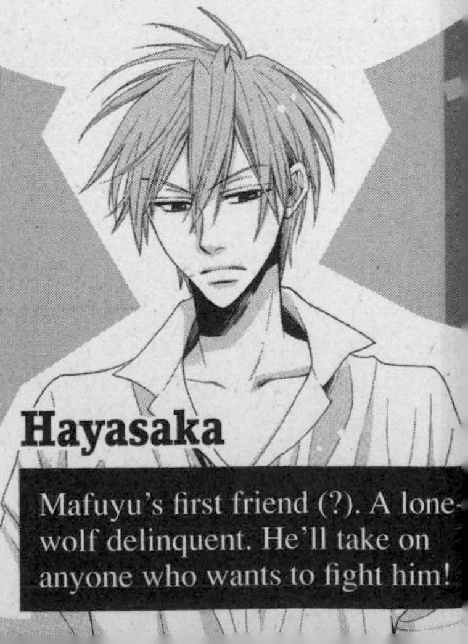

Hayasaka

Mafuyu's first friend (?). A lone-wolf delinquent. He'll take on anyone who wants to fight him!

ORESAMA TEACHER

Volume 5
CONTENTS

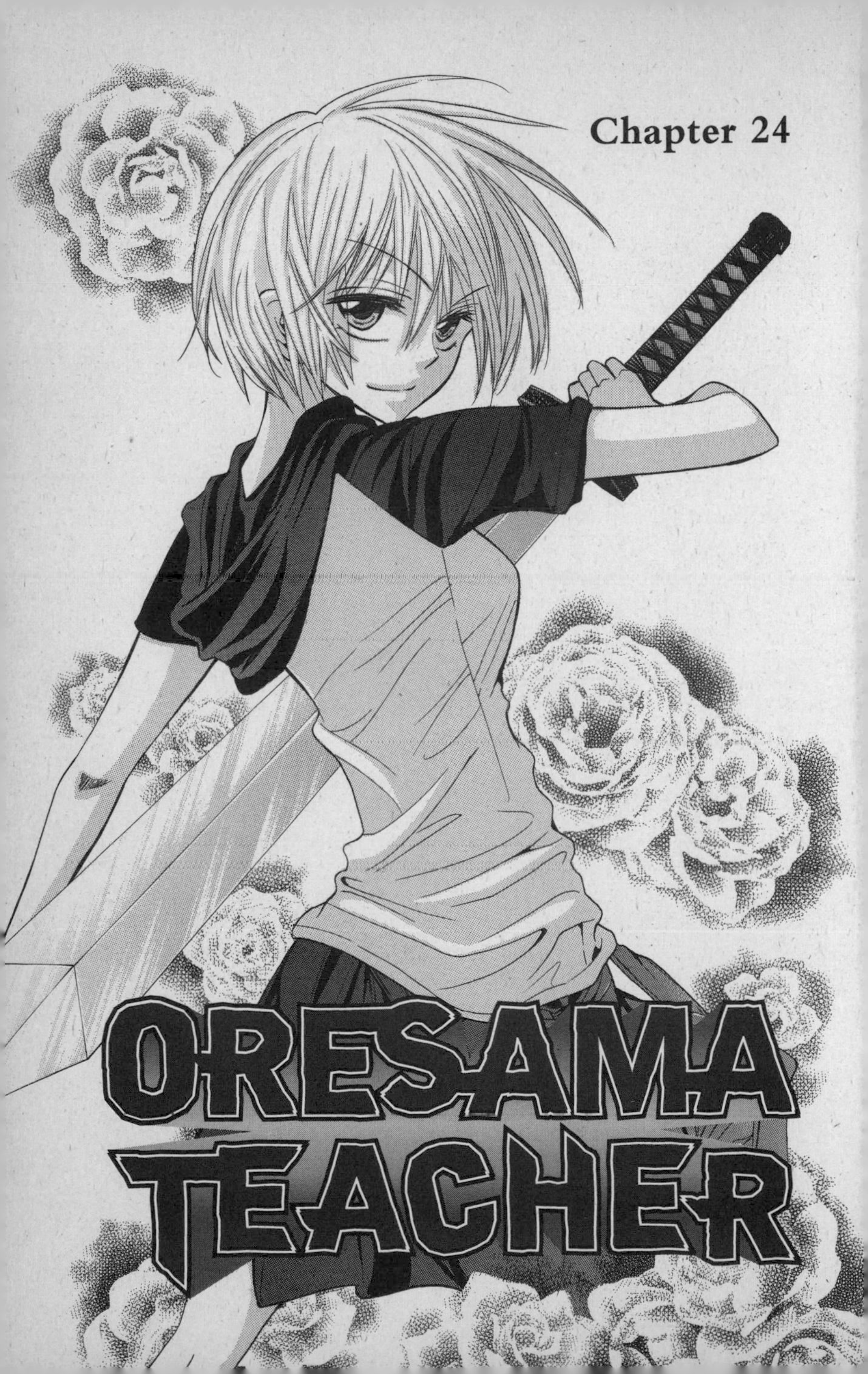
Chapter 24
ORESAMA
TEACHER

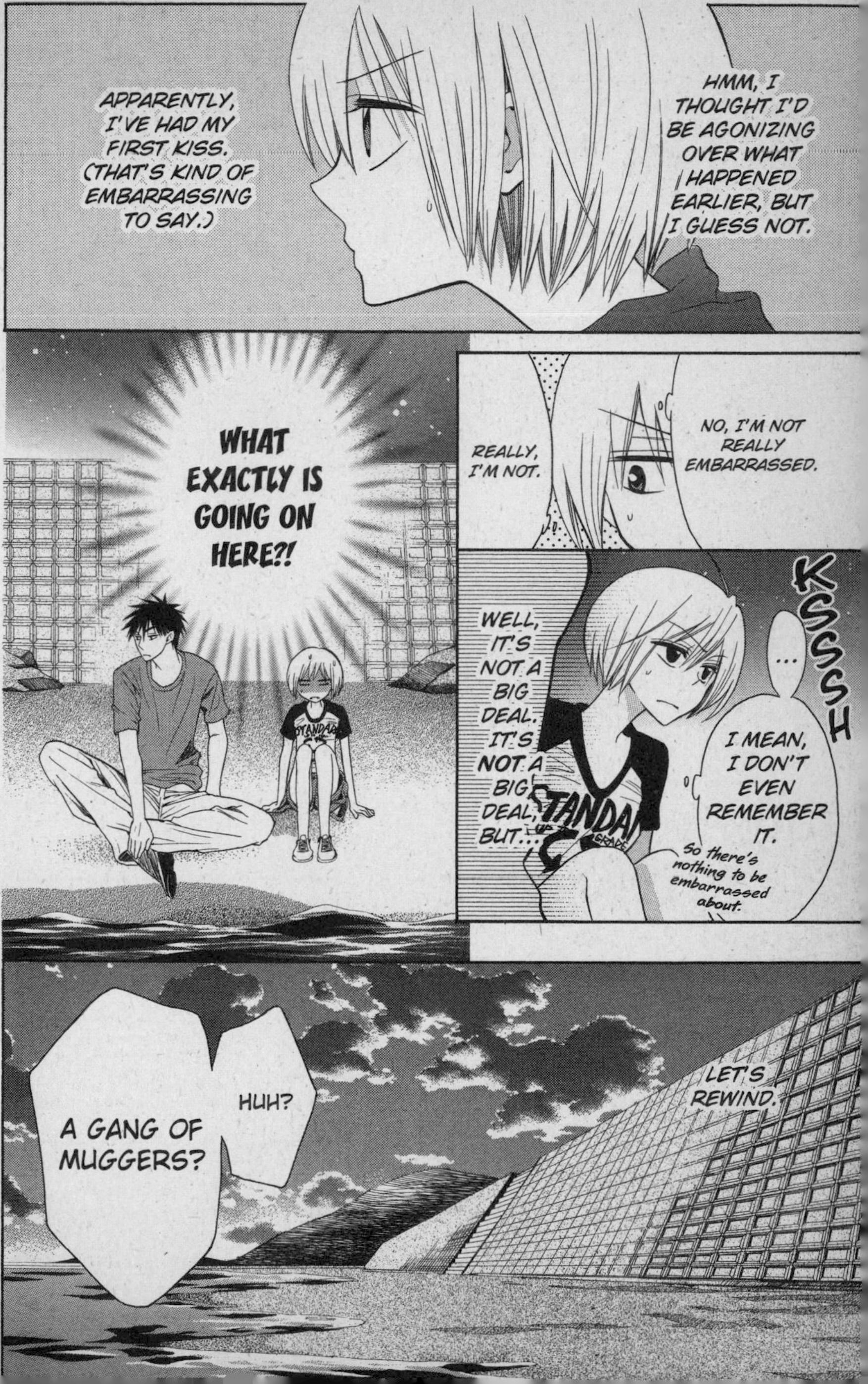
HMM, I THOUGHT I'D BE AGONIZING OVER WHAT HAPPENED EARLIER, BUT I GUESS NOT.
APPARENTLY, I'VE HAD MY FIRST KISS. (THAT'S KIND OF EMBARRASSING TO SAY.)
NO, I'M NOT REALLY EMBARRASSED.
REALLY, I'M NOT.
KSSSH
...
I MEAN, I DON'T EVEN REMEMBER IT.
So there's nothing to be embarrassed about.
WELL, IT'S NOT A BIG DEAL. IT'S NOT A BIG DEAL, BUT...
WHAT EXACTLY IS GOING ON HERE?!
LET'S REWIND.
HUH?
A GANG OF MUGGERS?

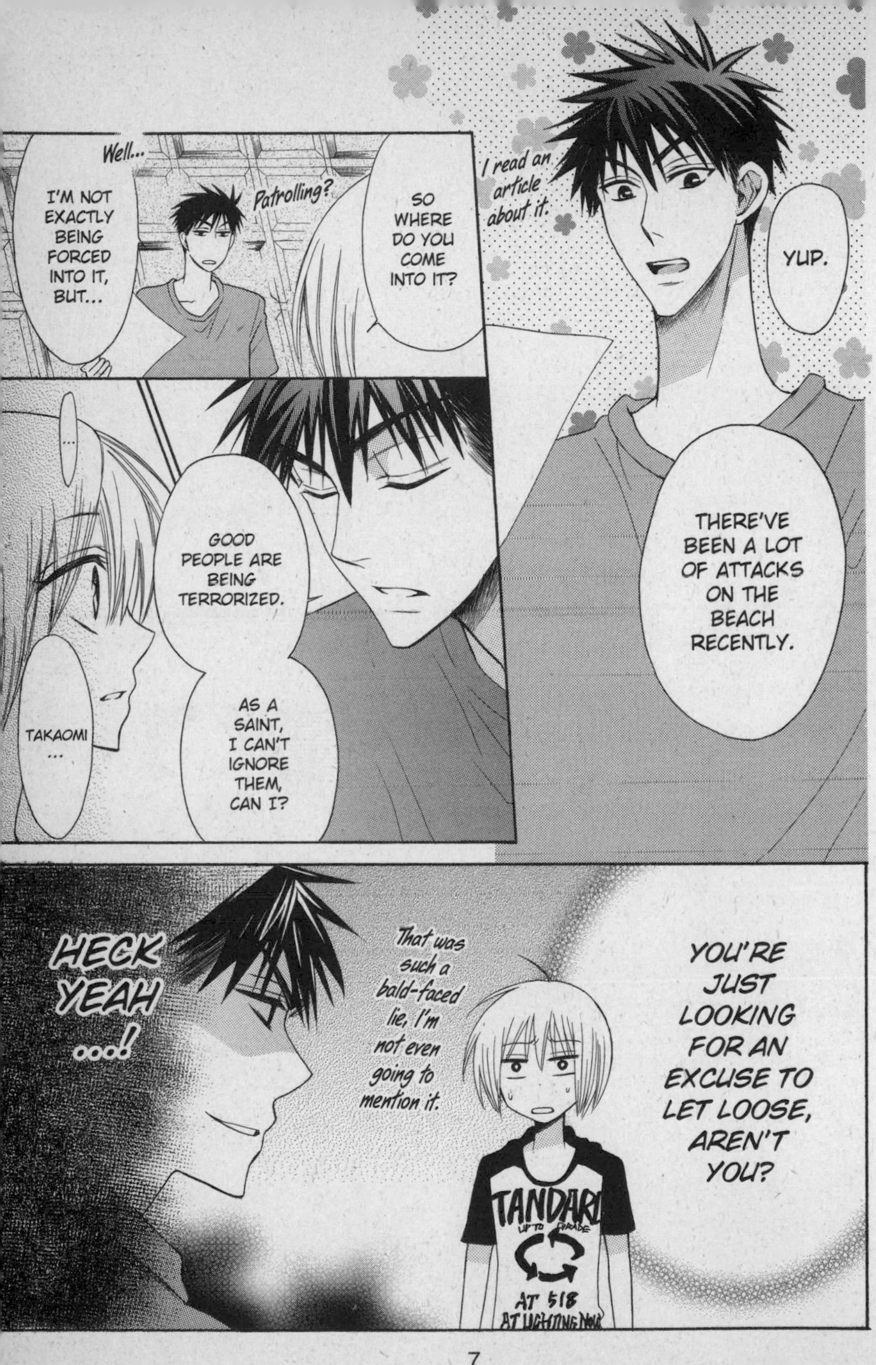
YUP.
I read an article about it.
THERE'VE BEEN A LOT OF ATTACKS ON THE BEACH RECENTLY.
SO WHERE DO YOU COME INTO IT?
Patrolling?
Well...
I'M NOT EXACTLY BEING FORCED INTO IT, BUT...
GOOD PEOPLE ARE BEING TERRORIZED.
...
AS A SAINT, I CAN'T IGNORE THEM, CAN I?
TAKAOMI...
YOU'RE JUST LOOKING FOR AN EXCUSE TO LET LOOSE, AREN'T YOU?
That was such a bald-faced lie, I'm not even going to mention it.
HECK YEAH...!

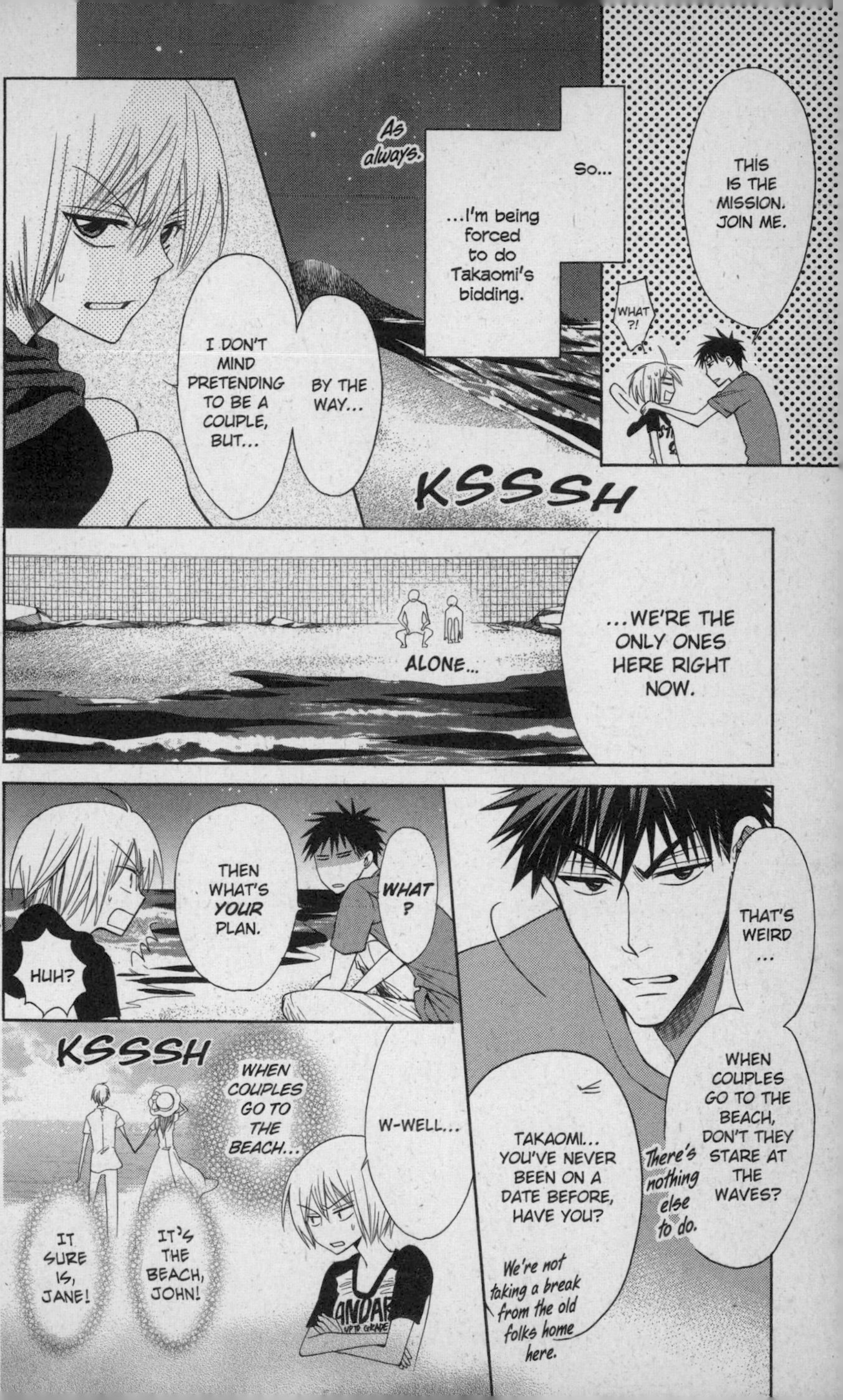
THIS IS THE MISSION. JOIN ME.
WHAT?!
So...
...I'm being forced to do Takaomi's bidding.
As always.
BY THE WAY...
I DON'T MIND PRETENDING TO BE A COUPLE, BUT...
KSSSH
...WE'RE THE ONLY ONES HERE RIGHT NOW.
ALONE...
THAT'S WEIRD...
WHAT?
THEN WHAT'S YOUR PLAN.
HUH?
WHEN COUPLES GO TO THE BEACH, DON'T THEY STARE AT THE WAVES?
There's nothing else to do.
TAKAOMI... YOU'VE NEVER BEEN ON A DATE BEFORE, HAVE YOU?
We're not taking a break from the old folks home here.
W-WELL...
WHEN COUPLES GO TO THE BEACH...
KSSSH
IT'S THE BEACH, JOHN!
IT SURE IS, JANE!

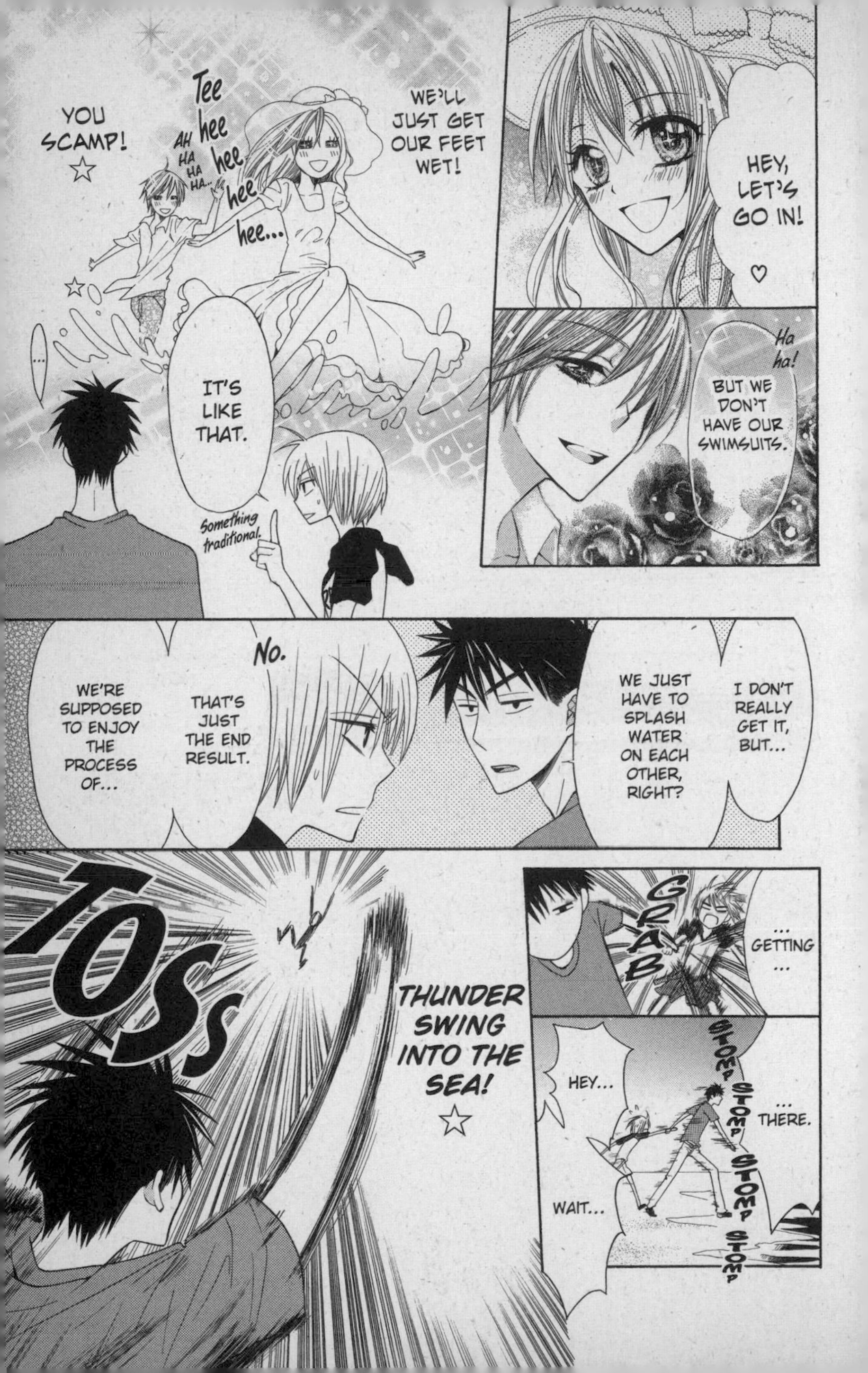
HEY, LET'S GO IN! ♡
Ha ha! BUT WE DON'T HAVE OUR SWIMSUITS.
WE'LL JUST GET OUR FEET WET!
Tee hee hee hee hee...
AH HA HA HA...
YOU SCAMP! ☆
...
IT'S LIKE THAT.
Something traditional.
I DON'T REALLY GET IT, BUT...
WE JUST HAVE TO SPLASH WATER ON EACH OTHER, RIGHT?
No.
THAT'S JUST THE END RESULT.
WE'RE SUPPOSED TO ENJOY THE PROCESS OF...
...GETTING...
GRAB
...THERE.
STOMP STOMP STOMP STOMP
HEY...
WAIT...
THUNDER SWING INTO THE SEA! ☆
TOSS

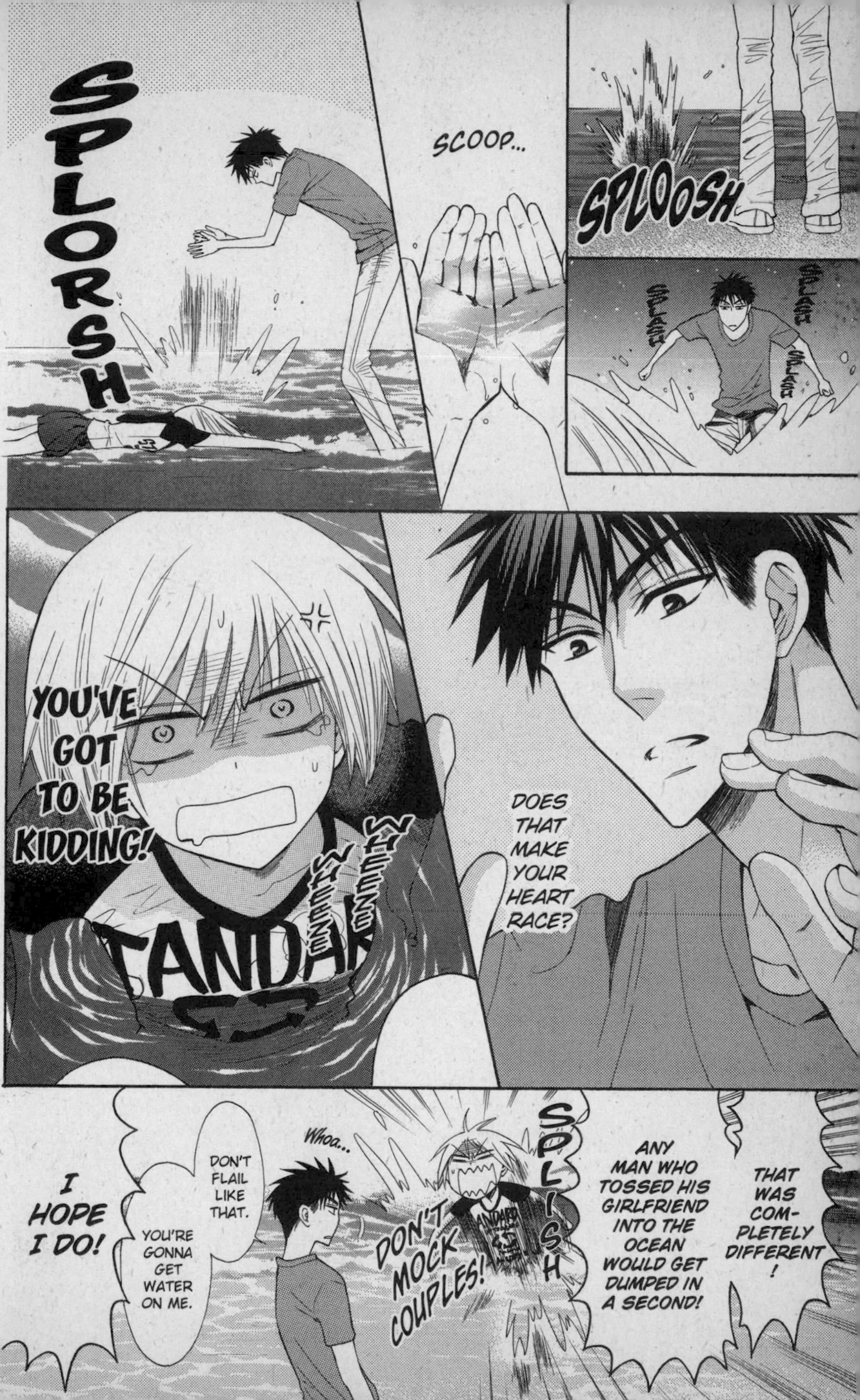
SPLOOSH
SPLASH SPLASH SPLASH
SCOOP...
SPLORSH
DOES THAT MAKE YOUR HEART RACE?
YOU'VE GOT TO BE KIDDING!
WHEEZE WHEEZE
TANDAR
THAT WAS COM- PLETELY DIFFERENT!
ANY MAN WHO TOSSED HIS GIRLFRIEND INTO THE OCEAN WOULD GET DUMPED IN A SECOND!
SPLISH
DON'T MOCK COUPLES!
Whoa...
DON'T FLAIL LIKE THAT.
YOU'RE GONNA GET WATER ON ME.
I HOPE I DO!

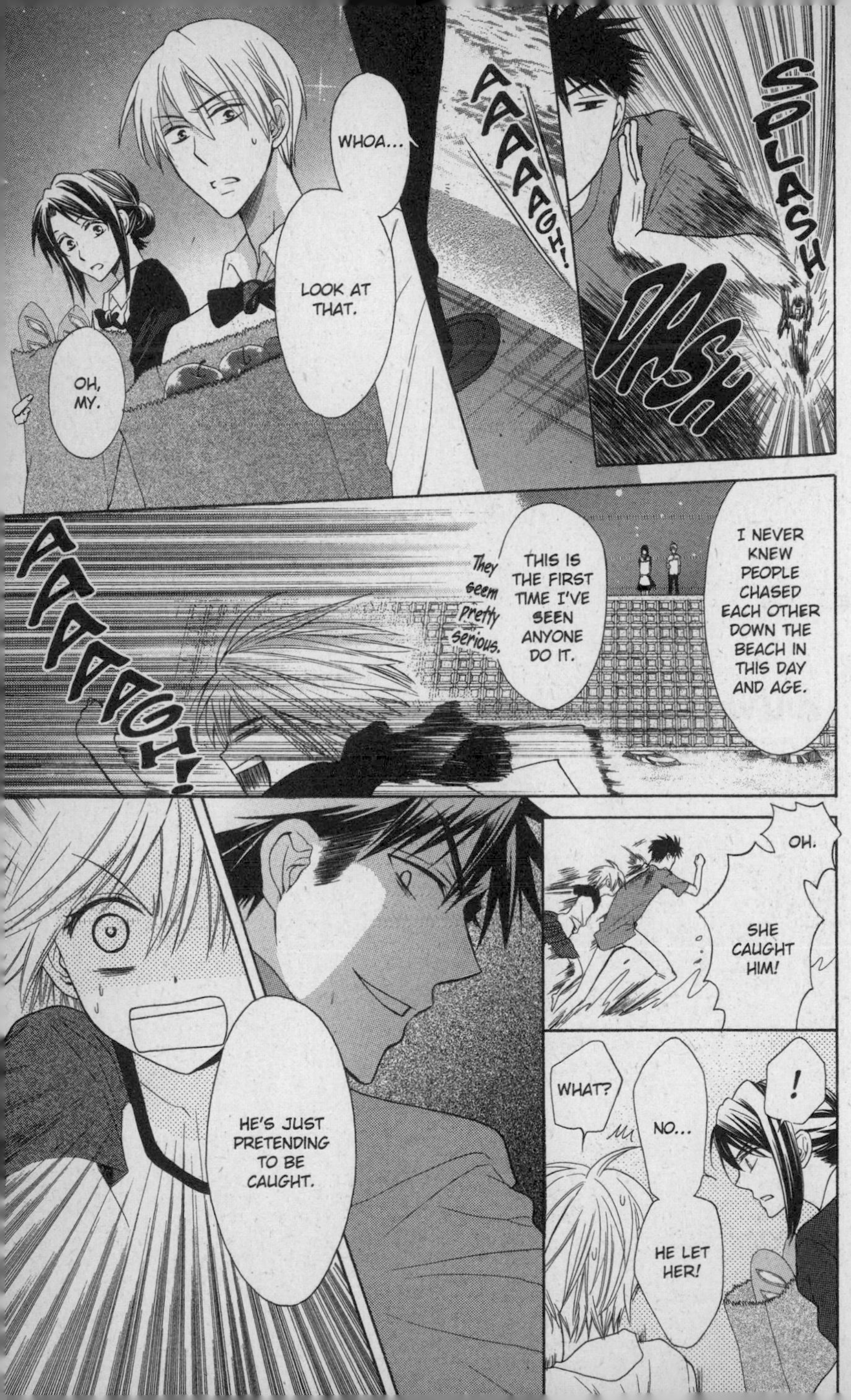
SPLASH
DASH
AAAAAGH!
WHOA...
LOOK AT THAT.
OH, MY.
I NEVER KNEW PEOPLE CHASED EACH OTHER DOWN THE BEACH IN THIS DAY AND AGE.
THIS IS THE FIRST TIME I'VE SEEN ANYONE DO IT.
They seem pretty serious.
AAAAAGH!
OH.
SHE CAUGHT HIM!
!
NO...
HE LET HER!
WHAT?
HE'S JUST PRETENDING TO BE CAUGHT.

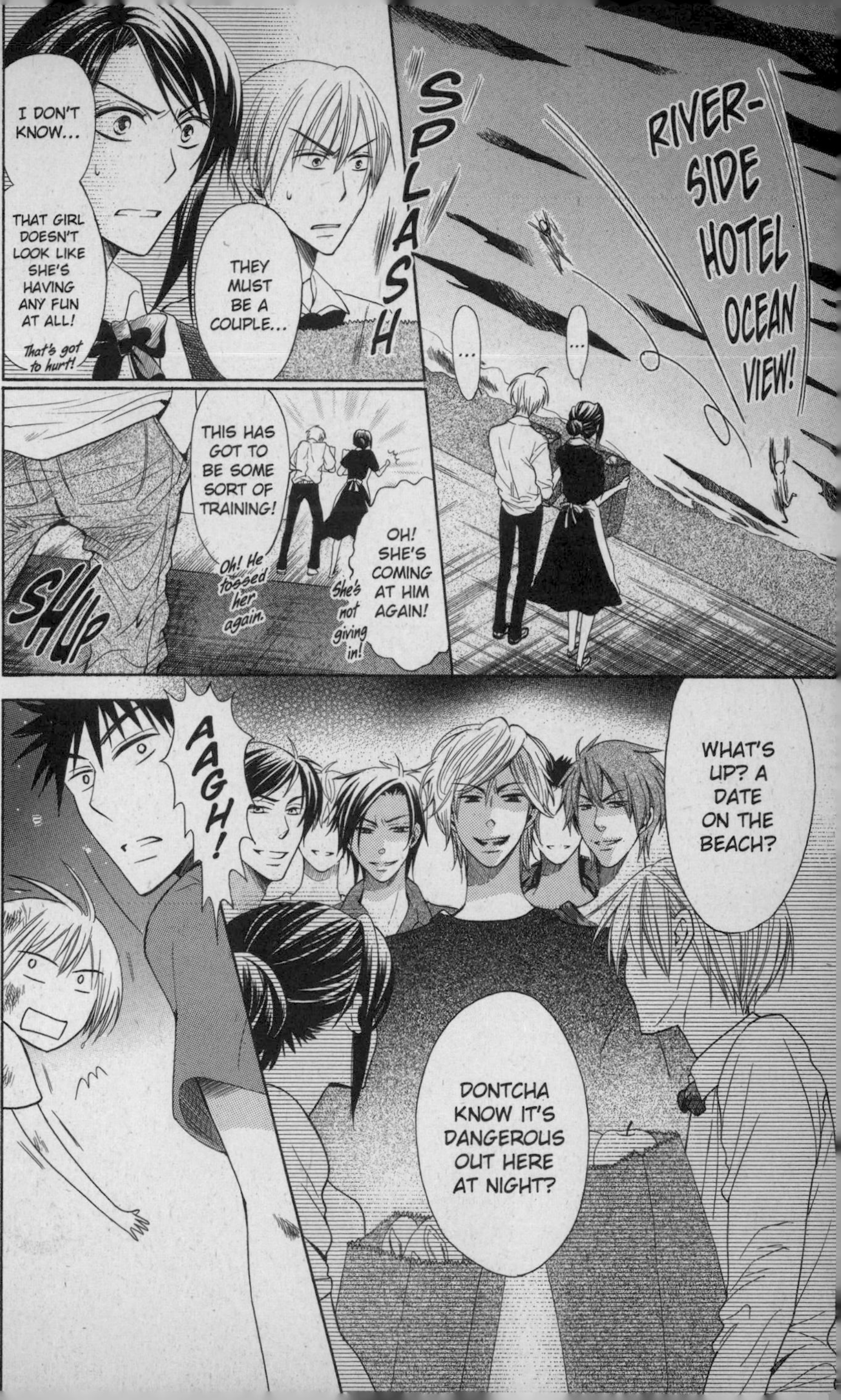
SPLASH
RIVER-SIDE HOTEL OCEAN VIEW!
...
...
THEY MUST BE A COUPLE...
I DON'T KNOW...
THAT GIRL DOESN'T LOOK LIKE SHE'S HAVING ANY FUN AT ALL!
That's got to hurt!
OH! SHE'S COMING AT HIM AGAIN!
She's not giving in!
THIS HAS GOT TO BE SOME SORT OF TRAINING!
Oh! He tossed her again.
SHUP
WHAT'S UP? A DATE ON THE BEACH?
AAGH!
DONTCHA KNOW IT'S DANGEROUS OUT HERE AT NIGHT?

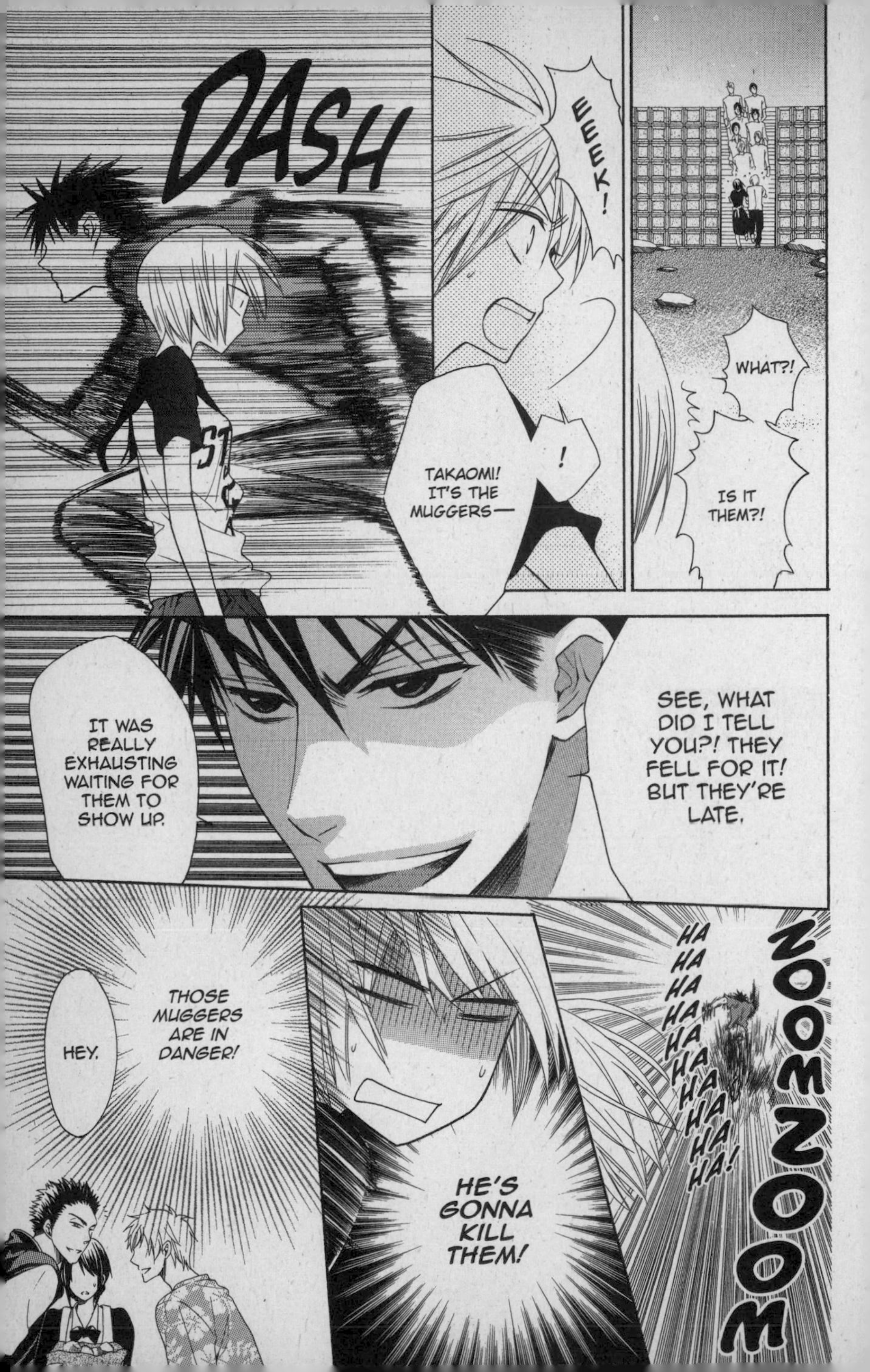
WHAT?!
IS IT THEM?!
EEEEK!
!
TAKAOMI! IT'S THE MUGGERS—
DASH
SEE, WHAT DID I TELL YOU?! THEY FELL FOR IT! BUT THEY'RE LATE.
IT WAS REALLY EXHAUSTING WAITING FOR THEM TO SHOW UP.
ZOOM ZOOM
HA HA HA HA HA HA HA HA HA HA HA!
HE'S GONNA KILL THEM!
THOSE MUGGERS ARE IN DANGER!
HEY.

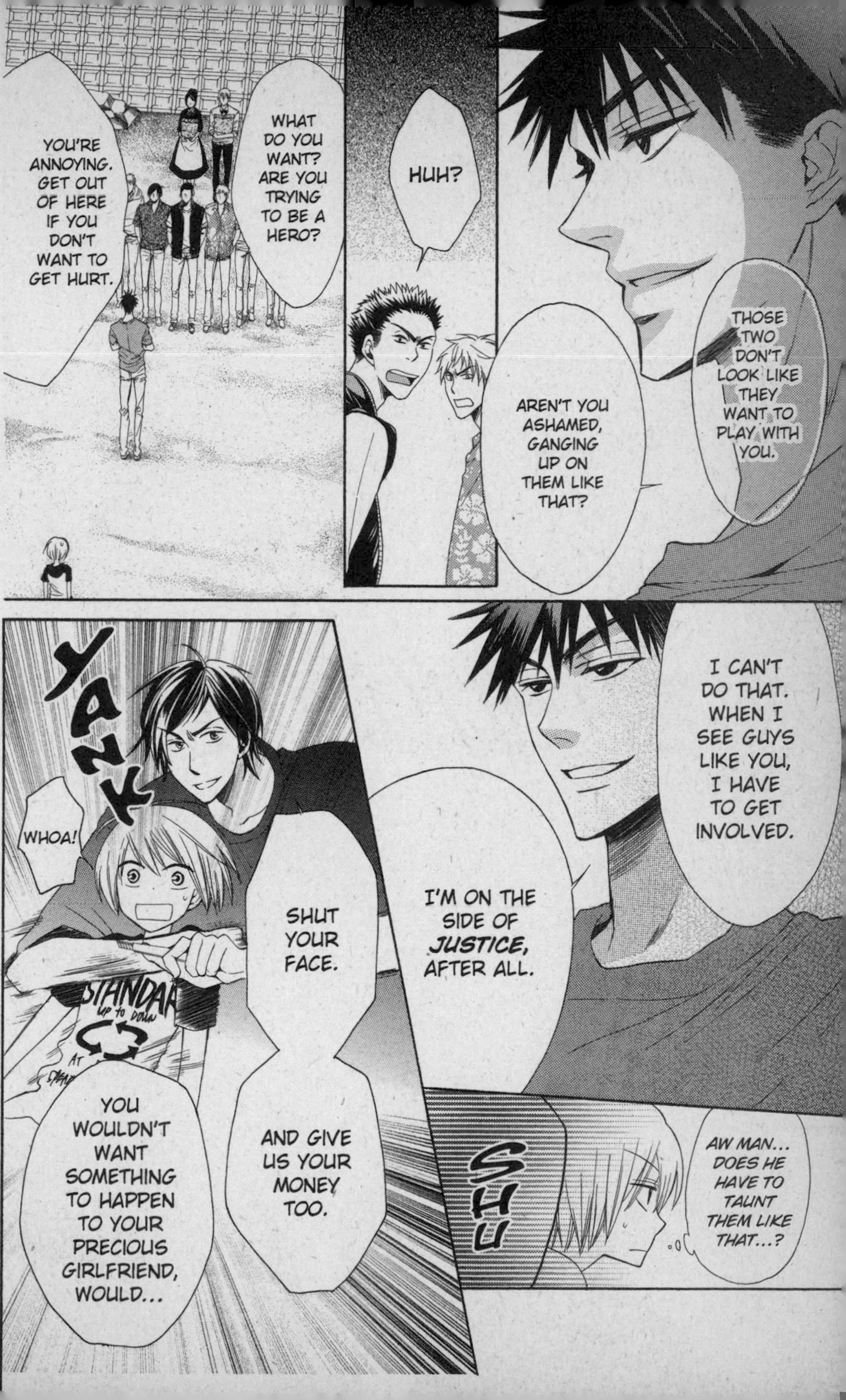
THOSE TWO DON'T LOOK LIKE THEY WANT TO PLAY WITH YOU.
AREN'T YOU ASHAMED, GANGING UP ON THEM LIKE THAT?
HUH?
WHAT DO YOU WANT? ARE YOU TRYING TO BE A HERO?
YOU'RE ANNOYING. GET OUT OF HERE IF YOU DON'T WANT TO GET HURT.
I CAN'T DO THAT. WHEN I SEE GUYS LIKE YOU, I HAVE TO GET INVOLVED.
I'M ON THE SIDE OF *JUSTICE*, AFTER ALL.
SHU
AW MAN... DOES HE HAVE TO TAUNT THEM LIKE THAT...?
YANK
WHOA!
SHUT YOUR FACE.
AND GIVE US YOUR MONEY TOO.
YOU WOULDN'T WANT SOMETHING TO HAPPEN TO YOUR PRECIOUS GIRLFRIEND, WOULD...

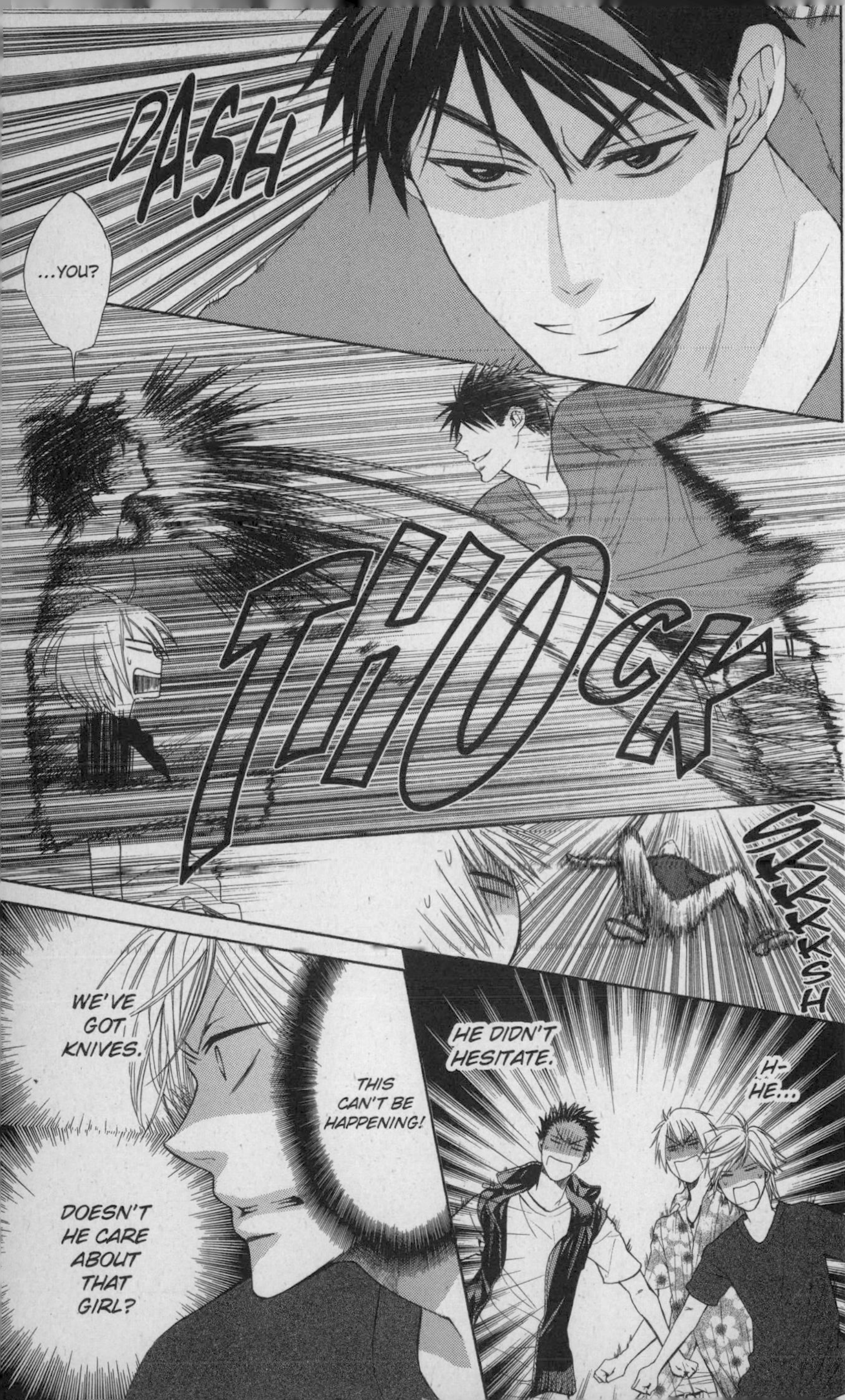
DASH
...YOU?
THOCK
SKKKKSH
H- HE...
HE DIDN'T HESITATE.
THIS CAN'T BE HAPPENING!
WE'VE GOT KNIVES.
DOESN'T HE CARE ABOUT THAT GIRL?

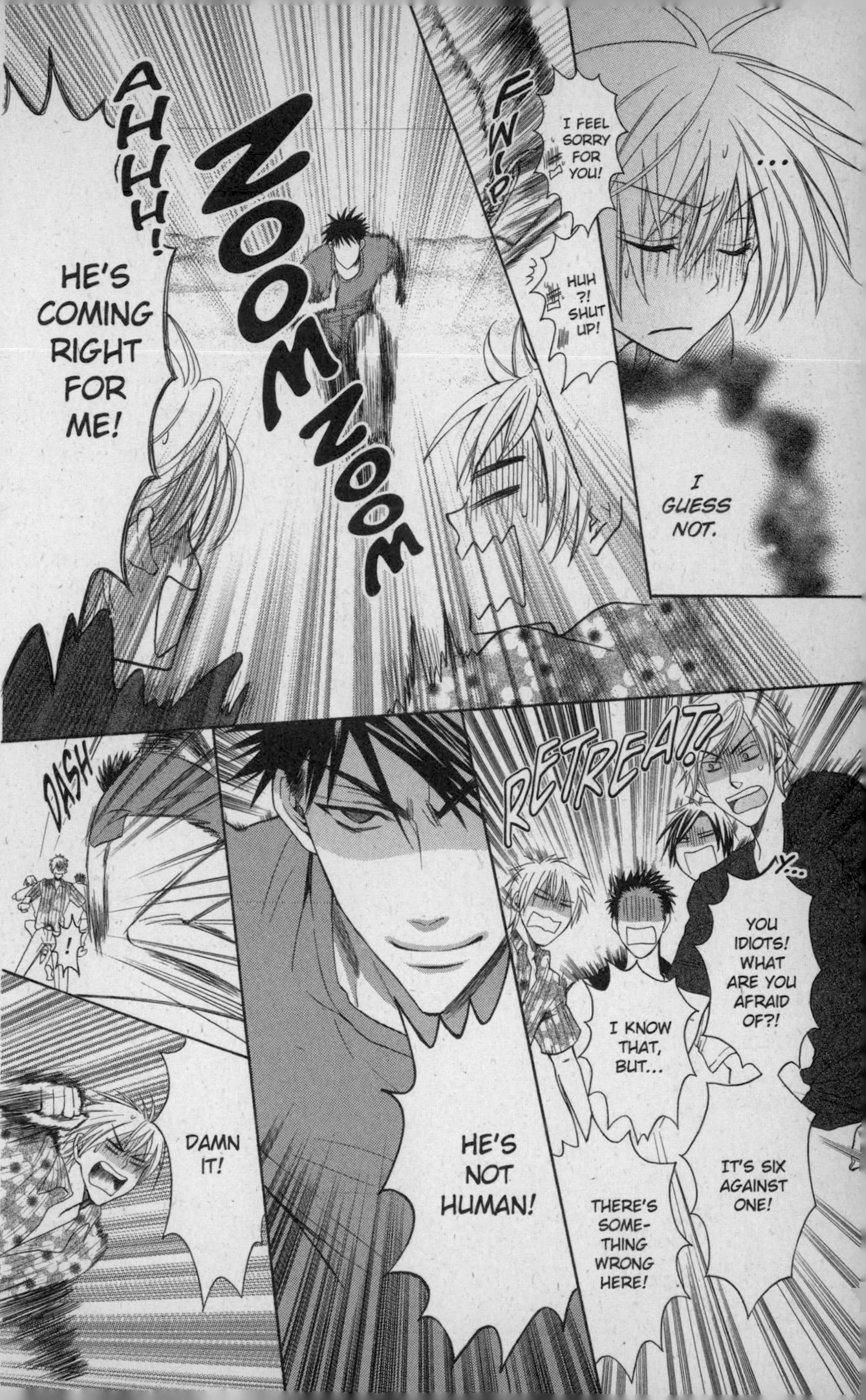
FWIP
I FEEL SORRY FOR YOU!
...
HUH ?! SHUT UP!
I GUESS NOT.
NOOMNOOM
AHHHH!
HE'S COMING RIGHT FOR ME!
RETREAT!
Y...
YOU IDIOTS! WHAT ARE YOU AFRAID OF?!
IT'S SIX AGAINST ONE!
I KNOW THAT, BUT...
THERE'S SOME-THING WRONG HERE!
HE'S NOT HUMAN!
DASH
!
DAMN IT!

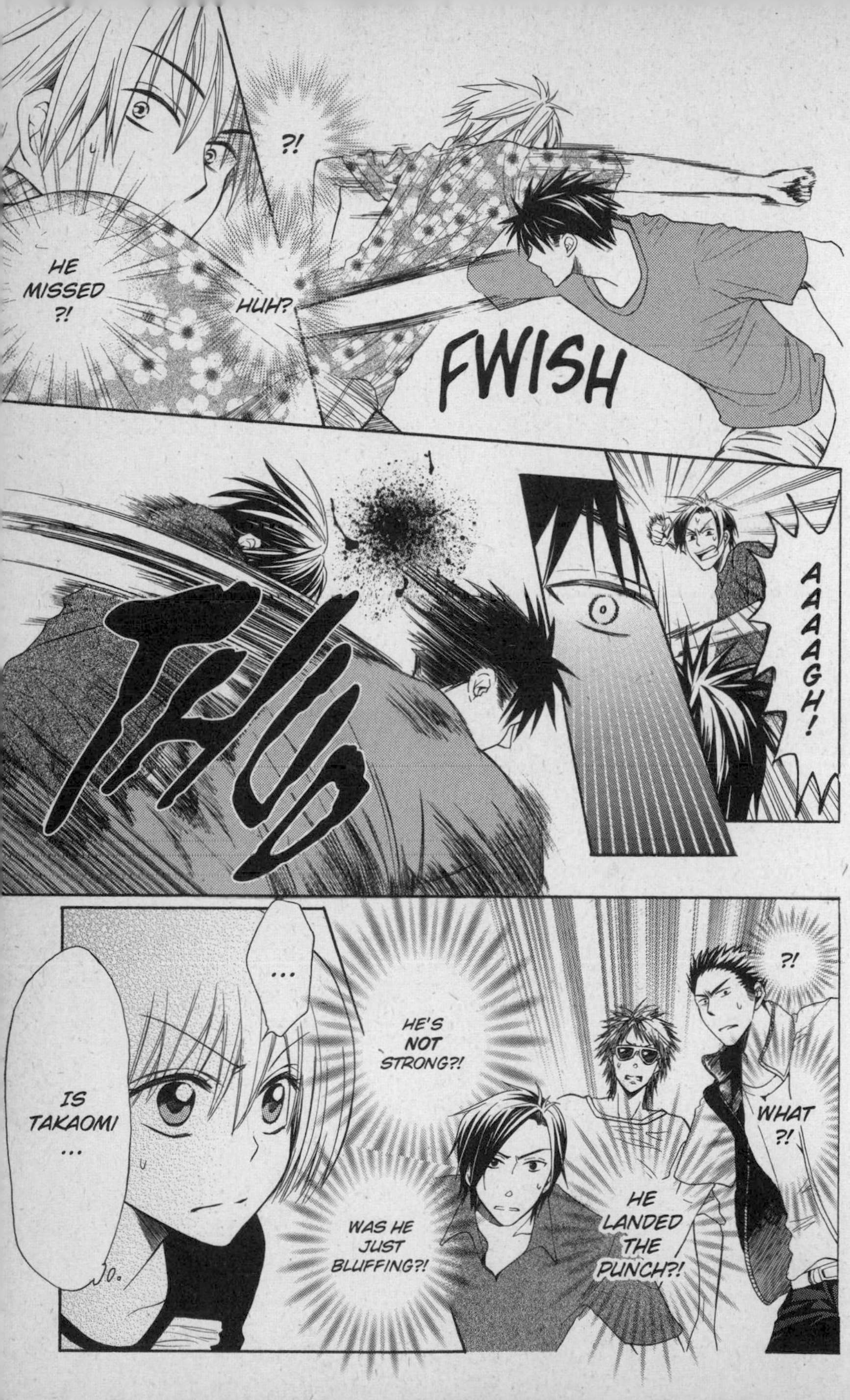
?!
HUH?
HE MISSED ?!
FWISH
AAAAGH!
THUD
?!
WHAT ?!
HE'S NOT STRONG?!
HE LANDED THE PUNCH?!
WAS HE JUST BLUFFING?!
...
IS TAKAOMI ...

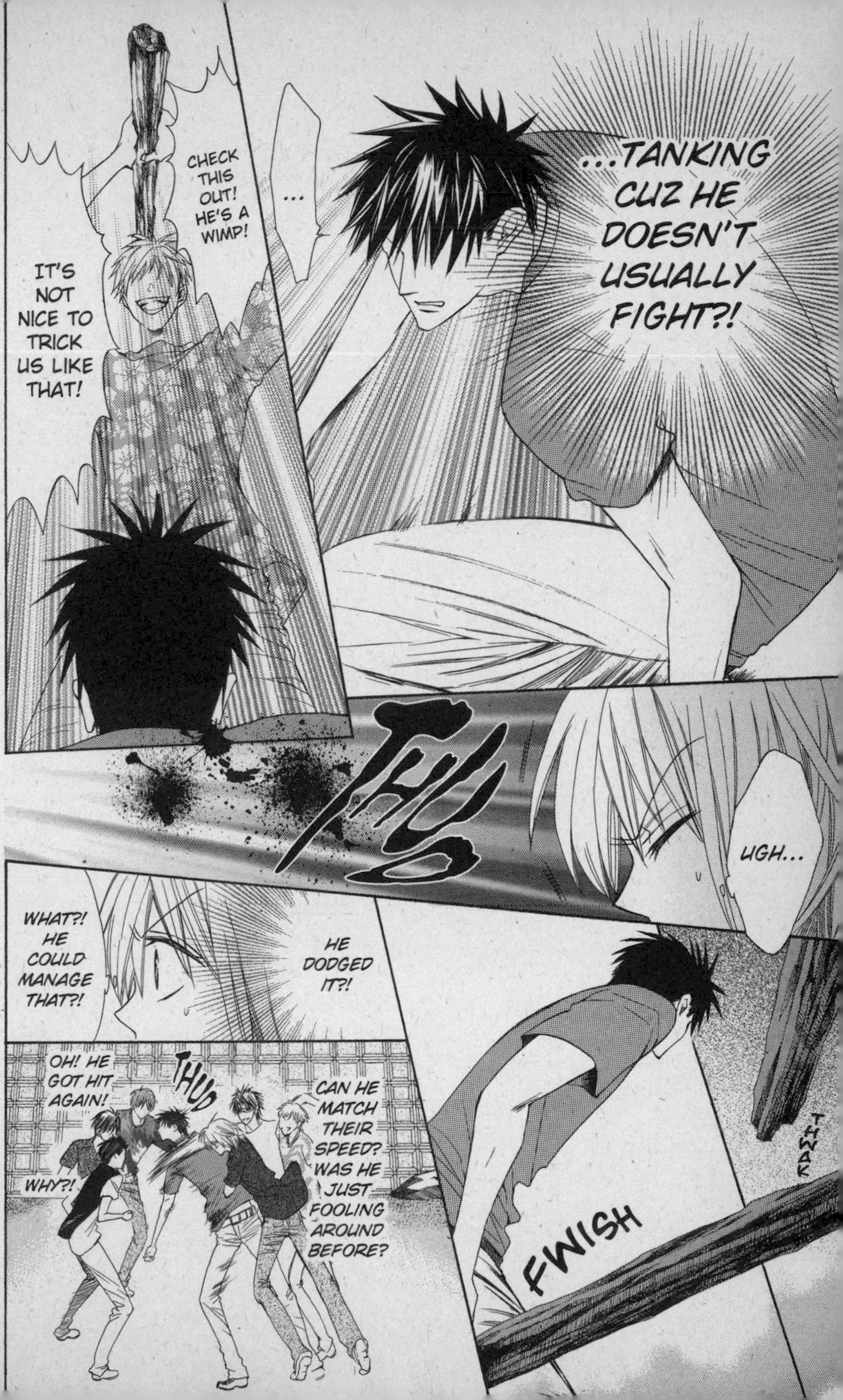
...TANKING CUZ HE DOESN'T USUALLY FIGHT?!
...
CHECK THIS OUT! HE'S A WIMP!
IT'S NOT NICE TO TRICK US LIKE THAT!
THUD
UGH...
THWAK
FWISH
HE DODGED IT?!
WHAT?! HE COULD MANAGE THAT?!
CAN HE MATCH THEIR SPEED? WAS HE JUST FOOLING AROUND BEFORE?
THUD
OH! HE GOT HIT AGAIN!
WHY?!

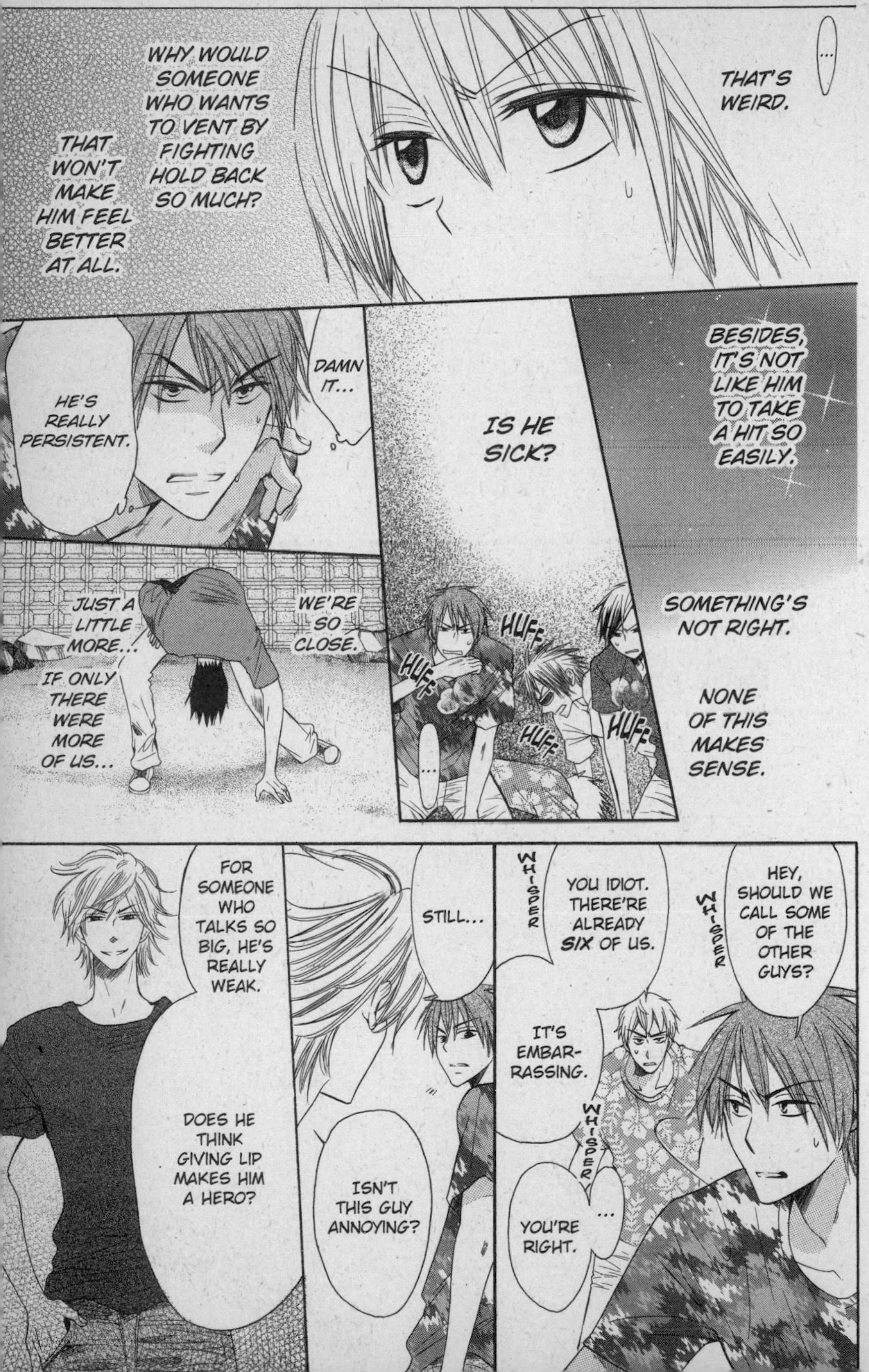
...
THAT'S WEIRD.
WHY WOULD SOMEONE WHO WANTS TO VENT BY FIGHTING HOLD BACK SO MUCH?
THAT WON'T MAKE HIM FEEL BETTER AT ALL.
BESIDES, IT'S NOT LIKE HIM TO TAKE A HIT SO EASILY.
IS HE SICK?
SOMETHING'S NOT RIGHT.
NONE OF THIS MAKES SENSE.
HUFF
HUFF
HUFF
HUFF
...
DAMN IT...
HE'S REALLY PERSISTENT.
WE'RE SO CLOSE.
JUST A LITTLE MORE...
IF ONLY THERE WERE MORE OF US...
HEY, SHOULD WE CALL SOME OF THE OTHER GUYS?
WHISPER
YOU IDIOT. THERE'RE ALREADY SIX OF US.
WHISPER
IT'S EMBARRASSING.
WHISPER
... YOU'RE RIGHT.
STILL...
ISN'T THIS GUY ANNOYING?
FOR SOMEONE WHO TALKS SO BIG, HE'S REALLY WEAK.
DOES HE THINK GIVING LIP MAKES HIM A HERO?

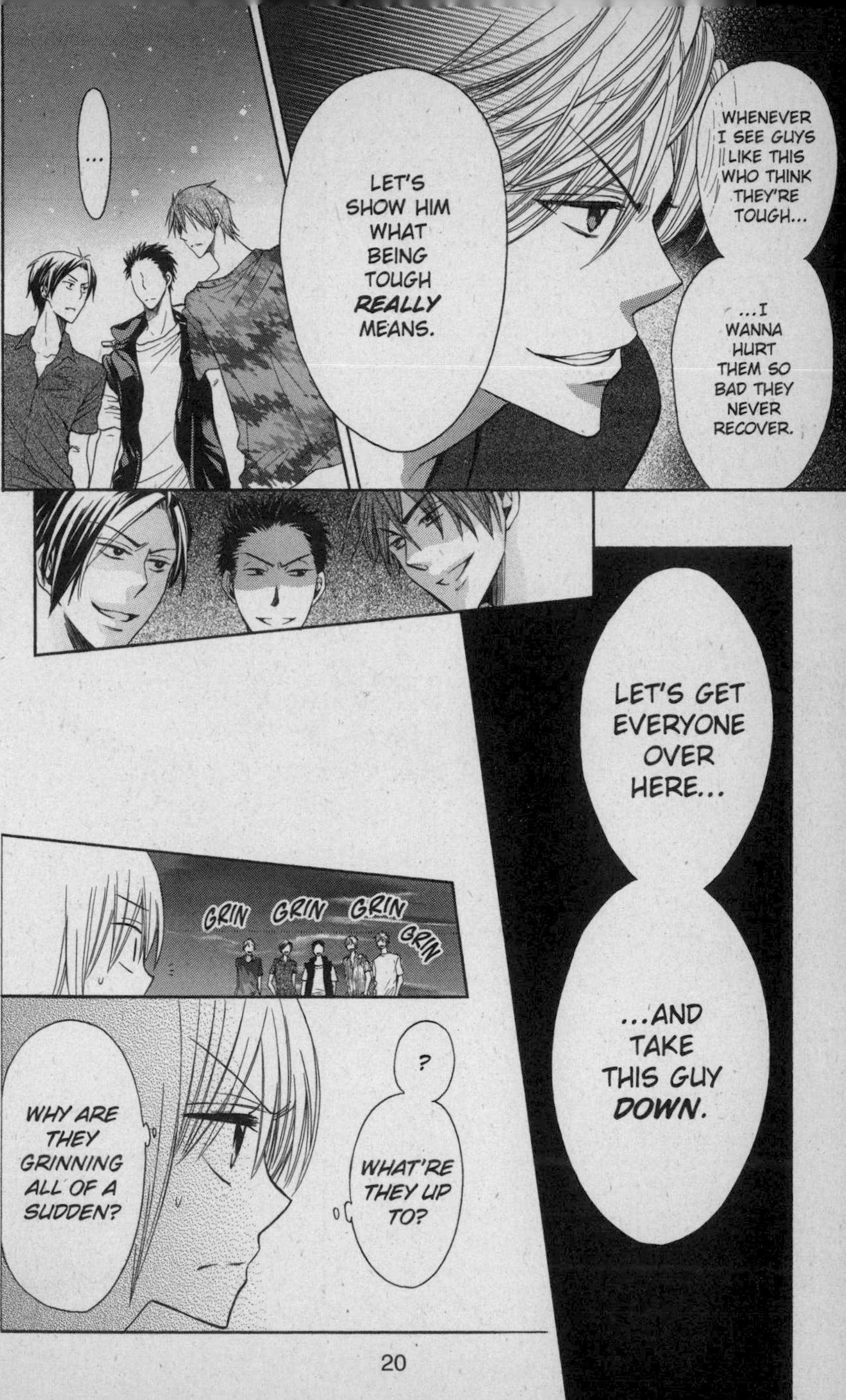
WHENEVER I SEE GUYS LIKE THIS WHO THINK THEY'RE TOUGH...
...I WANNA HURT THEM SO BAD THEY NEVER RECOVER.
LET'S SHOW HIM WHAT BEING TOUGH *REALLY* MEANS.
...
LET'S GET EVERYONE OVER HERE...
...AND TAKE THIS GUY *DOWN*.
GRIN GRIN GRIN GRIN
?
WHAT'RE THEY UP TO?
WHY ARE THEY GRINNING ALL OF A SUDDEN?

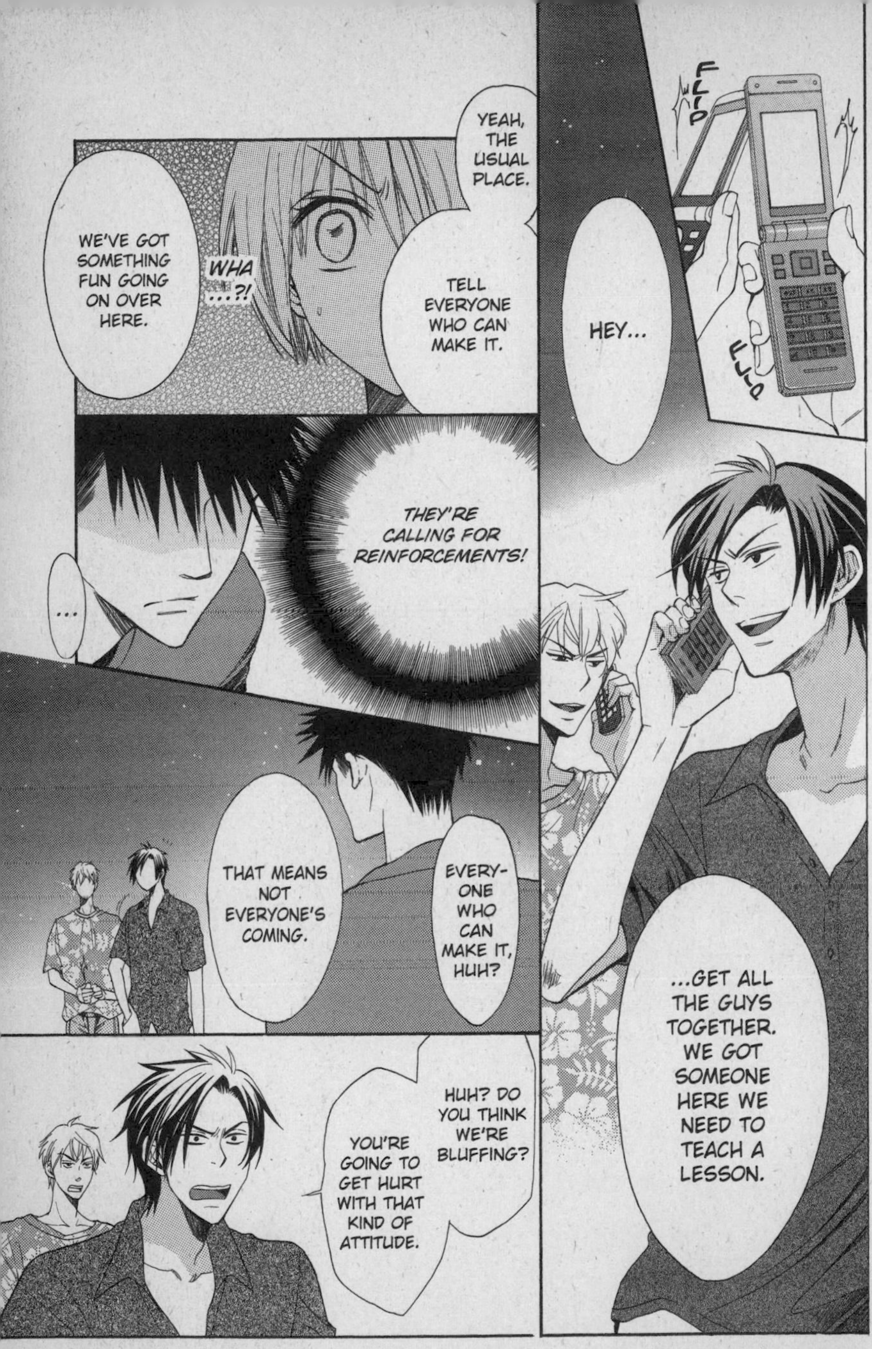
FLIP
FLIP
HEY...
...GET ALL THE GUYS TOGETHER. WE GOT SOMEONE HERE WE NEED TO TEACH A LESSON.
YEAH, THE USUAL PLACE.
TELL EVERYONE WHO CAN MAKE IT.
WHA ...?!
WE'VE GOT SOMETHING FUN GOING ON OVER HERE.
THEY'RE CALLING FOR REINFORCEMENTS!
...
EVERY-ONE WHO CAN MAKE IT, HUH?
THAT MEANS NOT EVERYONE'S COMING.
HUH? DO YOU THINK WE'RE BLUFFING?
YOU'RE GOING TO GET HURT WITH THAT KIND OF ATTITUDE.

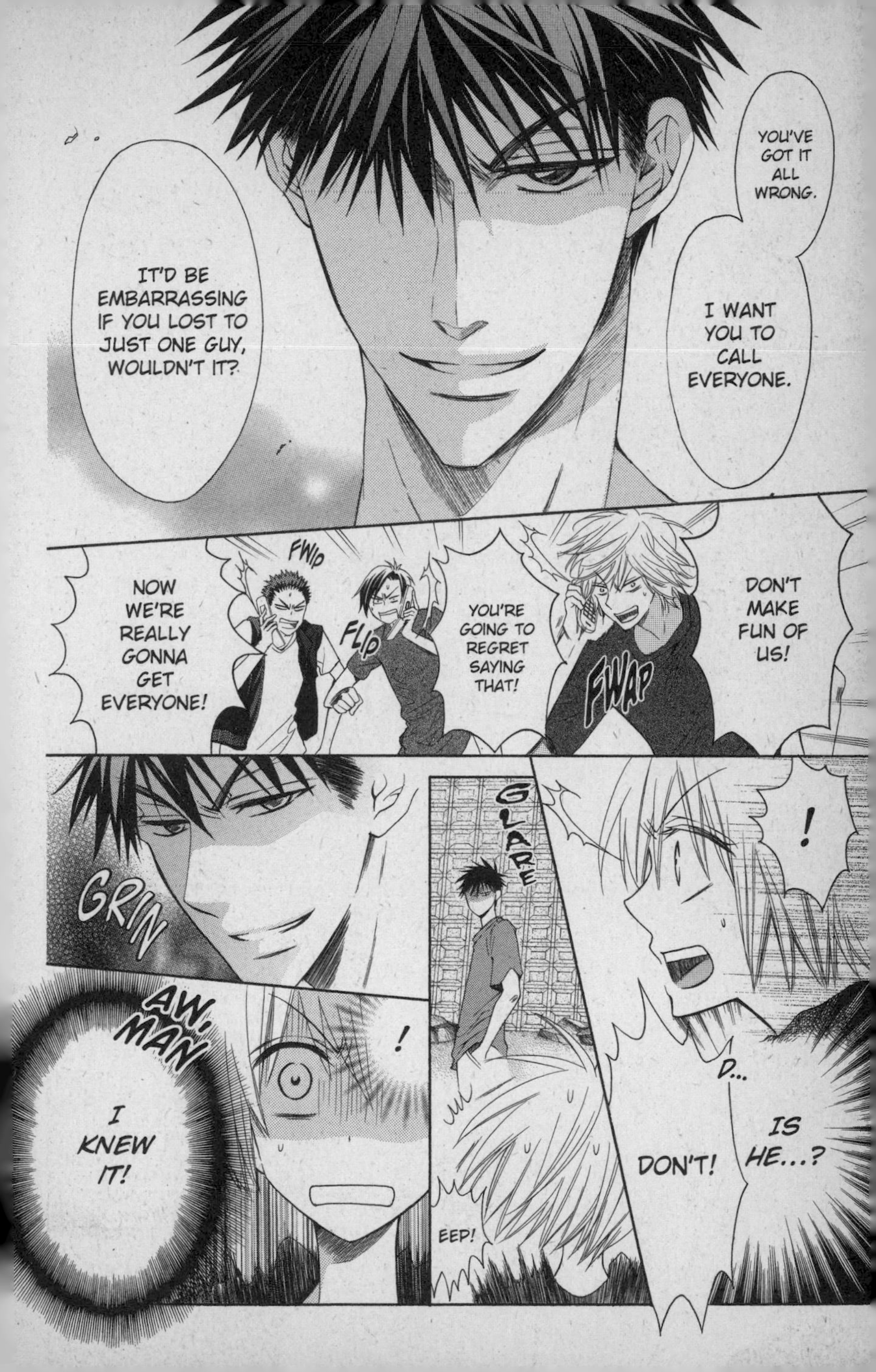
YOU'VE GOT IT ALL WRONG.
I WANT YOU TO CALL EVERYONE.
IT'D BE EMBARRASSING IF YOU LOST TO JUST ONE GUY, WOULDN'T IT?
DON'T MAKE FUN OF US!
FWAP
YOU'RE GOING TO REGRET SAYING THAT!
FLIP
FWIP
NOW WE'RE REALLY GONNA GET EVERYONE!
!
D...
IS HE...?
DON'T!
GLARE
EEP!
GRIN
!
AW, MAN
I KNEW IT!

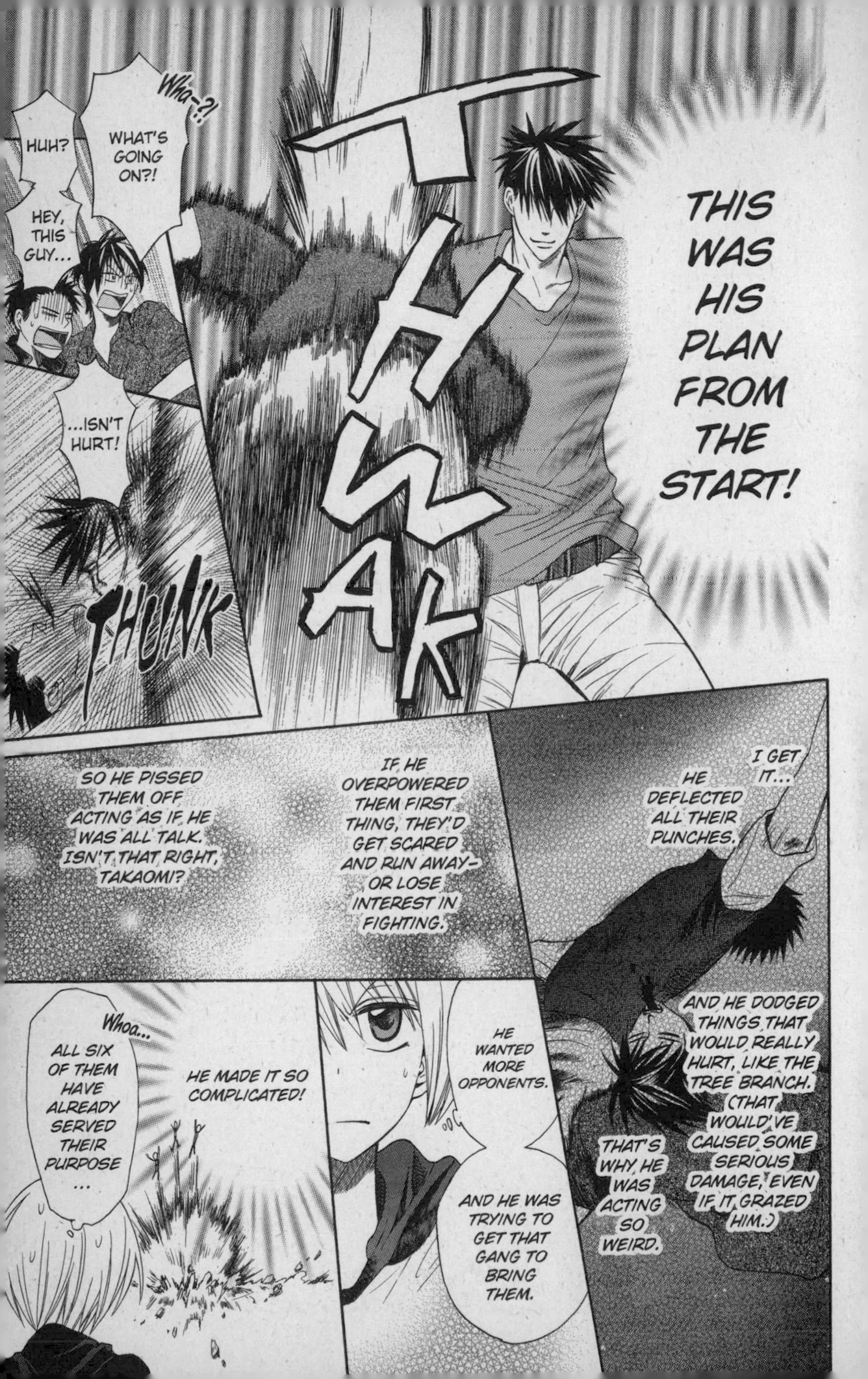
THIS WAS HIS PLAN FROM THE START!
HWAK
Wha-?!
WHAT'S GOING ON?!
HUH?
HEY, THIS GUY...
...ISN'T HURT!
THUNK
I GET IT...
HE DEFLECTED ALL THEIR PUNCHES.
AND HE DODGED THINGS THAT WOULD REALLY HURT, LIKE THE TREE BRANCH. (THAT WOULD'VE CAUSED SOME SERIOUS DAMAGE, EVEN IF IT GRAZED HIM.)
THAT'S WHY HE WAS ACTING SO WEIRD.
IF HE OVERPOWERED THEM FIRST THING, THEY'D GET SCARED AND RUN AWAY--OR LOSE INTEREST IN FIGHTING.
SO HE PISSED THEM OFF ACTING AS IF HE WAS ALL TALK. ISN'T THAT RIGHT, TAKAOMI?
HE WANTED MORE OPPONENTS.
AND HE WAS TRYING TO GET THAT GANG TO BRING THEM.
HE MADE IT SO COMPLICATED!
Whoa...
ALL SIX OF THEM HAVE ALREADY SERVED THEIR PURPOSE ...

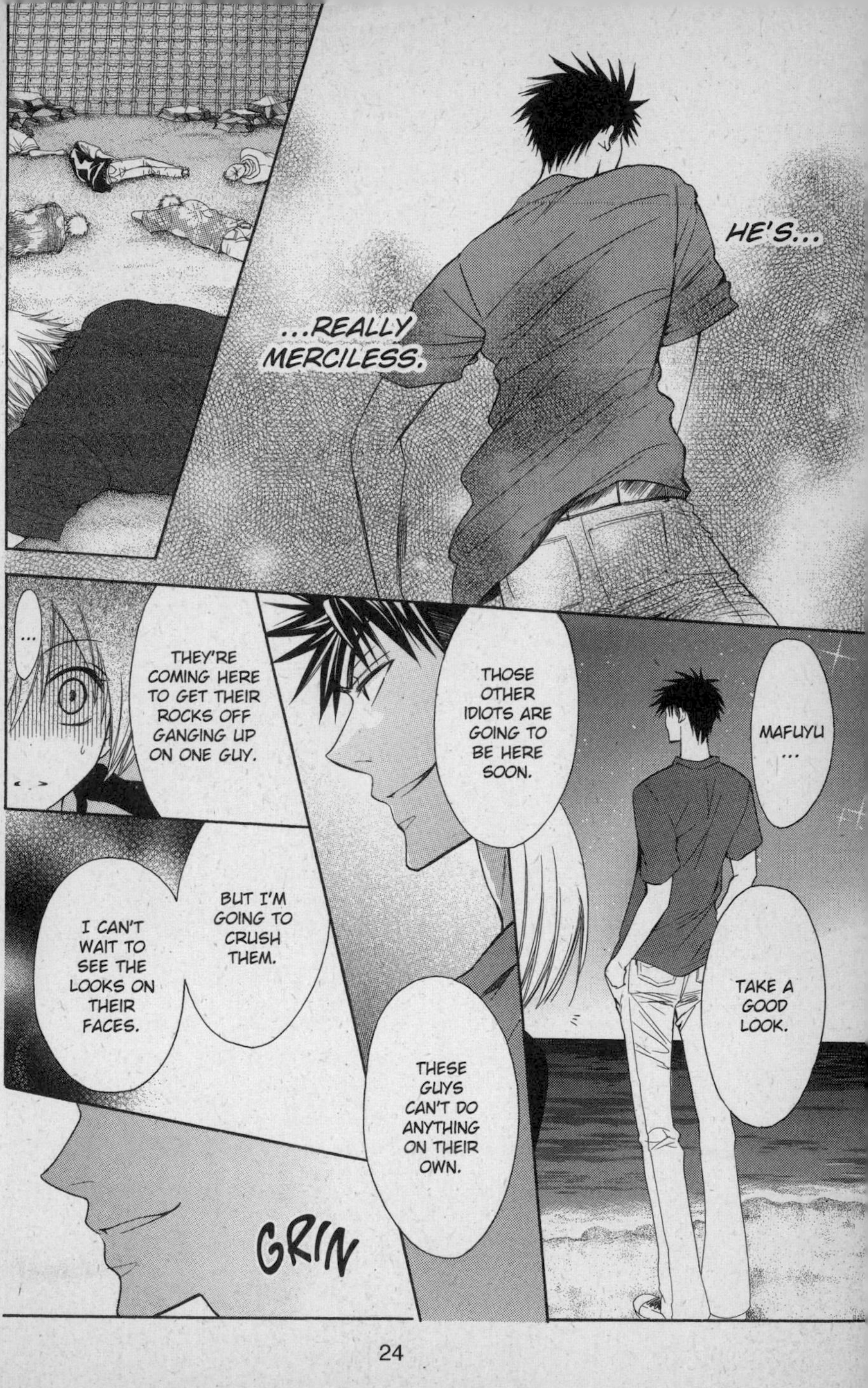
HE'S...
...REALLY MERCILESS.
MAFUYU...
TAKE A GOOD LOOK.
THOSE OTHER IDIOTS ARE GOING TO BE HERE SOON.
THESE GUYS CAN'T DO ANYTHING ON THEIR OWN.
...
THEY'RE COMING HERE TO GET THEIR ROCKS OFF GANGING UP ON ONE GUY.
BUT I'M GOING TO CRUSH THEM.
I CAN'T WAIT TO SEE THE LOOKS ON THEIR FACES.
GRIN

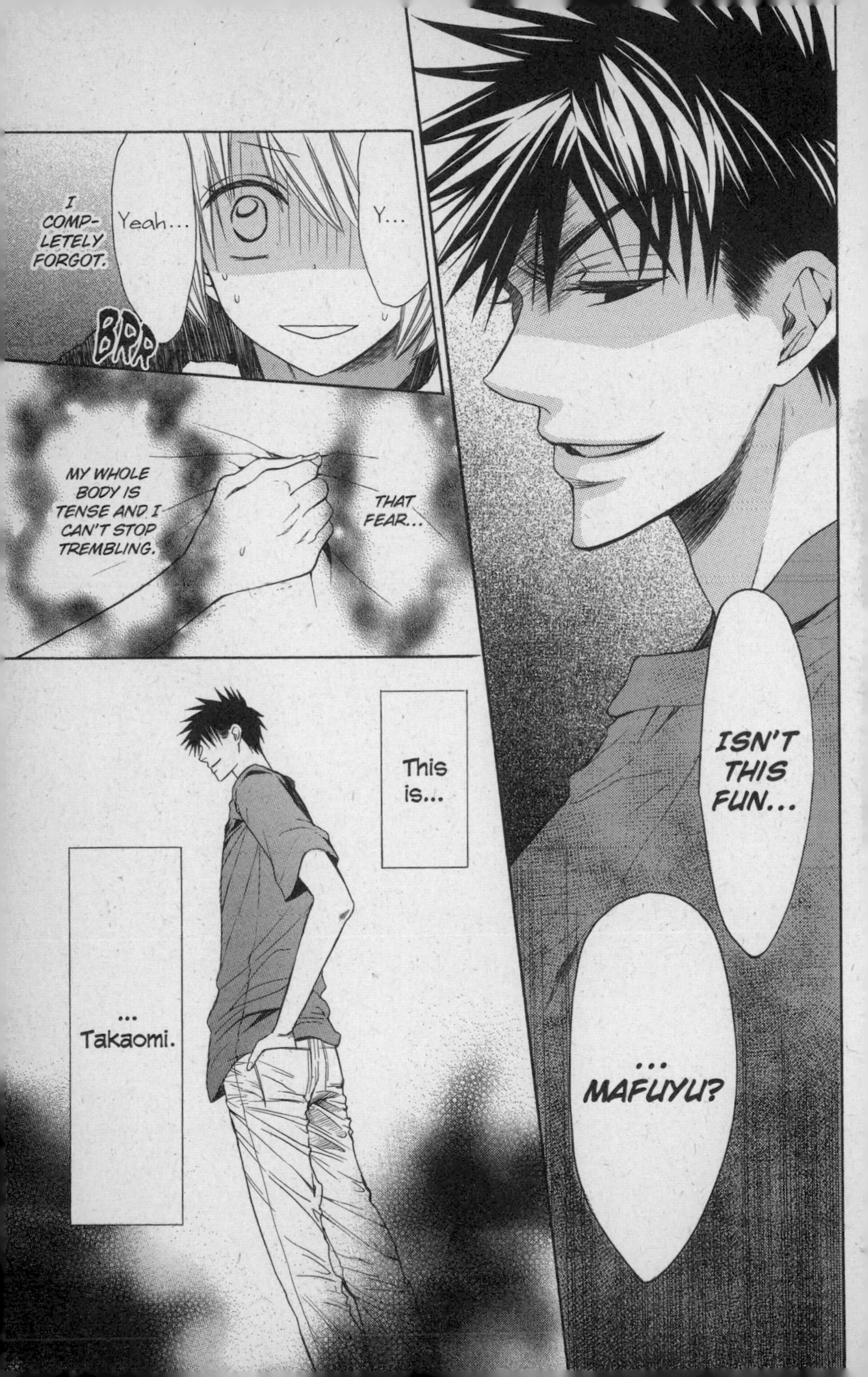
ISN'T THIS FUN...
... MAFUYU?
Y...
Yeah...
I COMPLETELY FORGOT.
BRR
THAT FEAR...
MY WHOLE BODY IS TENSE AND I CAN'T STOP TREMBLING.
This is...
... Takaomi.

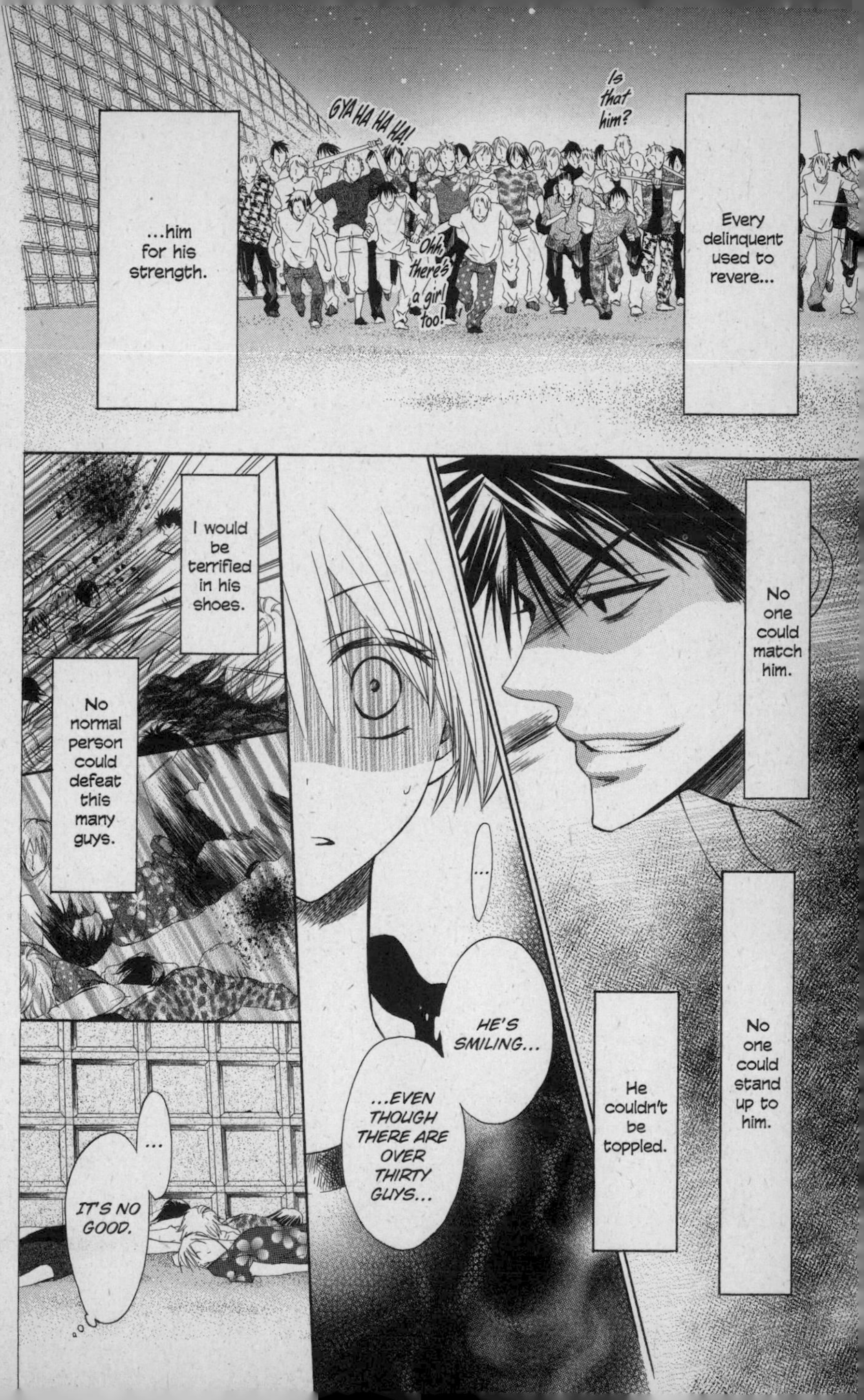
Every delinquent used to revere...
Is that him?
GYA HA HA HA!
Ohh, there's a girl too!
...him for his strength.
No one could match him.
No one could stand up to him.
He couldn't be toppled.
HE'S SMILING...
...EVEN THOUGH THERE ARE OVER THIRTY GUYS...
...
I would be terrified in his shoes.
No normal person could defeat this many guys.
...
IT'S NO GOOD.

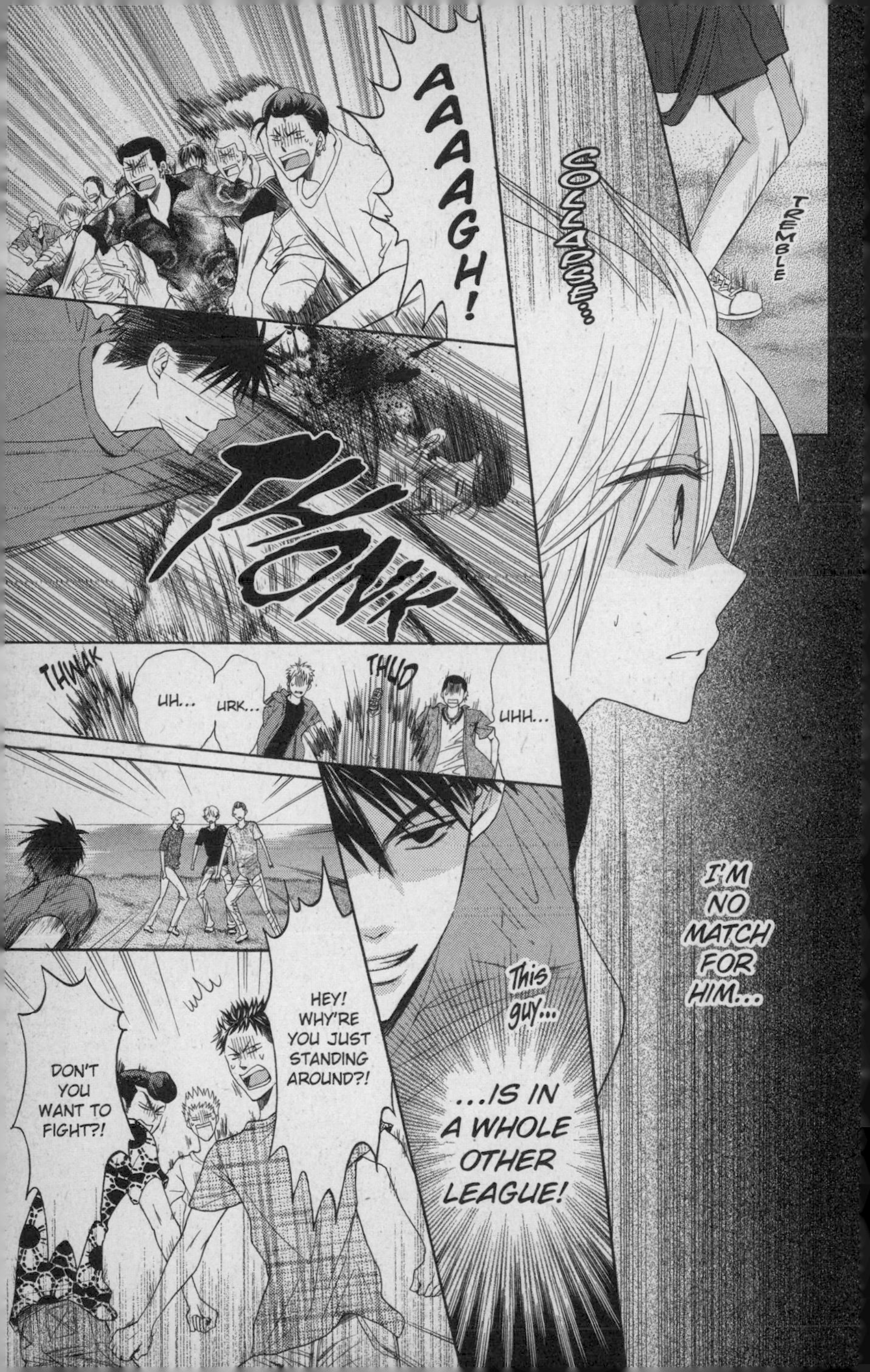
TREMBLE
COLLAPSE...
AAAAGH!
THONK
UHH...
THUD
URK...
UH...
THWAK
I'M NO MATCH FOR HIM...
This guy...
...IS IN A WHOLE OTHER LEAGUE!
HEY! WHY'RE YOU JUST STANDING AROUND?!
DON'T YOU WANT TO FIGHT?!

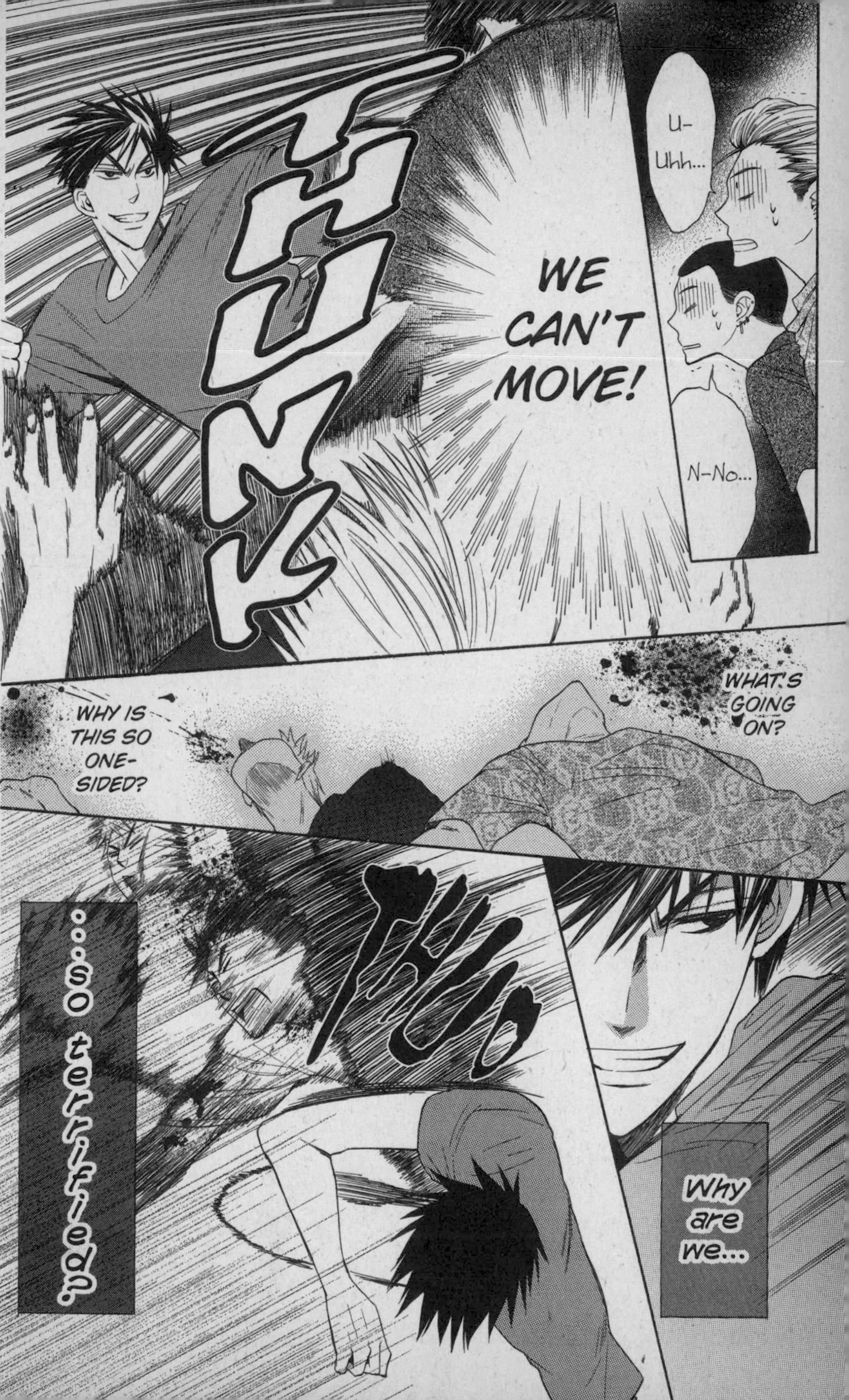
U- Uhh...
N-No...
WE CAN'T MOVE!
WHAT'S GOING ON?
WHY IS THIS SO ONE-SIDED?
Why are we...
THUD
...so terrified.

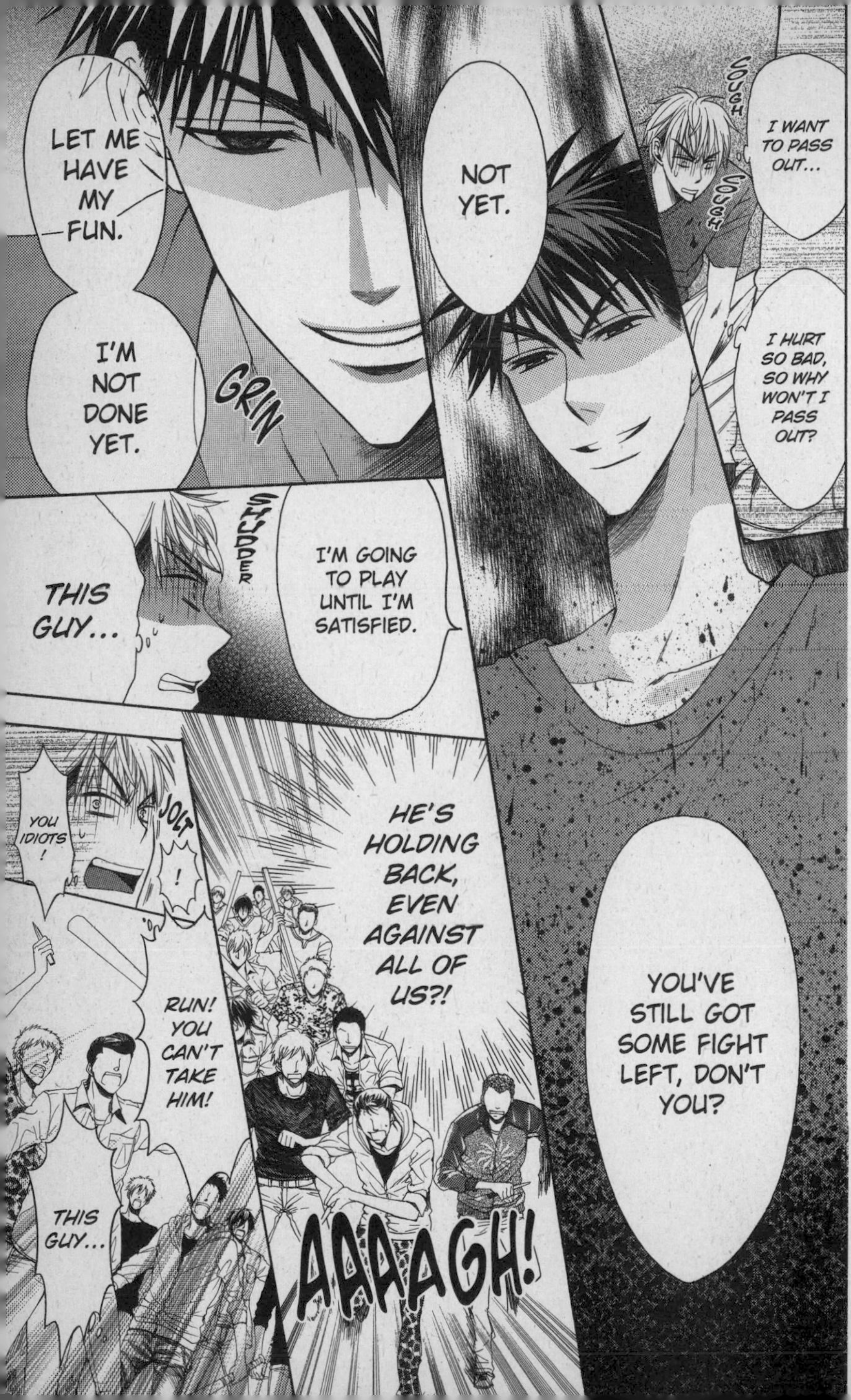
COUGH
I WANT TO PASS OUT...
COUGH
I HURT SO BAD, SO WHY WON'T I PASS OUT?
NOT YET.
YOU'VE STILL GOT SOME FIGHT LEFT, DON'T YOU?
LET ME HAVE MY FUN.
I'M NOT DONE YET.
GRIN
I'M GOING TO PLAY UNTIL I'M SATISFIED.
SHUDDER
THIS GUY...
HE'S HOLDING BACK, EVEN AGAINST ALL OF US?!
AAAAGH!
JOLT
!
YOU IDIOTS!
RUN! YOU CAN'T TAKE HIM!
THIS GUY...

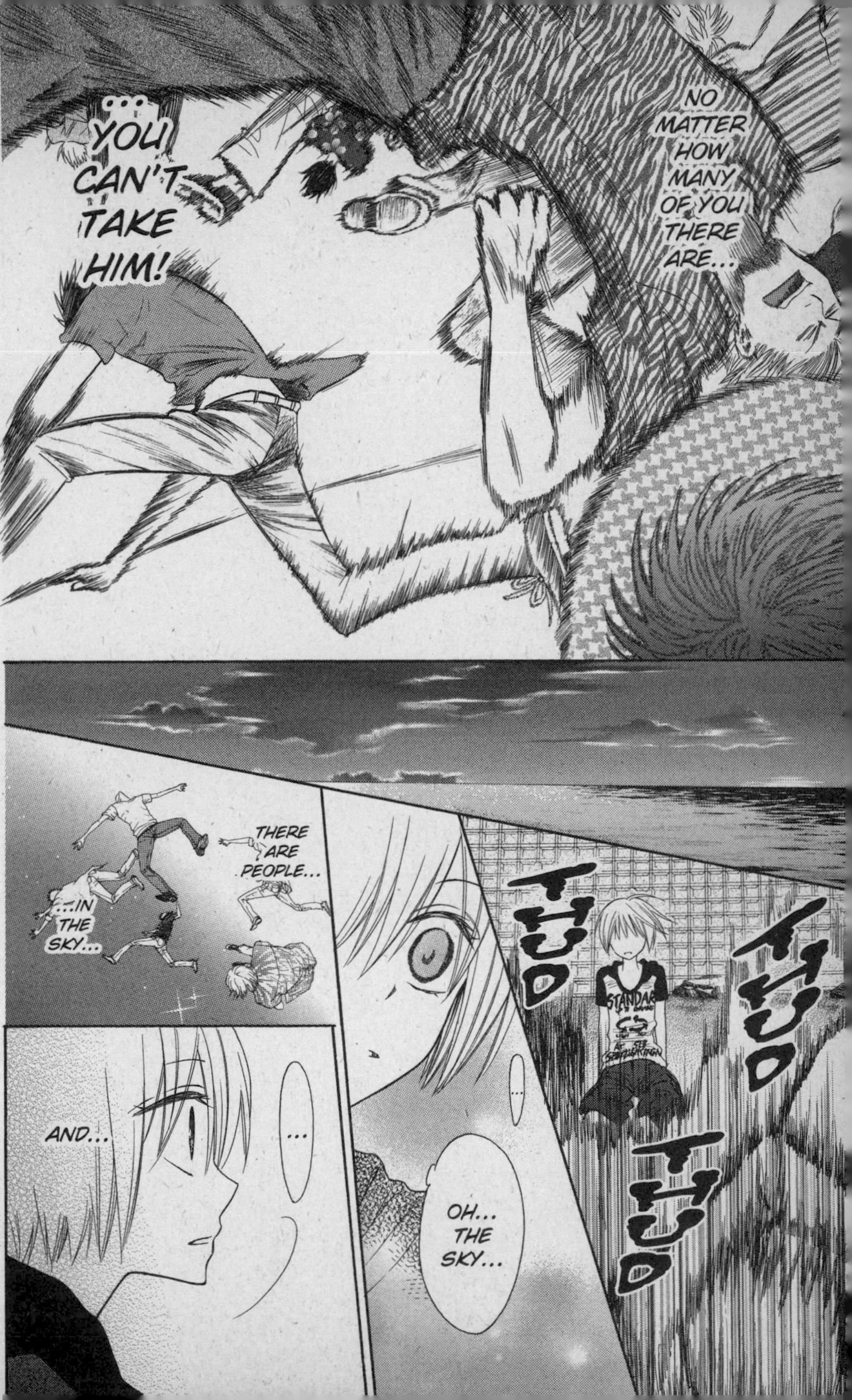
NO MATTER HOW MANY OF YOU THERE ARE...
...YOU CAN'T TAKE HIM!
...
OH... THE SKY...
THERE ARE PEOPLE...
...IN THE SKY...
...
AND...

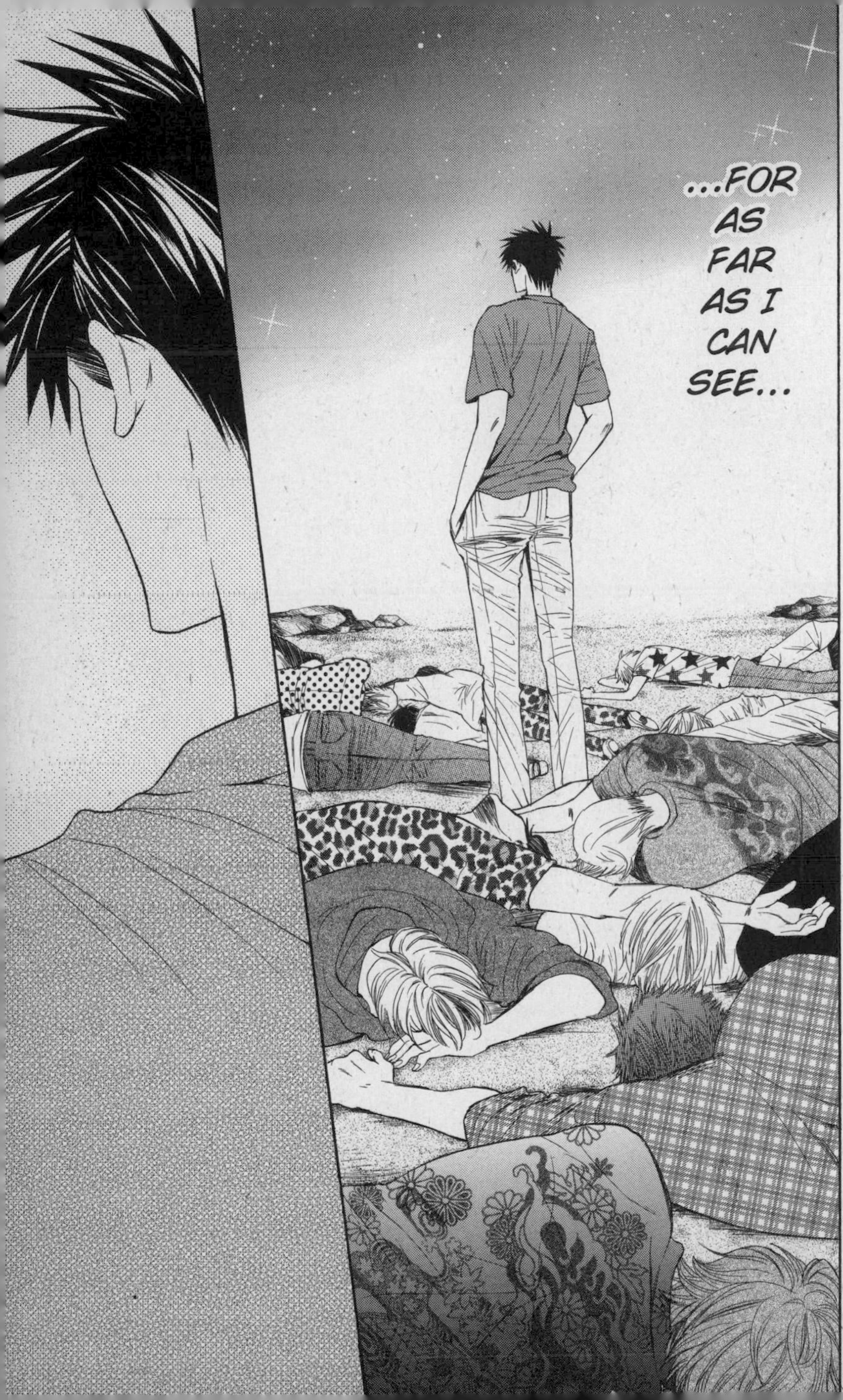
...FOR AS FAR AS I CAN SEE...

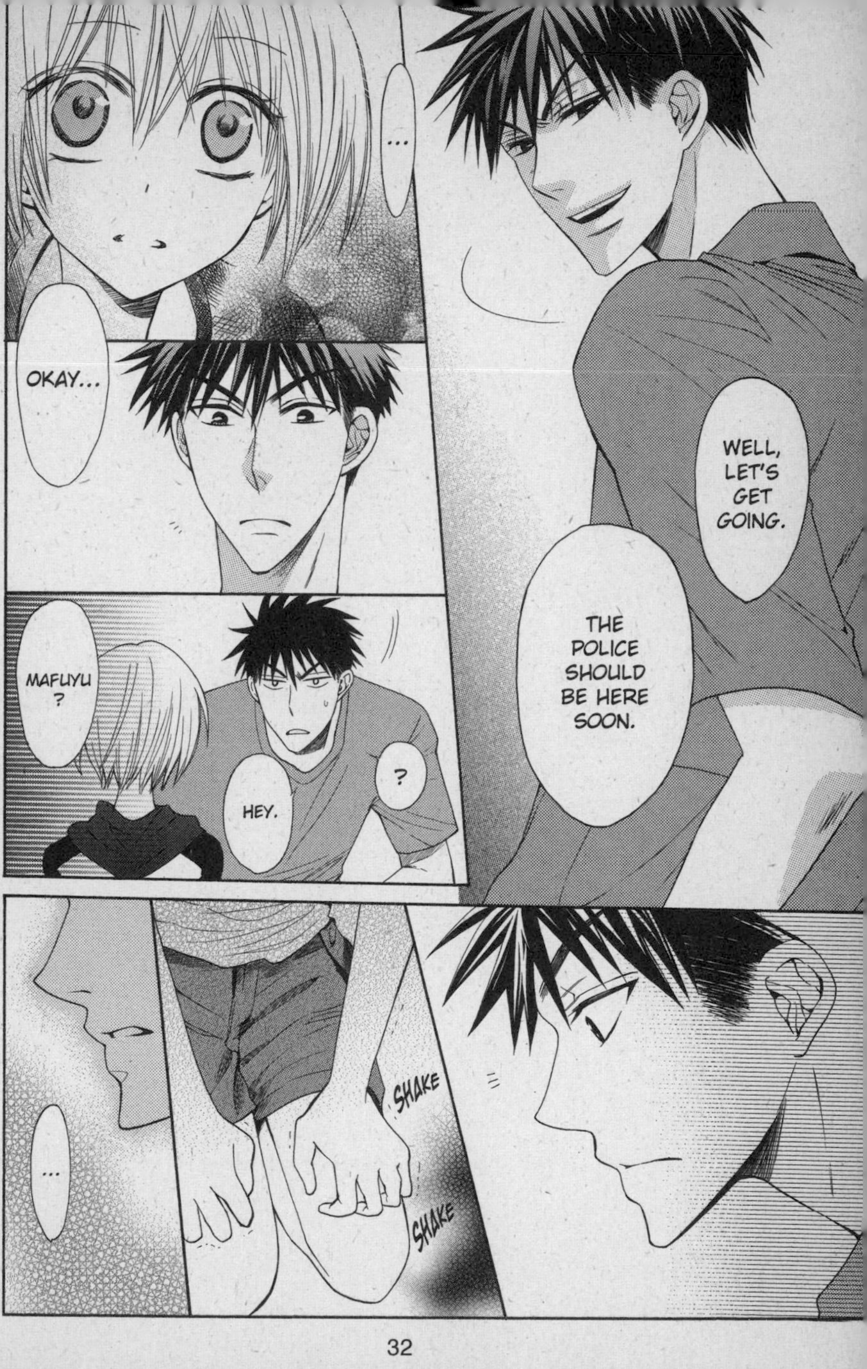
WELL, LET'S GET GOING.
THE POLICE SHOULD BE HERE SOON.
...
OKAY...
?
HEY.
MAFUYU ?
SHAKE
SHAKE
...

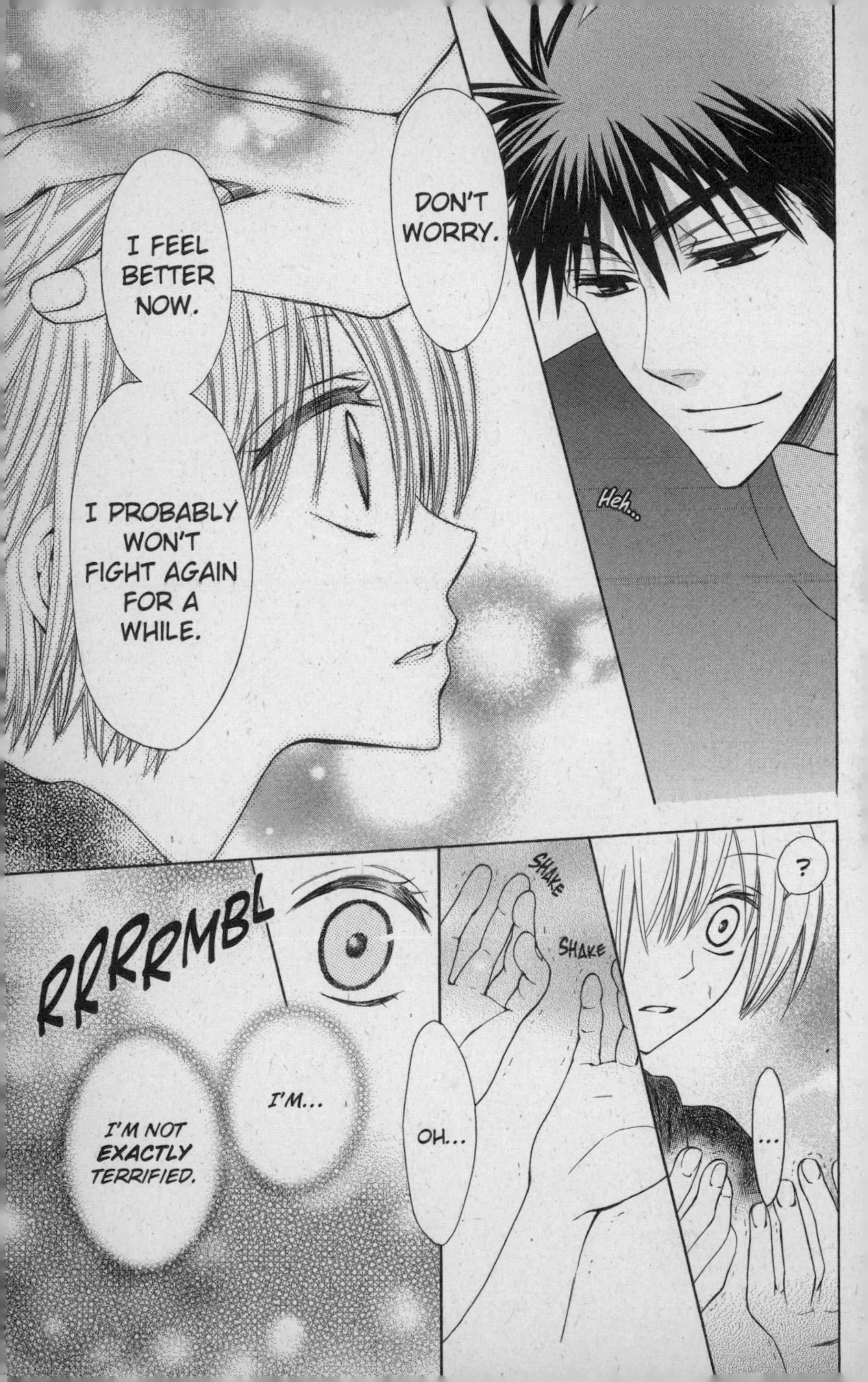
DON'T WORRY.
Heh...
I FEEL BETTER NOW.
I PROBABLY WON'T FIGHT AGAIN FOR A WHILE.
?
...
SHAKE
SHAKE
OH...
RRRRMBL
I'M...
I'M NOT EXACTLY TERRIFIED.

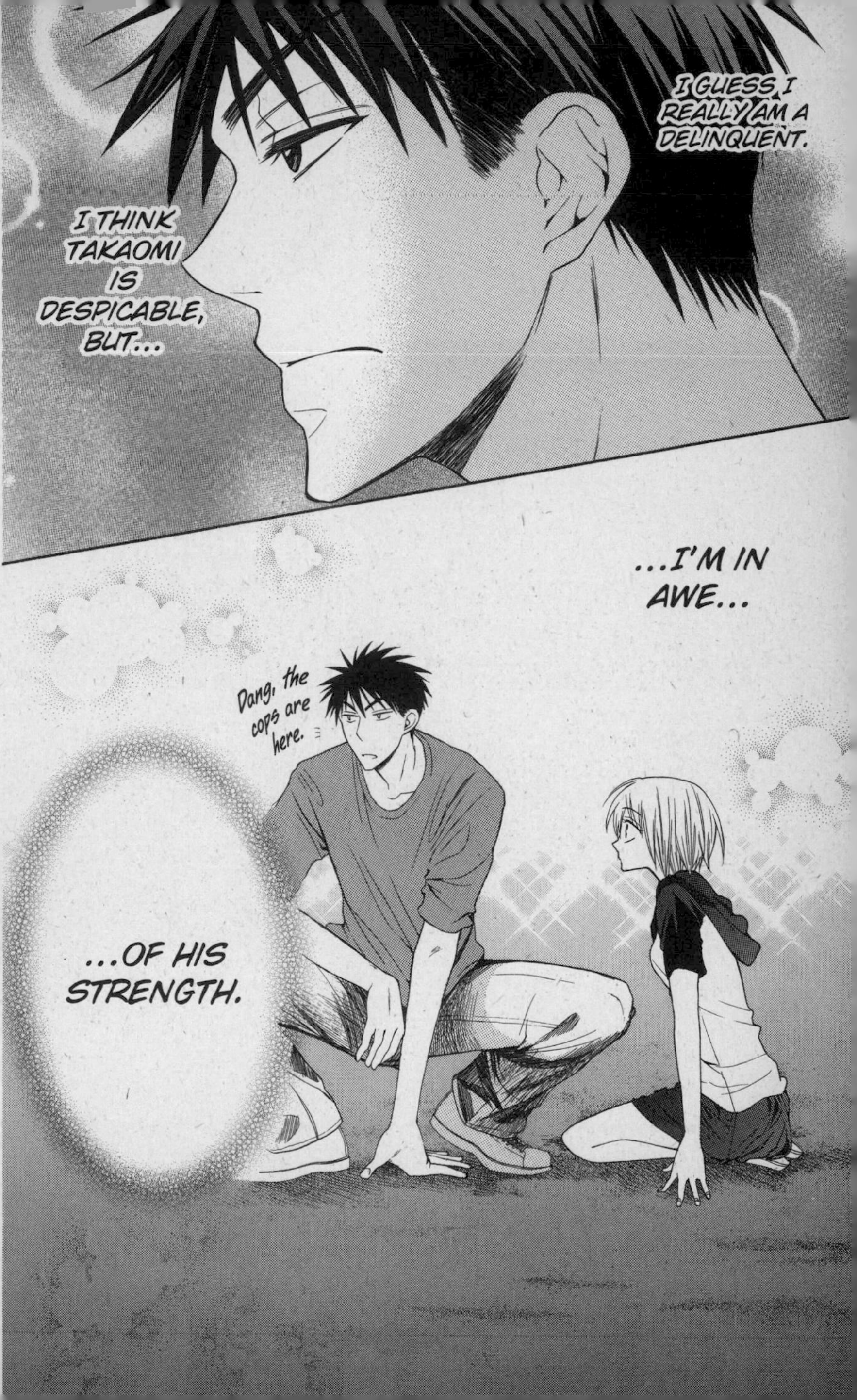
I GUESS I REALLY AM A DELINQUENT.
I THINK TAKAOMI IS DESPICABLE, BUT...
...I'M IN AWE...
Dang, the cops are here.
...OF HIS STRENGTH.

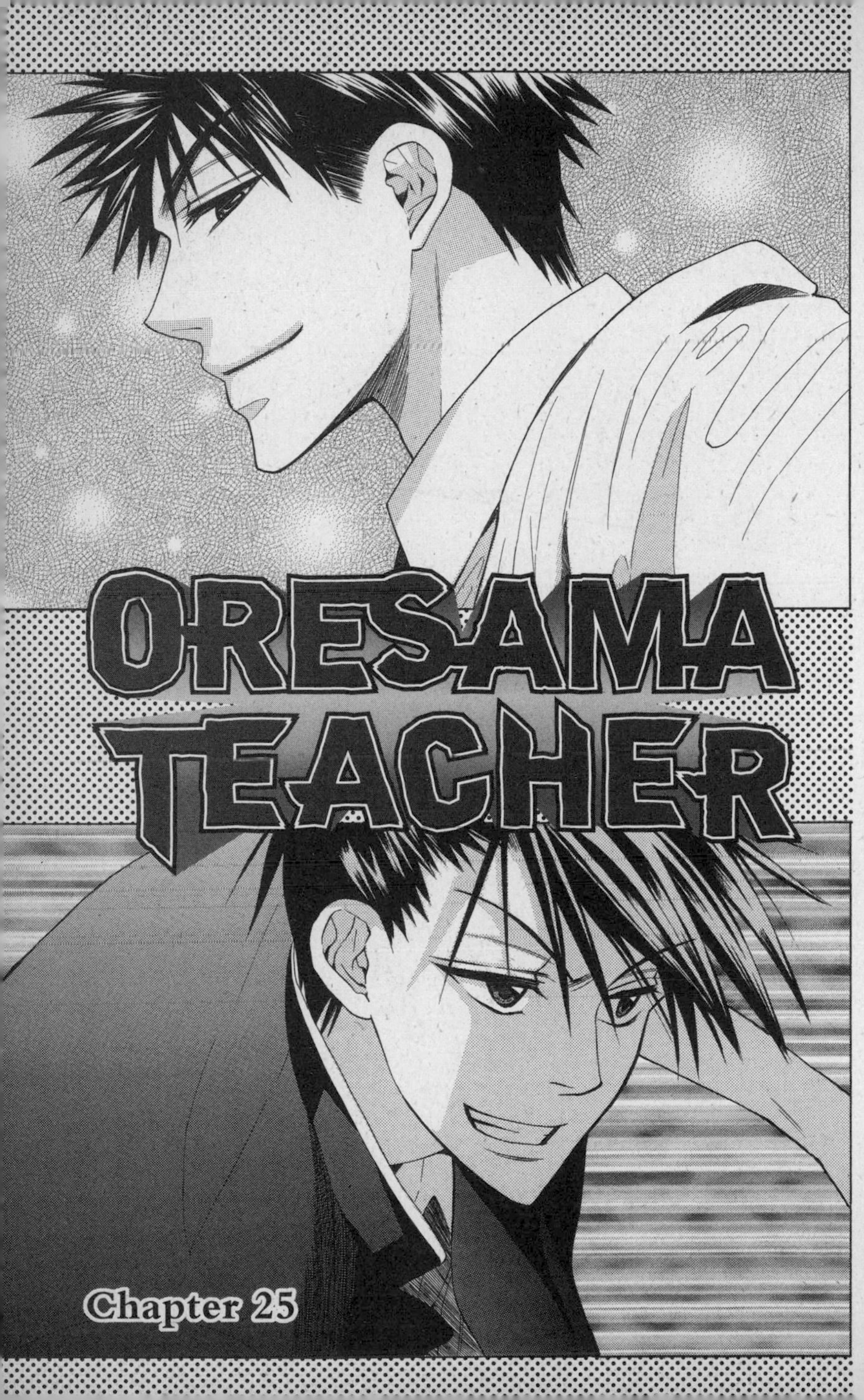
ORESAMA TEACHER
Chapter 25

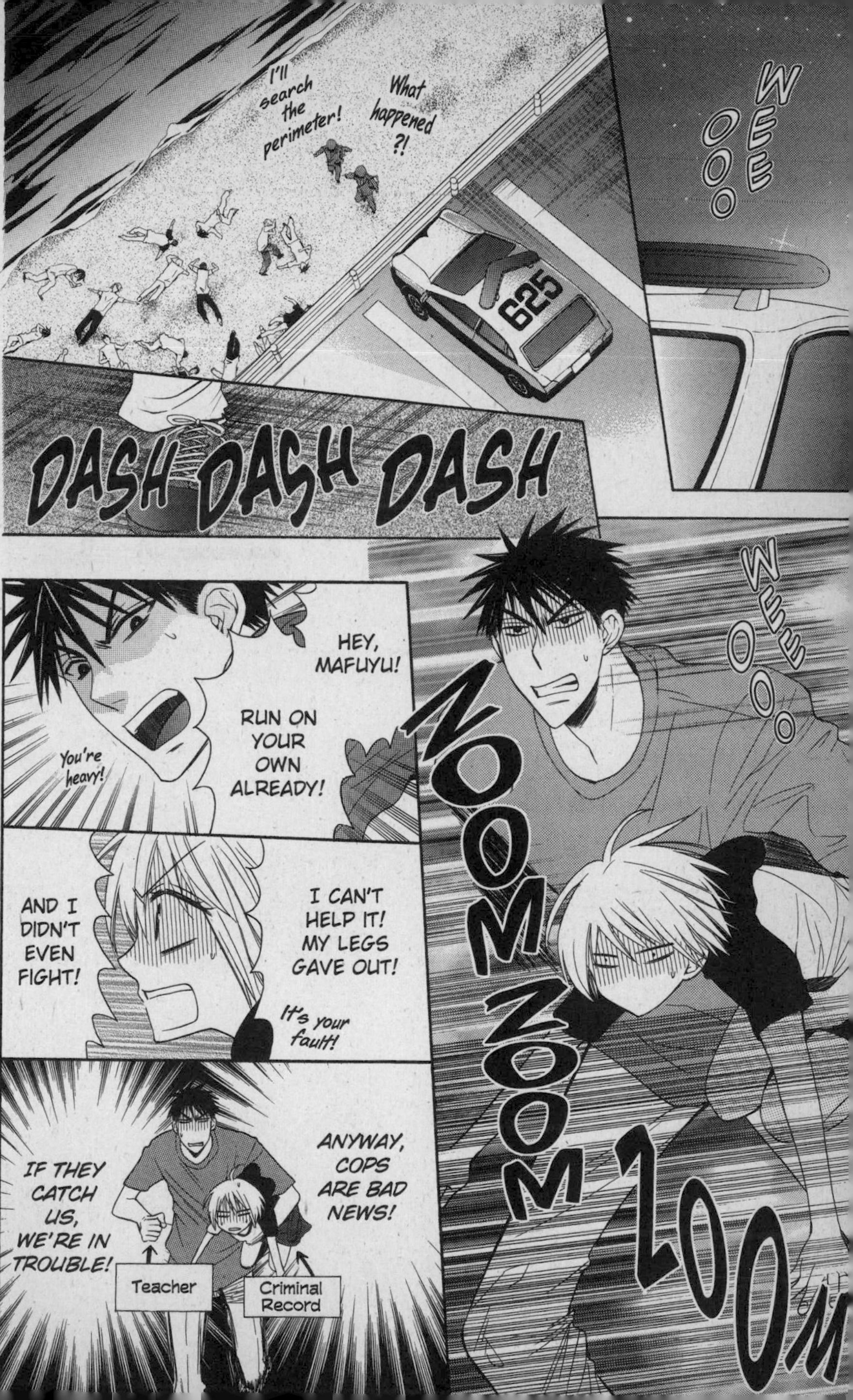
WEEE OOOO
What happened?!
I'll search the perimeter!
DASH DASH DASH
WEEE OOOO
ZOOM ZOOM
ZOOM
HEY, MAFUYU!
RUN ON YOUR OWN ALREADY!
You're heavy!
I CAN'T HELP IT! MY LEGS GAVE OUT!
AND I DIDN'T EVEN FIGHT!
It's your fault!
ANYWAY, COPS ARE BAD NEWS!
IF THEY CATCH US, WE'RE IN TROUBLE!
Teacher
Criminal Record

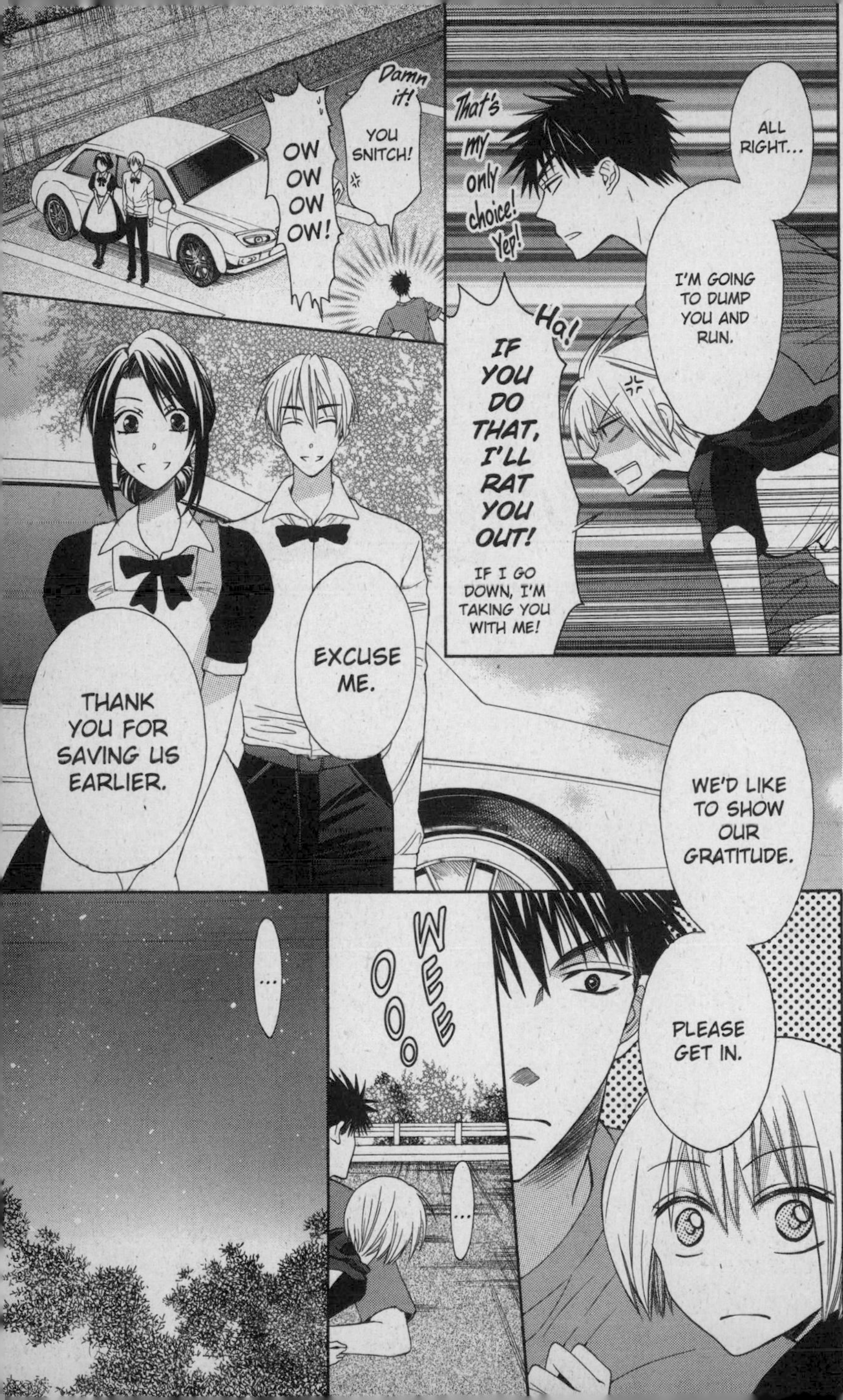

That's my only choice! Yep!
ALL RIGHT...
I'M GOING TO DUMP YOU AND RUN.
Ha!
IF YOU DO THAT, I'LL RAT YOU OUT!
IF I GO DOWN, I'M TAKING YOU WITH ME!
Damn it!
YOU SNITCH!
OW OW OW OW!
EXCUSE ME.
THANK YOU FOR SAVING US EARLIER.
WE'D LIKE TO SHOW OUR GRATITUDE.
PLEASE GET IN.
WEEOOO
...
...

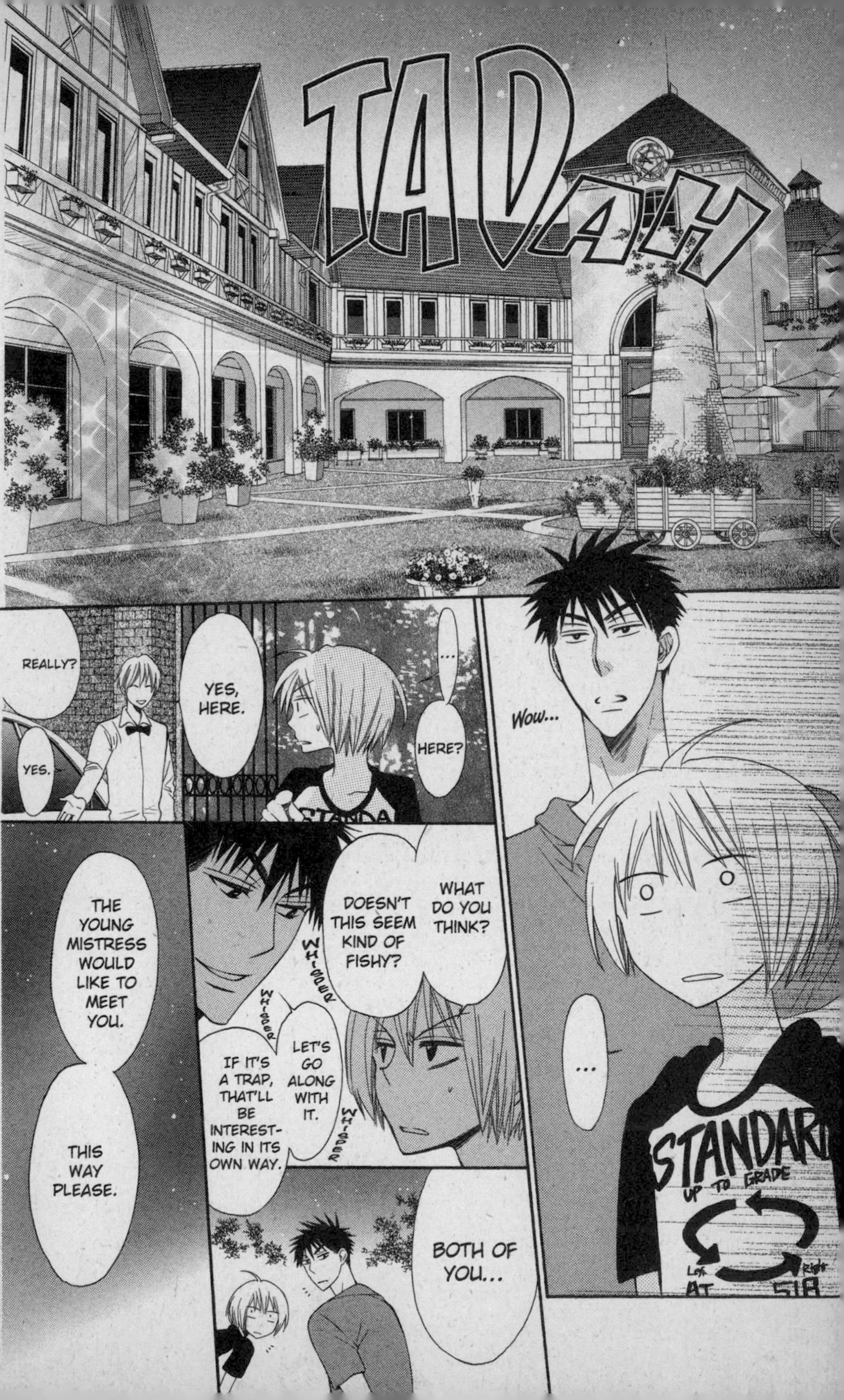
TADAH
Wow...
...
STANDARD
UP TO GRADE
Left
Right
AT
SIR
...
HERE?
YES, HERE.
REALLY?
YES.
WHAT DO YOU THINK?
DOESN'T THIS SEEM KIND OF FISHY?
WHISPER
WHISPER
LET'S GO ALONG WITH IT.
IF IT'S A TRAP, THAT'LL BE INTERESTING IN ITS OWN WAY.
WHISPER
BOTH OF YOU...
THE YOUNG MISTRESS WOULD LIKE TO MEET YOU.
THIS WAY PLEASE.

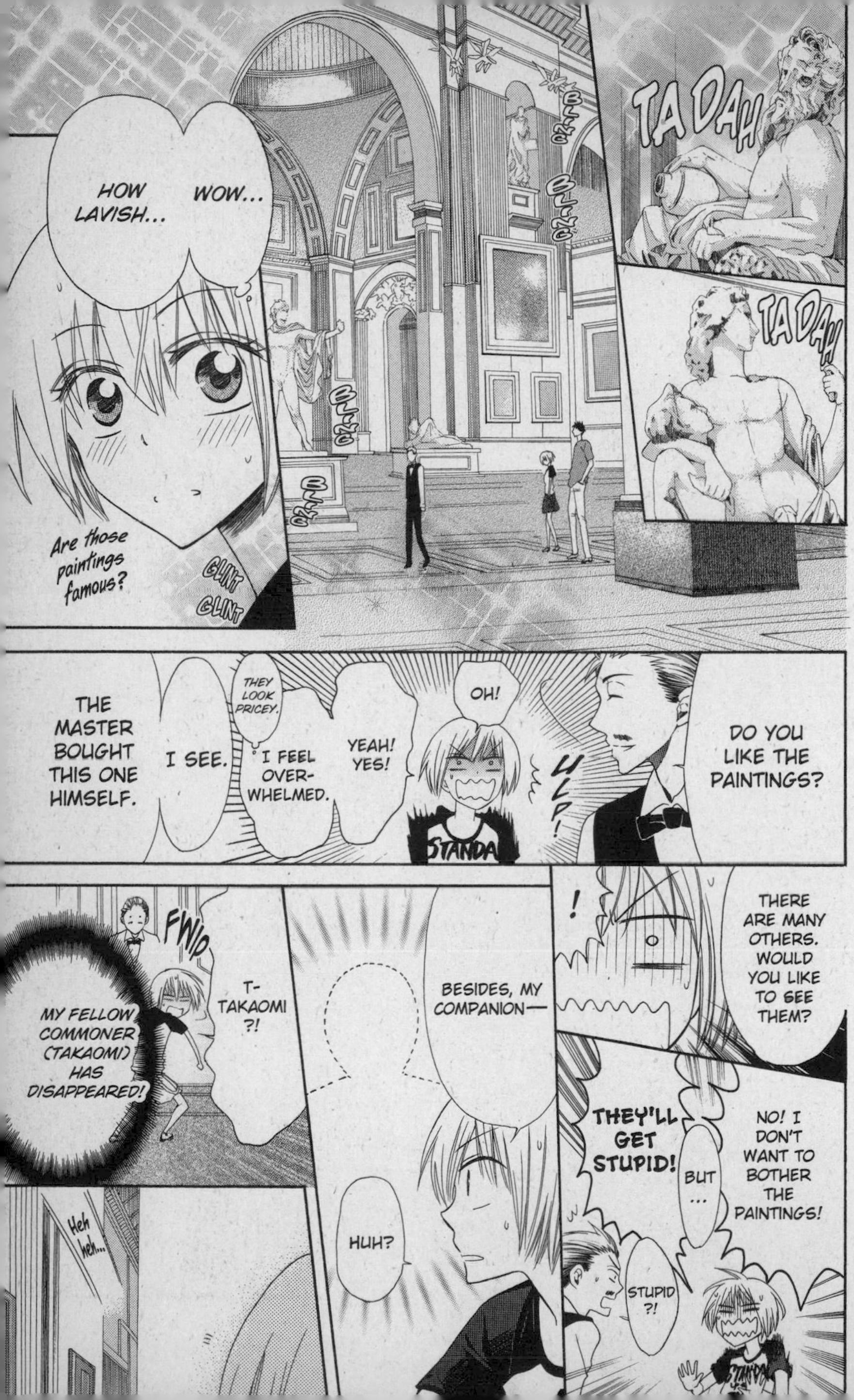
TA DAH
TA DAH
BLING
BLING
BLING
BLING
WOW... HOW LAVISH...
Are those paintings famous?
GLINT GLINT
DO YOU LIKE THE PAINTINGS?
ULP!
OH!
YEAH! YES!
THEY LOOK PRICEY.
I FEEL OVER-WHELMED.
I SEE.
THE MASTER BOUGHT THIS ONE HIMSELF.
THERE ARE MANY OTHERS. WOULD YOU LIKE TO SEE THEM?
!
NO! I DON'T WANT TO BOTHER THE PAINTINGS!
BUT...
THEY'LL GET STUPID!
STUPID?!
BESIDES, MY COMPANION—
HUH?
FWIP
T-TAKAOMI?!
MY FELLOW COMMONER (TAKAOMI) HAS DISAPPEARED!
Heh heh...

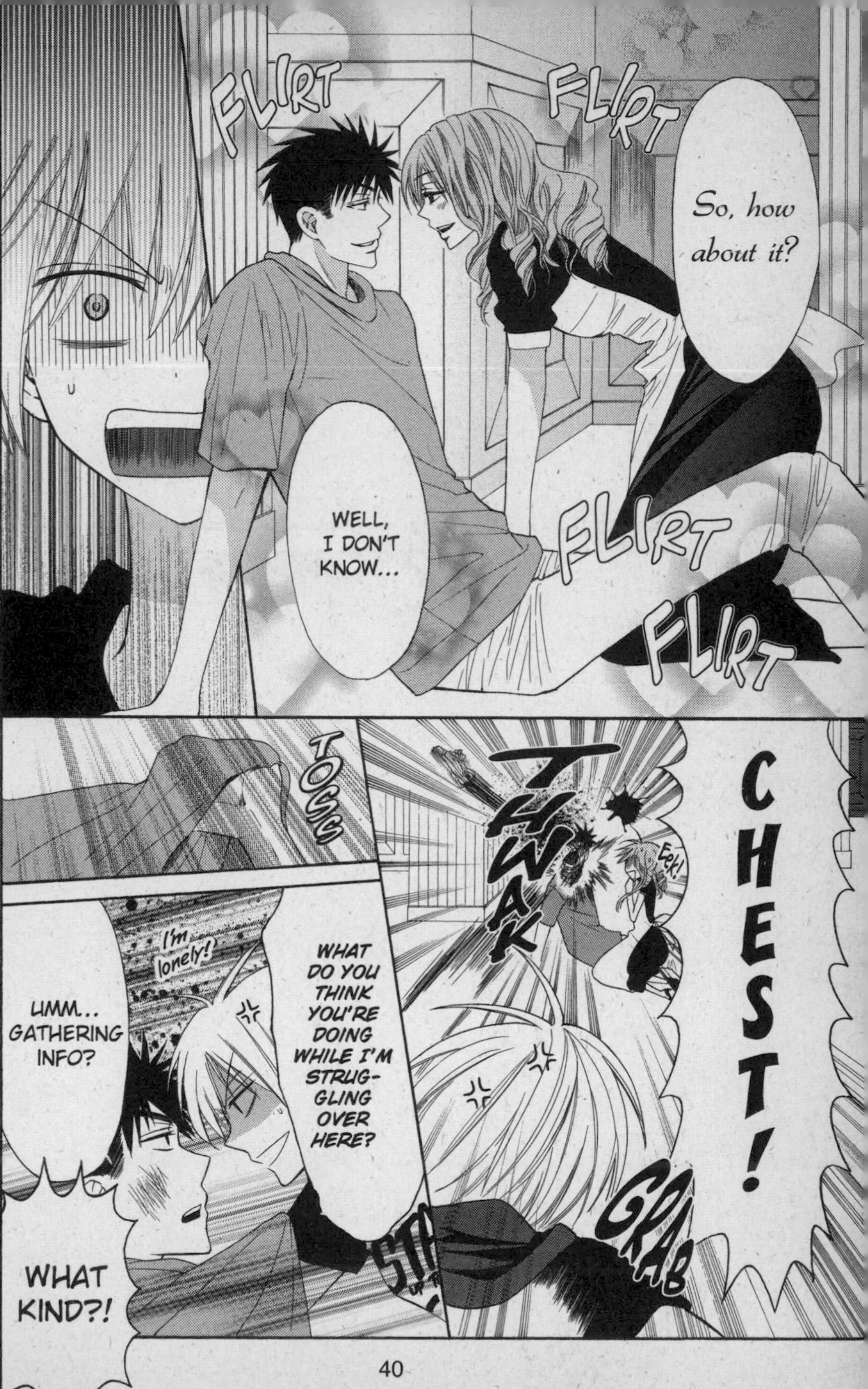
FLIRT
FLIRT
So, how about it?
WELL, I DON'T KNOW...
FLIRT
FLIRT
CHEST!
THWAK
Eek!
GRAB
TOSS
WHAT DO YOU THINK YOU'RE DOING WHILE I'M STRUG-GLING OVER HERE?
I'm lonely!
UMM... GATHERING INFO?
WHAT KIND?!

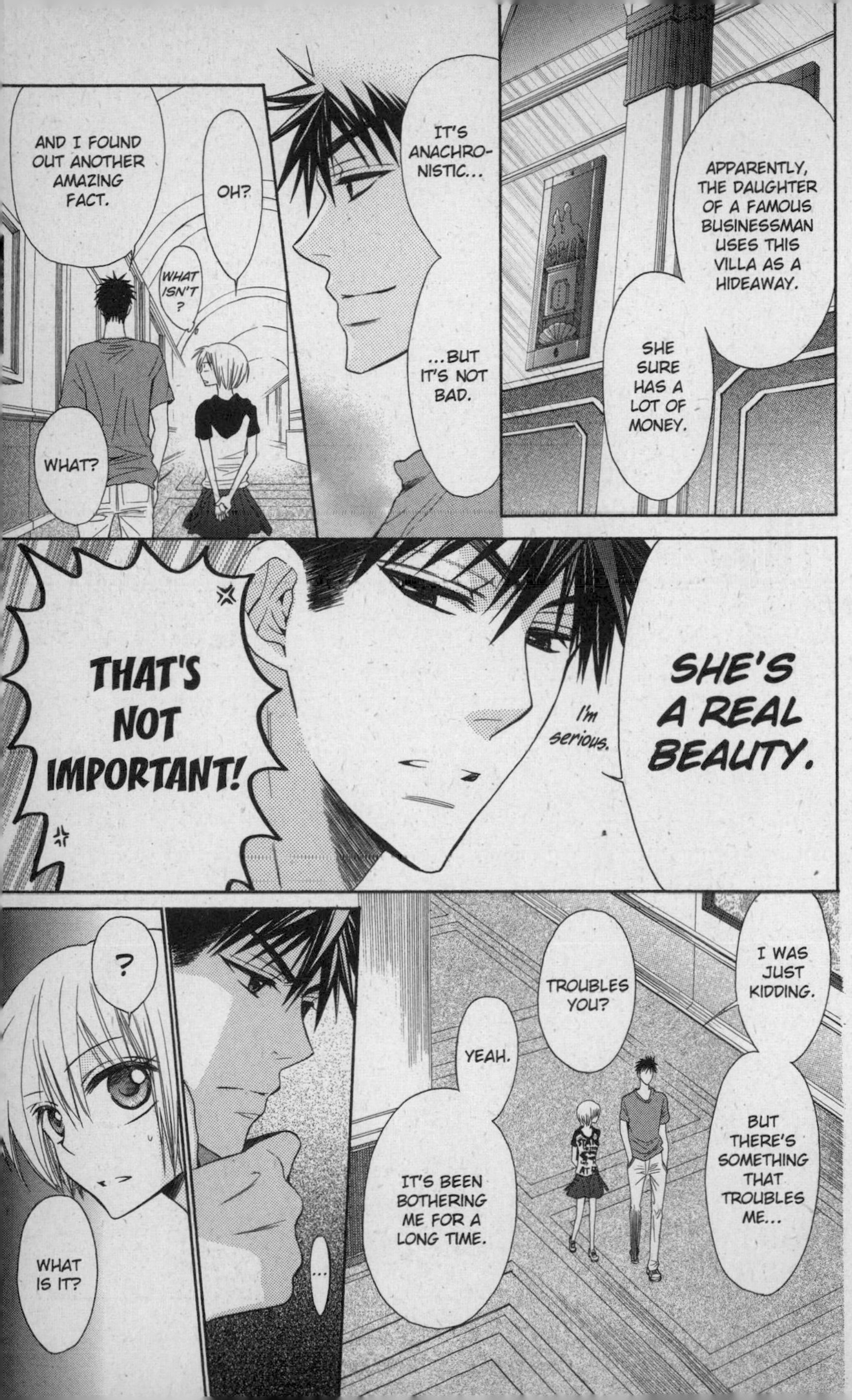
APPARENTLY, THE DAUGHTER OF A FAMOUS BUSINESSMAN USES THIS VILLA AS A HIDEAWAY.
SHE SURE HAS A LOT OF MONEY.
IT'S ANACHRO-NISTIC...
...BUT IT'S NOT BAD.
OH?
WHAT ISN'T?
AND I FOUND OUT ANOTHER AMAZING FACT.
WHAT?
SHE'S A REAL BEAUTY.
I'm serious.
THAT'S NOT IMPORTANT!
I WAS JUST KIDDING.
BUT THERE'S SOMETHING THAT TROUBLES ME...
TROUBLES YOU?
YEAH.
IT'S BEEN BOTHERING ME FOR A LONG TIME.
?
WHAT IS IT?
...

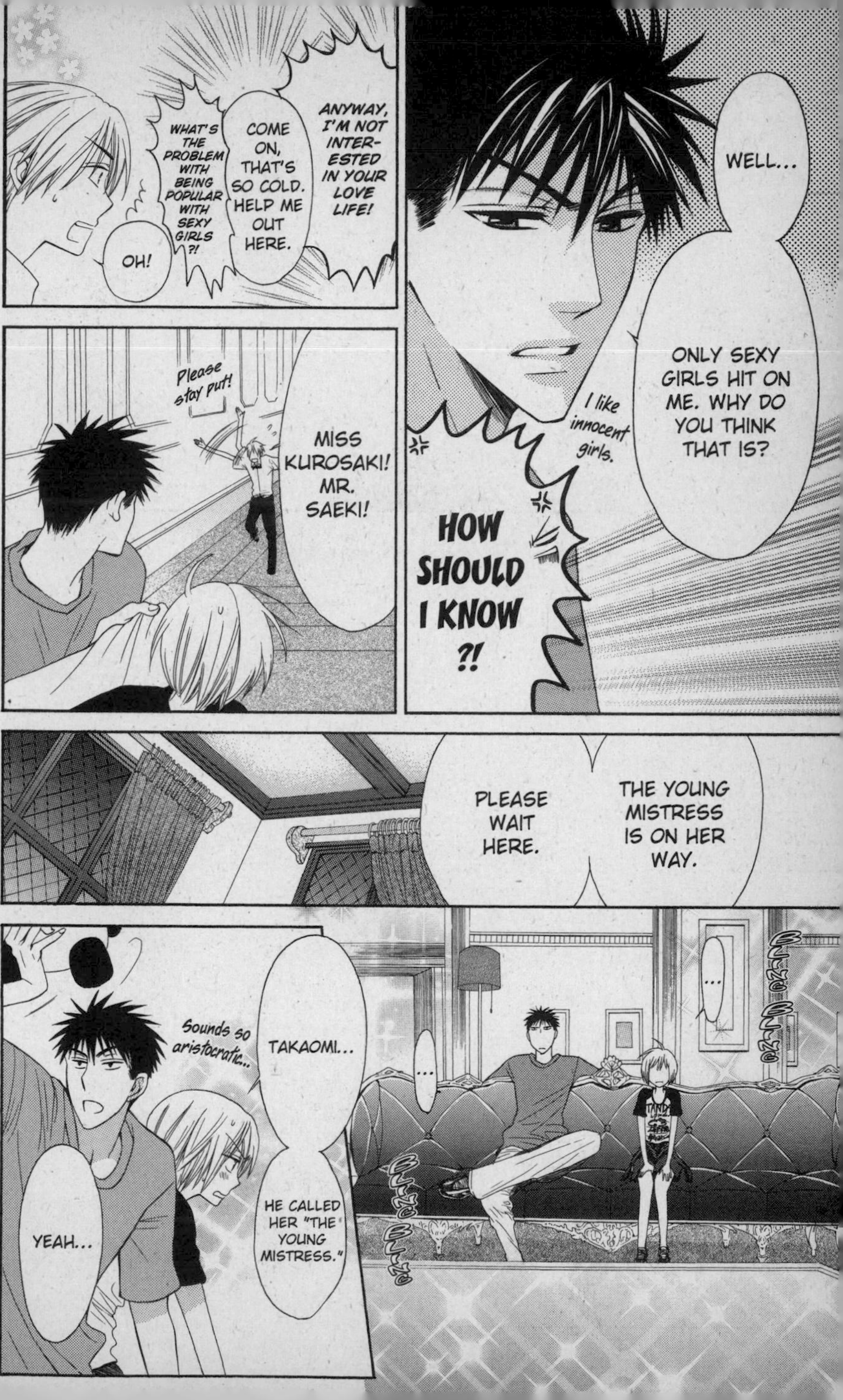
WELL...
ONLY SEXY GIRLS HIT ON ME. WHY DO YOU THINK THAT IS?
I like innocent girls.
HOW SHOULD I KNOW ?!
ANYWAY, I'M NOT INTER-ESTED IN YOUR LOVE LIFE!
COME ON, THAT'S SO COLD. HELP ME OUT HERE.
WHAT'S THE PROBLEM WITH BEING POPULAR WITH SEXY GIRLS ?!
OH!
MISS KUROSAKI! MR. SAEKI!
Please stay put!
THE YOUNG MISTRESS IS ON HER WAY.
PLEASE WAIT HERE.
...
...
TAKAOMI...
Sounds so aristocratic...
HE CALLED HER "THE YOUNG MISTRESS."
YEAH...

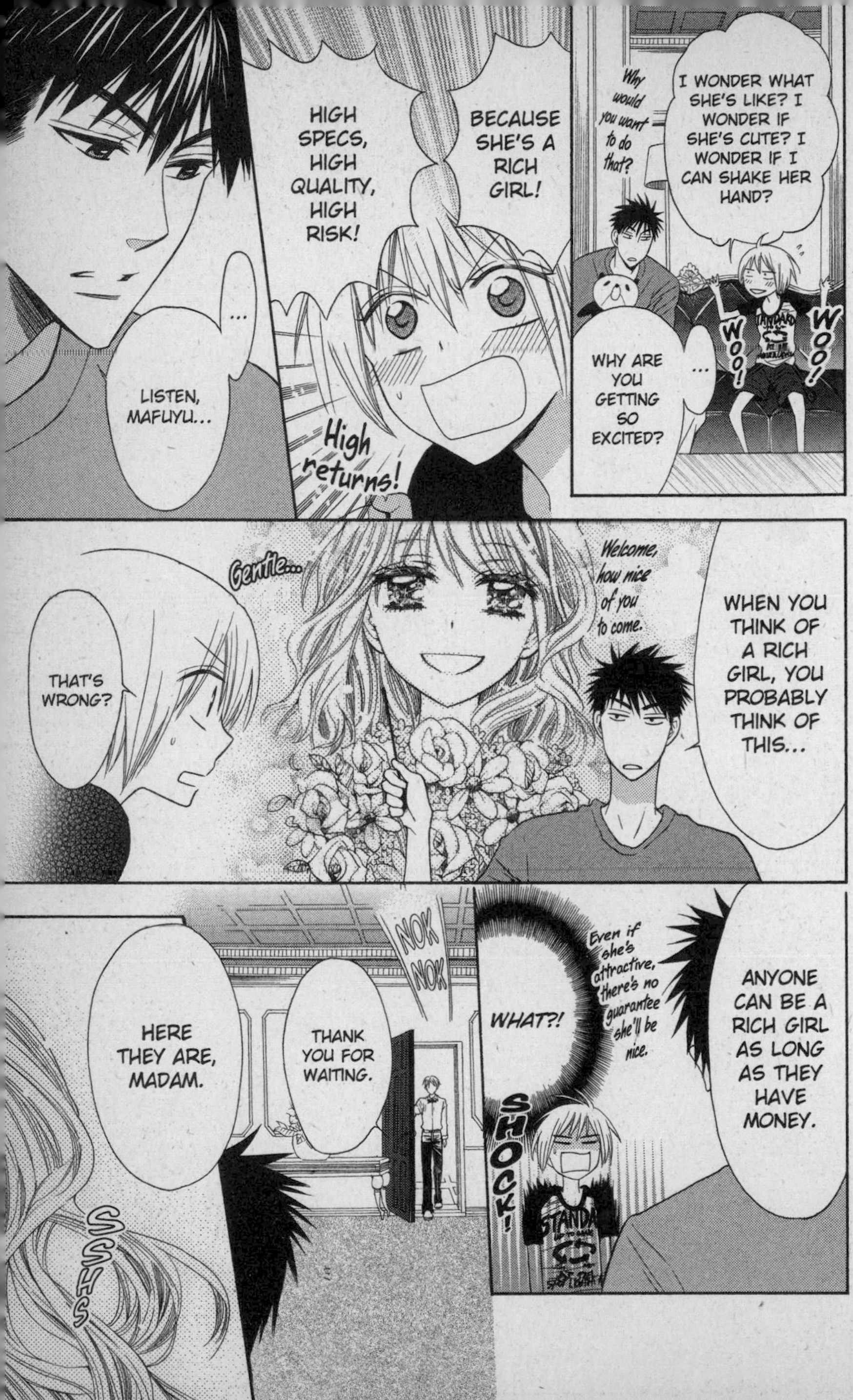
I WONDER WHAT SHE'S LIKE? I WONDER IF SHE'S CUTE? I WONDER IF I CAN SHAKE HER HAND?
Why would you want to do that?
WOO!
WOO!
...
WHY ARE YOU GETTING SO EXCITED?
BECAUSE SHE'S A RICH GIRL!
HIGH SPECS, HIGH QUALITY, HIGH RISK!
High returns!
...
LISTEN, MAFUYU...
WHEN YOU THINK OF A RICH GIRL, YOU PROBABLY THINK OF THIS...
Welcome, how nice of you to come.
Gentle...
THAT'S WRONG?
ANYONE CAN BE A RICH GIRL AS LONG AS THEY HAVE MONEY.
Even if she's attractive, there's no guarantee she'll be nice.
WHAT?!
SHOCK!
NOK NOK
THANK YOU FOR WAITING.
HERE THEY ARE, MADAM.
SSHS

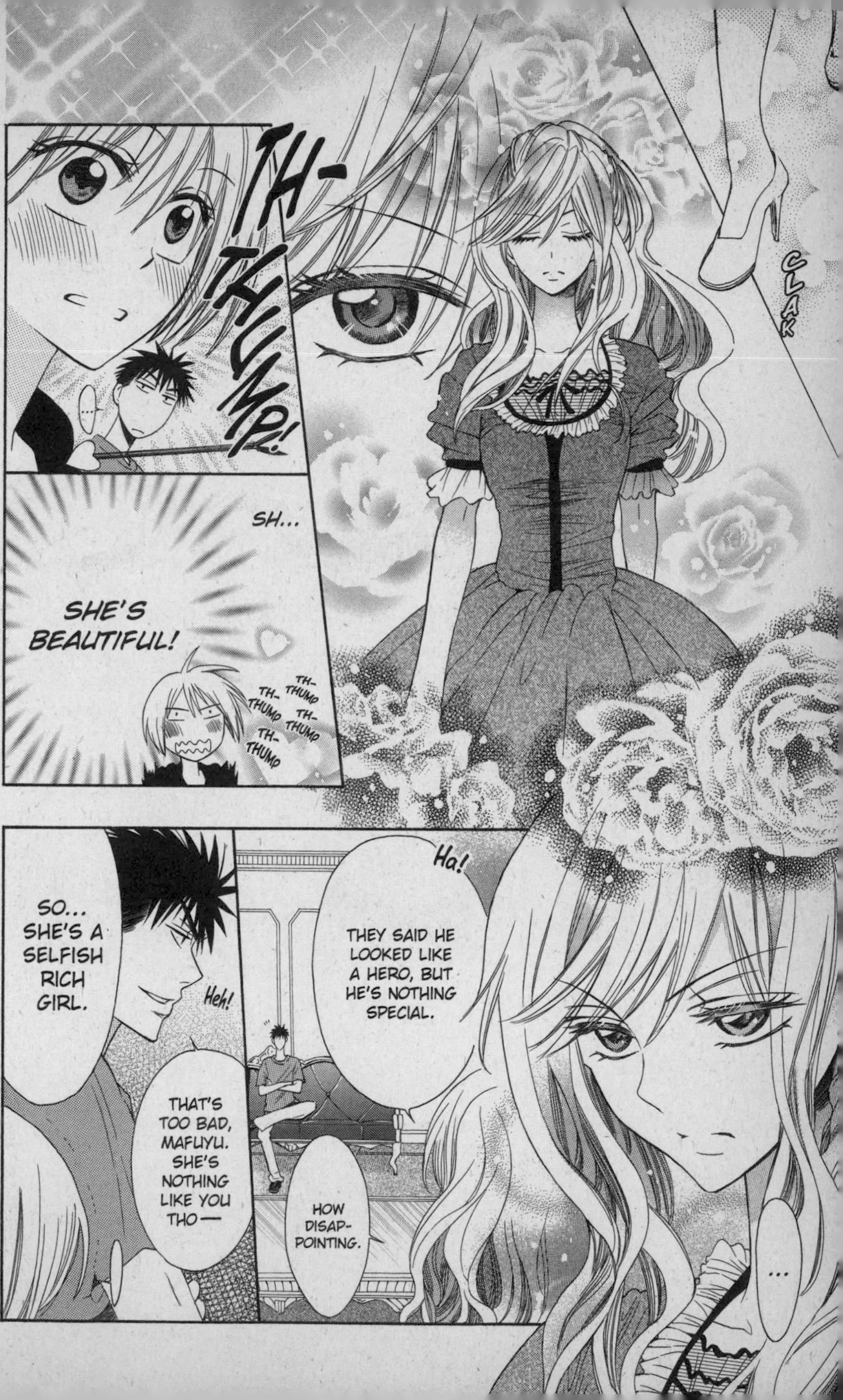
CLAK
TH-THUMP!
...
SH...
SHE'S BEAUTIFUL!
TH-THUMP TH-THUMP TH-THUMP TH-THUMP
...
Ha!
THEY SAID HE LOOKED LIKE A HERO, BUT HE'S NOTHING SPECIAL.
HOW DISAP-POINTING.
SO... SHE'S A SELFISH RICH GIRL.
Heh!
THAT'S TOO BAD, MAFUYU. SHE'S NOTHING LIKE YOU THO—

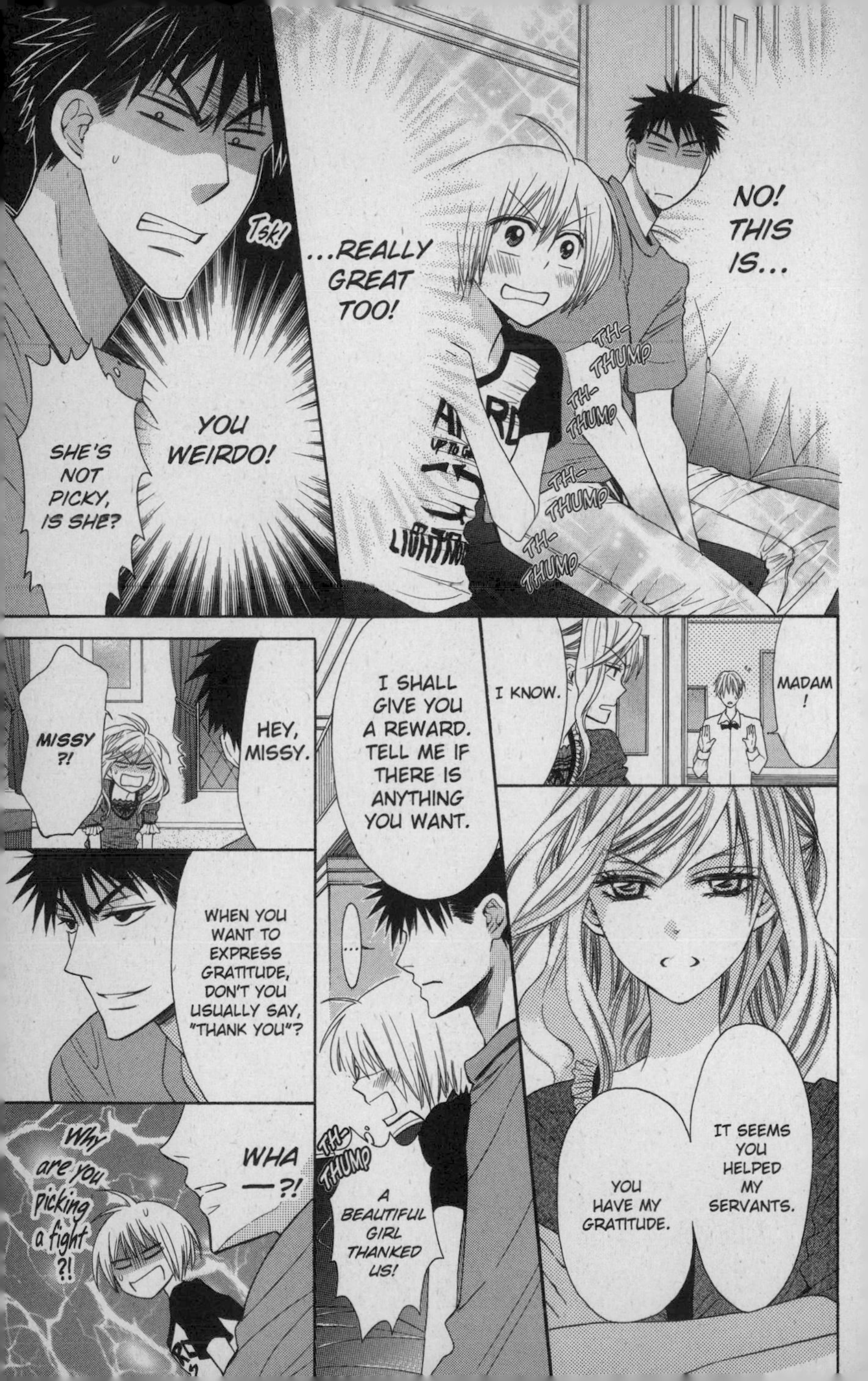
NO! THIS IS...
...REALLY GREAT TOO!
TH-THUMP
TH-THUMP
TH-THUMP
TH-THUMP
Tsk!
YOU WEIRDO!
SHE'S NOT PICKY, IS SHE?
MADAM!
I KNOW.
IT SEEMS YOU HELPED MY SERVANTS.
YOU HAVE MY GRATITUDE.
I SHALL GIVE YOU A REWARD. TELL ME IF THERE IS ANYTHING YOU WANT.
...
TH-THUMP
A BEAUTIFUL GIRL THANKED US!
HEY, MISSY.
MISSY?!
WHEN YOU WANT TO EXPRESS GRATITUDE, DON'T YOU USUALLY SAY, "THANK YOU"?
WHA—?!
Why are you picking a fight?!

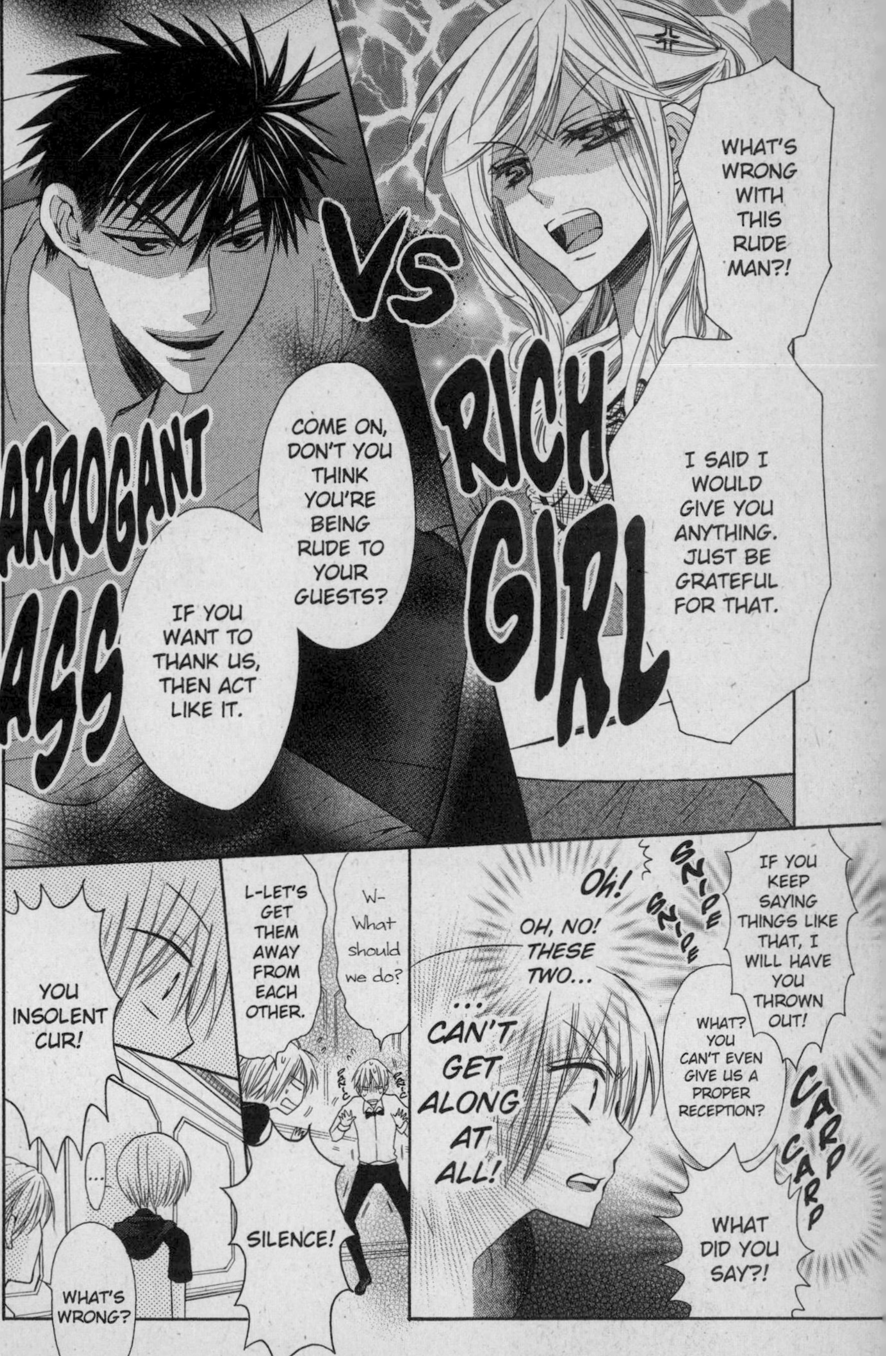
WHAT'S WRONG WITH THIS RUDE MAN?!
I SAID I WOULD GIVE YOU ANYTHING. JUST BE GRATEFUL FOR THAT.
RICH GIRL
VS
ARROGANT ASS
COME ON, DON'T YOU THINK YOU'RE BEING RUDE TO YOUR GUESTS?
IF YOU WANT TO THANK US, THEN ACT LIKE IT.
IF YOU KEEP SAYING THINGS LIKE THAT, I WILL HAVE YOU THROWN OUT!
SNIDE SNIDE
Oh!
OH, NO! THESE TWO...
...CAN'T GET ALONG AT ALL!
WHAT? YOU CAN'T EVEN GIVE US A PROPER RECEPTION?
CARP CARP
WHAT DID YOU SAY?!
W- What should we do?
L-LET'S GET THEM AWAY FROM EACH OTHER.
SILENCE!
YOU INSOLENT CUR!
...
WHAT'S WRONG?

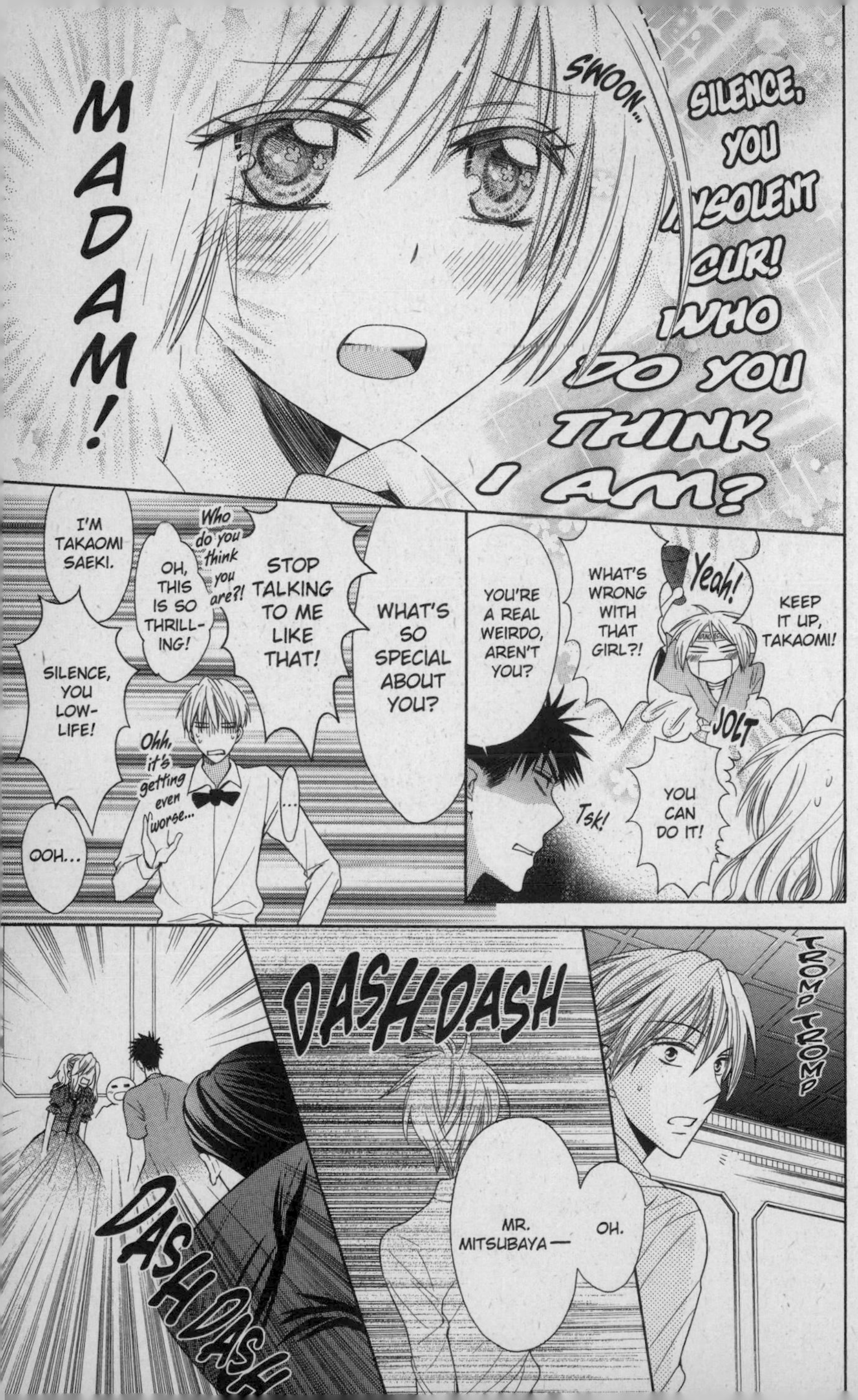
SILENCE, YOU INSOLENT CUR! WHO DO YOU THINK I AM?
SWOON...
MADAM!
KEEP IT UP, TAKAOMI!
Yeah!
WHAT'S WRONG WITH THAT GIRL?!
YOU'RE A REAL WEIRDO, AREN'T YOU?
JOLT
YOU CAN DO IT!
Tsk!
WHAT'S SO SPECIAL ABOUT YOU?
STOP TALKING TO ME LIKE THAT!
Who do you think you are?!
OH, THIS IS SO THRILL-ING!
I'M TAKAOMI SAEKI.
SILENCE, YOU LOW-LIFE!
...
Ohh, it's getting even worse...
OOH...
TROMP TROMP TROMP
OH.
MR. MITSUBAYA—
DASH DASH
DASH DASH

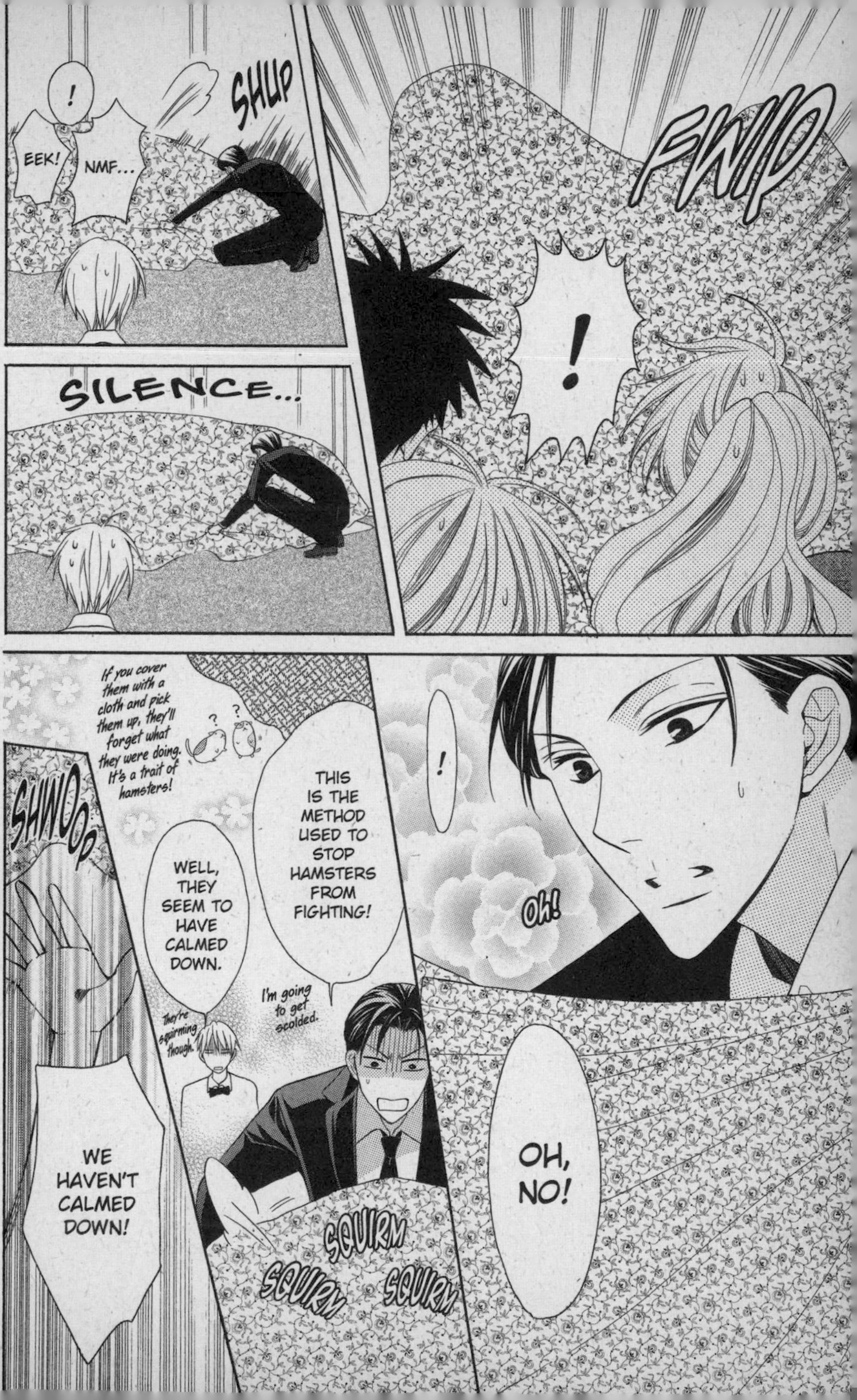
FWIP
!
SHUP
!
EEK!
NMF...
SILENCE...
!
OH!
OH, NO!
If you cover them with a cloth and pick them up, they'll forget what they were doing. It's a trait of hamsters!
THIS IS THE METHOD USED TO STOP HAMSTERS FROM FIGHTING!
WELL, THEY SEEM TO HAVE CALMED DOWN.
I'm going to get scolded.
They're squirming though.
SQUIRM
SQUIRM
SQUIRM
SHWOOP
WE HAVEN'T CALMED DOWN!

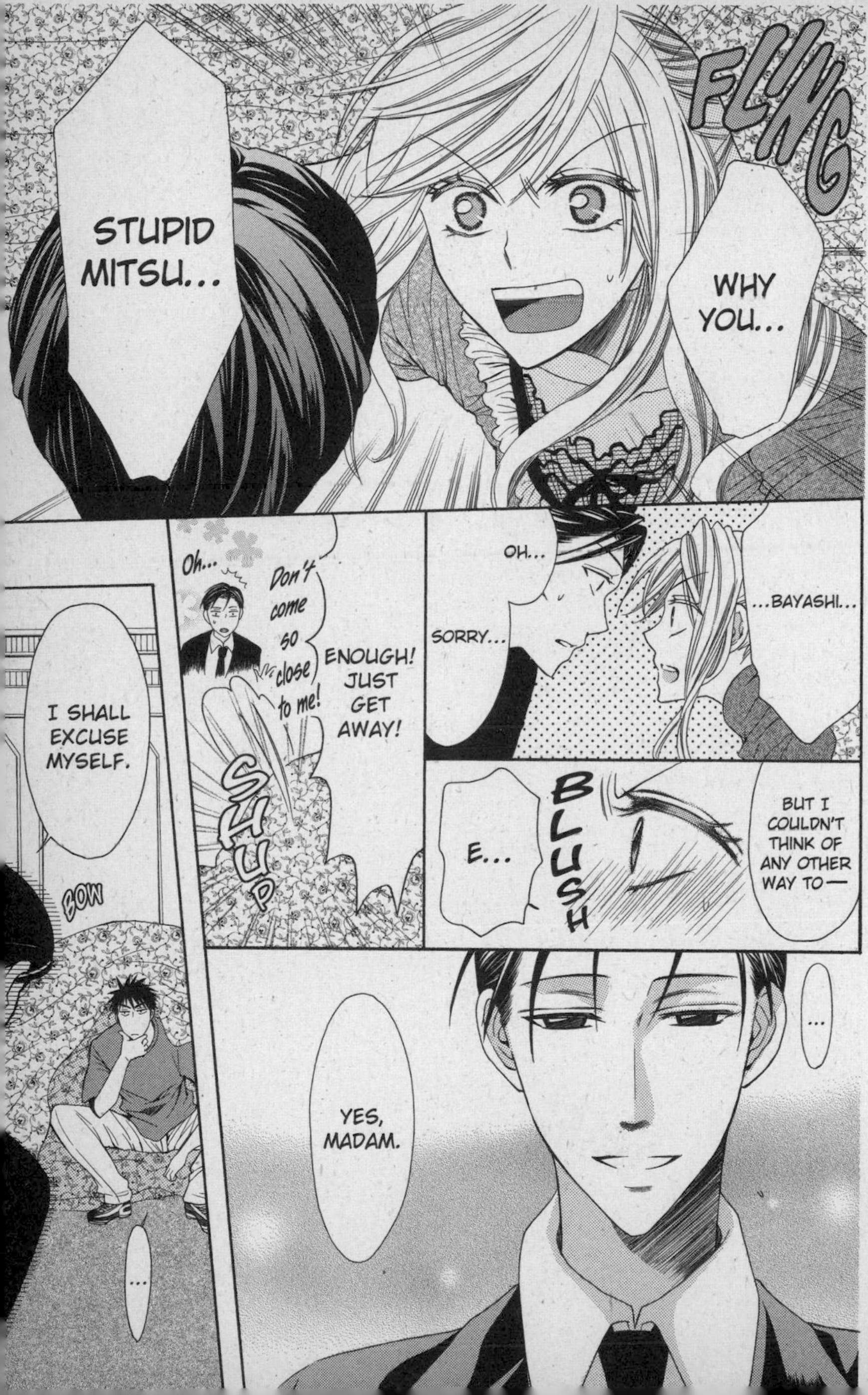
FLING
WHY YOU...
STUPID MITSU...
...BAYASHI...
OH...
SORRY...
BUT I COULDN'T THINK OF ANY OTHER WAY TO—
BLUSH
E...
ENOUGH! JUST GET AWAY!
Don't come so close to me!
Oh...
SHUP
...
YES, MADAM.
I SHALL EXCUSE MYSELF.
BOW
...

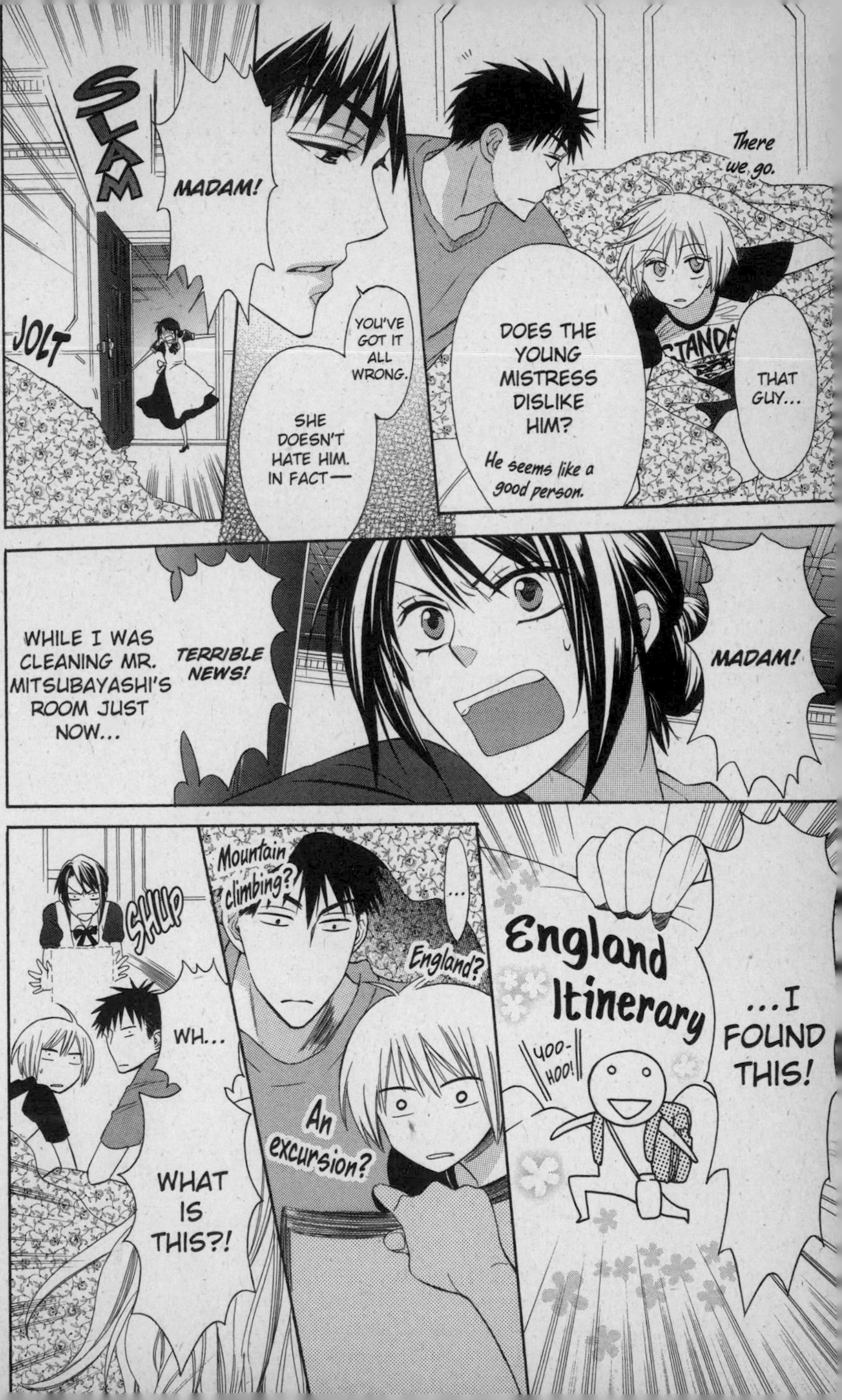
There we go.
THAT GUY...
DOES THE YOUNG MISTRESS DISLIKE HIM?
He seems like a good person.
YOU'VE GOT IT ALL WRONG.
SHE DOESN'T HATE HIM. IN FACT—
SLAM
MADAM!
JOLT
MADAM!
TERRIBLE NEWS!
WHILE I WAS CLEANING MR. MITSUBAYASHI'S ROOM JUST NOW...
...I FOUND THIS!
England Itinerary
YOO-HOO!
...
Mountain climbing?
England?
An excursion?
SHUP
WH...
WHAT IS THIS?!

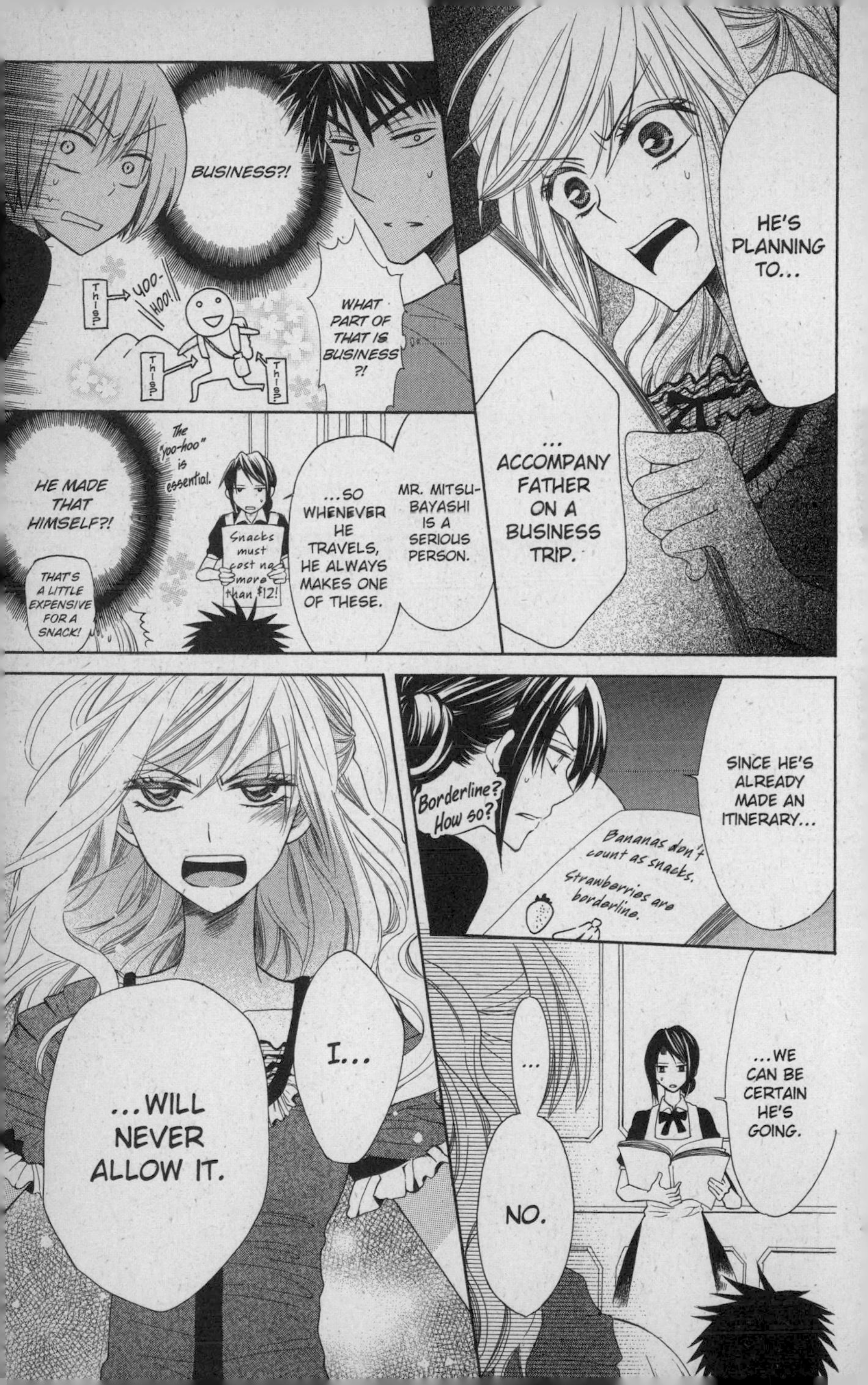
HE'S PLANNING TO...
...ACCOMPANY FATHER ON A BUSINESS TRIP.
BUSINESS?!
WHAT PART OF THAT IS BUSINESS?!
This.
YOO-HOO!
This.
This.
MR. MITSU-BAYASHI IS A SERIOUS PERSON.
...SO WHENEVER HE TRAVELS, HE ALWAYS MAKES ONE OF THESE.
The "yoo-hoo" is essential.
Snacks must cost no more than $12!
HE MADE THAT HIMSELF?!
THAT'S A LITTLE EXPENSIVE FOR A SNACK!
SINCE HE'S ALREADY MADE AN ITINERARY...
Borderline? How so?
Bananas don't count as snacks. Strawberries are borderline.
...WE CAN BE CERTAIN HE'S GOING.
...
NO.
I...
...WILL NEVER ALLOW IT.

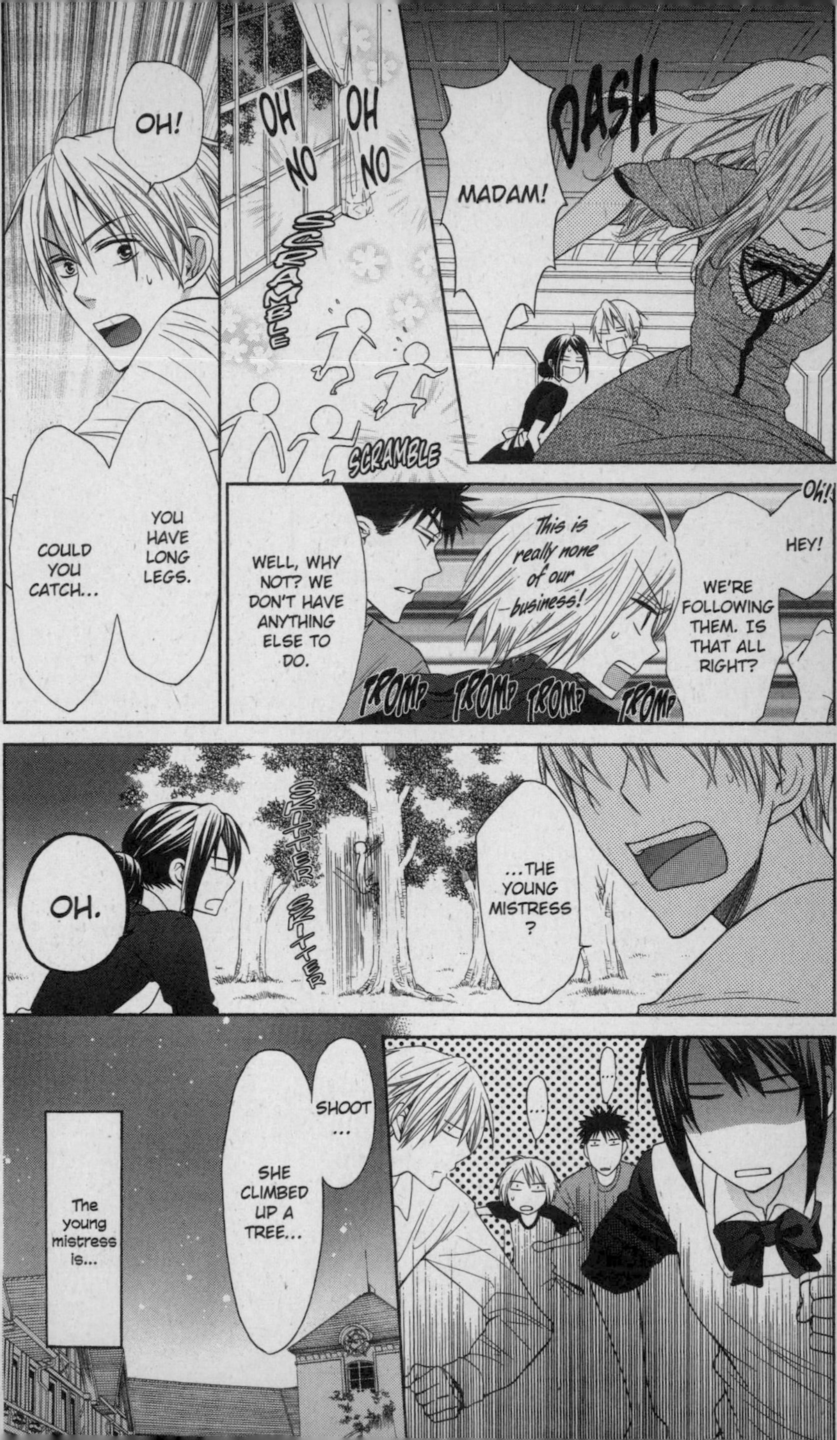
OASH
MADAM!
OH NO
OH NO
SCRAMBLE
SCRAMBLE
Oh!
HEY!
WE'RE FOLLOWING THEM. IS THAT ALL RIGHT?
This is really none of our business!
WELL, WHY NOT? WE DON'T HAVE ANYTHING ELSE TO DO.
TROMP TROMP TROMP TROMP
OH!
YOU HAVE LONG LEGS.
COULD YOU CATCH...
...THE YOUNG MISTRESS?
SKITTER SKITTER
OH.
...
...
SHOOT...
SHE CLIMBED UP A TREE...
The young mistress is...

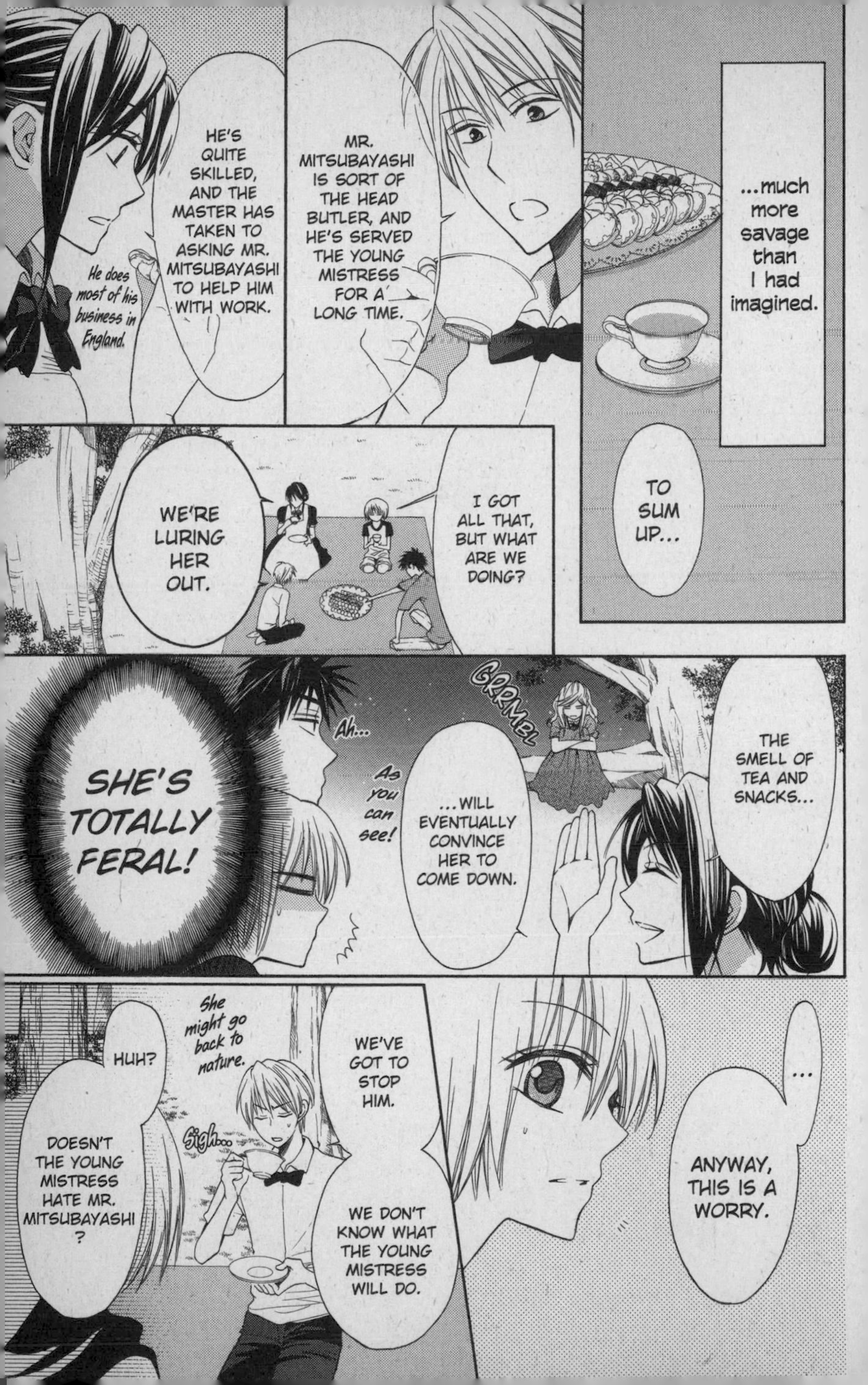
...much more savage than I had imagined.
TO SUM UP...
MR. MITSUBAYASHI IS SORT OF THE HEAD BUTLER, AND HE'S SERVED THE YOUNG MISTRESS FOR A LONG TIME.
HE'S QUITE SKILLED, AND THE MASTER HAS TAKEN TO ASKING MR. MITSUBAYASHI TO HELP HIM WITH WORK.
He does most of his business in England.
I GOT ALL THAT, BUT WHAT ARE WE DOING?
WE'RE LURING HER OUT.
THE SMELL OF TEA AND SNACKS...
GRRMBL
...WILL EVENTUALLY CONVINCE HER TO COME DOWN.
As you can see!
Ah...
SHE'S TOTALLY FERAL!
...
ANYWAY, THIS IS A WORRY.
WE'VE GOT TO STOP HIM.
WE DON'T KNOW WHAT THE YOUNG MISTRESS WILL DO.
She might go back to nature.
Sigh...
HUH?
DOESN'T THE YOUNG MISTRESS HATE MR. MITSUBAYASHI?

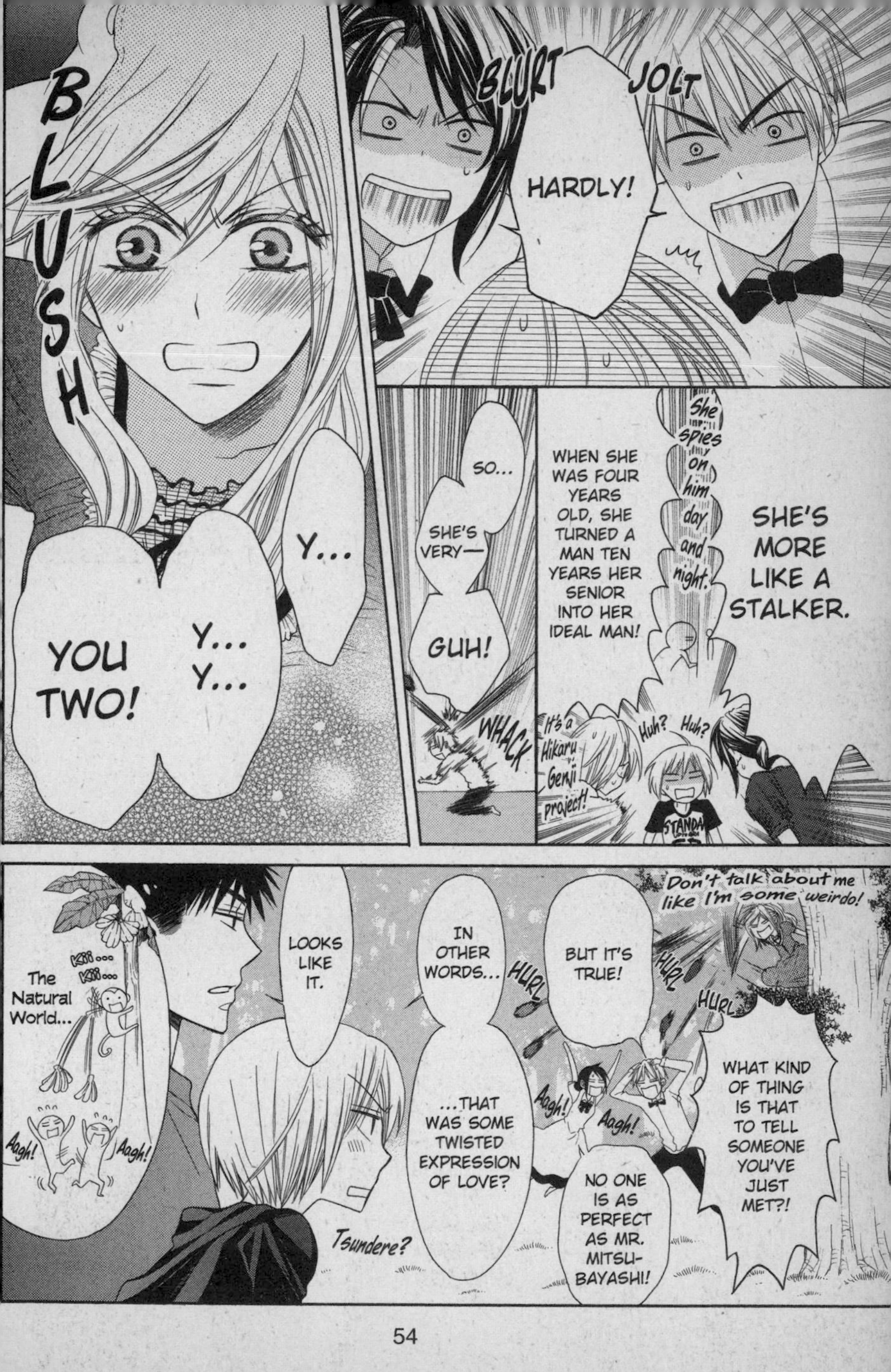
BLURT
JOLT
HARDLY!
SHE'S MORE LIKE A STALKER.
She spies on him day and night.
WHEN SHE WAS FOUR YEARS OLD, SHE TURNED A MAN TEN YEARS HER SENIOR INTO HER IDEAL MAN!
Huh?
Huh?
It's a Hikaru Genji project!
SO...
SHE'S VERY—
GUH!
WHACK
BLUSH
Y...
Y... Y...
YOU TWO!
Don't talk about me like I'm some weirdo!
HURL
HURL
HURL
WHAT KIND OF THING IS THAT TO TELL SOMEONE YOU'VE JUST MET?!
BUT IT'S TRUE!
NO ONE IS AS PERFECT AS MR. MITSUBAYASHI!
Aagh!
Aagh!
IN OTHER WORDS...
...THAT WAS SOME TWISTED EXPRESSION OF LOVE?
HURL
LOOKS LIKE IT.
Tsundere?
The Natural World...
Kii... Kii...
Aagh!
Aagh!

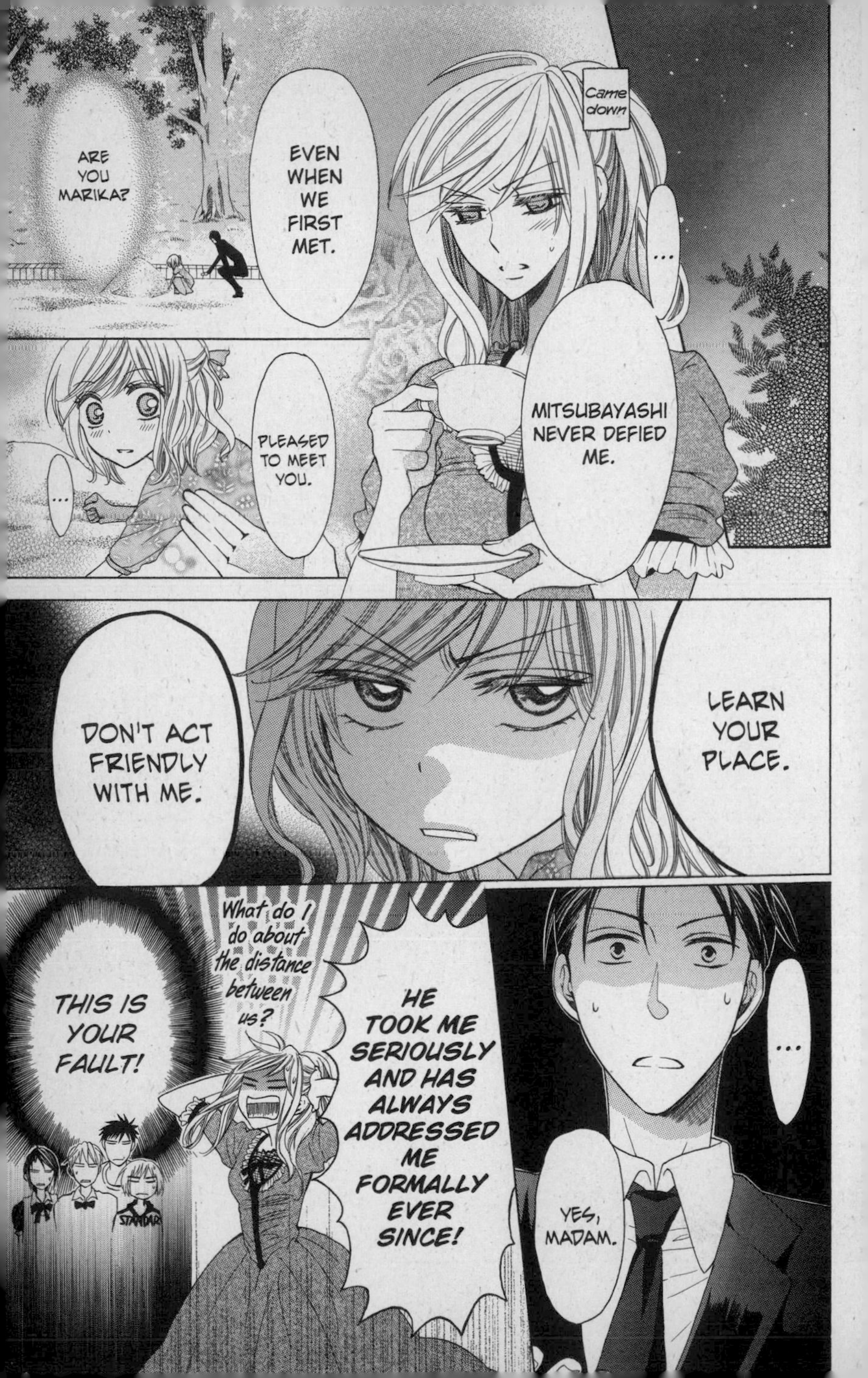
Came down
...
MITSUBAYASHI NEVER DEFIED ME.
EVEN WHEN WE FIRST MET.
ARE YOU MARIKA?
PLEASED TO MEET YOU.
...
LEARN YOUR PLACE.
DON'T ACT FRIENDLY WITH ME.
...
YES, MADAM.
HE TOOK ME SERIOUSLY AND HAS ALWAYS ADDRESSED ME FORMALLY EVER SINCE!
What do I do about the distance between us?
THIS IS YOUR FAULT!

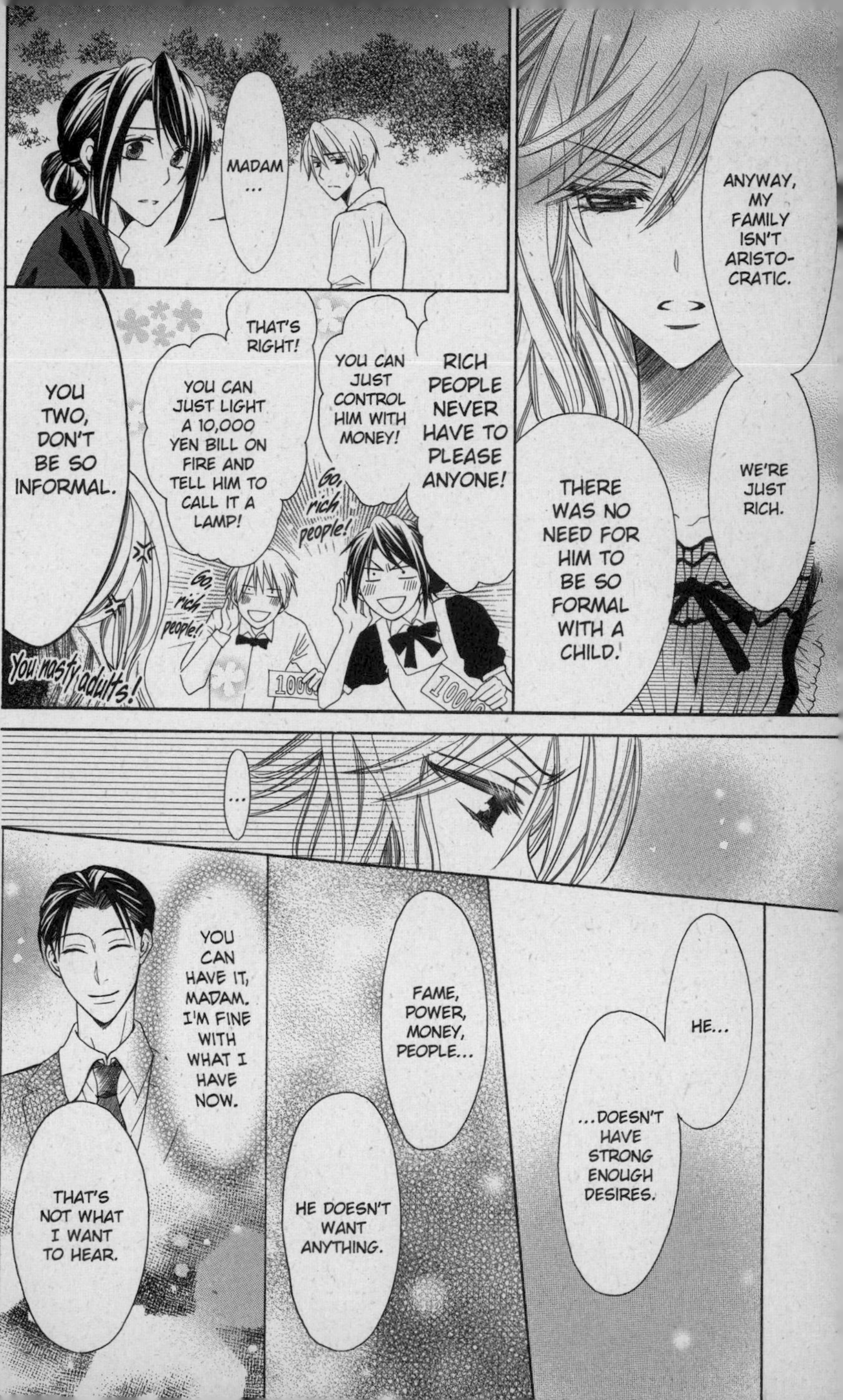
ANYWAY, MY FAMILY ISN'T ARISTO-CRATIC.
WE'RE JUST RICH.
THERE WAS NO NEED FOR HIM TO BE SO FORMAL WITH A CHILD.
MADAM...
RICH PEOPLE NEVER HAVE TO PLEASE ANYONE!
YOU CAN JUST CONTROL HIM WITH MONEY!
THAT'S RIGHT!
YOU CAN JUST LIGHT A 10,000 YEN BILL ON FIRE AND TELL HIM TO CALL IT A LAMP!
Go, rich people!
Go, rich people!
YOU TWO, DON'T BE SO INFORMAL.
You nasty adults!
...
HE...
...DOESN'T HAVE STRONG ENOUGH DESIRES.
FAME, POWER, MONEY, PEOPLE...
HE DOESN'T WANT ANYTHING.
YOU CAN HAVE IT, MADAM. I'M FINE WITH WHAT I HAVE NOW.
THAT'S NOT WHAT I WANT TO HEAR.

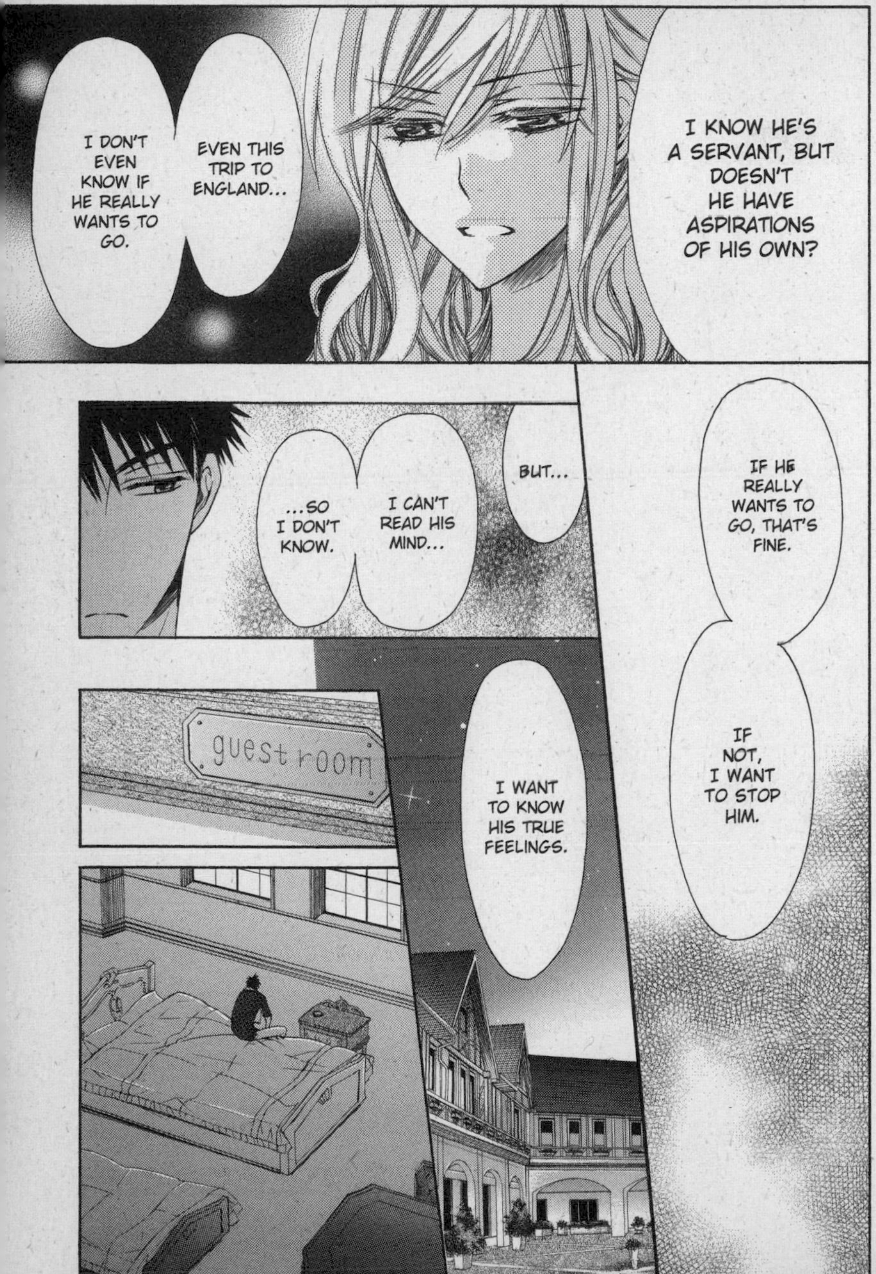
I KNOW HE'S A SERVANT, BUT DOESN'T HE HAVE ASPIRATIONS OF HIS OWN?
EVEN THIS TRIP TO ENGLAND...
I DON'T EVEN KNOW IF HE REALLY WANTS TO GO.
IF HE REALLY WANTS TO GO, THAT'S FINE.
IF NOT, I WANT TO STOP HIM.
BUT...
I CAN'T READ HIS MIND...
...SO I DON'T KNOW.
guest room
I WANT TO KNOW HIS TRUE FEELINGS.

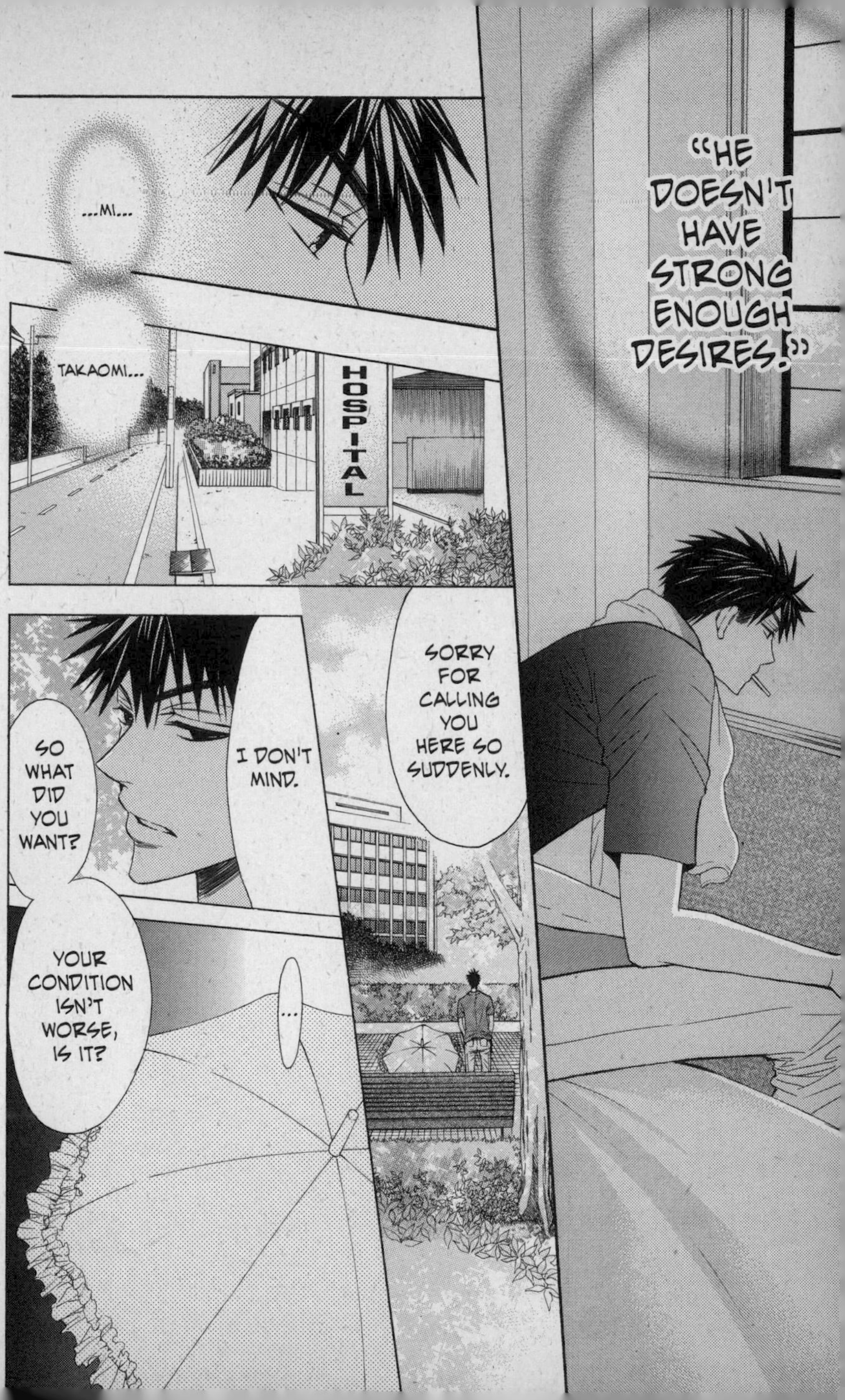
"HE DOESN'T HAVE STRONG ENOUGH DESIRES!"
...MI...
TAKAOMI...
HOSPITAL
SORRY FOR CALLING YOU HERE SO SUDDENLY.
I DON'T MIND.
SO WHAT DID YOU WANT?
...
YOUR CONDITION ISN'T WORSE, IS IT?

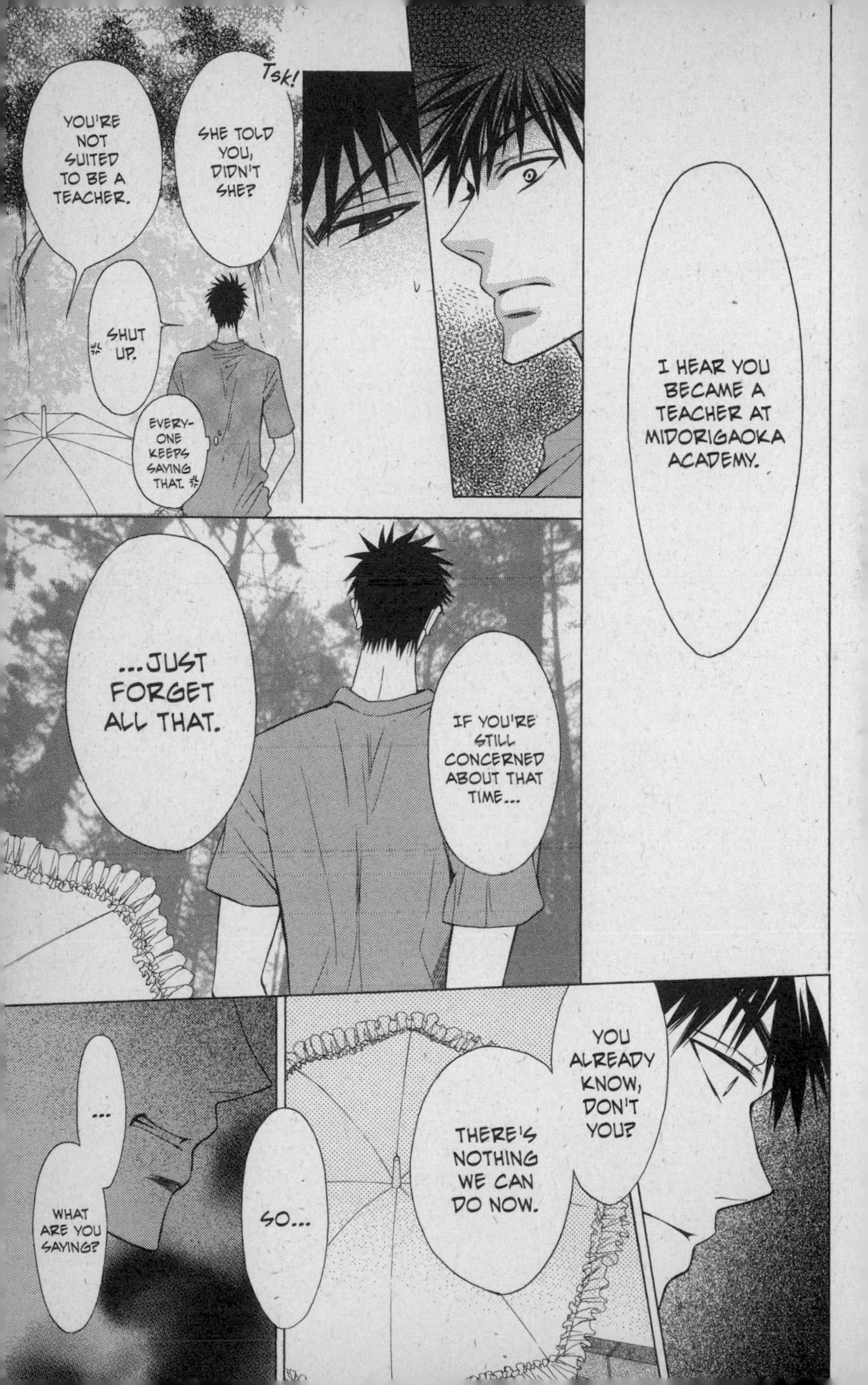
I HEAR YOU BECAME A TEACHER AT MIDORIGAOKA ACADEMY.
Tsk!
SHE TOLD YOU, DIDN'T SHE?
YOU'RE NOT SUITED TO BE A TEACHER.
SHUT UP.
EVERYONE KEEPS SAYING THAT.
IF YOU'RE STILL CONCERNED ABOUT THAT TIME...
...JUST FORGET ALL THAT.
YOU ALREADY KNOW, DON'T YOU?
THERE'S NOTHING WE CAN DO NOW.
SO...
...
WHAT ARE YOU SAYING?

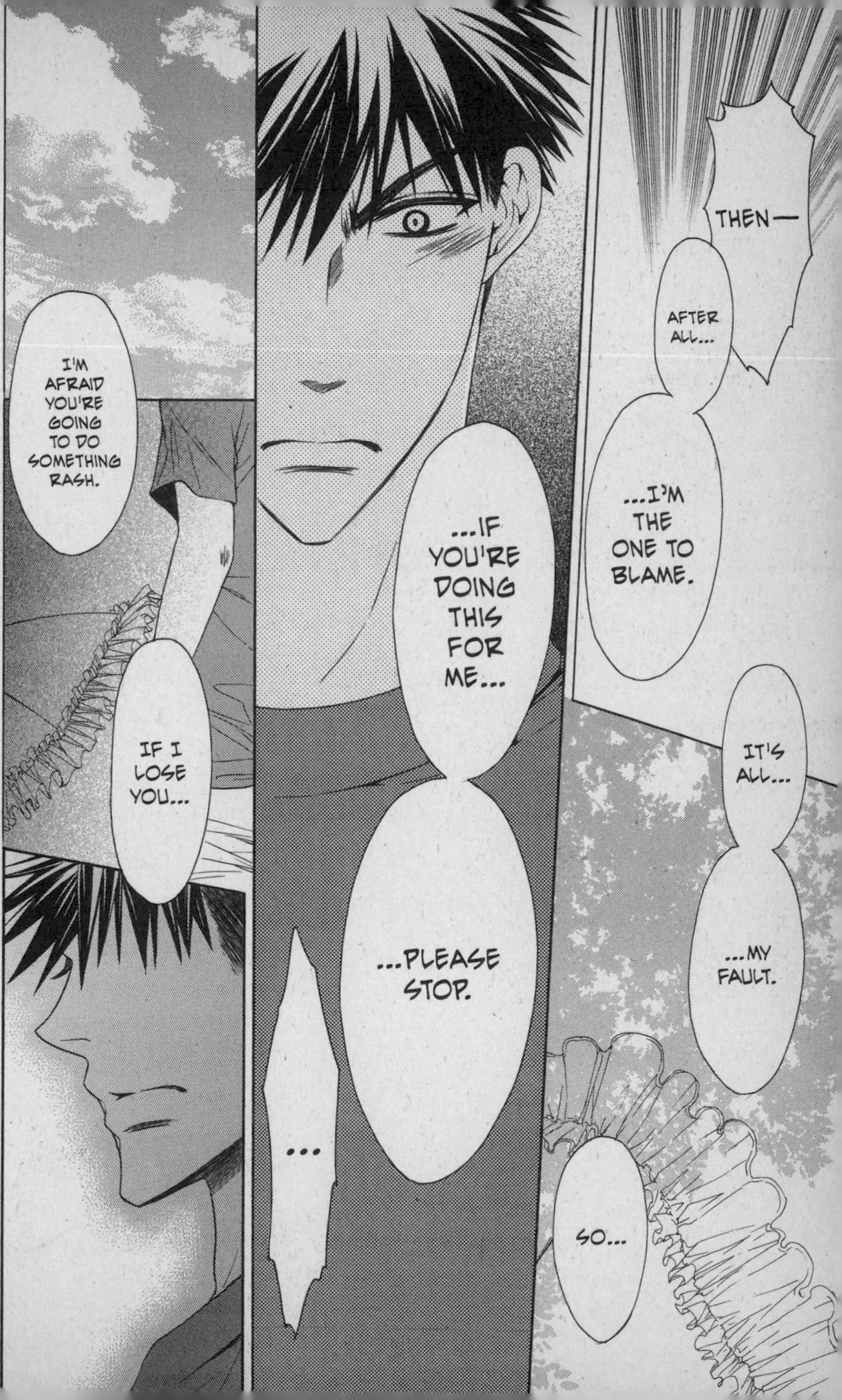
THEN—
AFTER ALL...
...I'M THE ONE TO BLAME.
IT'S ALL...
...MY FAULT.
SO...
...IF YOU'RE DOING THIS FOR ME...
...PLEASE STOP.
...
I'M AFRAID YOU'RE GOING TO DO SOMETHING RASH.
IF I LOSE YOU...

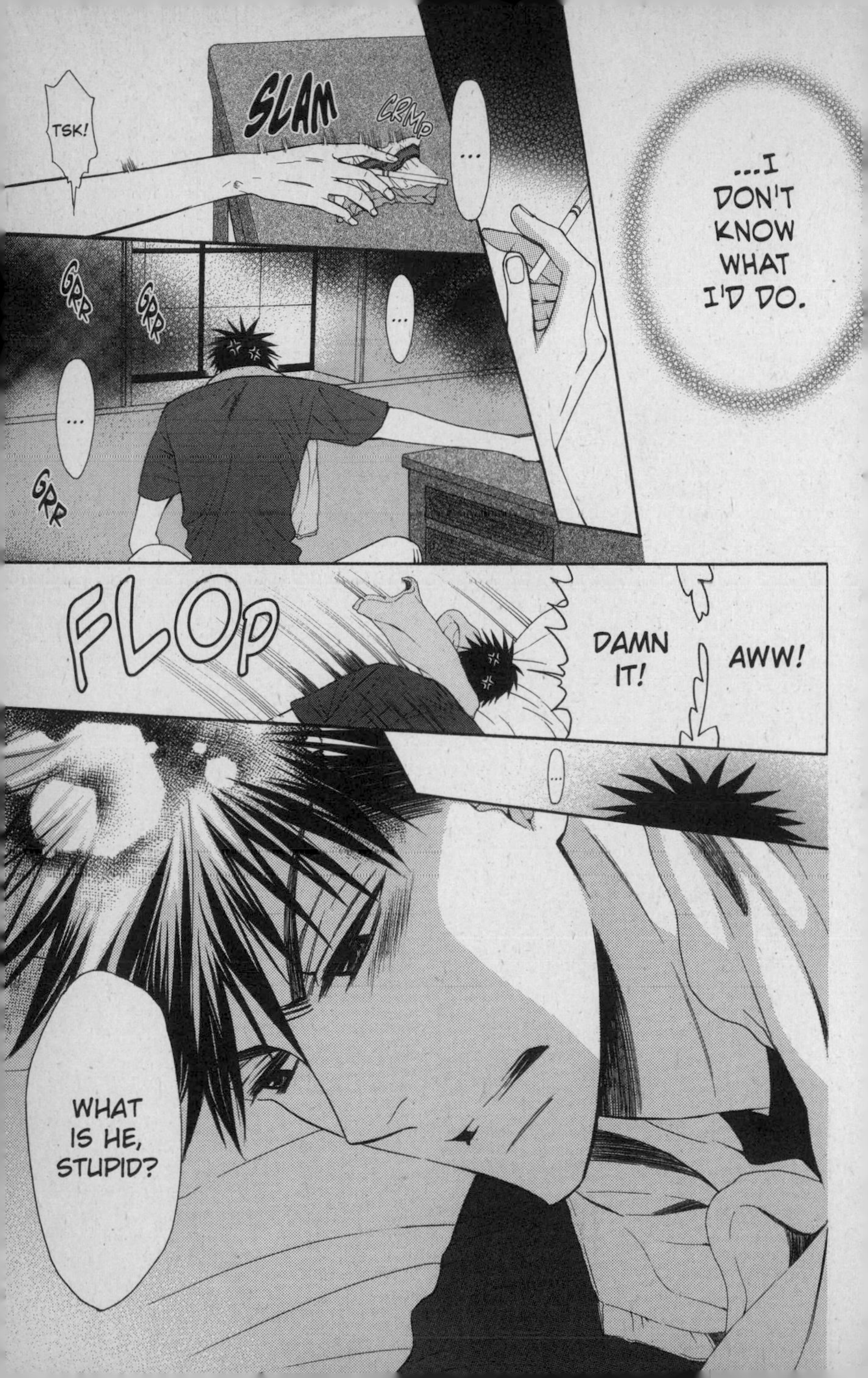
...I DON'T KNOW WHAT I'D DO.
...
TSK!
SLAM
CRMP
...
GRR
GRR
...
GRR
AWW!
DAMN IT!
FLOP
...
WHAT IS HE, STUPID?

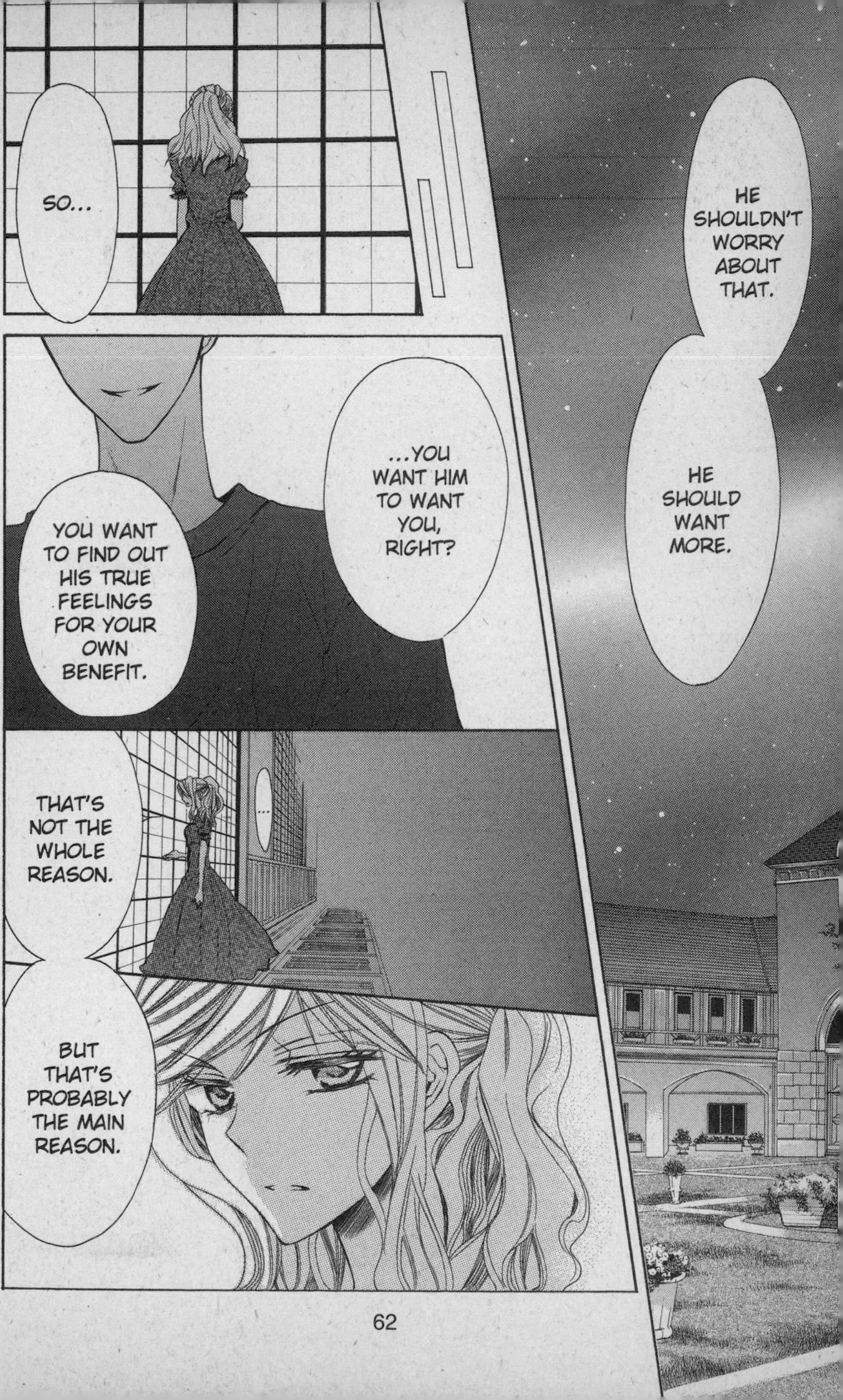
HE SHOULDN'T WORRY ABOUT THAT.
HE SHOULD WANT MORE.
SO...
...YOU WANT HIM TO WANT YOU, RIGHT?
YOU WANT TO FIND OUT HIS TRUE FEELINGS FOR YOUR OWN BENEFIT.
...
THAT'S NOT THE WHOLE REASON.
BUT THAT'S PROBABLY THE MAIN REASON.

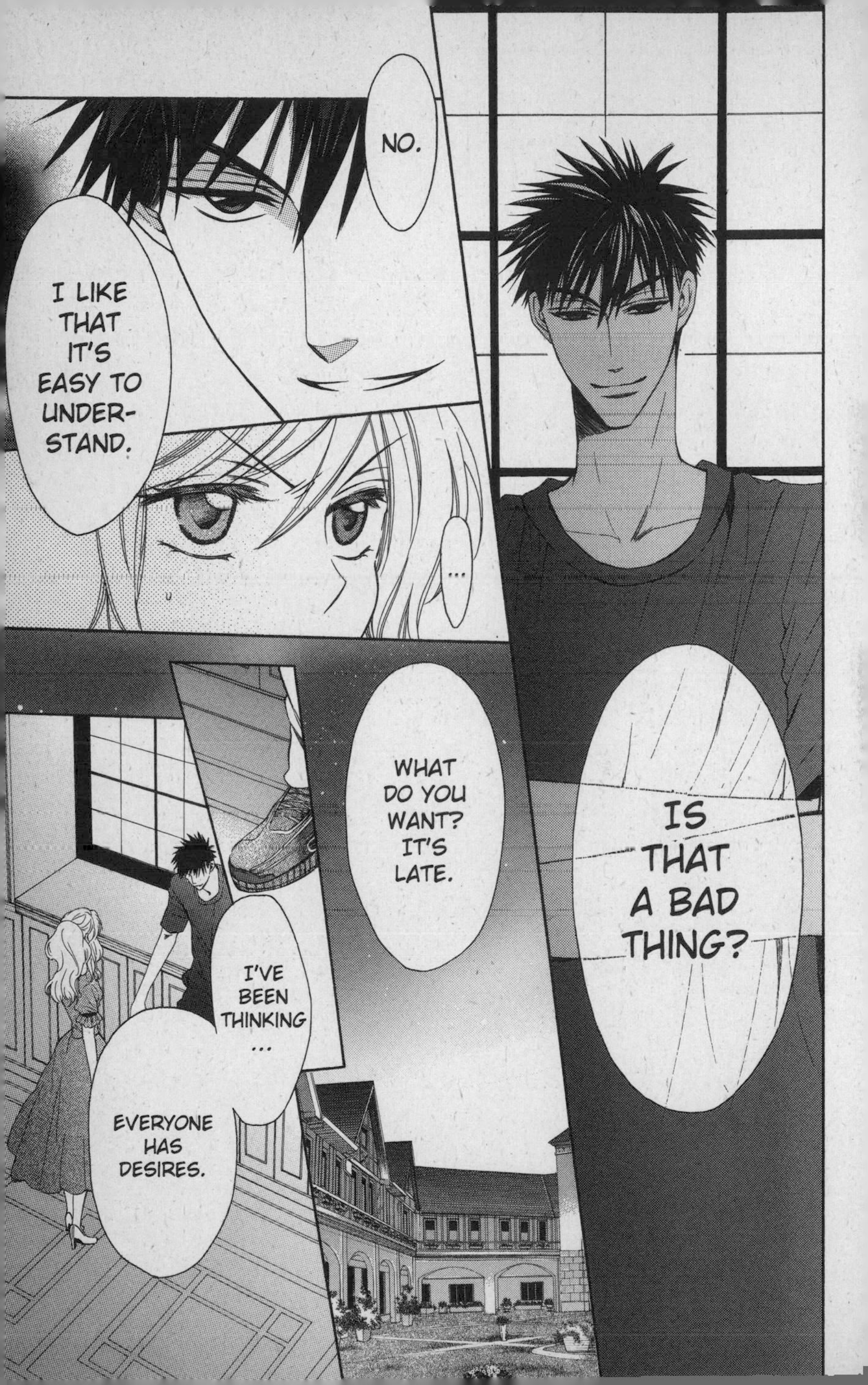
IS THAT A BAD THING?
NO.
I LIKE THAT IT'S EASY TO UNDER-STAND.
...
WHAT DO YOU WANT? IT'S LATE.
I'VE BEEN THINKING...
EVERYONE HAS DESIRES.

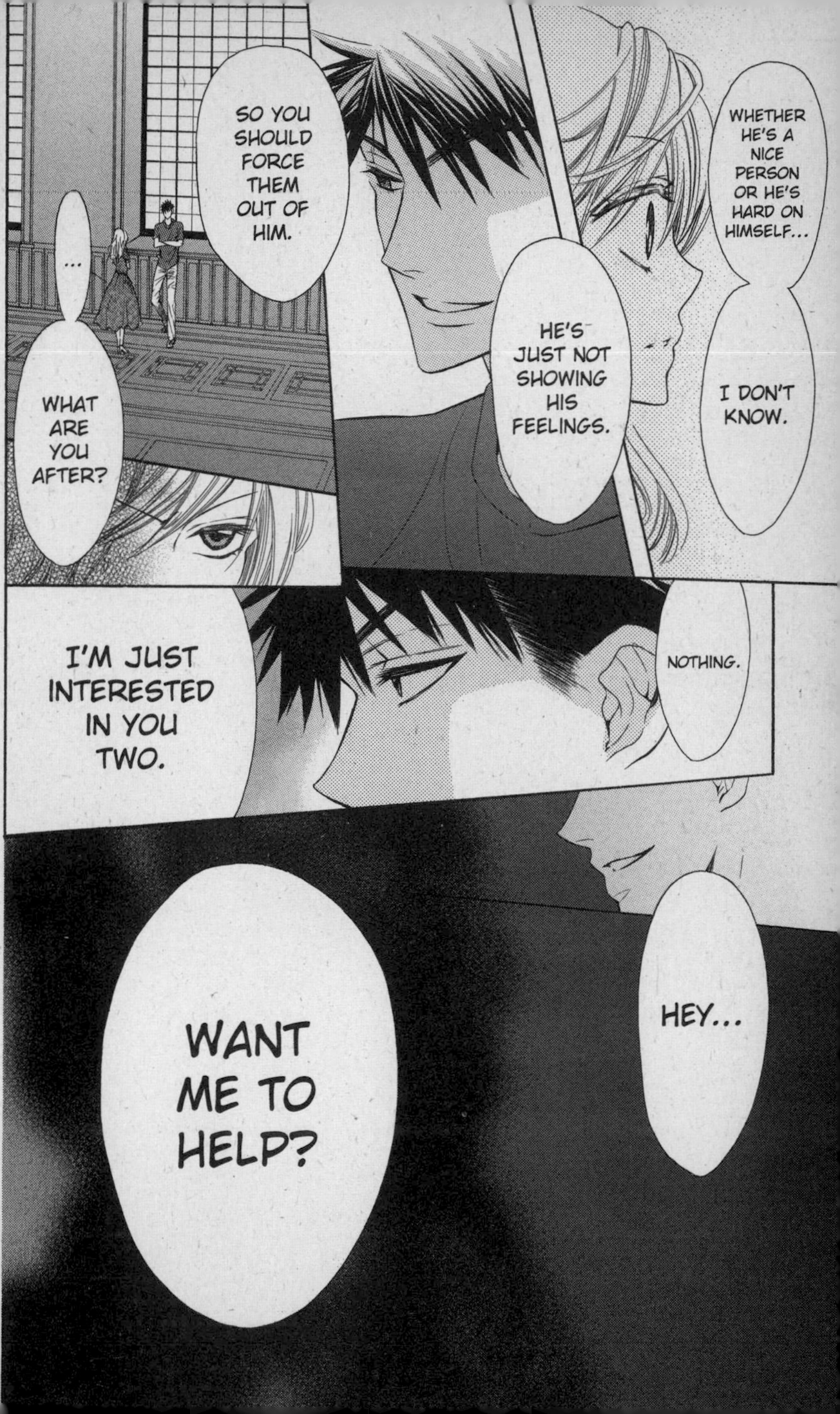
WHETHER HE'S A NICE PERSON OR HE'S HARD ON HIMSELF...
I DON'T KNOW.
HE'S JUST NOT SHOWING HIS FEELINGS.
SO YOU SHOULD FORCE THEM OUT OF HIM.
...
WHAT ARE YOU AFTER?
NOTHING.
I'M JUST INTERESTED IN YOU TWO.
HEY...
WANT ME TO HELP?

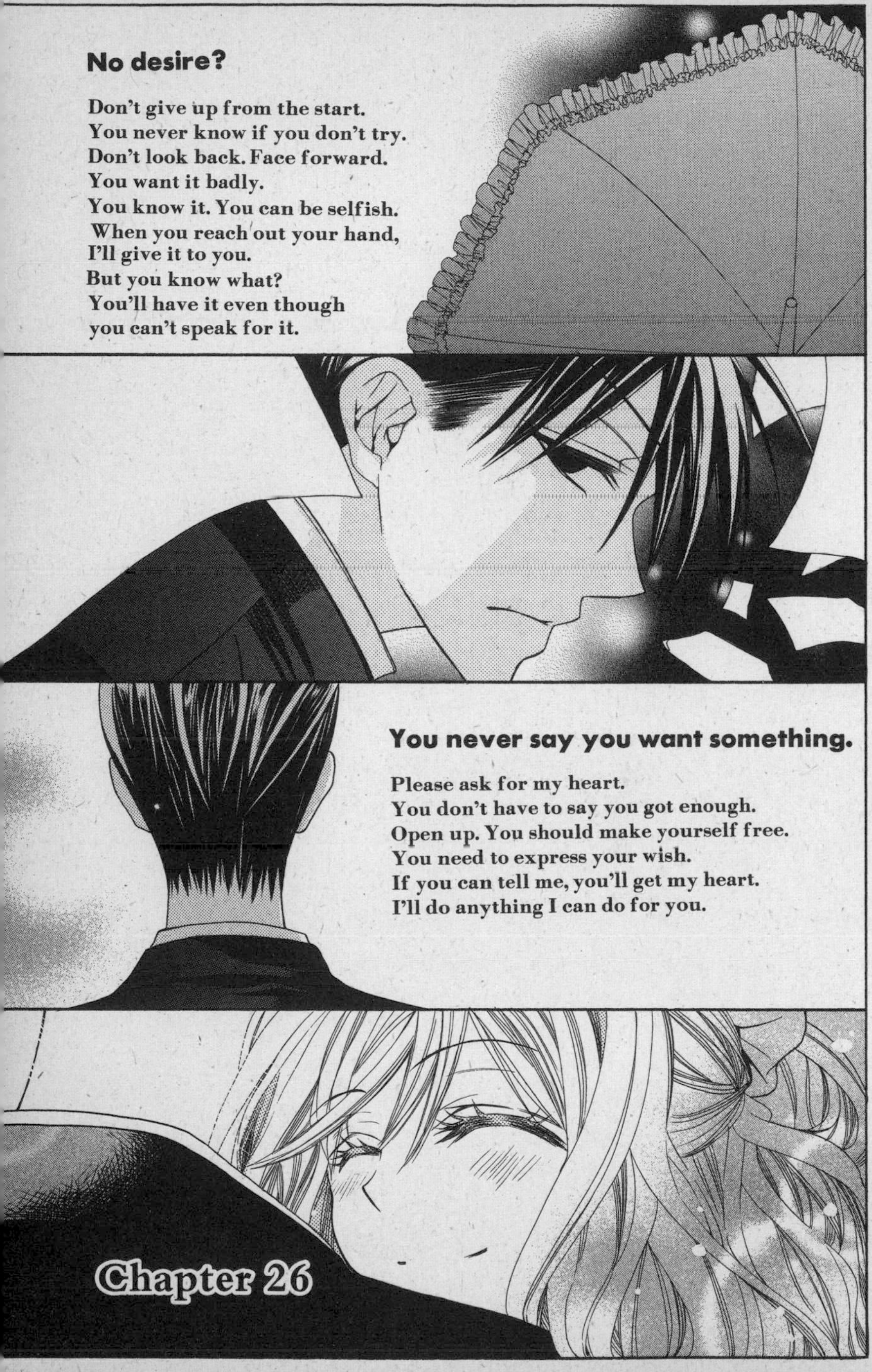
No desire?
Don't give up from the start.
You never know if you don't try.
Don't look back. Face forward.
You want it badly.
You know it. You can be selfish.
When you reach out your hand,
I'll give it to you.
But you know what?
You'll have it even though
you can't speak for it.
You never say you want something.
Please ask for my heart.
You don't have to say you got enough.
Open up. You should make yourself free.
You need to express your wish.
If you can tell me, you'll get my heart.
I'll do anything I can do for you.
Chapter 26

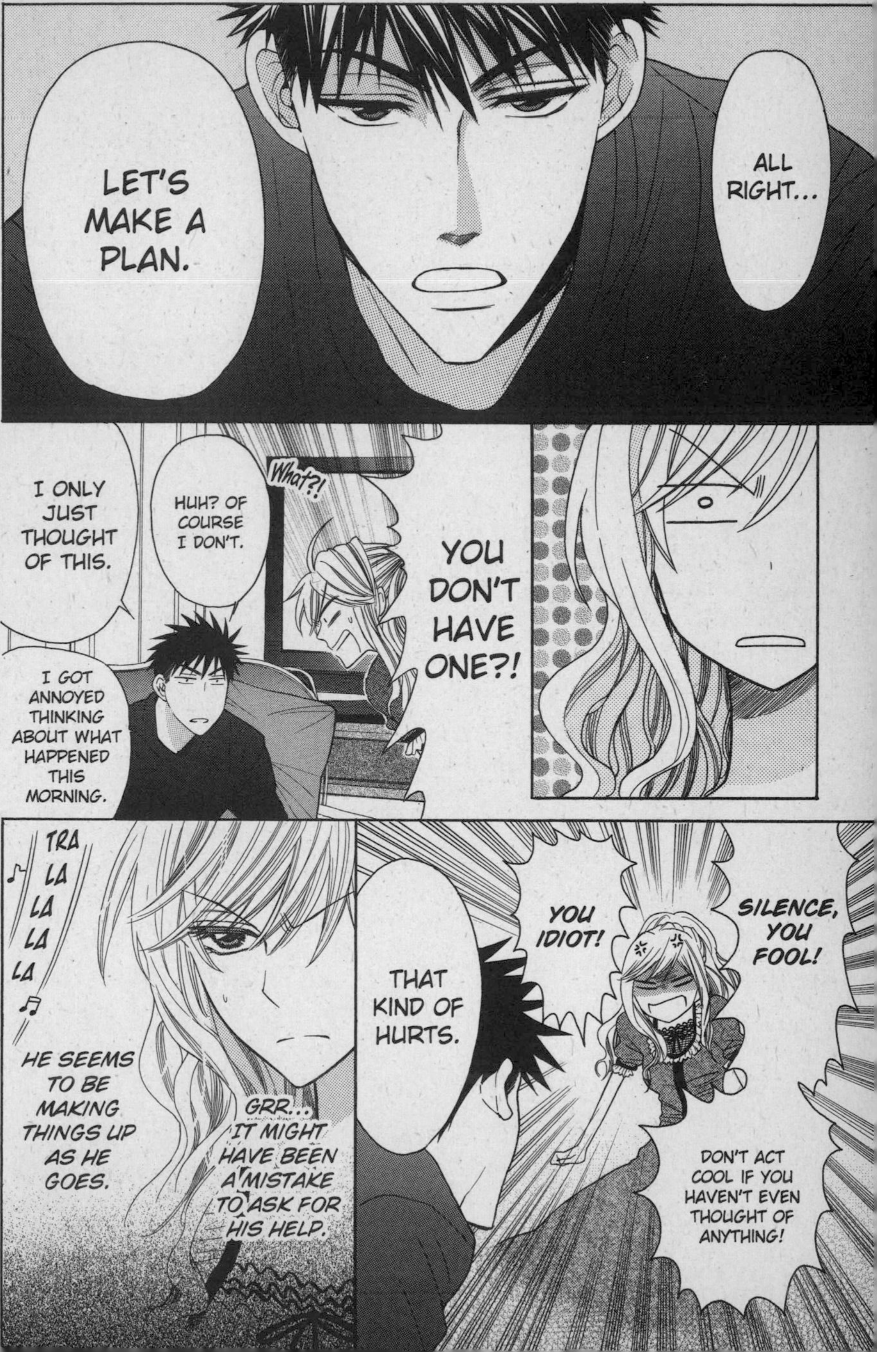
ALL RIGHT...
LET'S MAKE A PLAN.
YOU DON'T HAVE ONE?!
What?!
HUH? OF COURSE I DON'T.
I ONLY JUST THOUGHT OF THIS.
I GOT ANNOYED THINKING ABOUT WHAT HAPPENED THIS MORNING.
SILENCE, YOU FOOL!
YOU IDIOT!
THAT KIND OF HURTS.
DON'T ACT COOL IF YOU HAVEN'T EVEN THOUGHT OF ANYTHING!
GRR... IT MIGHT HAVE BEEN A MISTAKE TO ASK FOR HIS HELP.
TRA LA LA LA LA
HE SEEMS TO BE MAKING THINGS UP AS HE GOES.

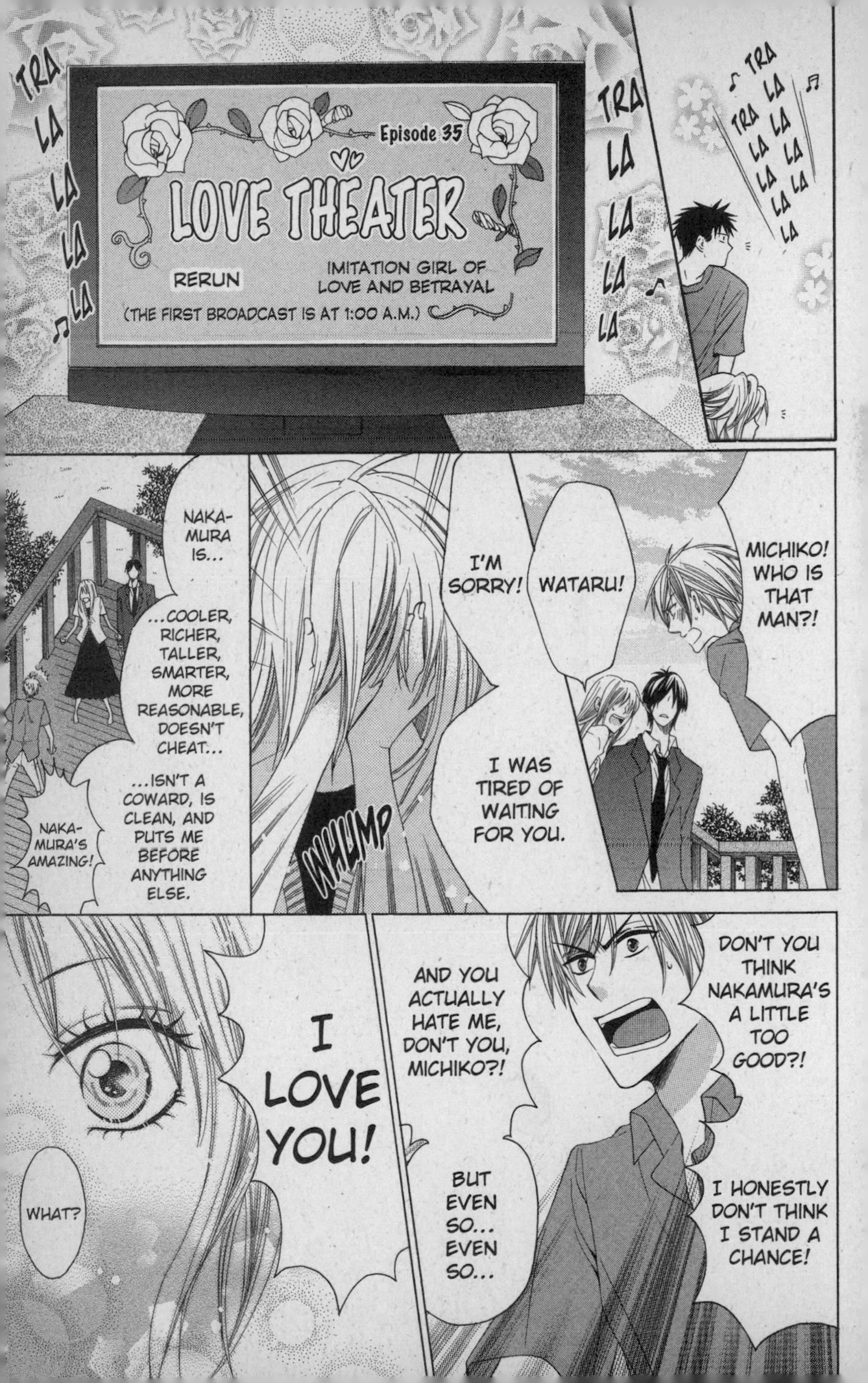

TRA TRA LA LA LA LA LA LA LA LA LA
TRA LA LA LA LA
TRA LA LA LA LA
Episode 35
LOVE THEATER
RERUN
IMITATION GIRL OF LOVE AND BETRAYAL
(THE FIRST BROADCAST IS AT 1:00 A.M.)
MICHIKO! WHO IS THAT MAN?!
WATARU!
I'M SORRY!
I WAS TIRED OF WAITING FOR YOU.
WHUMP
NAKAMURA IS...
...COOLER, RICHER, TALLER, SMARTER, MORE REASONABLE, DOESN'T CHEAT...
...ISN'T A COWARD, IS CLEAN, AND PUTS ME BEFORE ANYTHING ELSE.
NAKAMURA'S AMAZING!
DON'T YOU THINK NAKAMURA'S A LITTLE TOO GOOD?!
AND YOU ACTUALLY HATE ME, DON'T YOU, MICHIKO?!
I HONESTLY DON'T THINK I STAND A CHANCE!
BUT EVEN SO... EVEN SO...
I LOVE YOU!
WHAT?

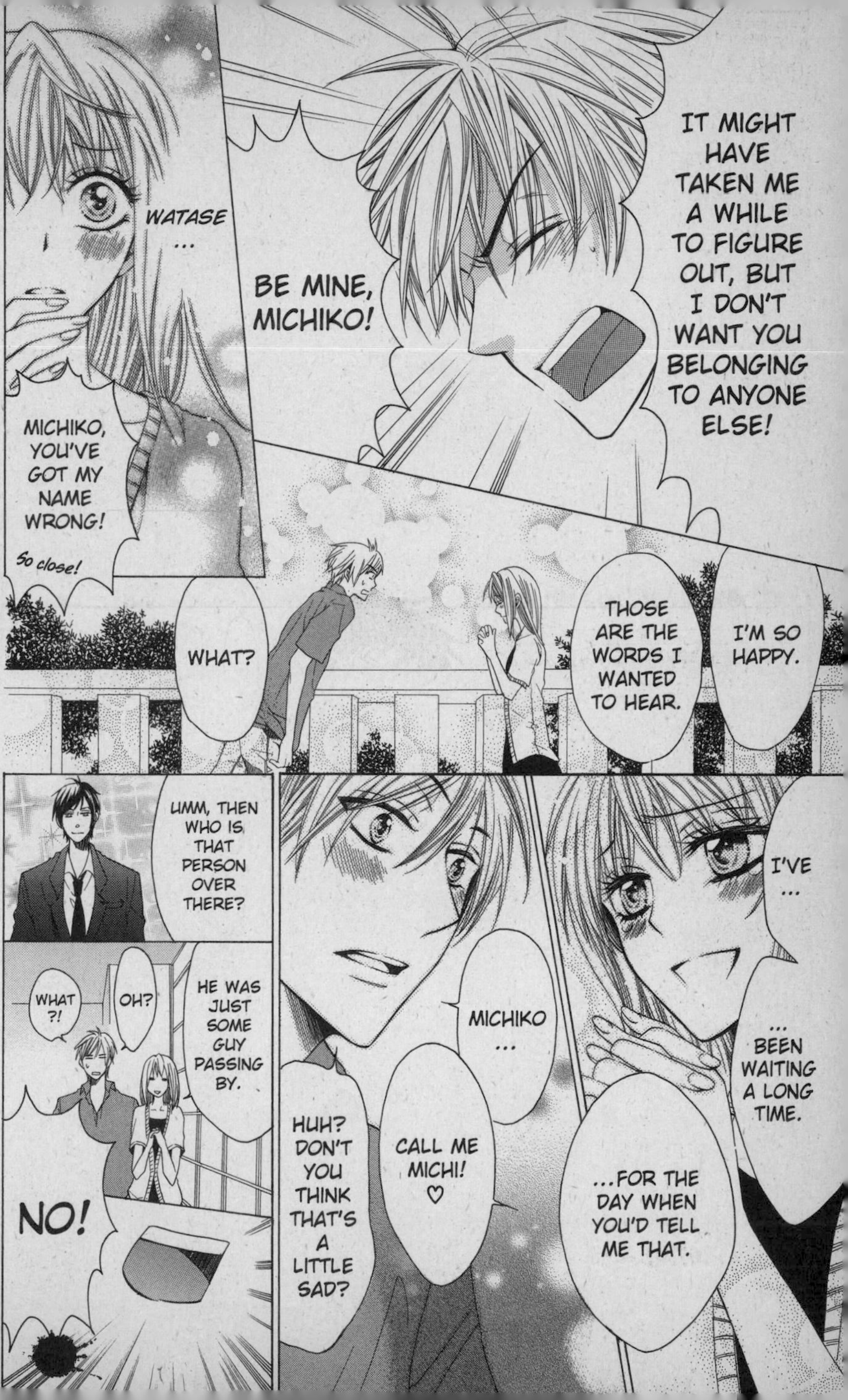
IT MIGHT HAVE TAKEN ME A WHILE TO FIGURE OUT, BUT I DON'T WANT YOU BELONGING TO ANYONE ELSE!
BE MINE, MICHIKO!
WATASE ...
MICHIKO, YOU'VE GOT MY NAME WRONG!
So close!
I'M SO HAPPY.
THOSE ARE THE WORDS I WANTED TO HEAR.
WHAT?
I'VE ...
... BEEN WAITING A LONG TIME.
...FOR THE DAY WHEN YOU'D TELL ME THAT.
MICHIKO ...
CALL ME MICHI! ♡
HUH? DON'T YOU THINK THAT'S A LITTLE SAD?
UMM, THEN WHO IS THAT PERSON OVER THERE?
HE WAS JUST SOME GUY PASSING BY.
OH?
WHAT?!
NO!

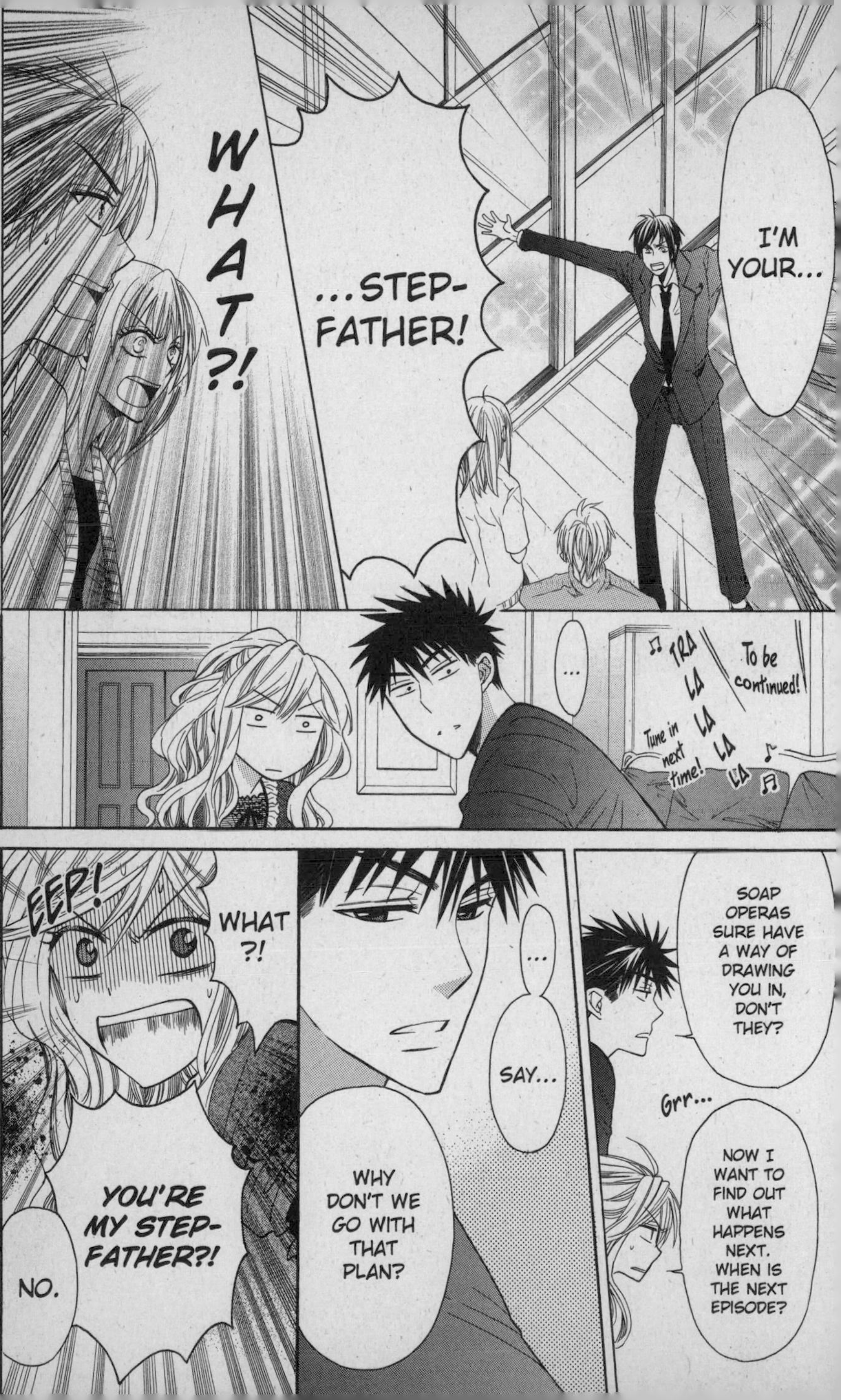
I'M YOUR...
...STEP-FATHER!
WHAT?!
To be continued!
TRA LA LA LA LA
Tune in next time!
...
SOAP OPERAS SURE HAVE A WAY OF DRAWING YOU IN, DON'T THEY?
Grr...
NOW I WANT TO FIND OUT WHAT HAPPENS NEXT. WHEN IS THE NEXT EPISODE?
...
SAY...
WHY DON'T WE GO WITH THAT PLAN?
EEP!
WHAT?!
YOU'RE MY STEP-FATHER?!
NO.

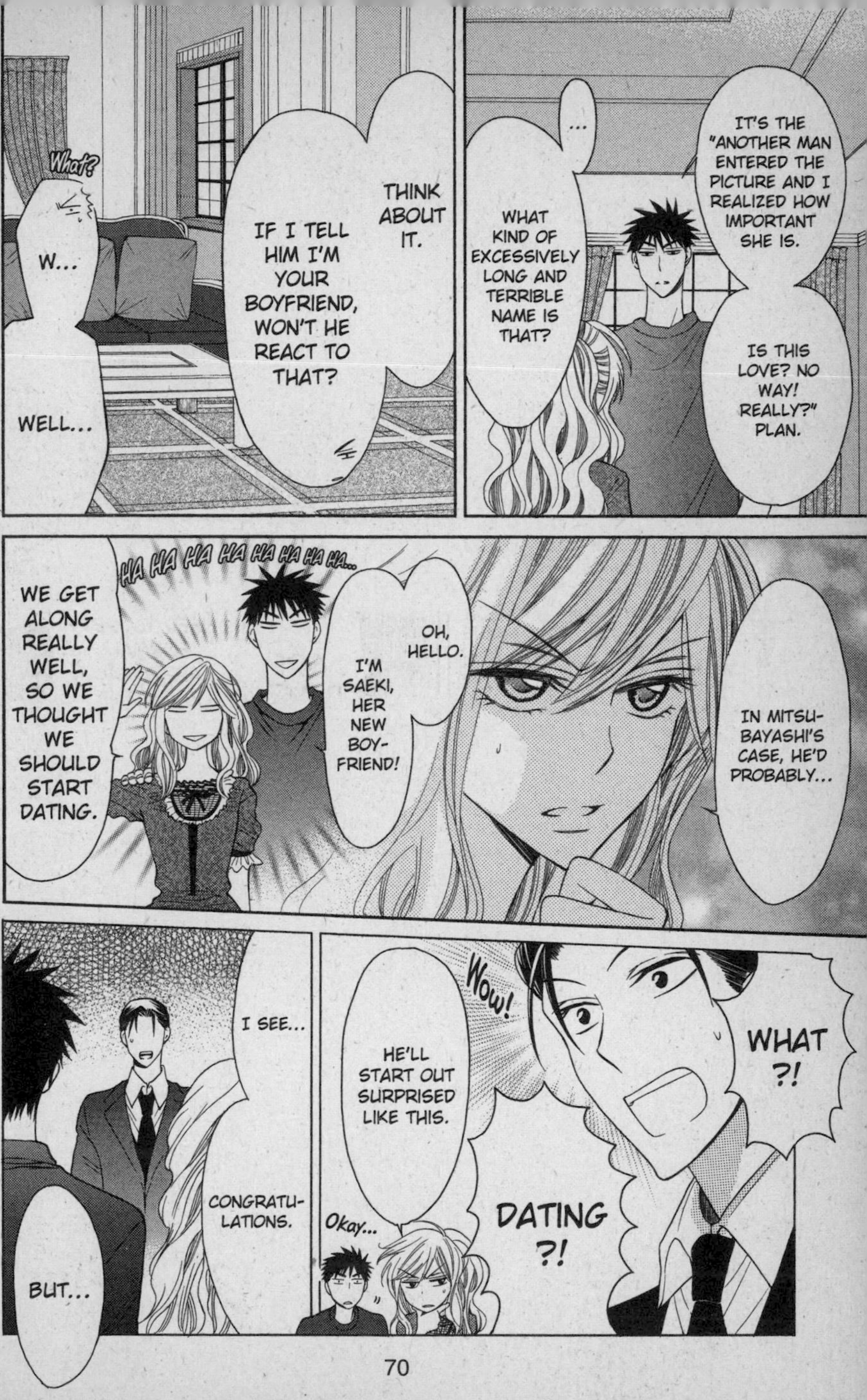
IT'S THE "ANOTHER MAN ENTERED THE PICTURE AND I REALIZED HOW IMPORTANT SHE IS.
IS THIS LOVE? NO WAY! REALLY?" PLAN.
...
WHAT KIND OF EXCESSIVELY LONG AND TERRIBLE NAME IS THAT?
THINK ABOUT IT.
IF I TELL HIM I'M YOUR BOYFRIEND, WON'T HE REACT TO THAT?
What?
W...
WELL...
IN MITSU-BAYASHI'S CASE, HE'D PROBABLY...
OH, HELLO.
I'M SAEKI, HER NEW BOY-FRIEND!
HA HA HA HA HA HA HA HA...
WE GET ALONG REALLY WELL, SO WE THOUGHT WE SHOULD START DATING.
WHAT ?!
Wow!
DATING ?!
HE'LL START OUT SURPRISED LIKE THIS.
Okay...
I SEE...
CONGRATU-LATIONS.
BUT...

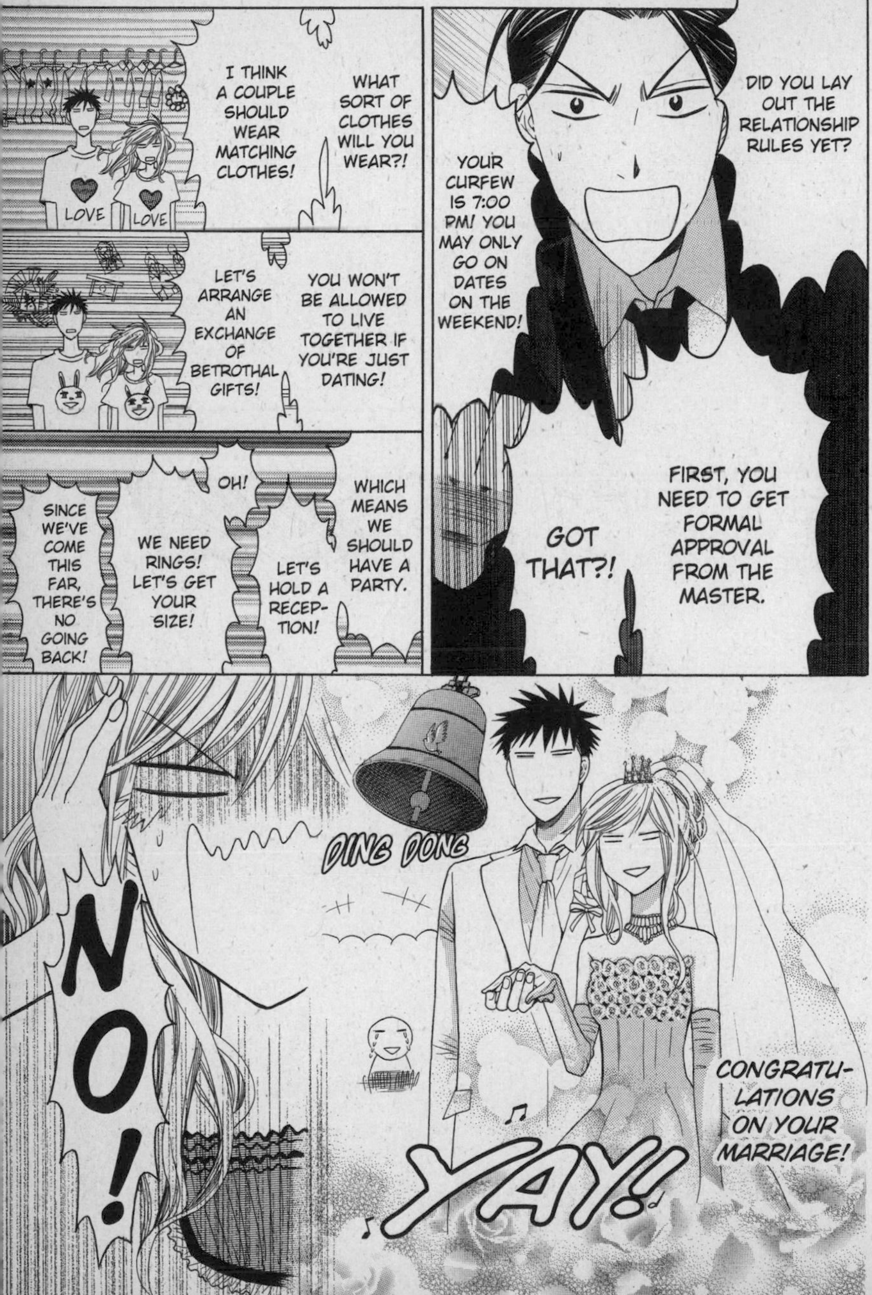
DID YOU LAY OUT THE RELATIONSHIP RULES YET?
YOUR CURFEW IS 7:00 PM! YOU MAY ONLY GO ON DATES ON THE WEEKEND!
FIRST, YOU NEED TO GET FORMAL APPROVAL FROM THE MASTER.
GOT THAT?!
WHAT SORT OF CLOTHES WILL YOU WEAR?!
I THINK A COUPLE SHOULD WEAR MATCHING CLOTHES!
LOVE
LOVE
YOU WON'T BE ALLOWED TO LIVE TOGETHER IF YOU'RE JUST DATING!
LET'S ARRANGE AN EXCHANGE OF BETROTHAL GIFTS!
WHICH MEANS WE SHOULD HAVE A PARTY.
LET'S HOLD A RECEPTION!
OH!
WE NEED RINGS! LET'S GET YOUR SIZE!
SINCE WE'VE COME THIS FAR, THERE'S NO GOING BACK!
CONGRATULATIONS ON YOUR MARRIAGE!
DING DONG
YAY!
NO!

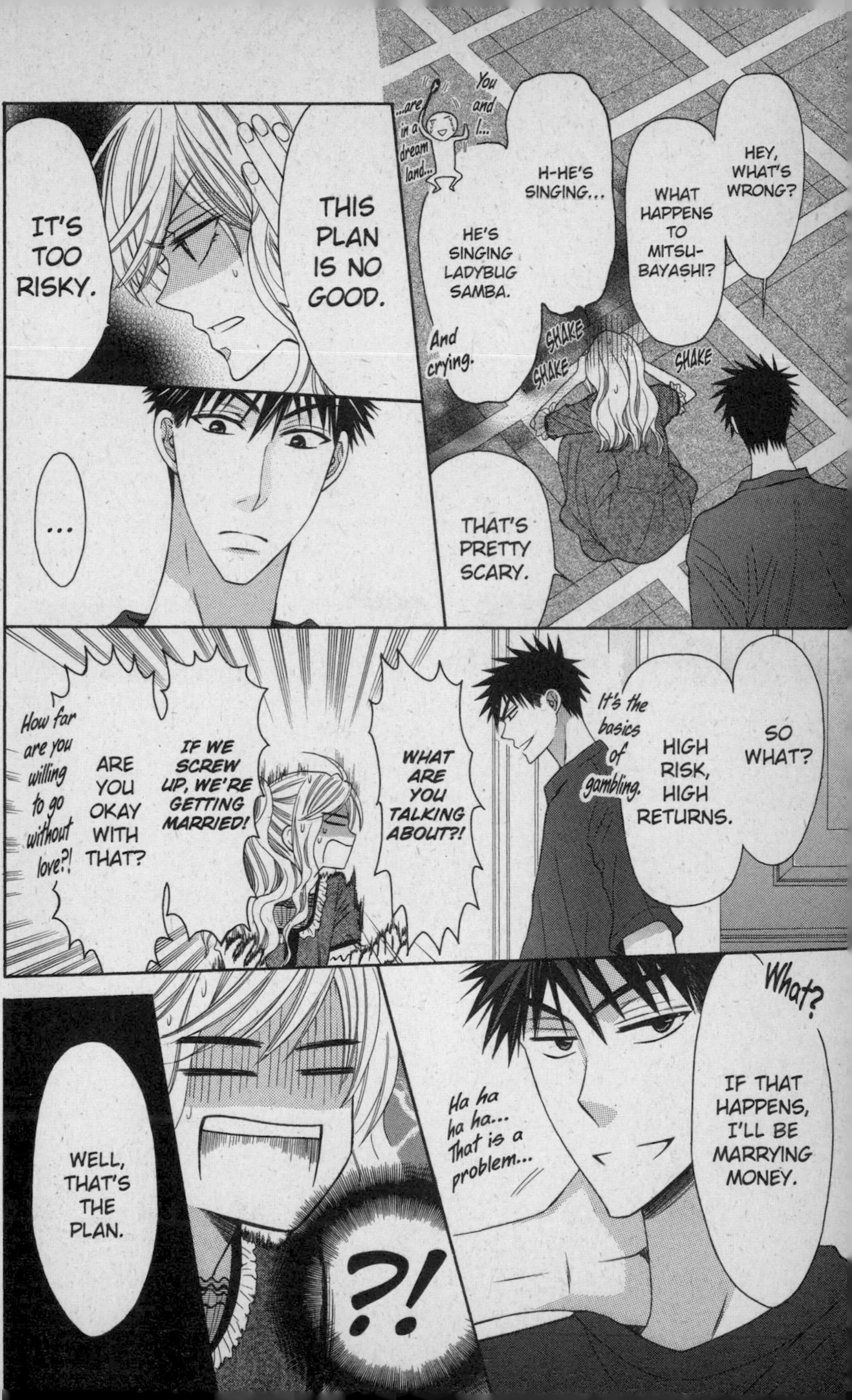
HEY, WHAT'S WRONG?
WHAT HAPPENS TO MITSU-BAYASHI?
H-HE'S SINGING...
You and I...
...are in a dream land...
HE'S SINGING LADYBUG SAMBA.
And crying.
SHAKE
SHAKE
SHAKE
THAT'S PRETTY SCARY.
THIS PLAN IS NO GOOD.
IT'S TOO RISKY.
...
SO WHAT?
HIGH RISK, HIGH RETURNS.
It's the basics of gambling.
WHAT ARE YOU TALKING ABOUT?!
IF WE SCREW UP, WE'RE GETTING MARRIED!
ARE YOU OKAY WITH THAT?
How far are you willing to go without love?!
What?
IF THAT HAPPENS, I'LL BE MARRYING MONEY.
Ha ha ha ha... That is a problem...
?!
WELL, THAT'S THE PLAN.

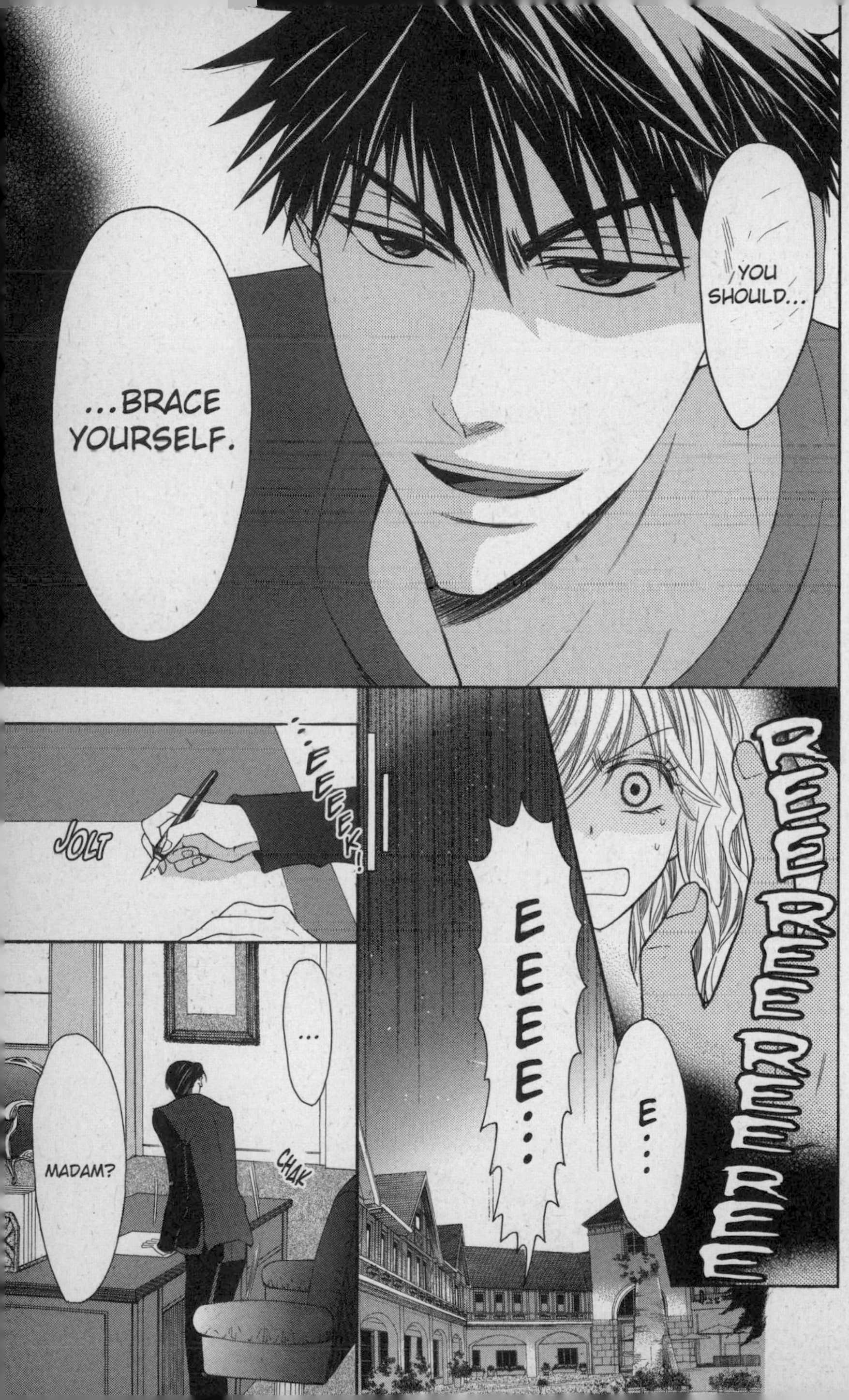
YOU SHOULD...
...BRACE YOURSELF.
REEEREEREEREE
E...
EEEE...
...EEEEK!
JOLT
...
MADAM?
CHAK

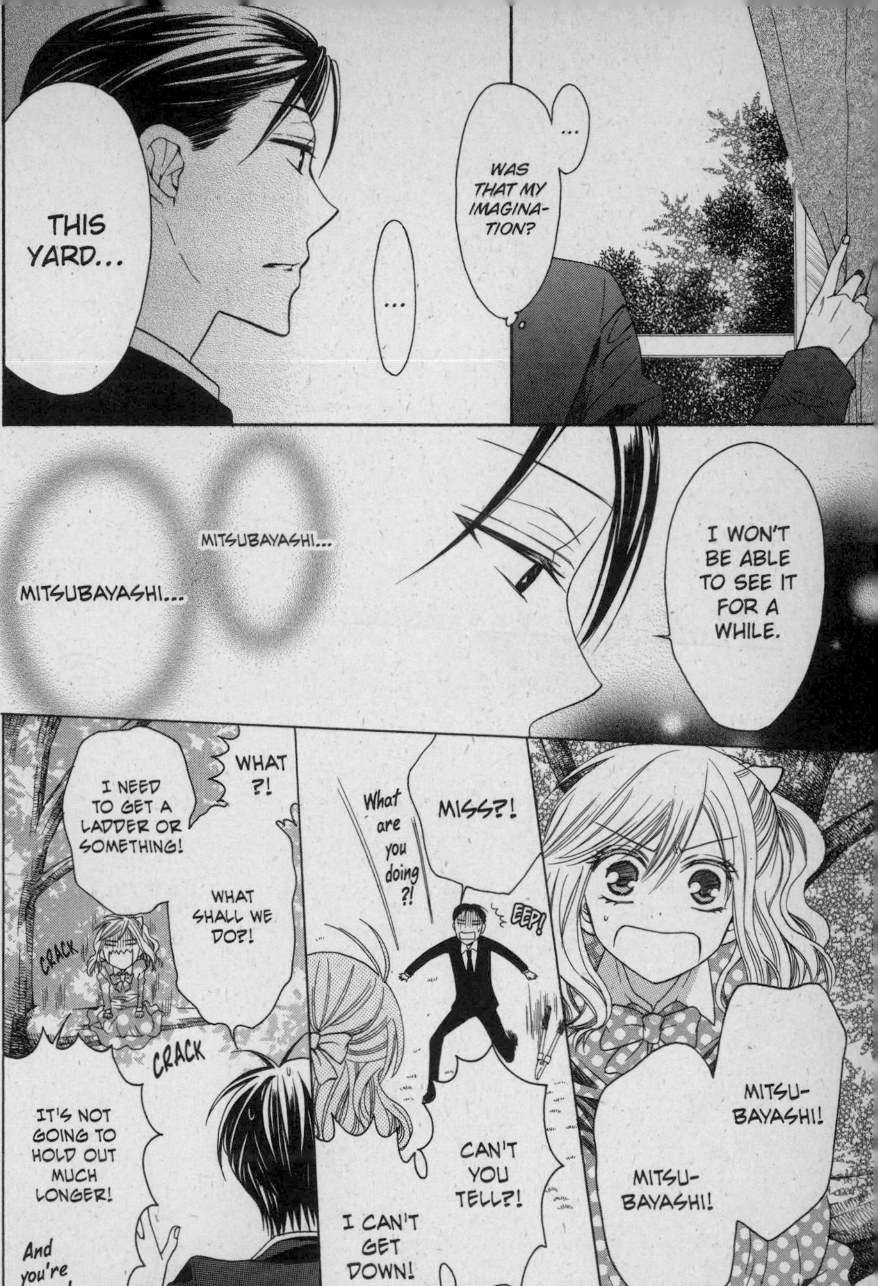
...
WAS THAT MY IMAGINATION?
...
THIS YARD...
I WON'T BE ABLE TO SEE IT FOR A WHILE.
MITSUBAYASHI...
MITSUBAYASHI...
MITSU-BAYASHI!
MITSU-BAYASHI!
MISS?!
What are you doing?!
EEP!
CAN'T YOU TELL?!
I CAN'T GET DOWN!
WHAT?!
I NEED TO GET A LADDER OR SOMETHING!
WHAT SHALL WE DO?!
CRACK
CRACK
IT'S NOT GOING TO HOLD OUT MUCH LONGER!
And you're slow!

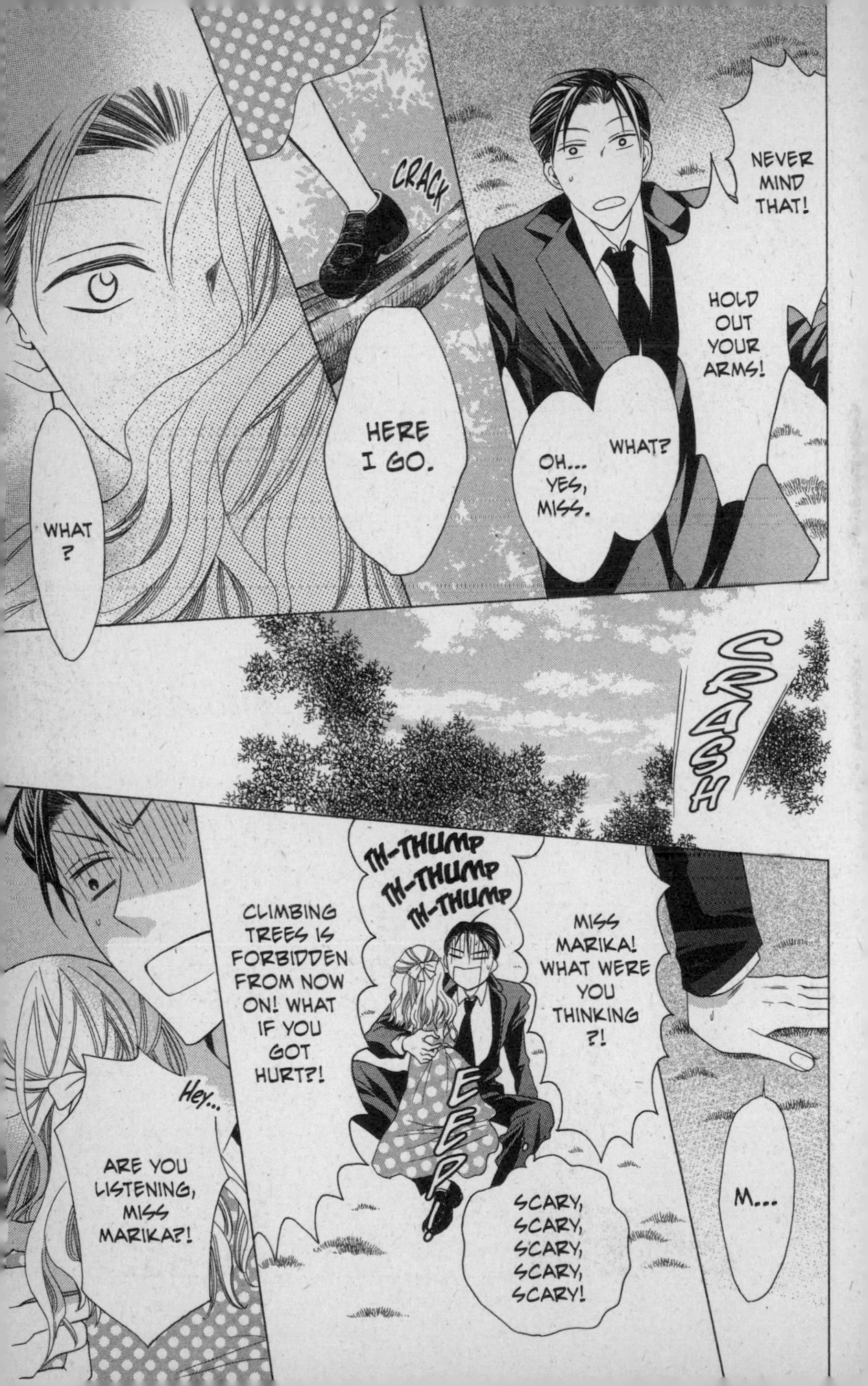
NEVER MIND THAT!
HOLD OUT YOUR ARMS!
WHAT?
OH... YES, MISS.
CRACK
HERE I GO.
WHAT ?
CRASH
M...
MISS MARIKA! WHAT WERE YOU THINKING?!
TH-THUMP TH-THUMP TH-THUMP
CLIMBING TREES IS FORBIDDEN FROM NOW ON! WHAT IF YOU GOT HURT?!
EEP!
SCARY, SCARY, SCARY, SCARY, SCARY!
Hey...
ARE YOU LISTENING, MISS MARIKA?!

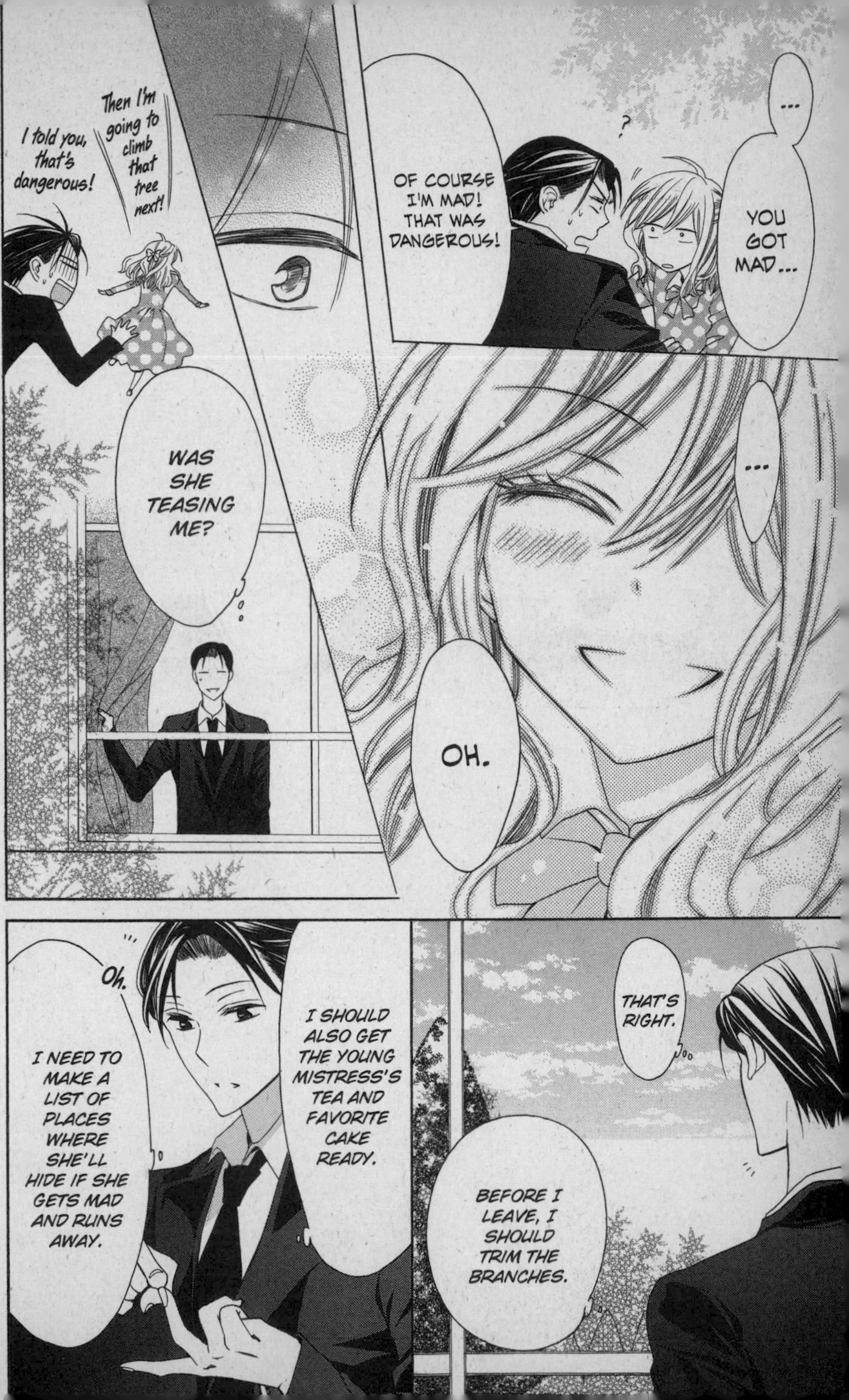
...
YOU GOT MAD...
?
OF COURSE I'M MAD! THAT WAS DANGEROUS!
Then I'm going to climb that tree next!
I told you, that's dangerous!
...
OH.
WAS SHE TEASING ME?
THAT'S RIGHT.
BEFORE I LEAVE, I SHOULD TRIM THE BRANCHES.
I SHOULD ALSO GET THE YOUNG MISTRESS'S TEA AND FAVORITE CAKE READY.
Oh.
I NEED TO MAKE A LIST OF PLACES WHERE SHE'LL HIDE IF SHE GETS MAD AND RUNS AWAY.

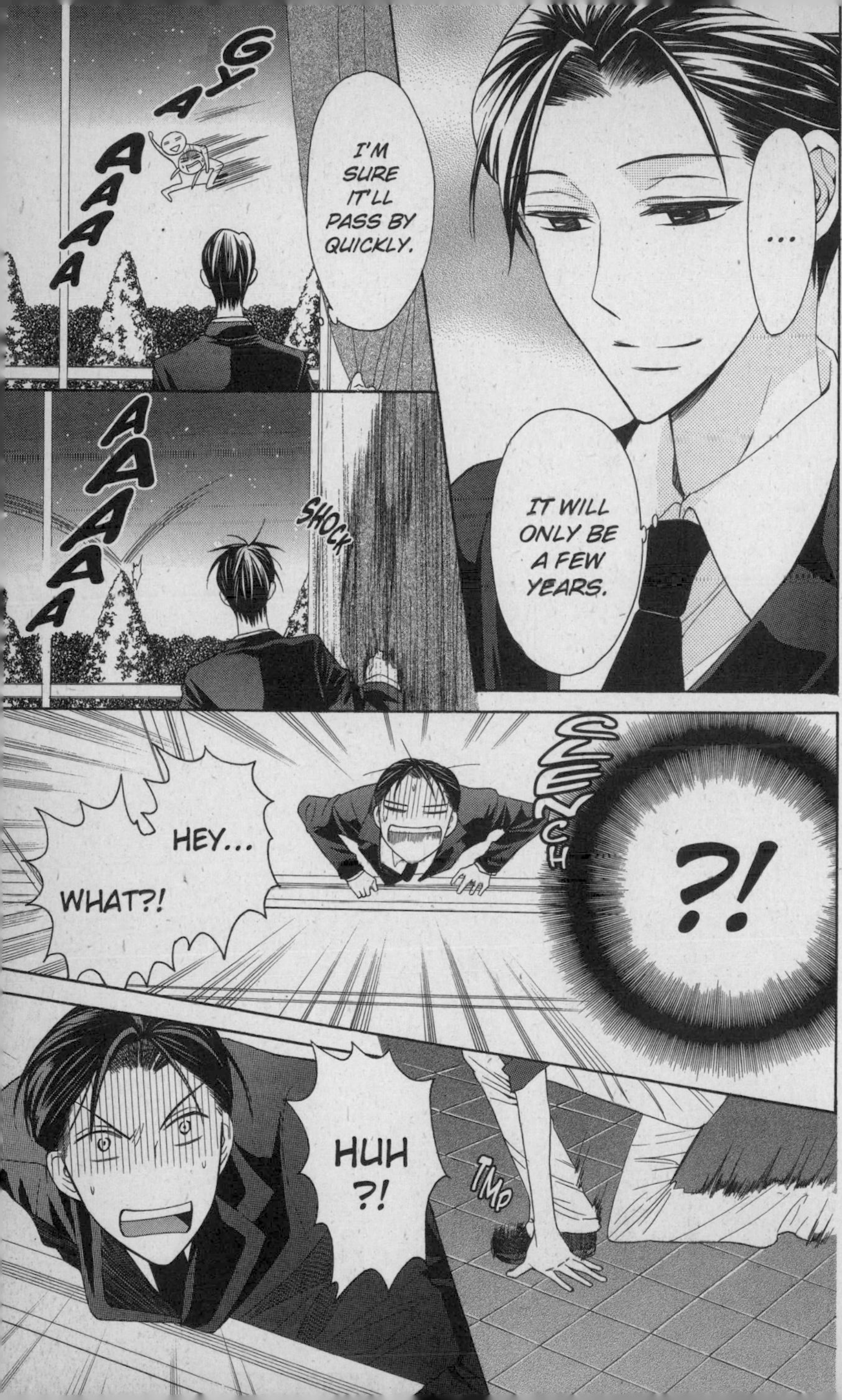
...
I'M SURE IT'LL PASS BY QUICKLY.
IT WILL ONLY BE A FEW YEARS.
GYAAAAAA
AAAAAAA
SHOCK
?!
CLENCH
HEY... WHAT?!
TMP
HUH ?!

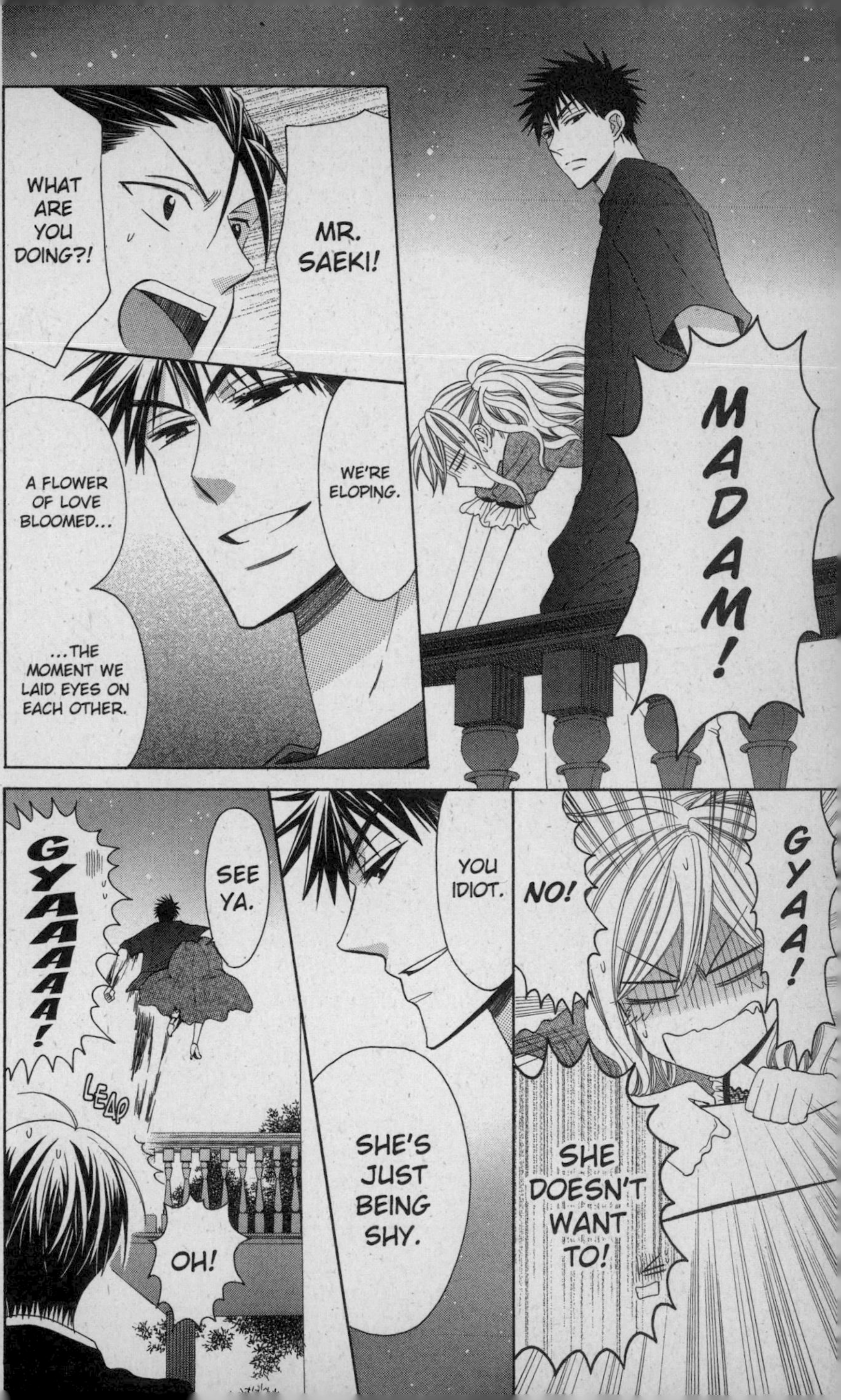
MADAM!
MR. SAEKI!
WHAT ARE YOU DOING?!
WE'RE ELOPING.
A FLOWER OF LOVE BLOOMED...
...THE MOMENT WE LAID EYES ON EACH OTHER.
GYAA!
NO!
SHE DOESN'T WANT TO!
YOU IDIOT.
SHE'S JUST BEING SHY.
SEE YA.
GYAAAAAA!
LEAP
OH!

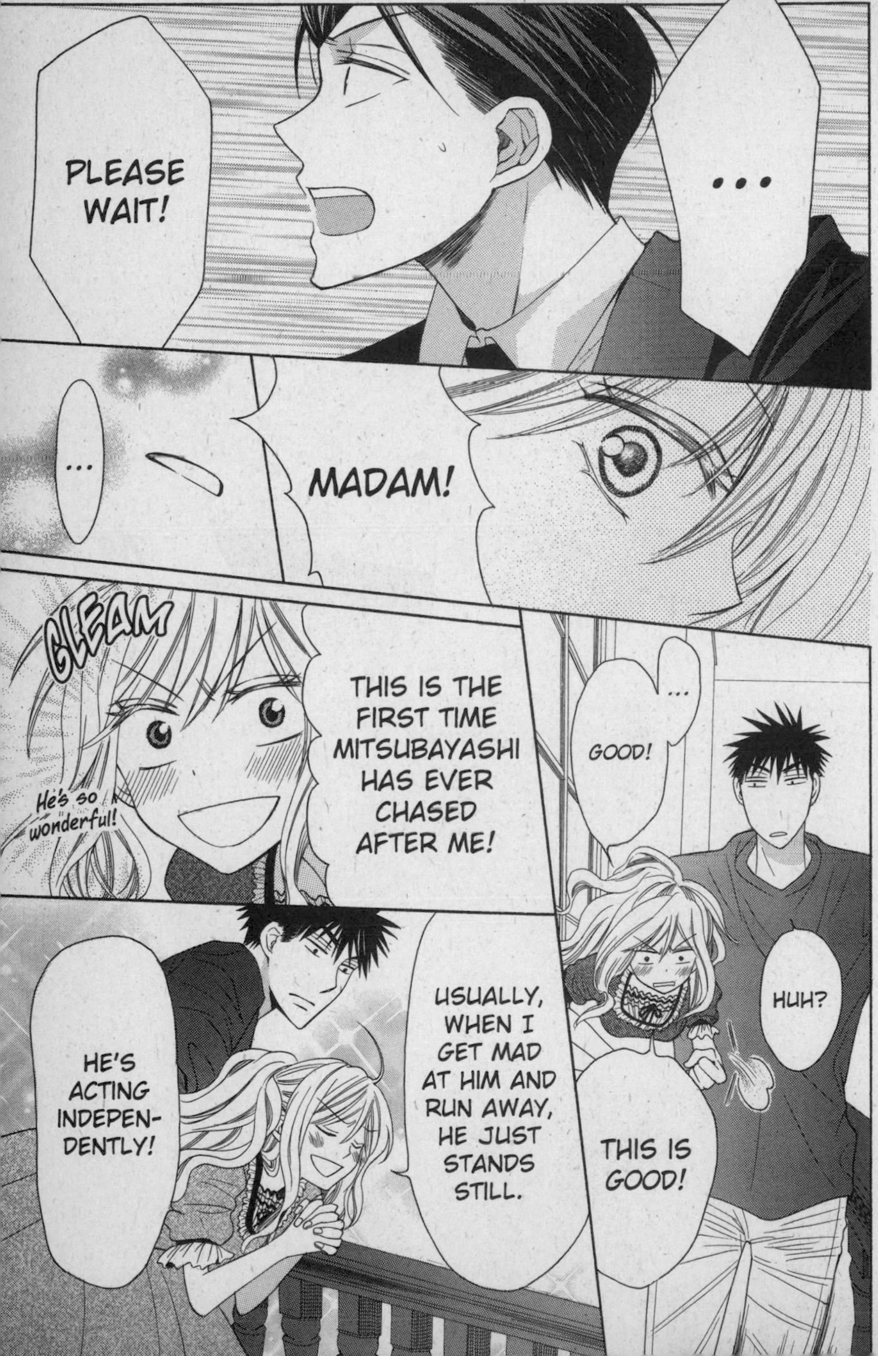
...
PLEASE WAIT!
MADAM!
...
... GOOD!
HUH?
THIS IS GOOD!
GLEAM
THIS IS THE FIRST TIME MITSUBAYASHI HAS EVER CHASED AFTER ME!
He's so wonderful!
USUALLY, WHEN I GET MAD AT HIM AND RUN AWAY, HE JUST STANDS STILL.
HE'S ACTING INDEPEN-DENTLY!

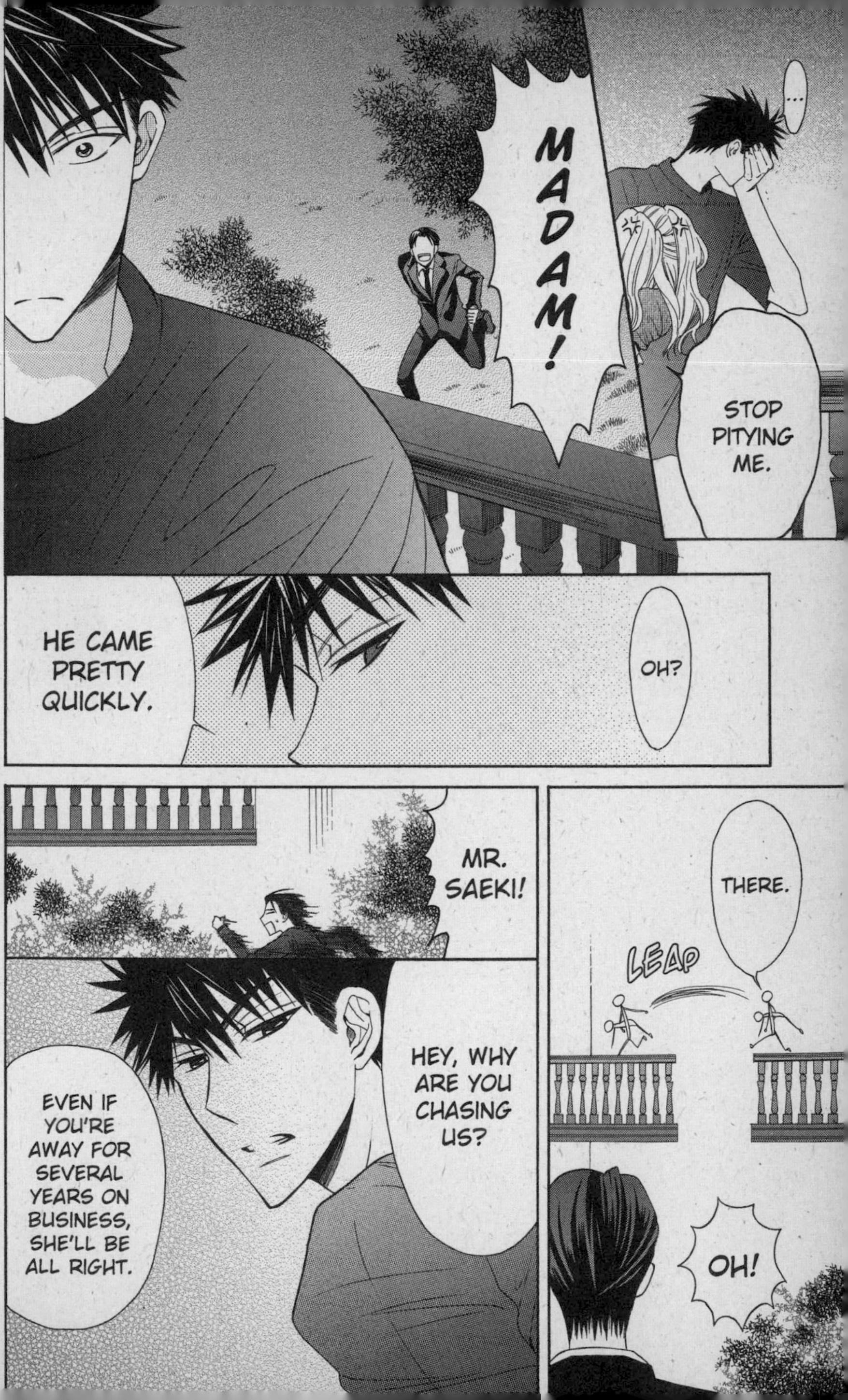
...
STOP PITYING ME.
MADAM!
OH?
HE CAME PRETTY QUICKLY.
THERE.
LEAP
OH!
MR. SAEKI!
HEY, WHY ARE YOU CHASING US?
EVEN IF YOU'RE AWAY FOR SEVERAL YEARS ON BUSINESS, SHE'LL BE ALL RIGHT.

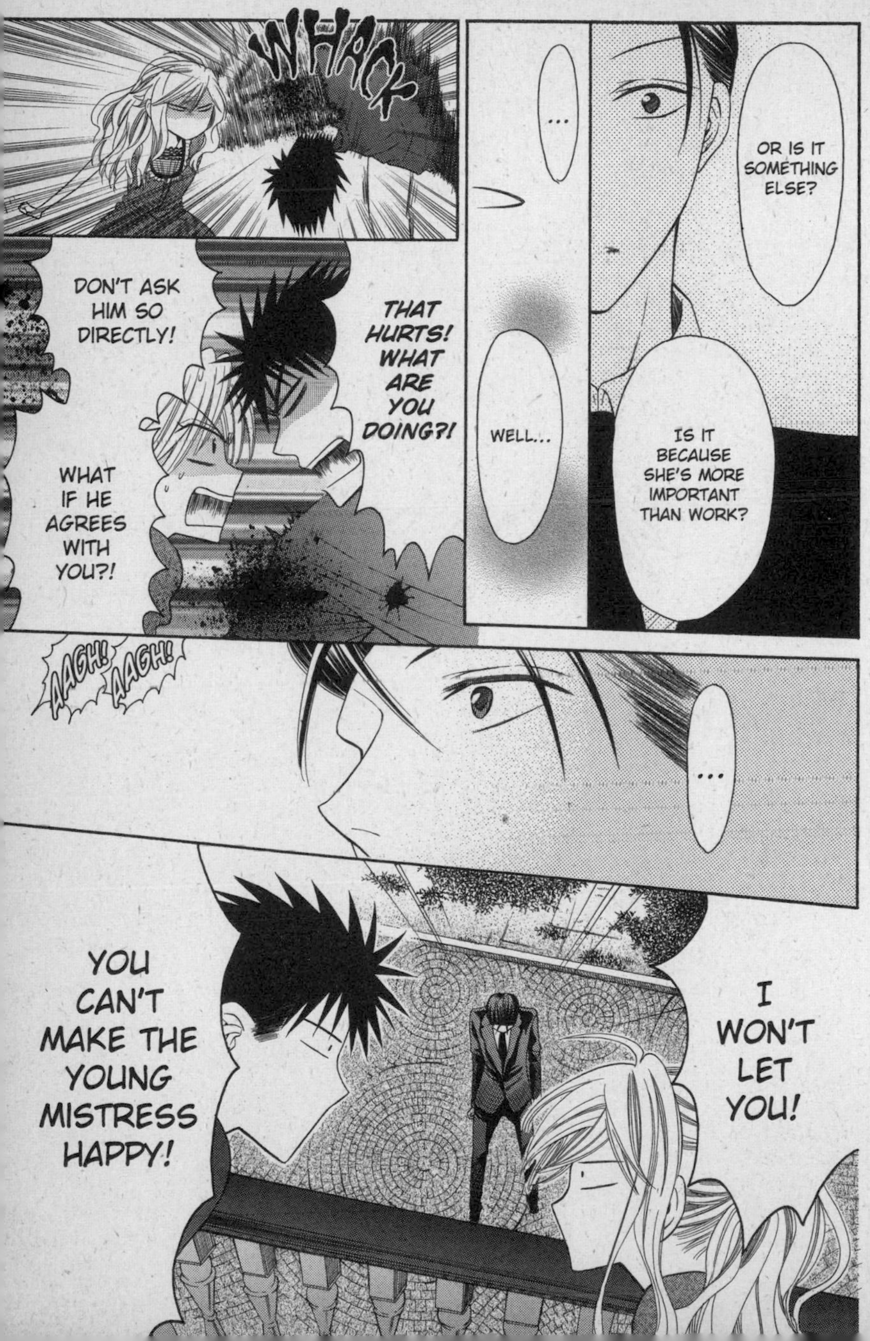
OR IS IT SOMETHING ELSE?
IS IT BECAUSE SHE'S MORE IMPORTANT THAN WORK?
...
WELL...
WHACK
THAT HURTS! WHAT ARE YOU DOING?!
DON'T ASK HIM SO DIRECTLY!
WHAT IF HE AGREES WITH YOU?!
...
AAGH! AAGH!
I WON'T LET YOU!
YOU CAN'T MAKE THE YOUNG MISTRESS HAPPY!

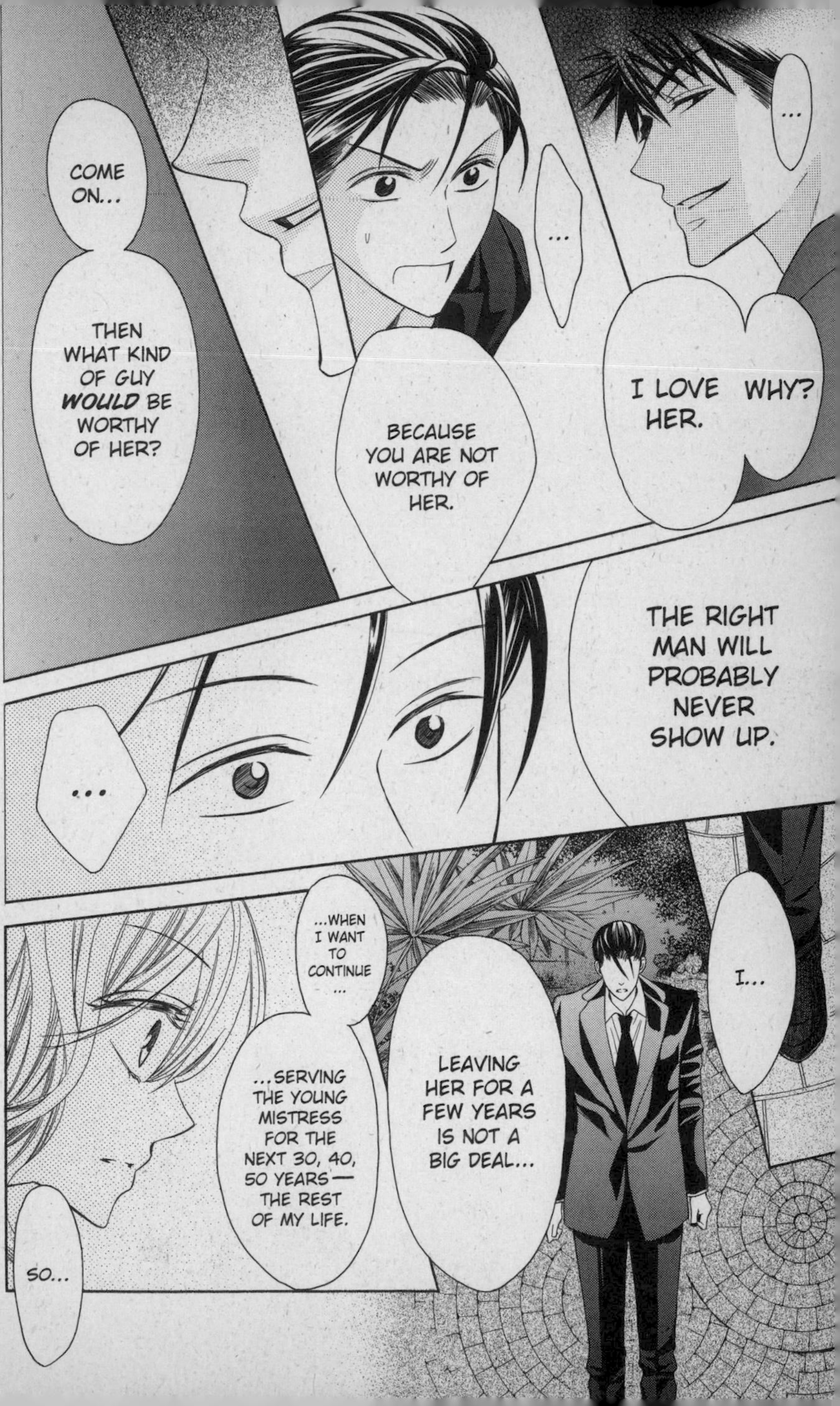
...
WHY?
I LOVE HER.
...
BECAUSE YOU ARE NOT WORTHY OF HER.
COME ON...
THEN WHAT KIND OF GUY *WOULD* BE WORTHY OF HER?
THE RIGHT MAN WILL PROBABLY NEVER SHOW UP.
...
I...
LEAVING HER FOR A FEW YEARS IS NOT A BIG DEAL...
...WHEN I WANT TO CONTINUE...
...SERVING THE YOUNG MISTRESS FOR THE NEXT 30, 40, 50 YEARS—THE REST OF MY LIFE.
SO...

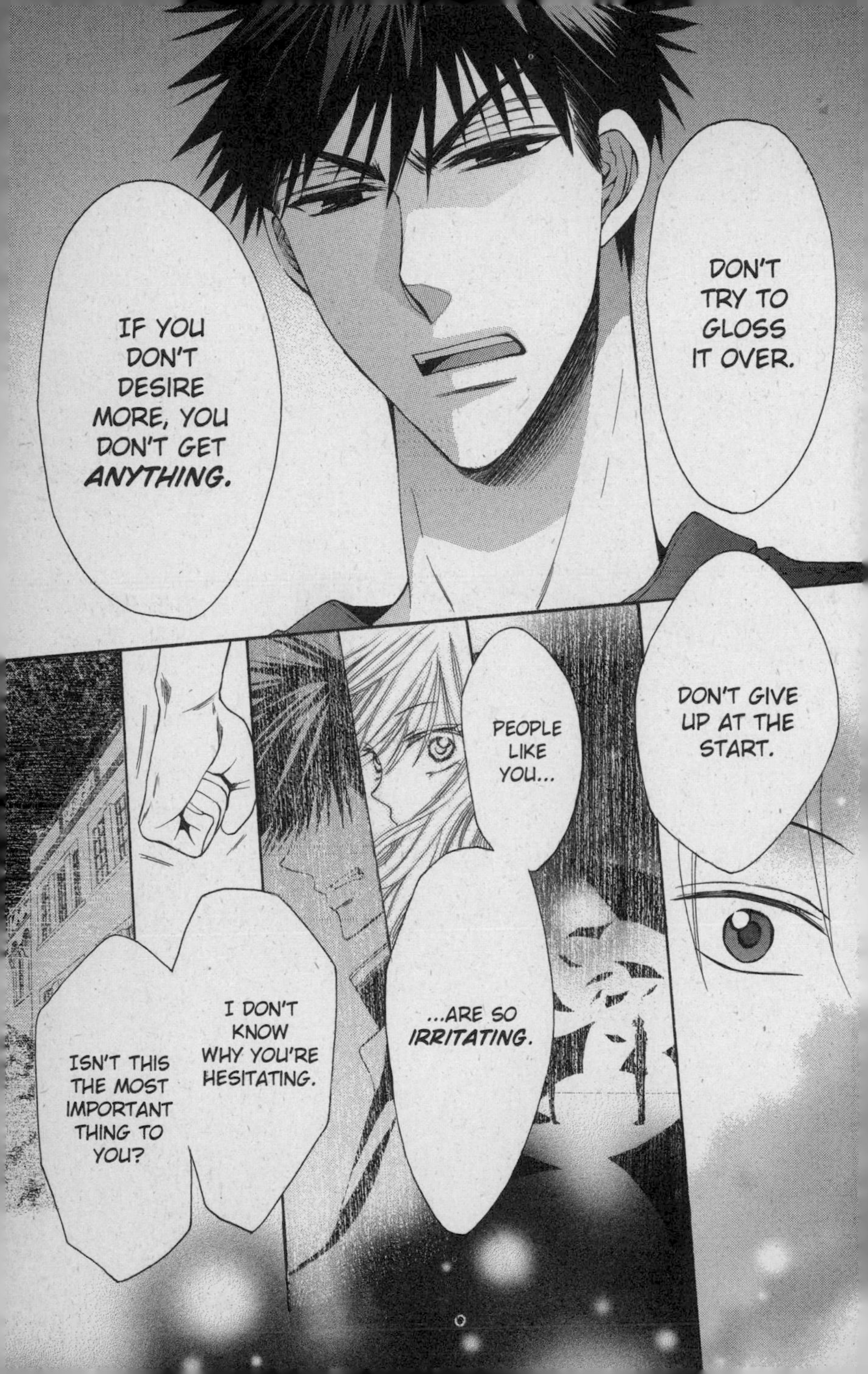
DON'T TRY TO GLOSS IT OVER.
IF YOU DON'T DESIRE MORE, YOU DON'T GET *ANYTHING.*
DON'T GIVE UP AT THE START.
PEOPLE LIKE YOU...
...ARE SO *IRRITATING.*
I DON'T KNOW WHY YOU'RE HESITATING.
ISN'T THIS THE MOST IMPORTANT THING TO YOU?

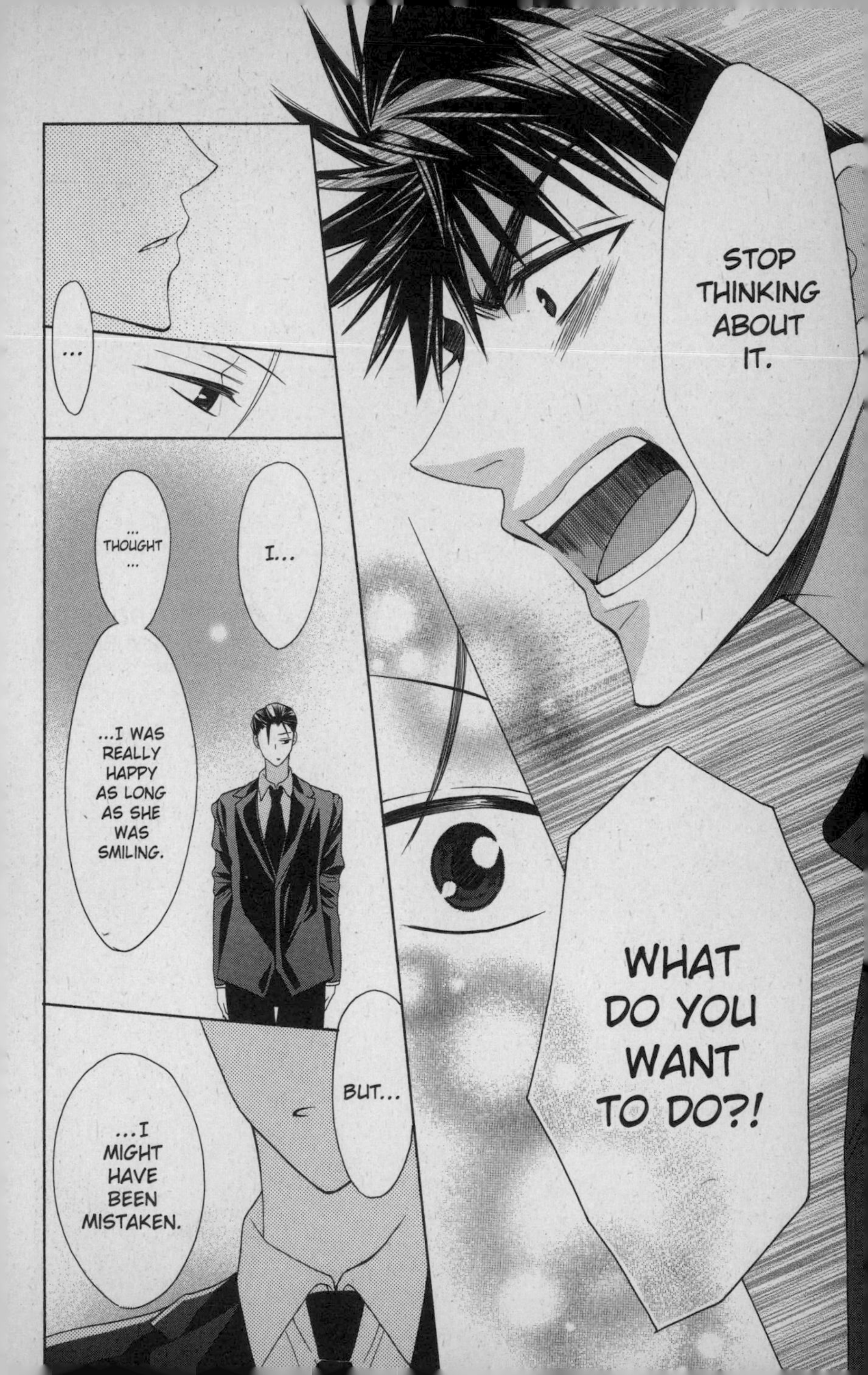
STOP THINKING ABOUT IT.
WHAT DO YOU WANT TO DO?!
...
I...
...THOUGHT...
...I WAS REALLY HAPPY AS LONG AS SHE WAS SMILING.
BUT...
...I MIGHT HAVE BEEN MISTAKEN.

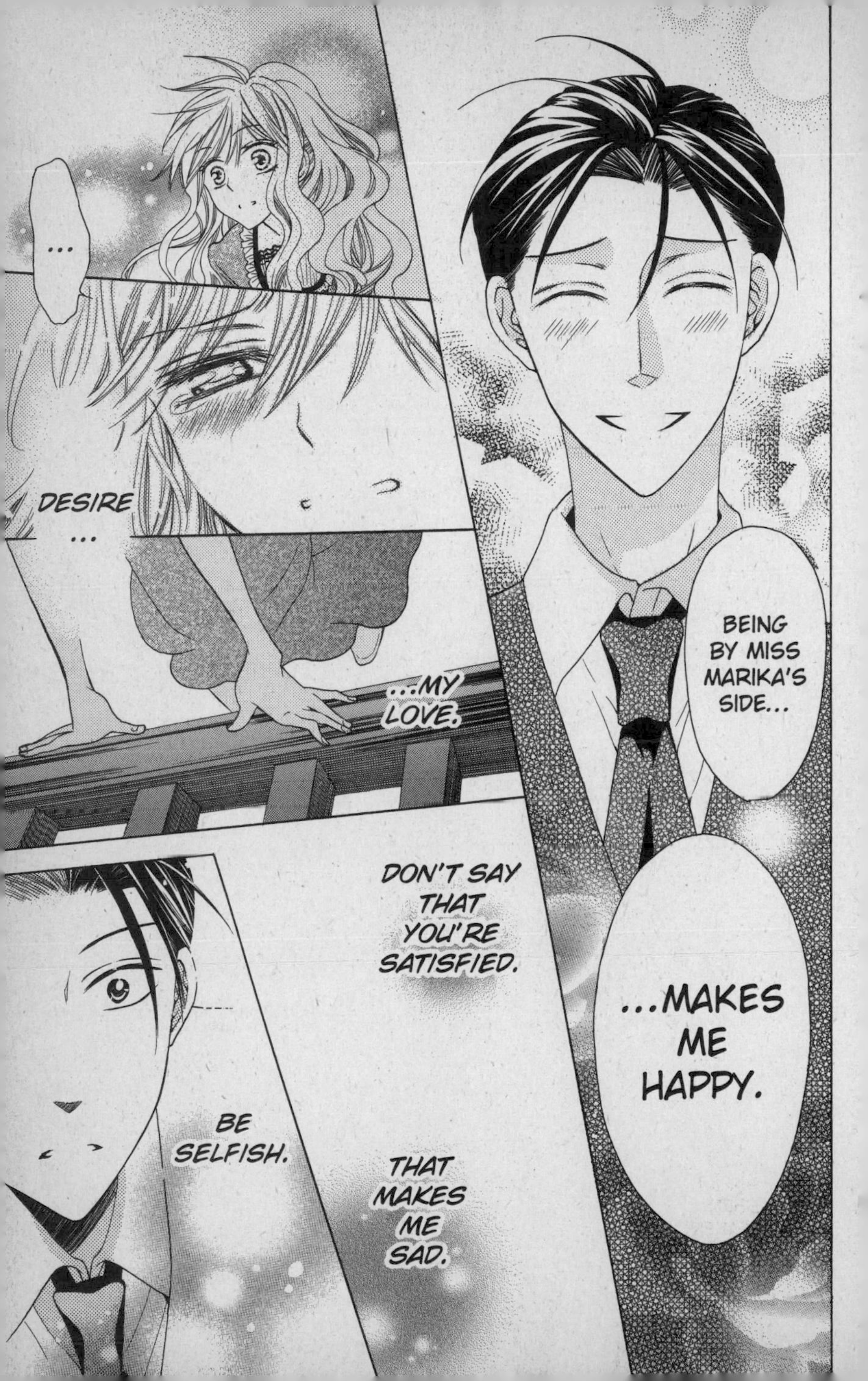
BEING BY MISS MARIKA'S SIDE...
...MAKES ME HAPPY.
...
DESIRE ...
...MY LOVE.
DON'T SAY THAT YOU'RE SATISFIED.
THAT MAKES ME SAD.
BE SELFISH.

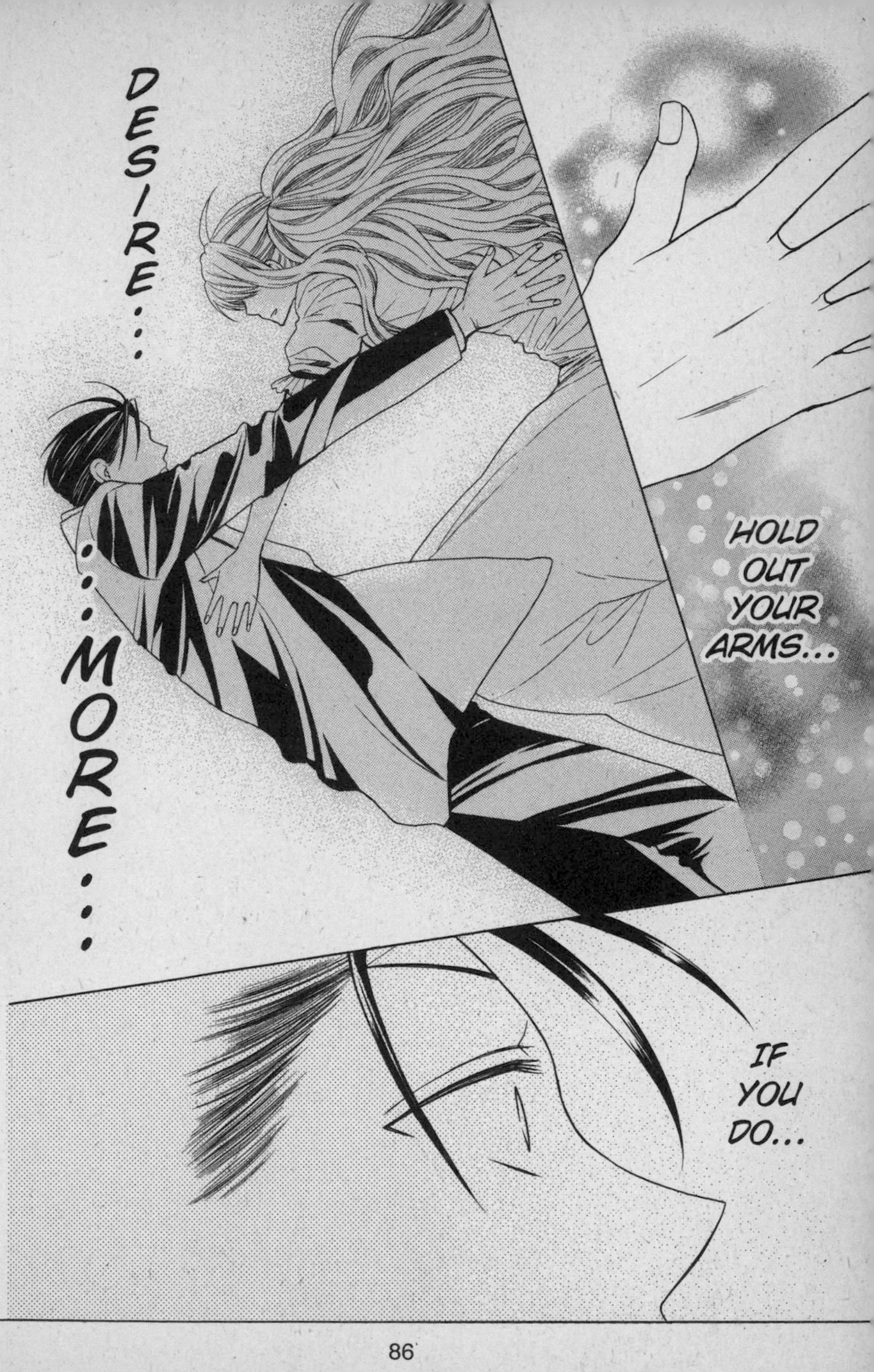
HOLD OUT YOUR ARMS...
DESIRE...
...MORE...
IF YOU DO...

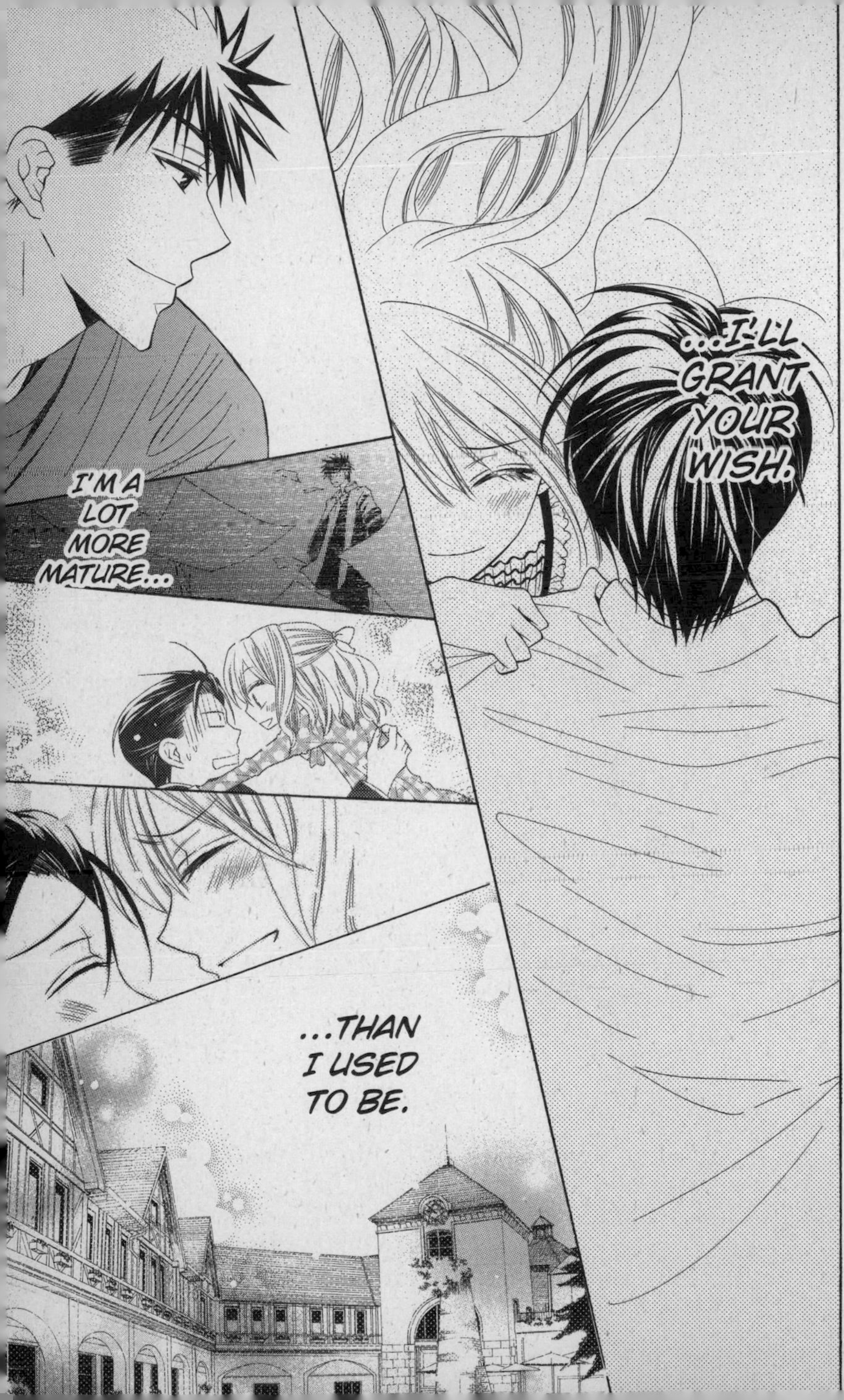
...I'LL GRANT YOUR WISH.
I'M A LOT MORE MATURE...
...THAN I USED TO BE.

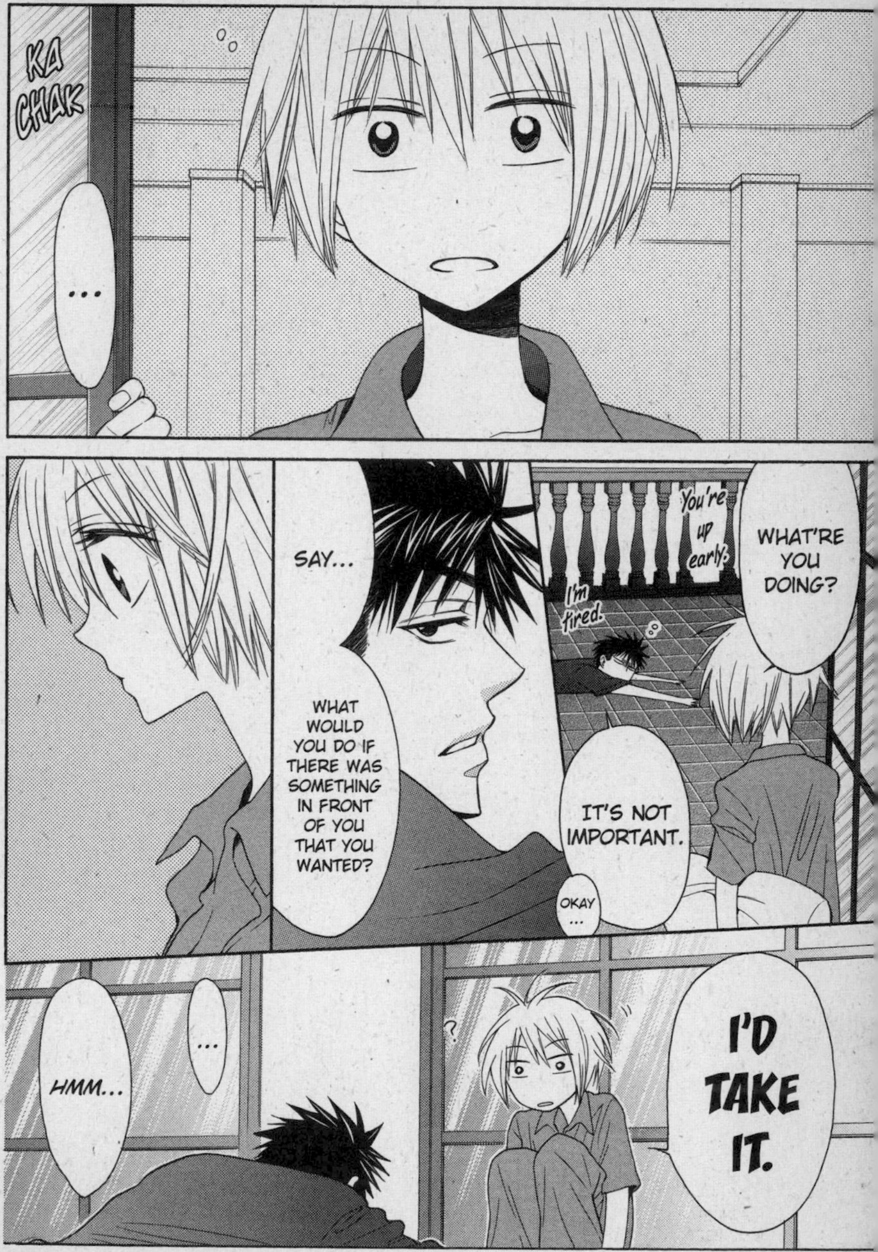
KA CHAK
...
WHAT'RE YOU DOING?
You're up early.
I'm tired.
IT'S NOT IMPORTANT.
OKAY ...
SAY...
WHAT WOULD YOU DO IF THERE WAS SOMETHING IN FRONT OF YOU THAT YOU WANTED?
I'D TAKE IT.
...
HMM...

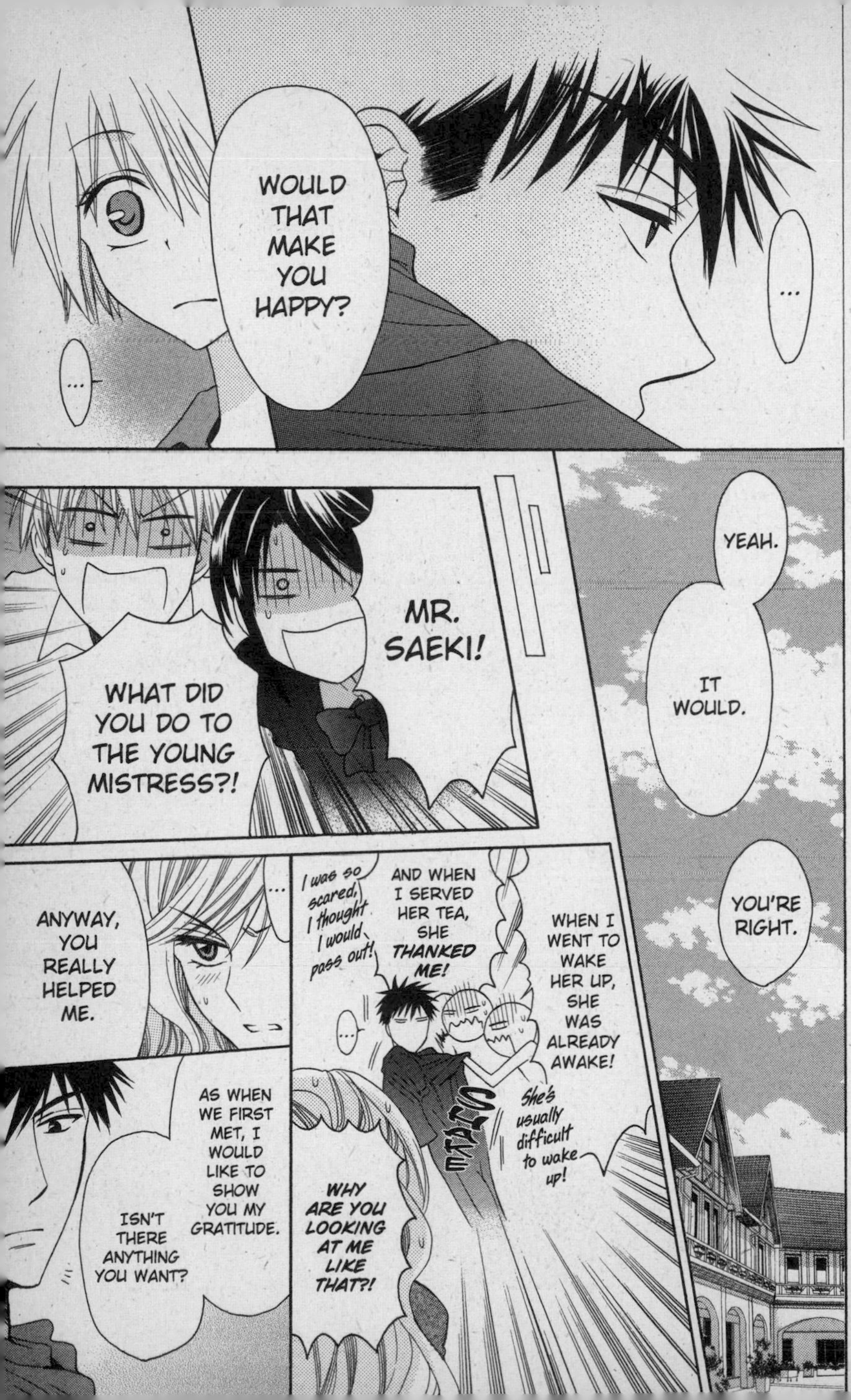
...
WOULD THAT MAKE YOU HAPPY?
...
YEAH.
IT WOULD.
YOU'RE RIGHT.
MR. SAEKI!
WHAT DID YOU DO TO THE YOUNG MISTRESS?!
WHEN I WENT TO WAKE HER UP, SHE WAS ALREADY AWAKE!
She's usually difficult to wake up!
AND WHEN I SERVED HER TEA, SHE THANKED ME!
I was so scared, I thought I would pass out!
...
SHAKE
WHY ARE YOU LOOKING AT ME LIKE THAT?!
...
ANYWAY, YOU REALLY HELPED ME.
AS WHEN WE FIRST MET, I WOULD LIKE TO SHOW YOU MY GRATITUDE.
ISN'T THERE ANYTHING YOU WANT?

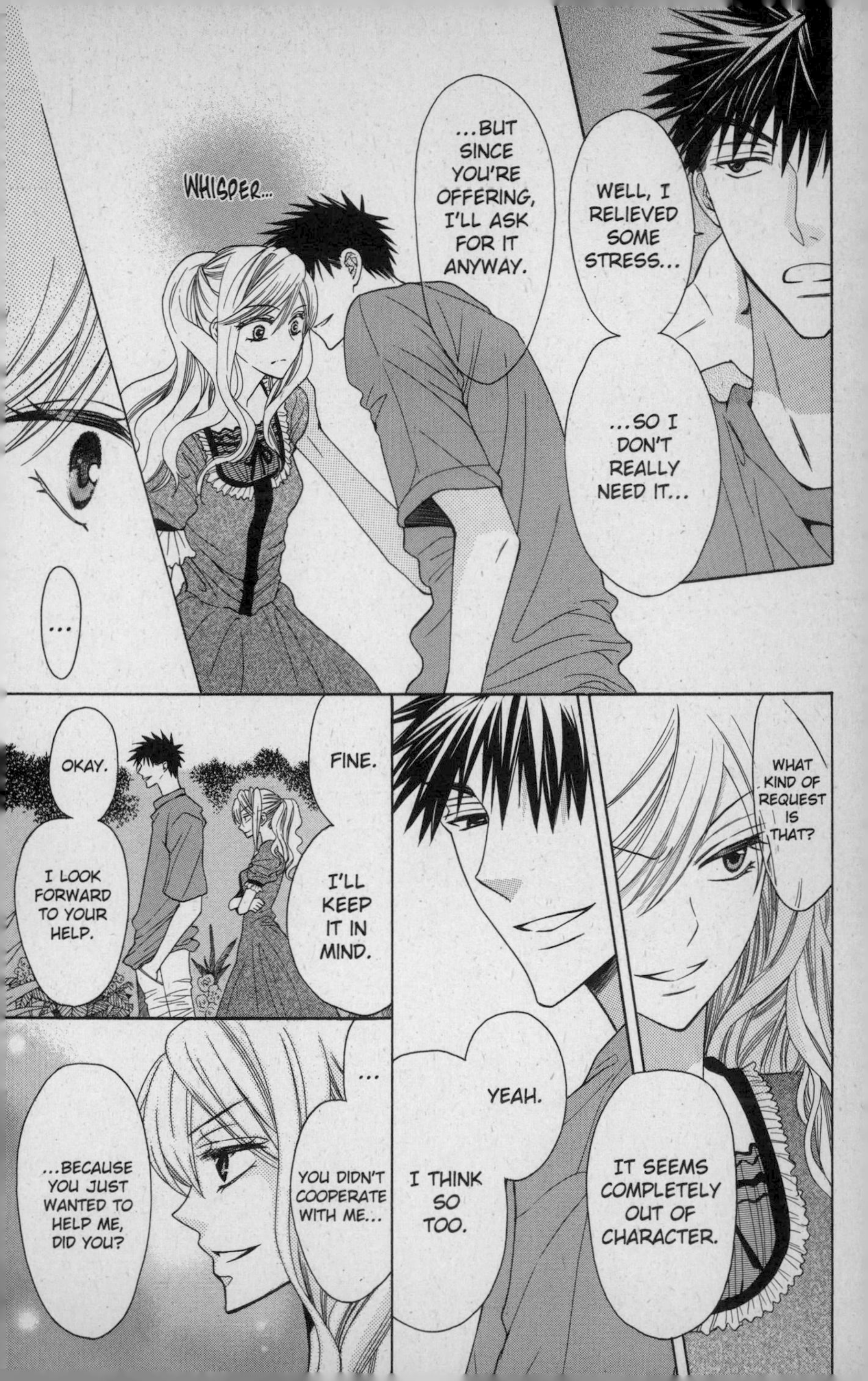
WELL, I RELIEVED SOME STRESS...
...SO I DON'T REALLY NEED IT...
...BUT SINCE YOU'RE OFFERING, I'LL ASK FOR IT ANYWAY.
WHISPER...
...
WHAT KIND OF REQUEST IS THAT?
IT SEEMS COMPLETELY OUT OF CHARACTER.
YEAH.
I THINK SO TOO.
FINE.
I'LL KEEP IT IN MIND.
OKAY.
I LOOK FORWARD TO YOUR HELP.
...
YOU DIDN'T COOPERATE WITH ME...
...BECAUSE YOU JUST WANTED TO HELP ME, DID YOU?

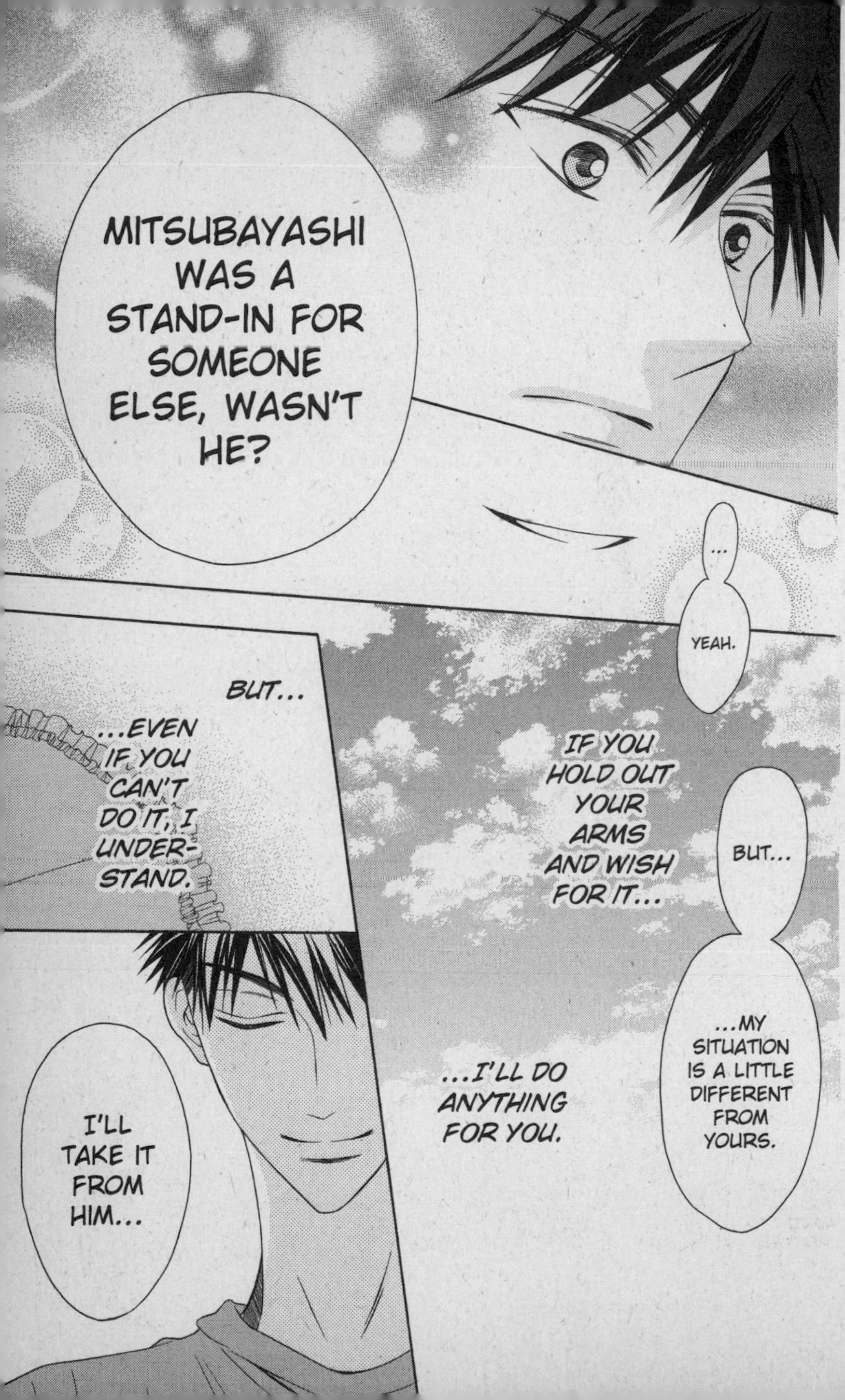
MITSUBAYASHI WAS A STAND-IN FOR SOMEONE ELSE, WASN'T HE?
...
YEAH.
BUT...
...MY SITUATION IS A LITTLE DIFFERENT FROM YOURS.
IF YOU HOLD OUT YOUR ARMS AND WISH FOR IT...
...I'LL DO ANYTHING FOR YOU.
BUT...
...EVEN IF YOU CAN'T DO IT, I UNDER-STAND.
I'LL TAKE IT FROM HIM...

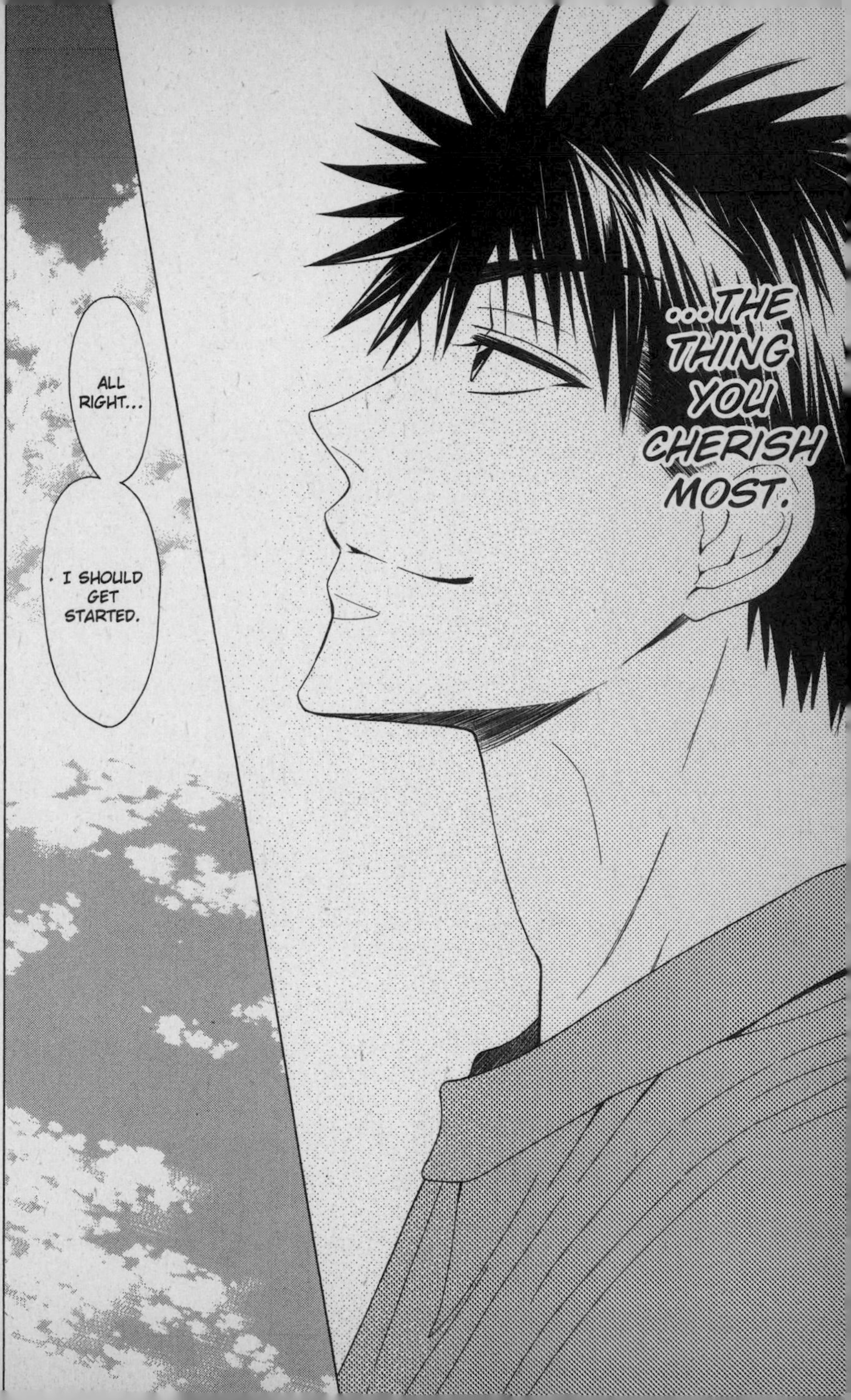
...THE THING YOU CHERISH MOST.
ALL RIGHT...
I SHOULD GET STARTED.

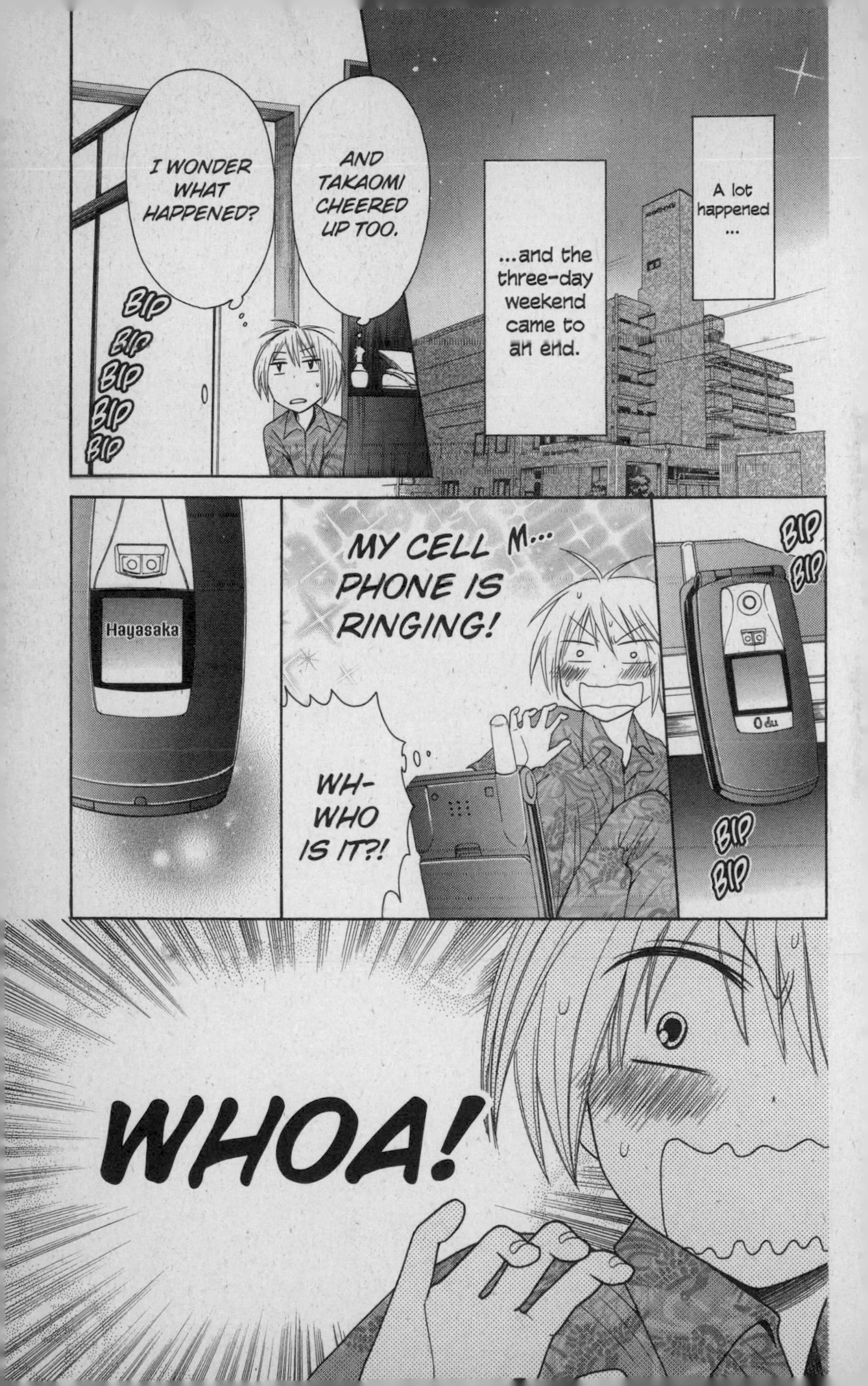
A lot happened ...
...and the three-day weekend came to an end.
AND TAKAOMI CHEERED UP TOO.
I WONDER WHAT HAPPENED?
BIP BIP BIP BIP BIP
BIP BIP
BIP BIP
M...
MY CELL PHONE IS RINGING!
WH- WHO IS IT?!
Hayasaka
WHOA!

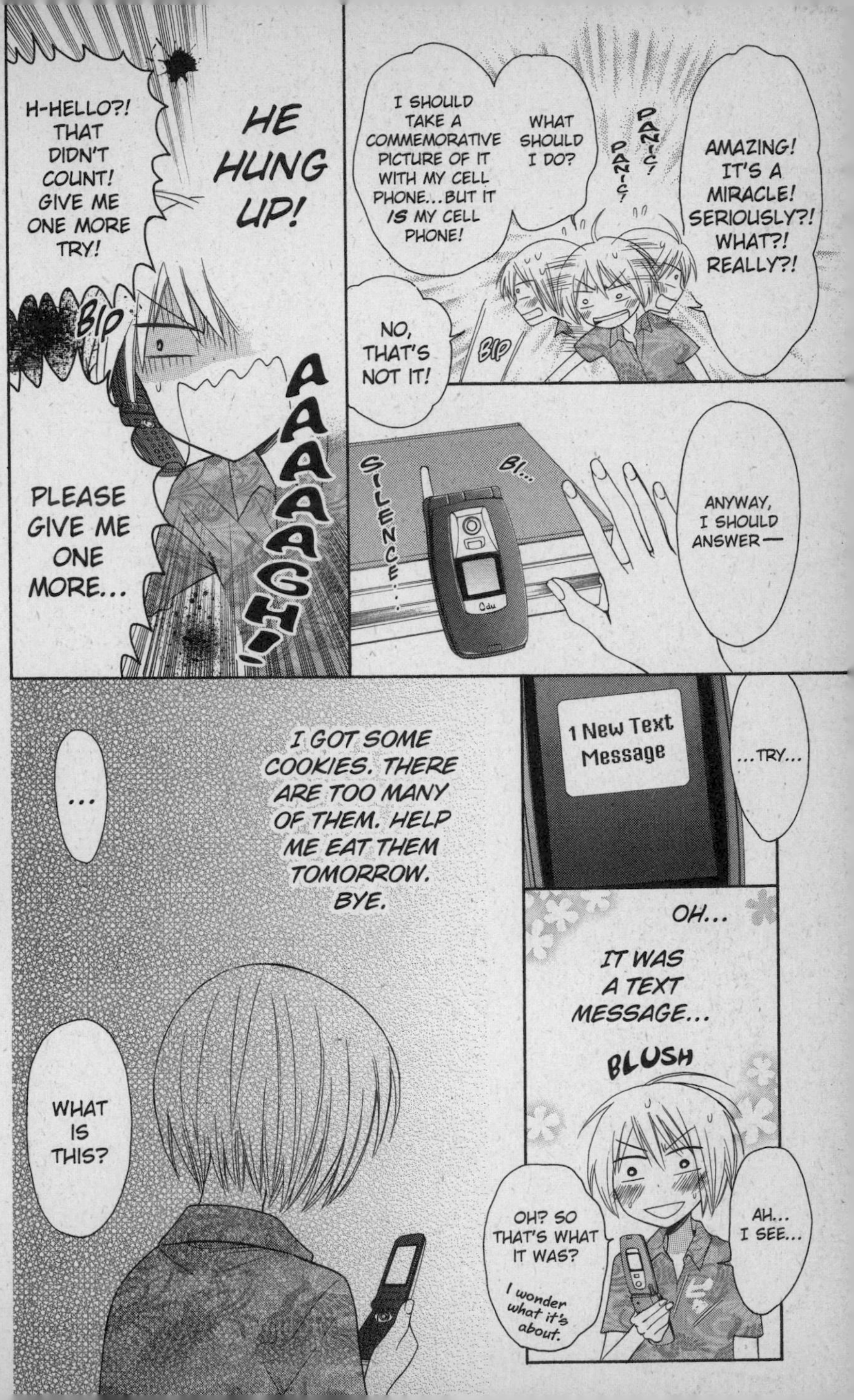

AMAZING! IT'S A MIRACLE! SERIOUSLY?! WHAT?! REALLY?!
PANIC! PANIC!
WHAT SHOULD I DO?
I SHOULD TAKE A COMMEMORATIVE PICTURE OF IT WITH MY CELL PHONE...BUT IT *IS* MY CELL PHONE!
BIP
NO, THAT'S NOT IT!
ANYWAY, I SHOULD ANSWER—
BI...
SILENCE...
HE HUNG UP!
H-HELLO?! THAT DIDN'T COUNT! GIVE ME ONE MORE TRY!
BIP
AAAAAAGH!
PLEASE GIVE ME ONE MORE...
...TRY...
1 New Text Message
OH...
IT WAS A TEXT MESSAGE...
BLUSH
AH... I SEE...
OH? SO THAT'S WHAT IT WAS?
I wonder what it's about.
I GOT SOME COOKIES. THERE ARE TOO MANY OF THEM. HELP ME EAT THEM TOMORROW. BYE.
...
WHAT IS THIS?

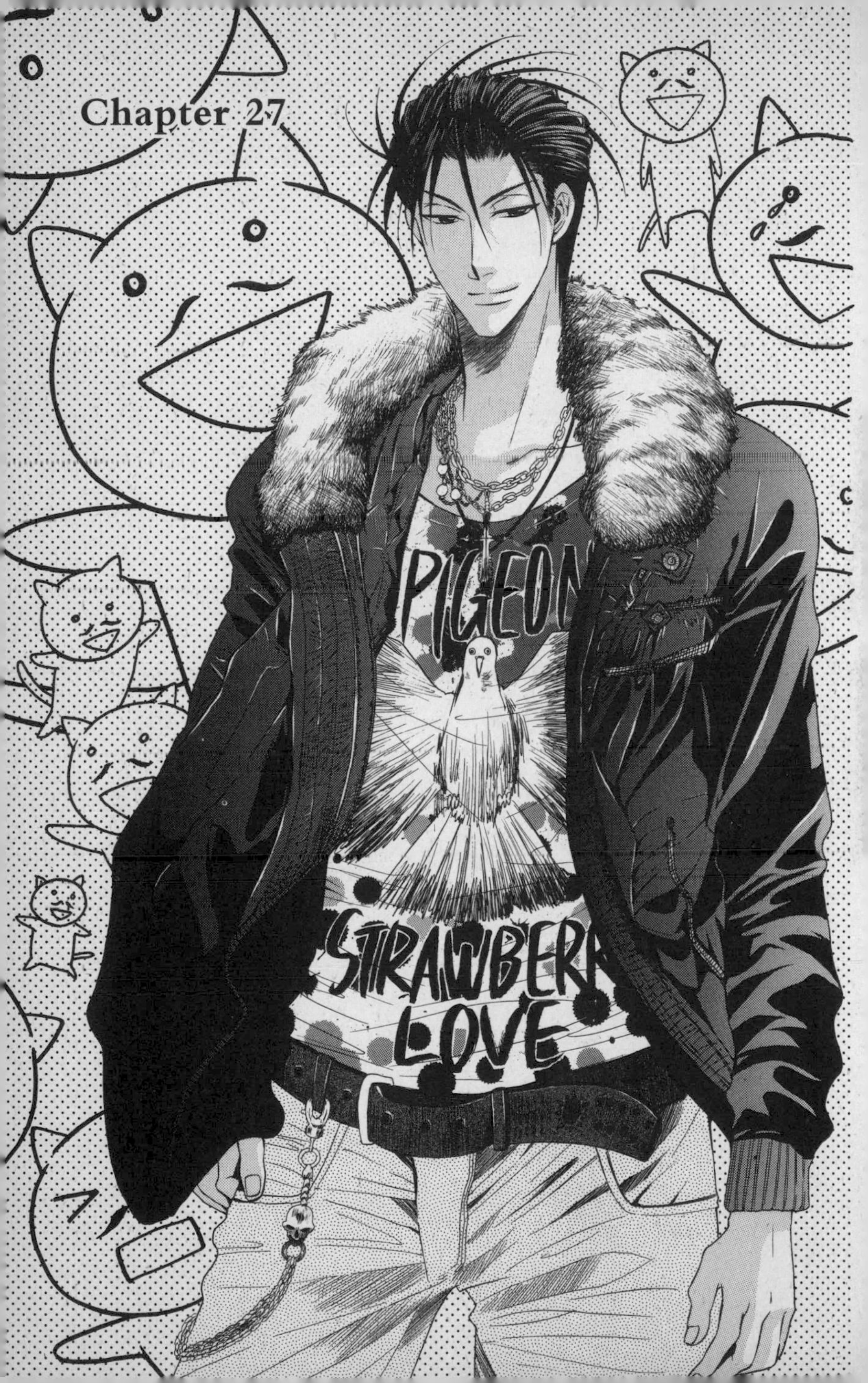
Chapter 27
PIGEON
STRAWBERR
LOVE

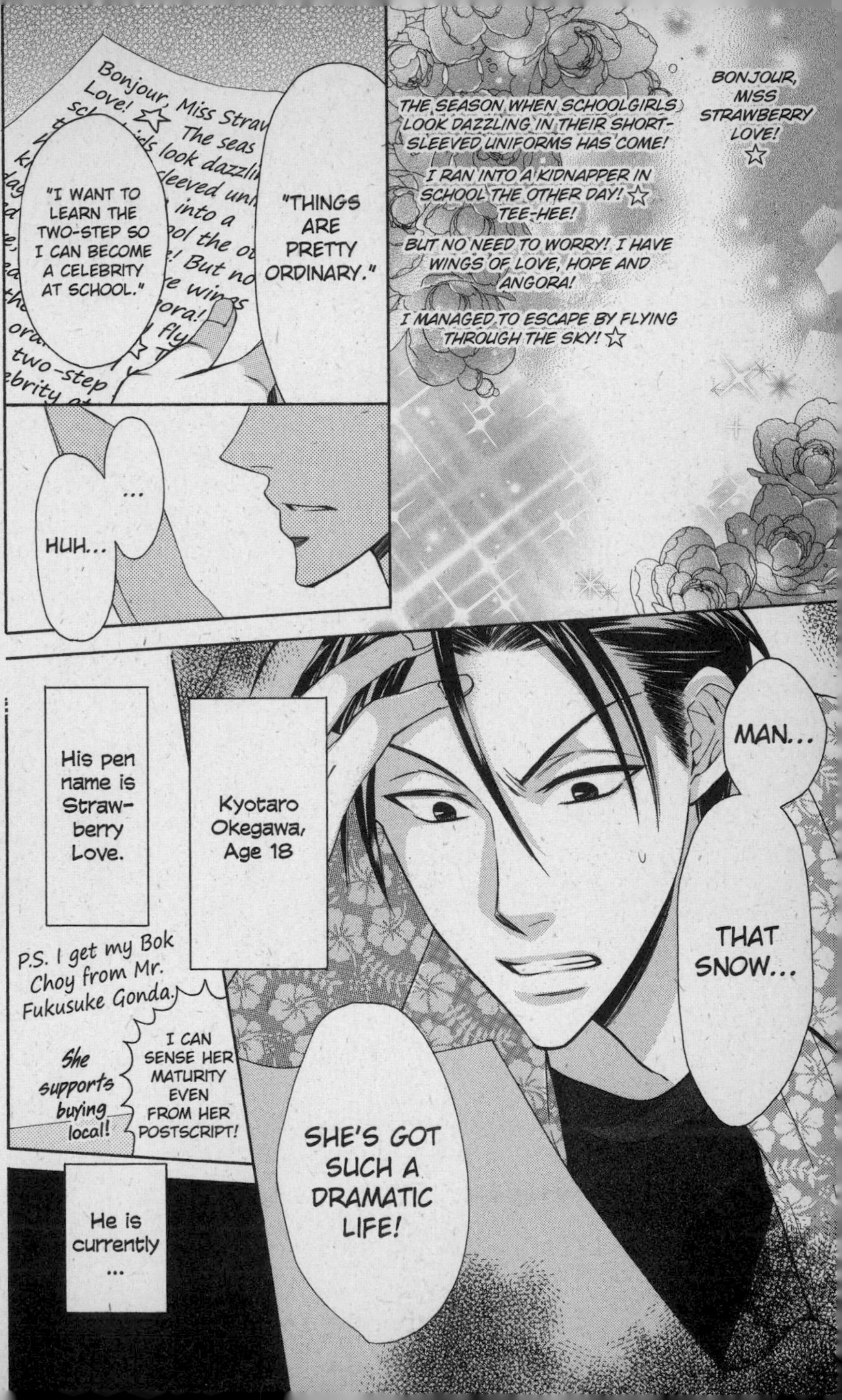
BONJOUR, MISS STRAWBERRY LOVE! ☆
THE SEASON WHEN SCHOOLGIRLS LOOK DAZZLING IN THEIR SHORT-SLEEVED UNIFORMS HAS COME!
I RAN INTO A KIDNAPPER IN SCHOOL THE OTHER DAY! ☆ TEE-HEE!
BUT NO NEED TO WORRY! I HAVE WINGS OF LOVE, HOPE AND ANGORA!
I MANAGED TO ESCAPE BY FLYING THROUGH THE SKY! ☆
"THINGS ARE PRETTY ORDINARY."
"I WANT TO LEARN THE TWO-STEP SO I CAN BECOME A CELEBRITY AT SCHOOL."
...
HUH...
MAN...
THAT SNOW...
SHE'S GOT SUCH A DRAMATIC LIFE!
Kyotaro Okegawa, Age 18
His pen name is Straw-berry Love.
P.S. I get my Bok Choy from Mr. Fukusuke Gonda.
I CAN SENSE HER MATURITY EVEN FROM HER POSTSCRIPT!
She supports buying local!
He is currently ...

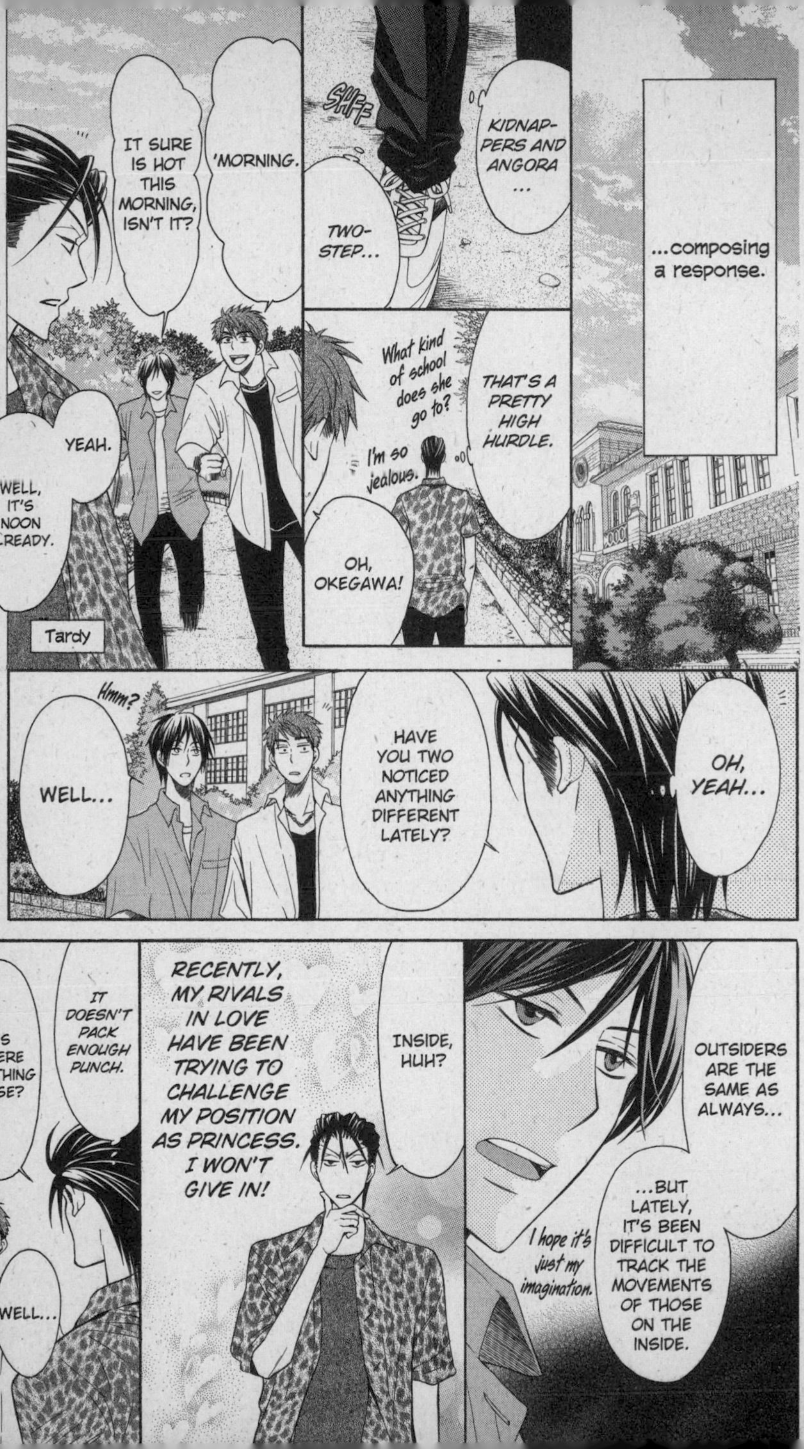
...composing a response.
SHFF
KIDNAPPERS AND ANGORA...
TWO-STEP...
THAT'S A PRETTY HIGH HURDLE.
What kind of school does she go to?
I'm so jealous.
OH, OKEGAWA!
'MORNING.
IT SURE IS HOT THIS MORNING, ISN'T IT?
YEAH.
WELL, IT'S NOON ALREADY.
Tardy
OH, YEAH...
HAVE YOU TWO NOTICED ANYTHING DIFFERENT LATELY?
Hmm?
WELL...
OUTSIDERS ARE THE SAME AS ALWAYS...
...BUT LATELY, IT'S BEEN DIFFICULT TO TRACK THE MOVEMENTS OF THOSE ON THE INSIDE.
I hope it's just my imagination.
INSIDE, HUH?
RECENTLY, MY RIVALS IN LOVE HAVE BEEN TRYING TO CHALLENGE MY POSITION AS PRINCESS. I WON'T GIVE IN!
IT DOESN'T PACK ENOUGH PUNCH.
IS THERE ANYTHING ELSE?
WELL...

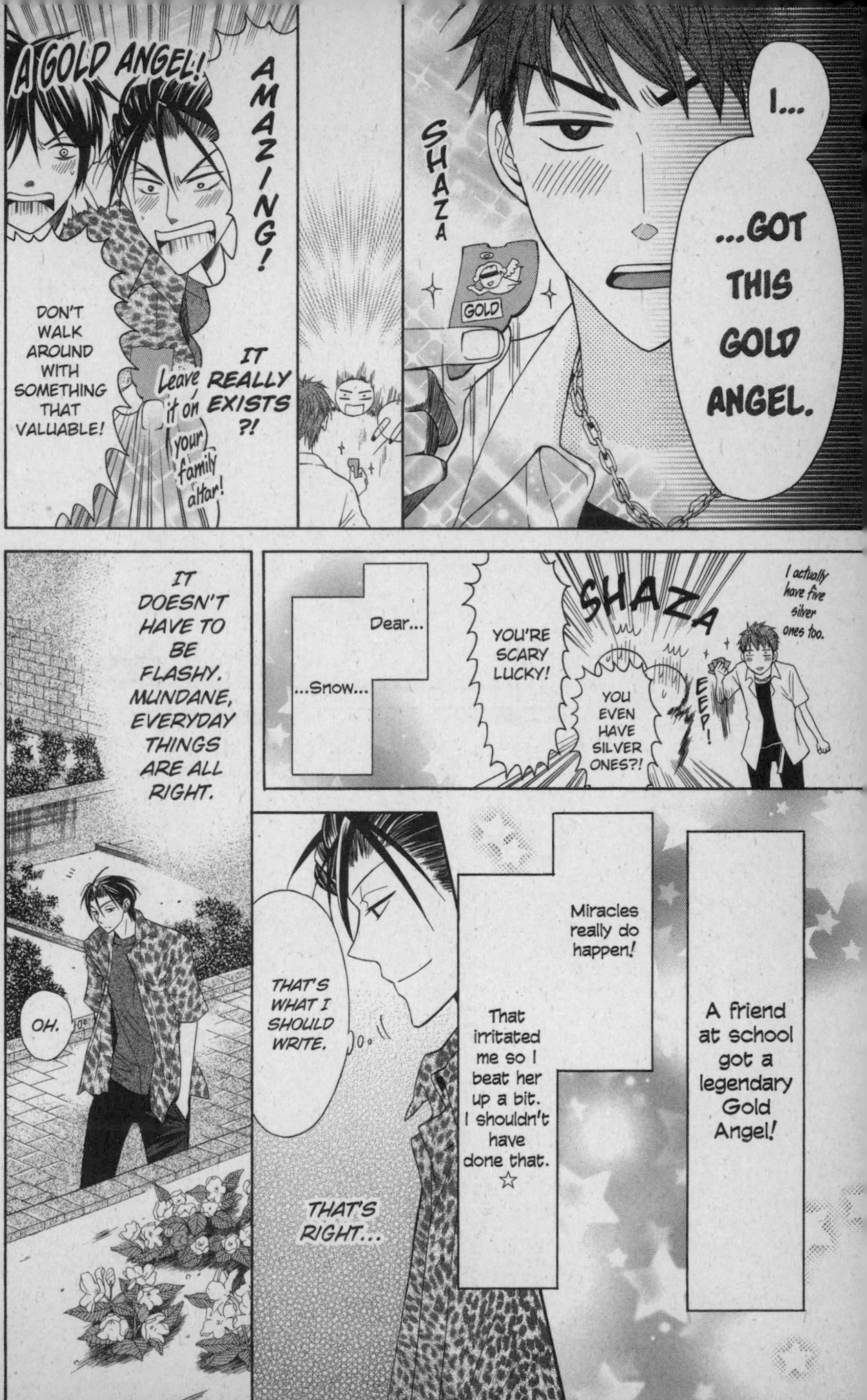
I...
...GOT THIS GOLD ANGEL.
SHAZA
A GOLD ANGEL!
AMAZING!
IT REALLY EXISTS?!
Leave it on your family altar!
DON'T WALK AROUND WITH SOMETHING THAT VALUABLE!
I actually have five silver ones too.
SHAZA
EEP!
YOU EVEN HAVE SILVER ONES?!
YOU'RE SCARY LUCKY!
Dear...
...Snow...
A friend at school got a legendary Gold Angel!
Miracles really do happen!
That irritated me so I beat her up a bit. I shouldn't have done that. ☆
THAT'S WHAT I SHOULD WRITE.
THAT'S RIGHT...
IT DOESN'T HAVE TO BE FLASHY. MUNDANE, EVERYDAY THINGS ARE ALL RIGHT.
OH.

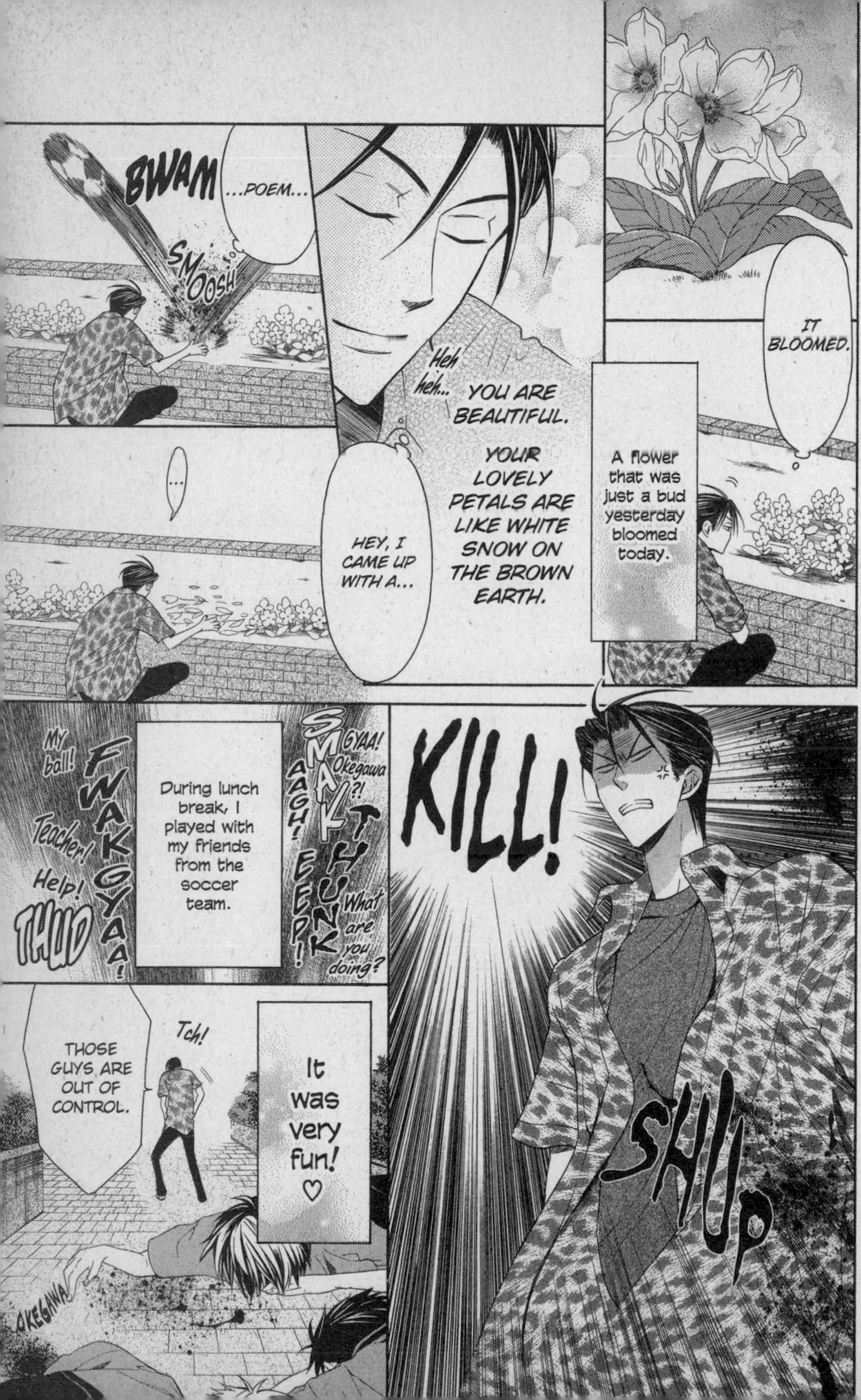
IT BLOOMED.
A flower that was just a bud yesterday bloomed today.
Heh heh...
YOU ARE BEAUTIFUL. YOUR LOVELY PETALS ARE LIKE WHITE SNOW ON THE BROWN EARTH.
HEY, I CAME UP WITH A...
...POEM...
BWAM
SMOOSH
...
KILL!
SHUP
GYAA! Okegawa?!
SMAK
AAGH!
THUNK
EEP!
What are you doing?
During lunch break, I played with my friends from the soccer team.
My ball!
FWAK
GYAAA!
Teacher! Help!
THUD
It was very fun! ♡
Tch!
THOSE GUYS ARE OUT OF CONTROL.
OKEGAWA

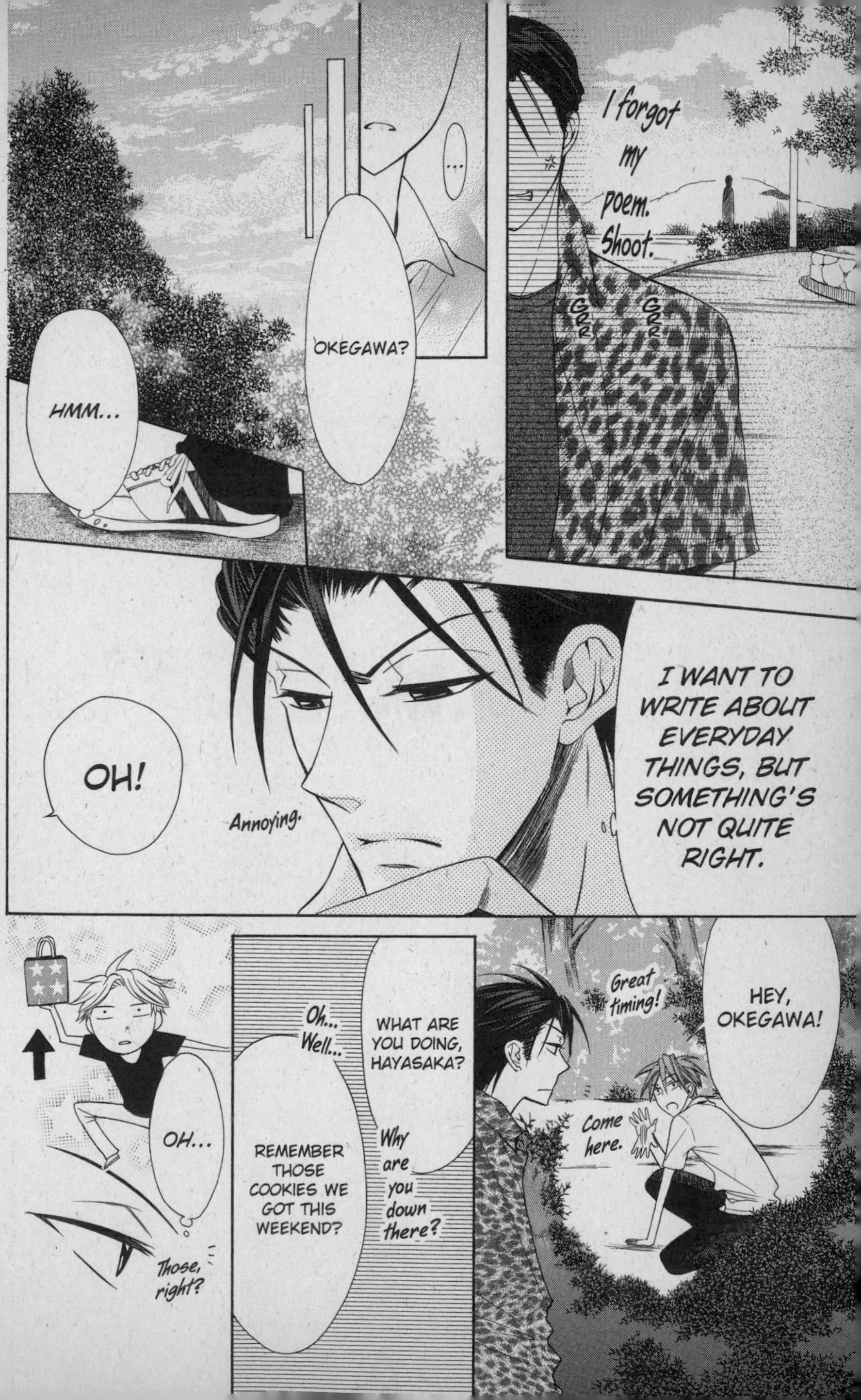
I forgot my poem. Shoot.
GRR GRR
...
OKEGAWA?
HMM...
I WANT TO WRITE ABOUT EVERYDAY THINGS, BUT SOMETHING'S NOT QUITE RIGHT.
Annoying.
OH!
HEY, OKEGAWA!
Great timing!
Come here.
WHAT ARE YOU DOING, HAYASAKA?
Oh... Well...
Why are you down there?
REMEMBER THOSE COOKIES WE GOT THIS WEEKEND?
OH...
Those, right?

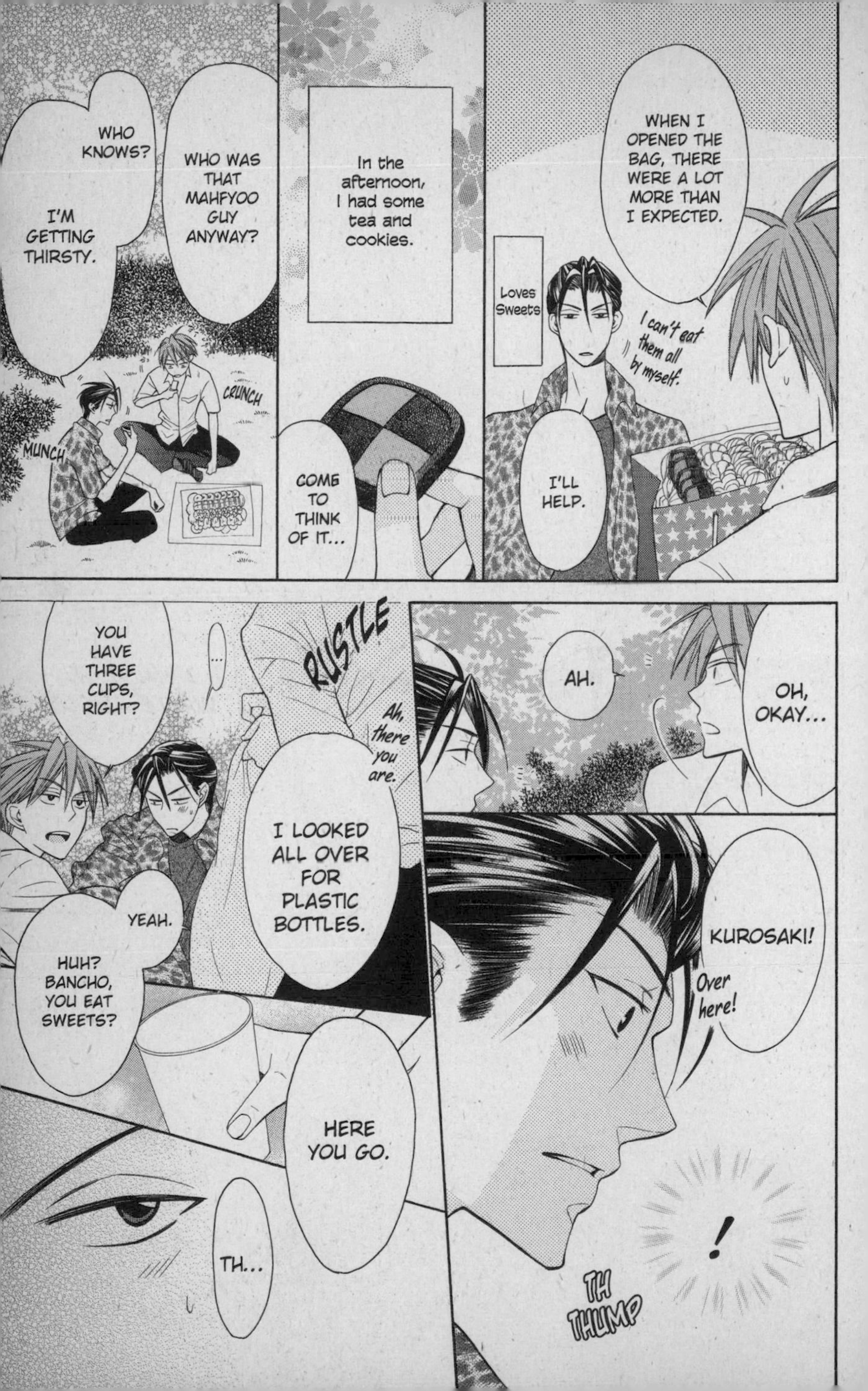
WHEN I OPENED THE BAG, THERE WERE A LOT MORE THAN I EXPECTED.
I can't eat them all by myself.
Loves Sweets
I'LL HELP.
In the afternoon, I had some tea and cookies.
COME TO THINK OF IT...
WHO WAS THAT MAHFYOO GUY ANYWAY?
WHO KNOWS?
I'M GETTING THIRSTY.
CRUNCH
MUNCH
OH, OKAY...
AH.
KUROSAKI!
Over here!
!
TH THUMP
RUSTLE
Ah, there you are.
I LOOKED ALL OVER FOR PLASTIC BOTTLES.
...
YOU HAVE THREE CUPS, RIGHT?
YEAH.
HUH? BANCHO, YOU EAT SWEETS?
HERE YOU GO.
TH...

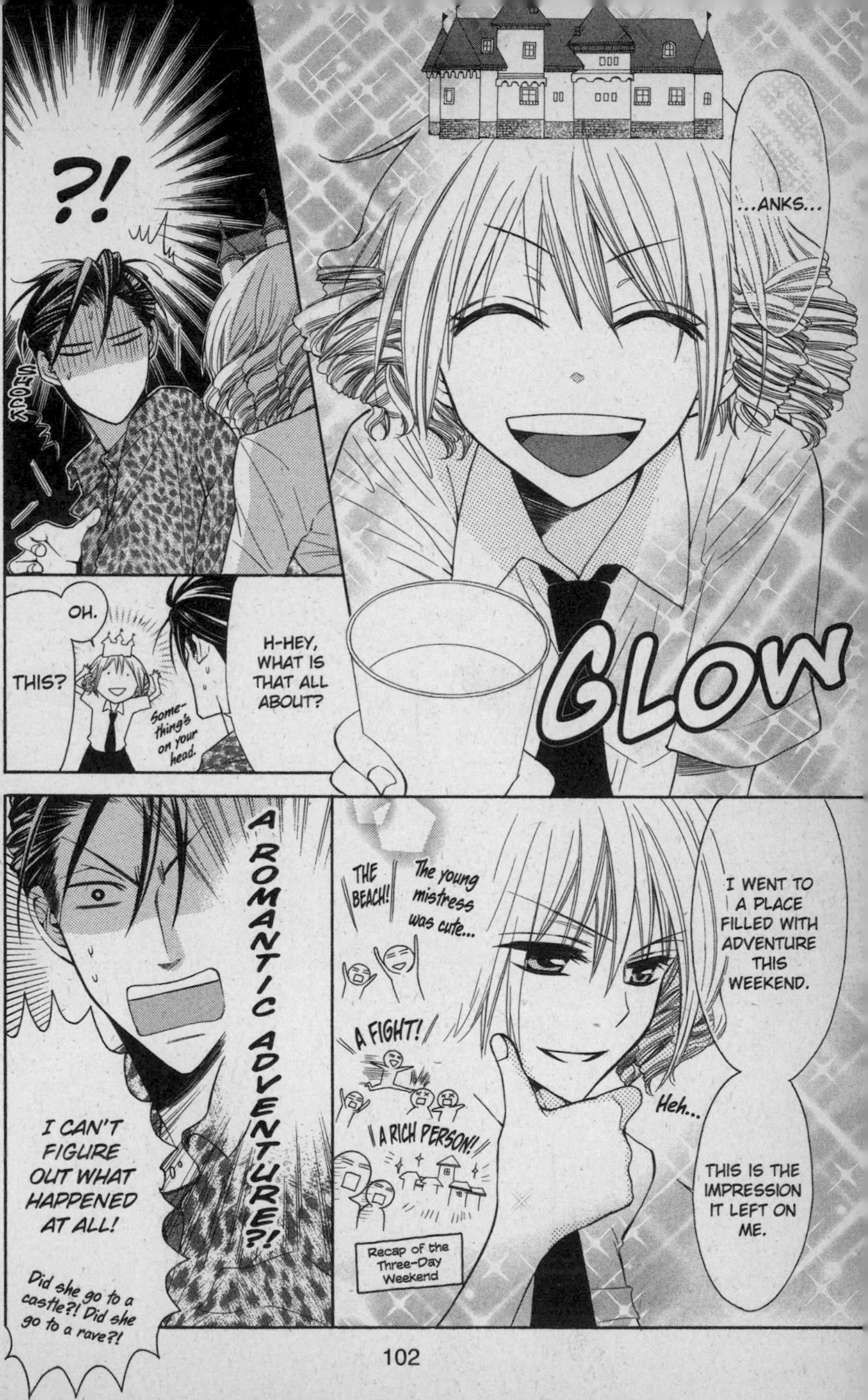
...ANKS...
GLOW
?!
THUMP
H-HEY, WHAT IS THAT ALL ABOUT?
Some-thing's on your head.
OH.
THIS?
I WENT TO A PLACE FILLED WITH ADVENTURE THIS WEEKEND.
Heh...
THIS IS THE IMPRESSION IT LEFT ON ME.
The young mistress was cute...
THE BEACH!
A FIGHT!
A RICH PERSON!
Recap of the Three-Day Weekend
A ROMANTIC ADVENTURE?!
I CAN'T FIGURE OUT WHAT HAPPENED AT ALL!
Did she go to a castle?! Did she go to a rave?!

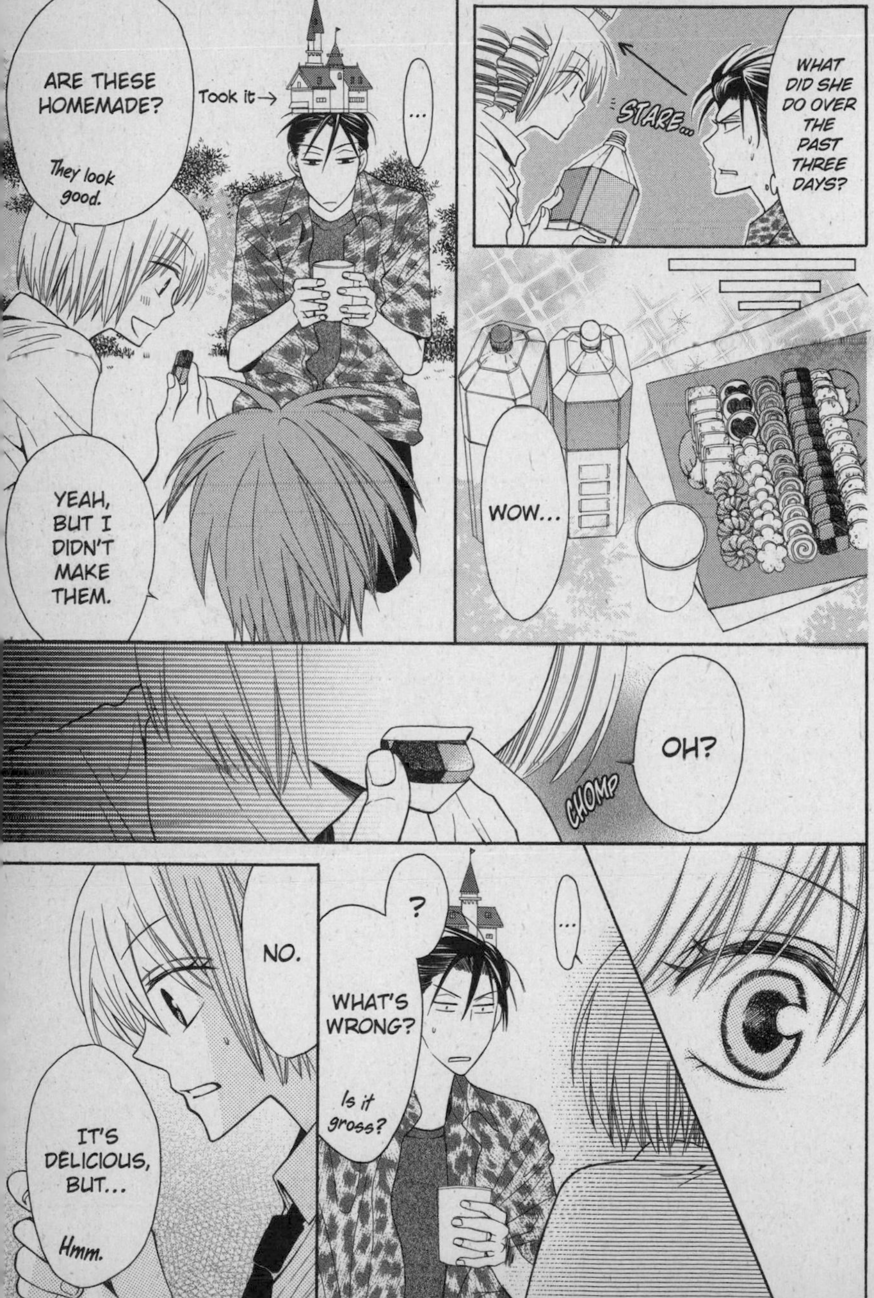
WHAT DID SHE DO OVER THE PAST THREE DAYS?
STARE...
WOW...
ARE THESE HOMEMADE?
They look good.
Took it →
...
YEAH, BUT I DIDN'T MAKE THEM.
OH?
CHOMP
...
?
WHAT'S WRONG?
Is it gross?
NO.
IT'S DELICIOUS, BUT...
Hmm.

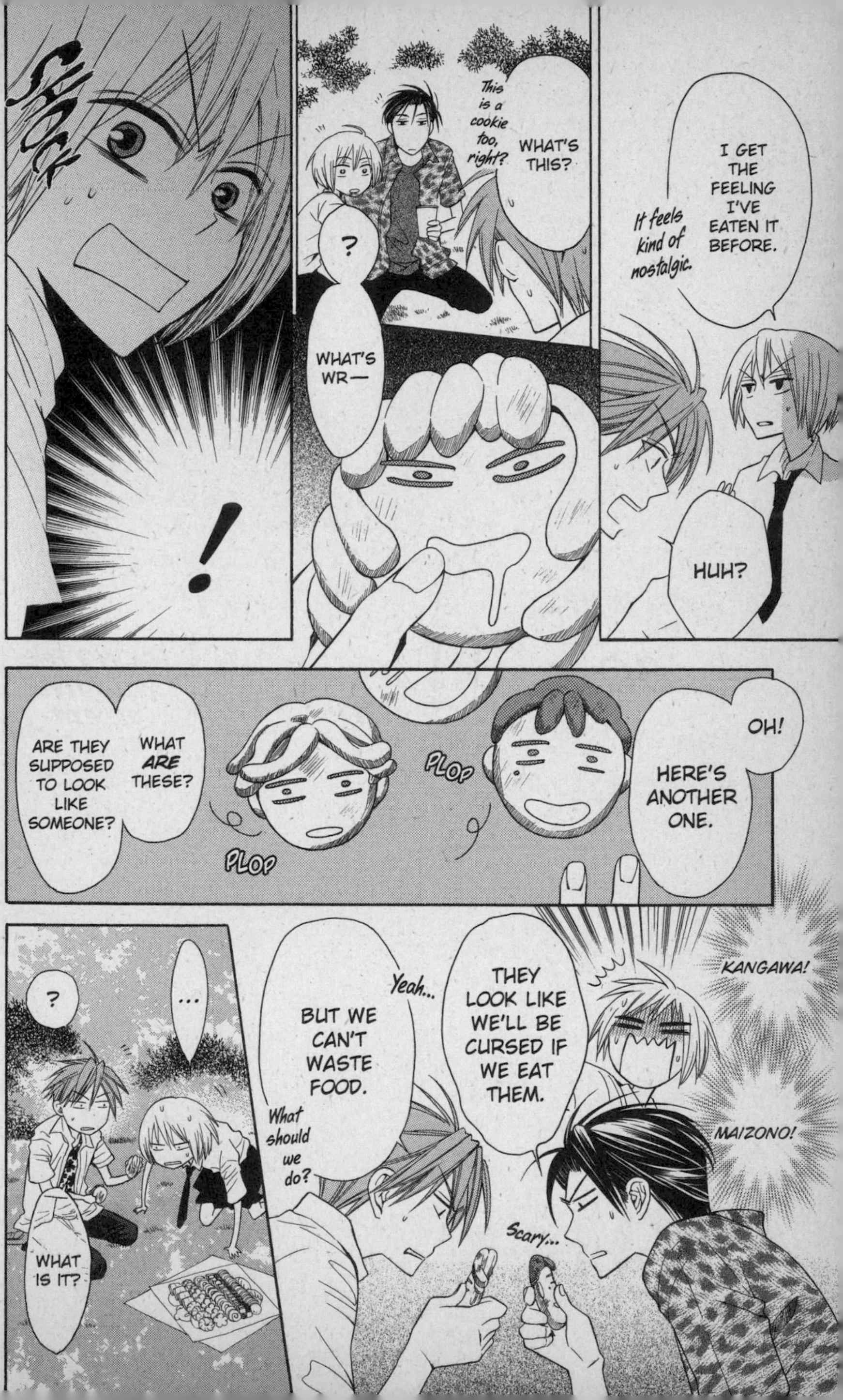
I GET THE FEELING I'VE EATEN IT BEFORE.
It feels kind of nostalgic.
HUH?
WHAT'S THIS?
This is a cookie too, right?
?
WHAT'S WR—
SHOCK
!
OH!
HERE'S ANOTHER ONE.
PLOP
WHAT *ARE* THESE?
ARE THEY SUPPOSED TO LOOK LIKE SOMEONE?
PLOP
KANGAWA!
MAIZONO!
THEY LOOK LIKE WE'LL BE CURSED IF WE EAT THEM.
Yeah...
BUT WE CAN'T WASTE FOOD.
What should we do?
Scary...
...
?
WHAT IS IT?

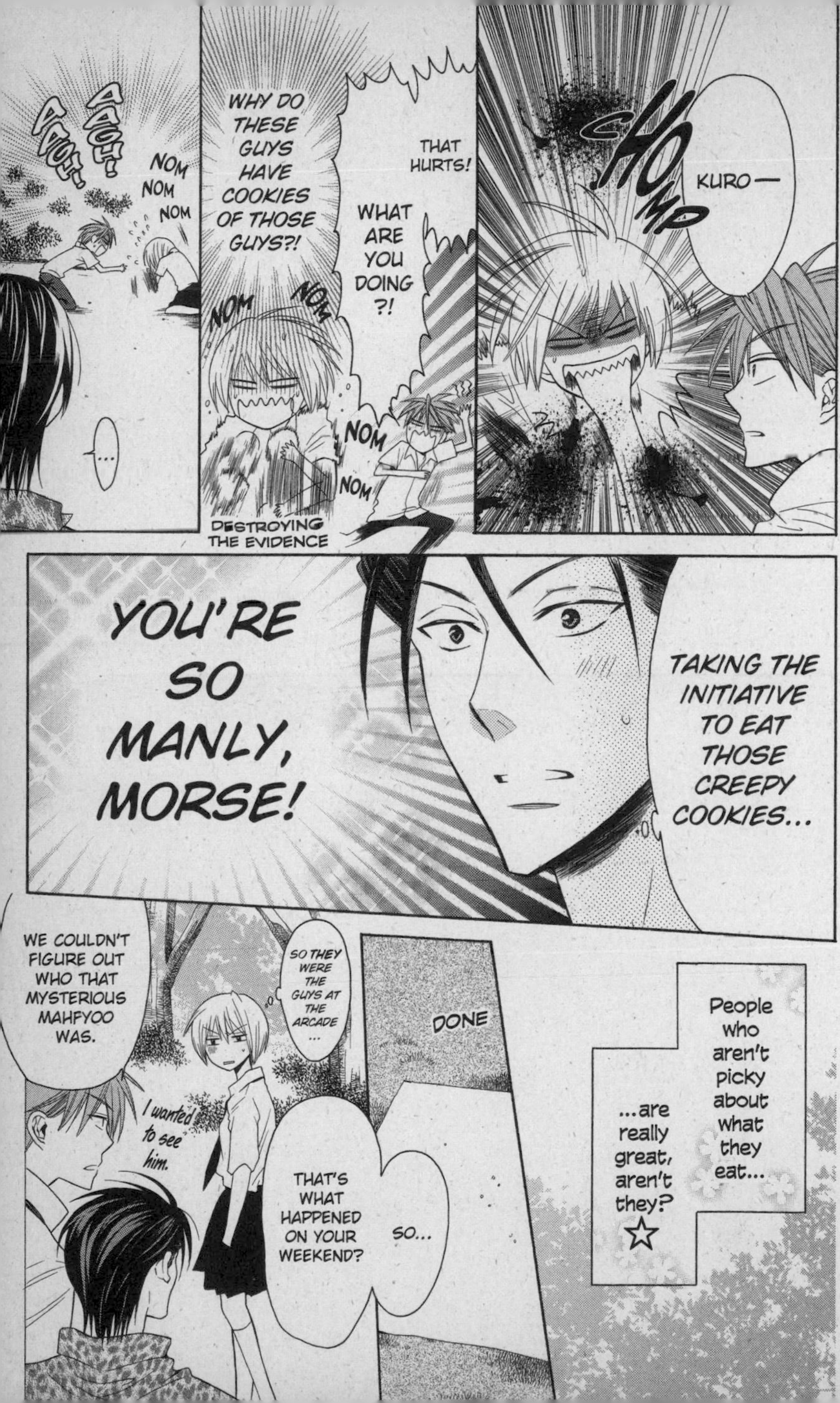
KURO—
CHOMP
THAT HURTS!
WHAT ARE YOU DOING?!
WHY DO THESE GUYS HAVE COOKIES OF THOSE GUYS?!
NOM NOM
NOM NOM
DESTROYING THE EVIDENCE
AAGH! AAGH!
NOM NOM NOM
...
TAKING THE INITIATIVE TO EAT THOSE CREEPY COOKIES...
YOU'RE SO MANLY, MORSE!
People who aren't picky about what they eat...
...are really great, aren't they? ☆
DONE
SO...
THAT'S WHAT HAPPENED ON YOUR WEEKEND?
SO THEY WERE THE GUYS AT THE ARCADE...
WE COULDN'T FIGURE OUT WHO THAT MYSTERIOUS MAHFYOO WAS.
I wanted to see him.

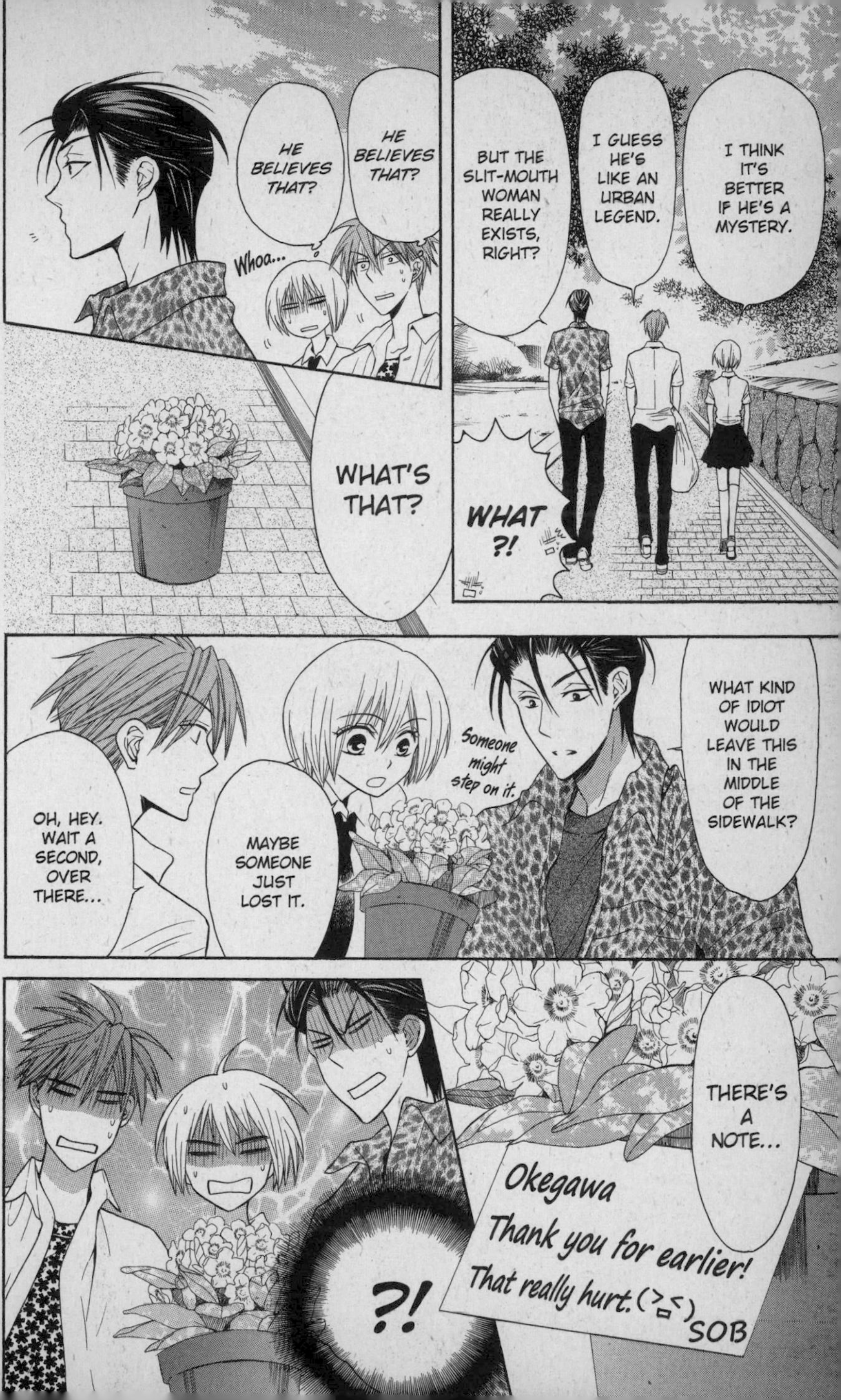
I THINK IT'S BETTER IF HE'S A MYSTERY.
I GUESS HE'S LIKE AN URBAN LEGEND.
BUT THE SLIT-MOUTH WOMAN REALLY EXISTS, RIGHT?
WHAT ?!
HE BELIEVES THAT?
HE BELIEVES THAT?
Whoa...
WHAT'S THAT?
WHAT KIND OF IDIOT WOULD LEAVE THIS IN THE MIDDLE OF THE SIDEWALK?
Someone might step on it.
MAYBE SOMEONE JUST LOST IT.
OH, HEY. WAIT A SECOND, OVER THERE...
THERE'S A NOTE...
Okegawa
Thank you for earlier!
That really hurt. (>_<) SOB
?!

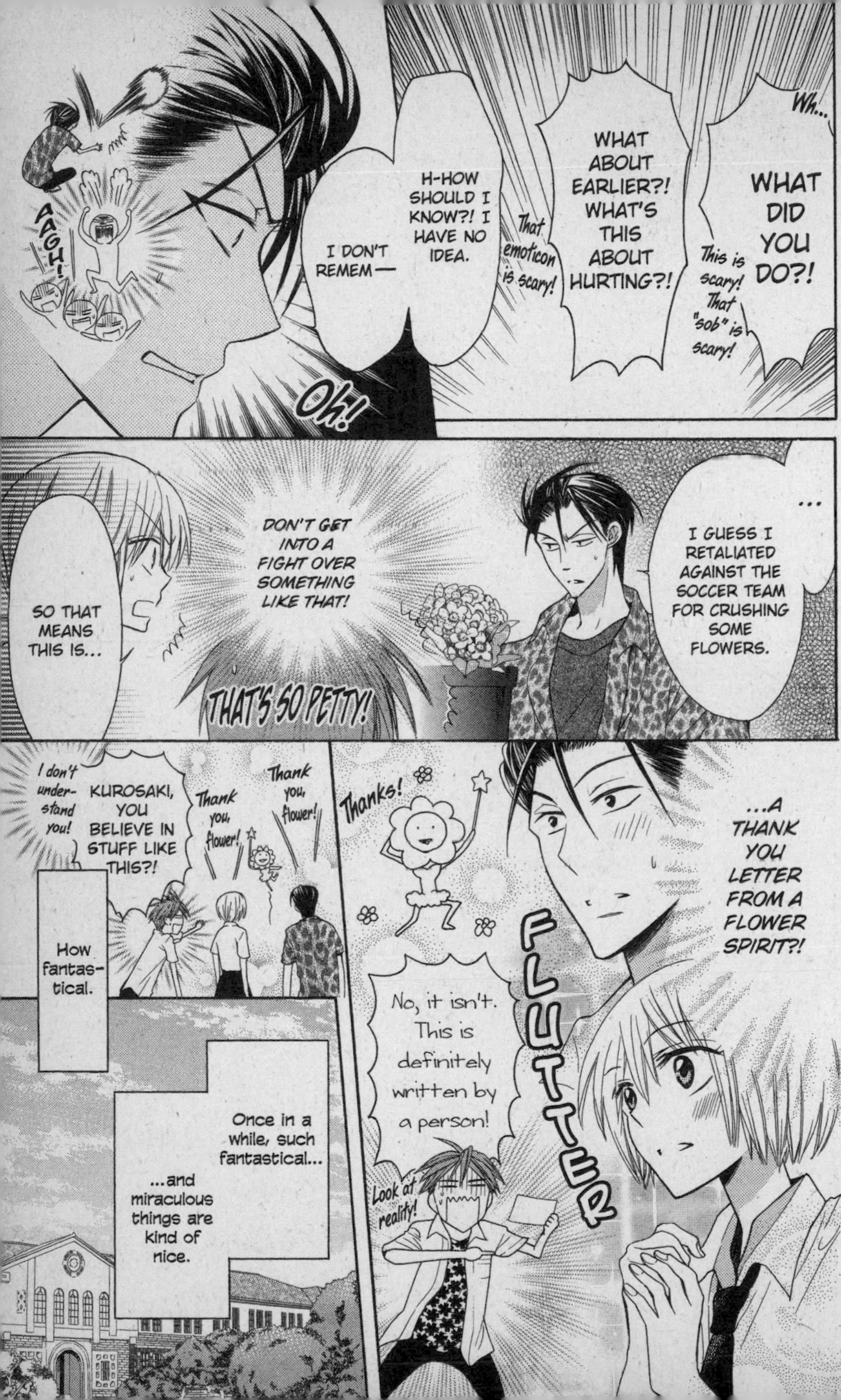
Wh...
WHAT DID YOU DO?!
This is scary! That "sob" is scary!
WHAT ABOUT EARLIER?! WHAT'S THIS ABOUT HURTING?!
That emoticon is scary!
H-HOW SHOULD I KNOW?! I HAVE NO IDEA.
I DON'T REMEM—
Oh!
AAGH!
...
I GUESS I RETALIATED AGAINST THE SOCCER TEAM FOR CRUSHING SOME FLOWERS.
DON'T GET INTO A FIGHT OVER SOMETHING LIKE THAT!
THAT'S SO PETTY!
SO THAT MEANS THIS IS...
...A THANK YOU LETTER FROM A FLOWER SPIRIT?!
FLUTTER
Thanks!
No, it isn't. This is definitely written by a person!
Look at reality!
Thank you, flower!
Thank you, flower!
KUROSAKI, YOU BELIEVE IN STUFF LIKE THIS?!
I don't under-stand you!
How fantas-tical.
Once in a while, such fantastical...
...and miraculous things are kind of nice.

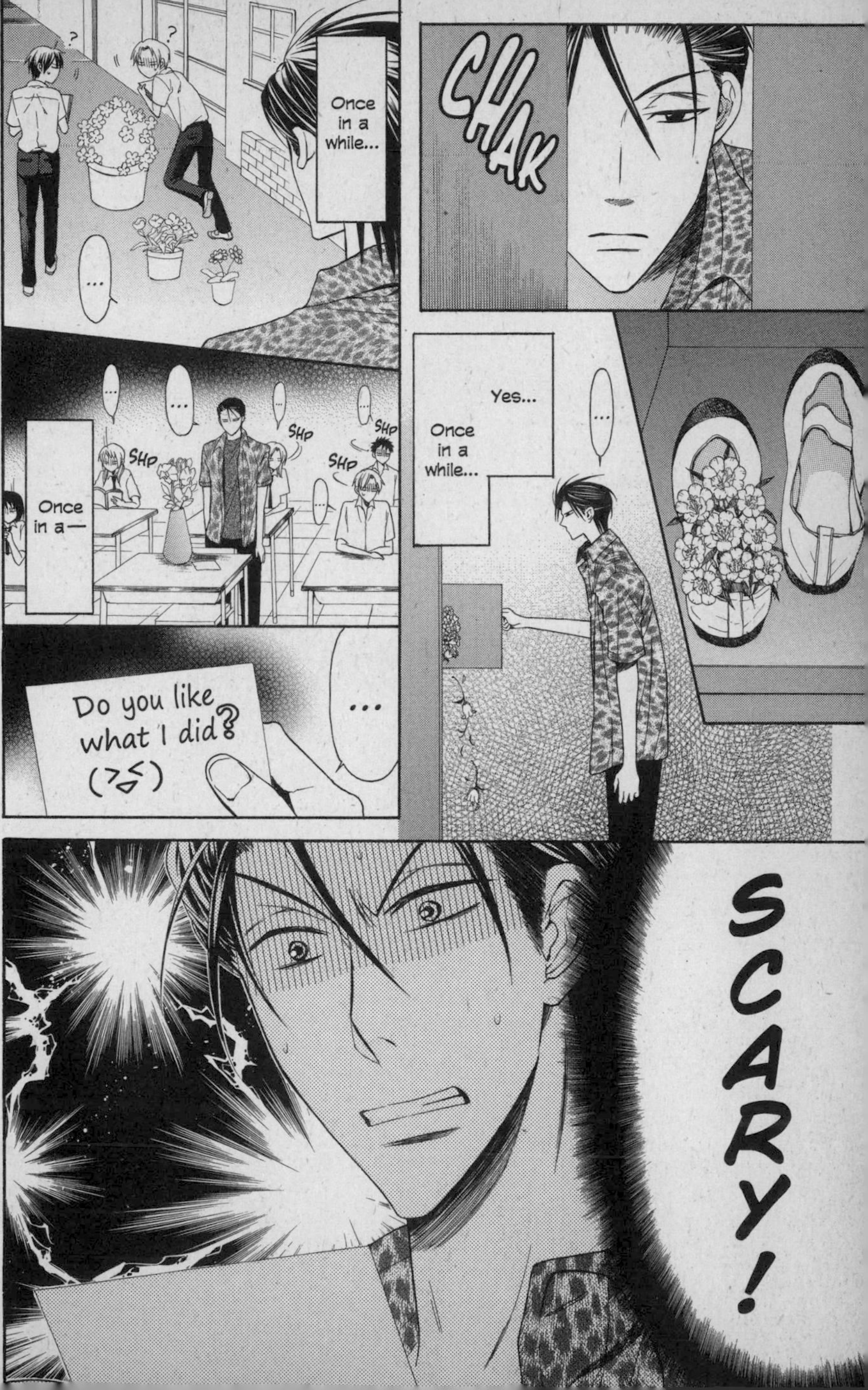
CHAK
Once in a while...
...
...
Yes...
Once in a while...
...
SHP
...
SHP
...
...
SHP
...
Once in a—
...
Do you like what I did? (>△<)
SCARY!

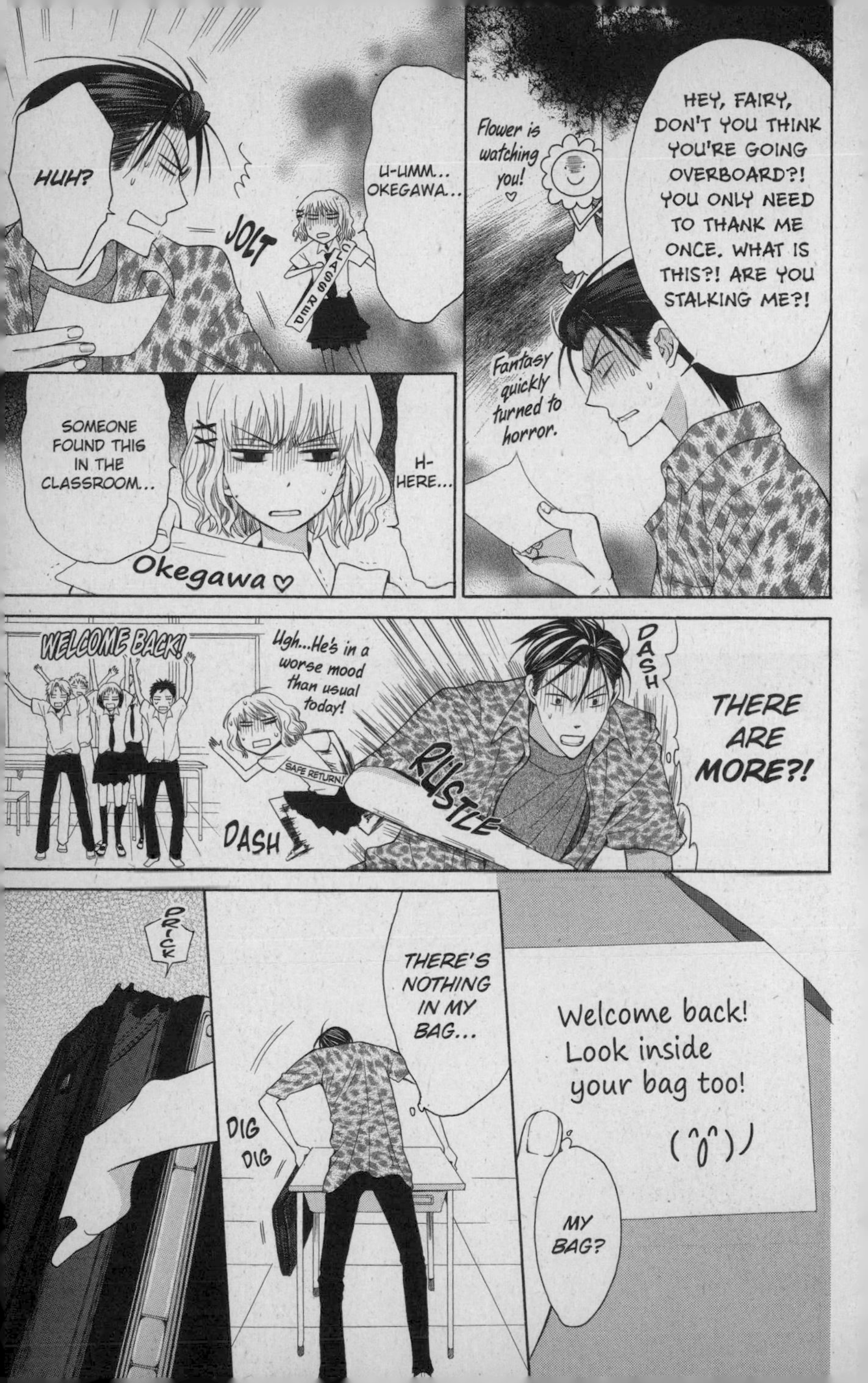
HEY, FAIRY, DON'T YOU THINK YOU'RE GOING OVERBOARD?! YOU ONLY NEED TO THANK ME ONCE. WHAT IS THIS?! ARE YOU STALKING ME?!
Flower is watching you! ♡
Fantasy quickly turned to horror.
U-UMM... OKEGAWA...
CLASS REP
JOLT
HUH?
H-HERE...
SOMEONE FOUND THIS IN THE CLASSROOM...
Okegawa ♡
THERE ARE MORE?!
DASH
RUSTLE
Ugh...He's in a worse mood than usual today!
SAFE RETURN!
WELCOME BACK!
DASH
Welcome back! Look inside your bag too!
(^o^)/
MY BAG?
THERE'S NOTHING IN MY BAG...
DIG DIG
PRICK

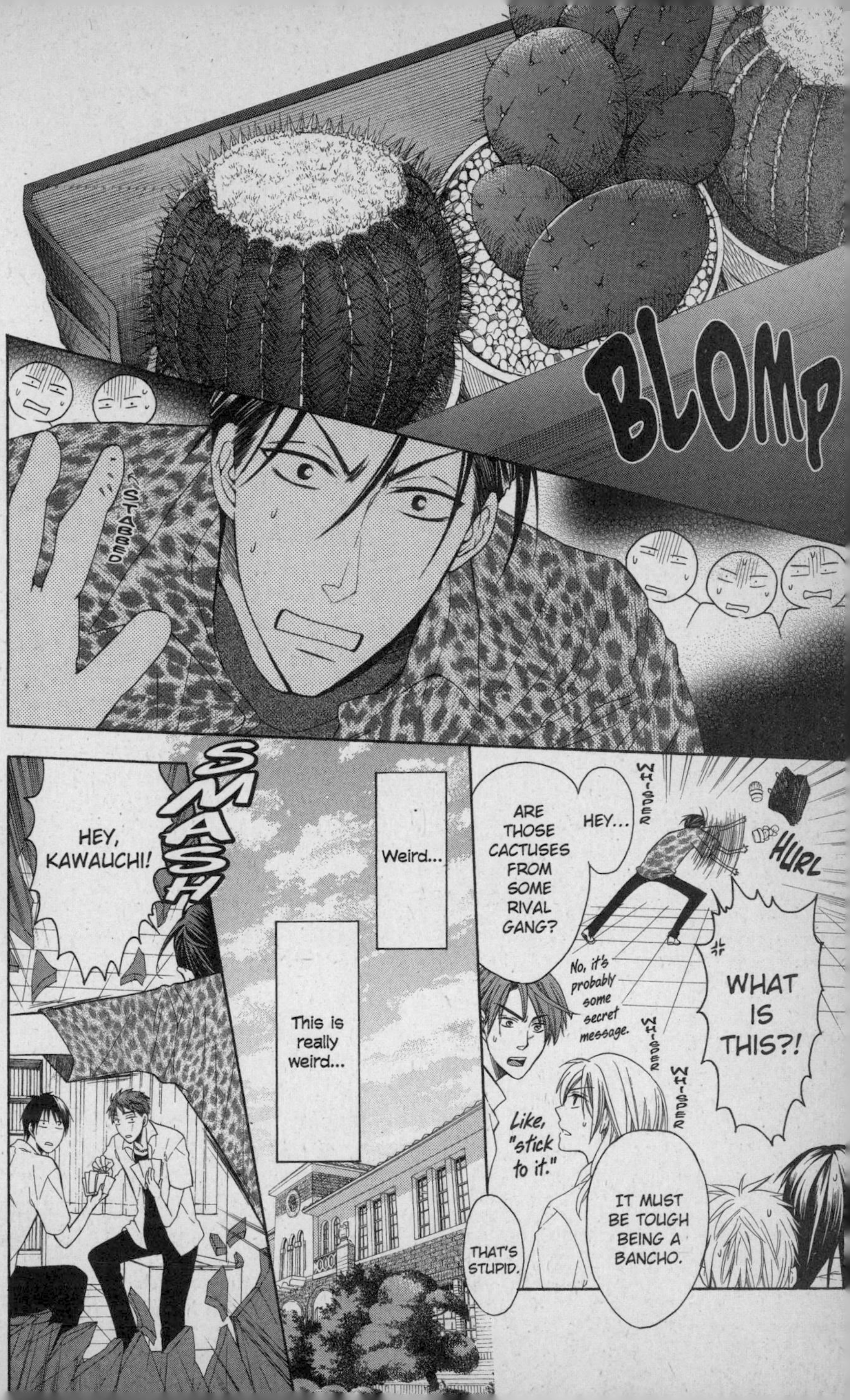
BLOMP
STABBED
HURL
WHAT IS THIS?!
WHISPER
HEY...
ARE THOSE CACTUSES FROM SOME RIVAL GANG?
No, it's probably some secret message.
WHISPER
WHISPER
Like, "stick to it."
IT MUST BE TOUGH BEING A BANCHO.
THAT'S STUPID.
Weird...
This is really weird...
SMASH!
HEY, KAWAUCHI!

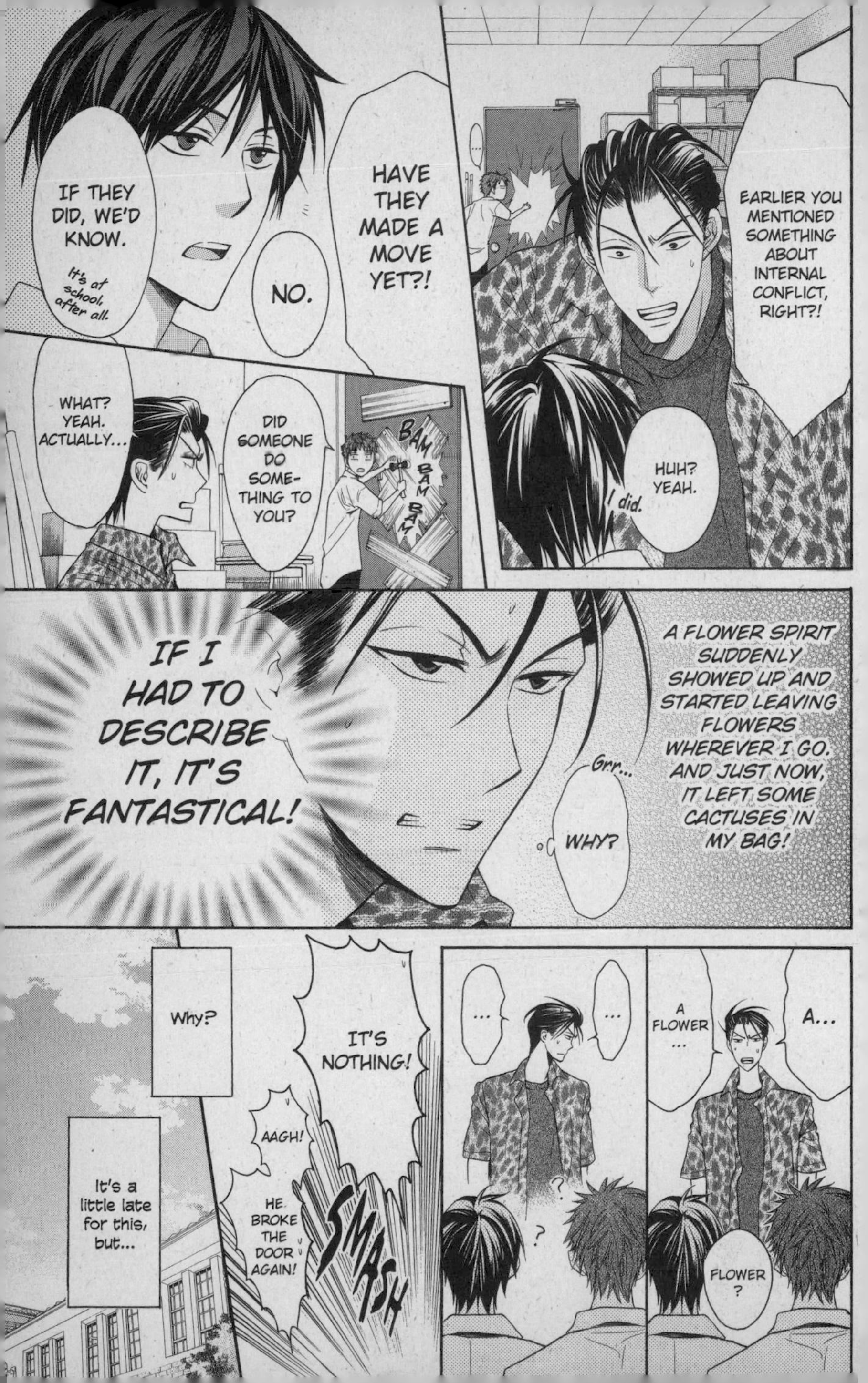
...
EARLIER YOU MENTIONED SOMETHING ABOUT INTERNAL CONFLICT, RIGHT?!
HUH? YEAH.
I did.
HAVE THEY MADE A MOVE YET?!
NO.
IF THEY DID, WE'D KNOW.
It's at school, after all.
DID SOMEONE DO SOMETHING TO YOU?
BAM BAM BAM
WHAT? YEAH. ACTUALLY...
A FLOWER SPIRIT SUDDENLY SHOWED UP AND STARTED LEAVING FLOWERS WHEREVER I GO. AND JUST NOW, IT LEFT SOME CACTUSES IN MY BAG!
Grr...
WHY?
IF I HAD TO DESCRIBE IT, IT'S FANTASTICAL!
A...
A FLOWER ...
FLOWER ?
...
...
?
?
IT'S NOTHING!
SMASH
AAGH!
HE BROKE THE DOOR AGAIN!
Why?
It's a little late for this, but...

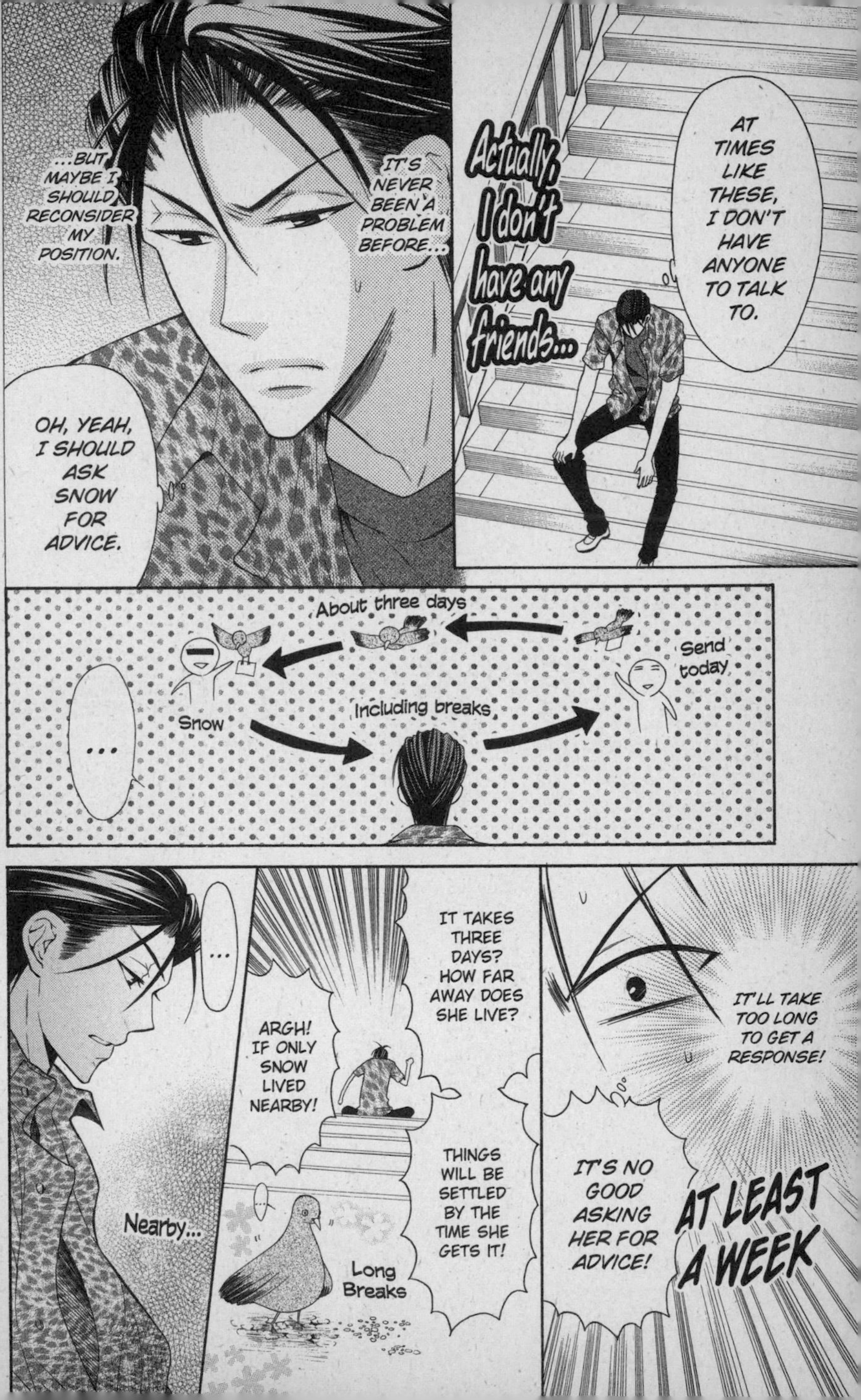
AT TIMES LIKE THESE, I DON'T HAVE ANYONE TO TALK TO.
Actually, I don't have any friends...
IT'S NEVER BEEN A PROBLEM BEFORE...
...BUT MAYBE I SHOULD RECONSIDER MY POSITION.
OH, YEAH, I SHOULD ASK SNOW FOR ADVICE.
Send today
About three days
Snow
Including breaks
...
IT'LL TAKE TOO LONG TO GET A RESPONSE!
IT'S NO GOOD ASKING HER FOR ADVICE!
AT LEAST A WEEK
IT TAKES THREE DAYS? HOW FAR AWAY DOES SHE LIVE?
ARGH! IF ONLY SNOW LIVED NEARBY!
THINGS WILL BE SETTLED BY THE TIME SHE GETS IT!
...
Long Breaks
...
Nearby...

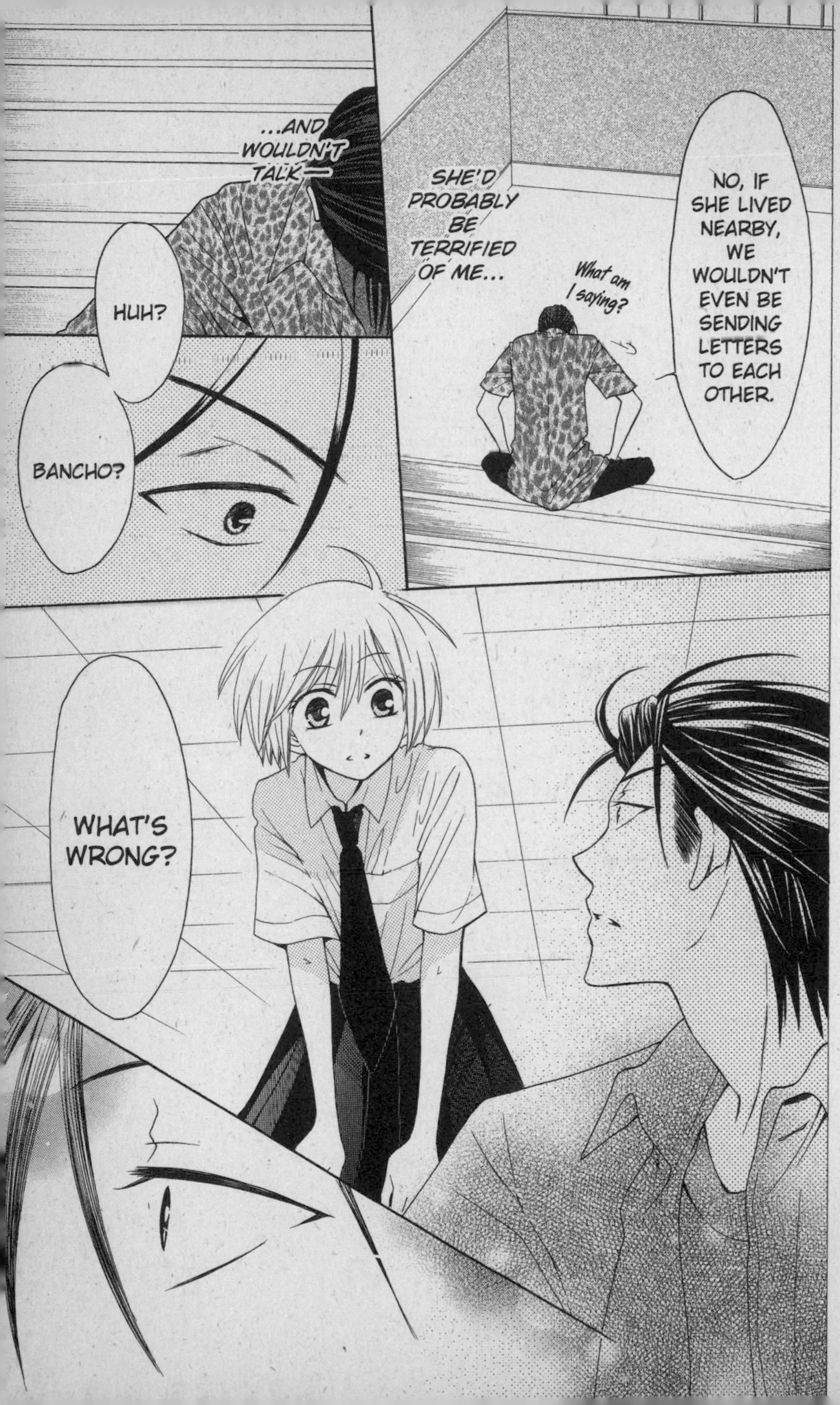
NO, IF SHE LIVED NEARBY, WE WOULDN'T EVEN BE SENDING LETTERS TO EACH OTHER.
What am I saying?
SHE'D PROBABLY BE TERRIFIED OF ME...
...AND WOULDN'T TALK—
HUH?
BANCHO?
WHAT'S WRONG?

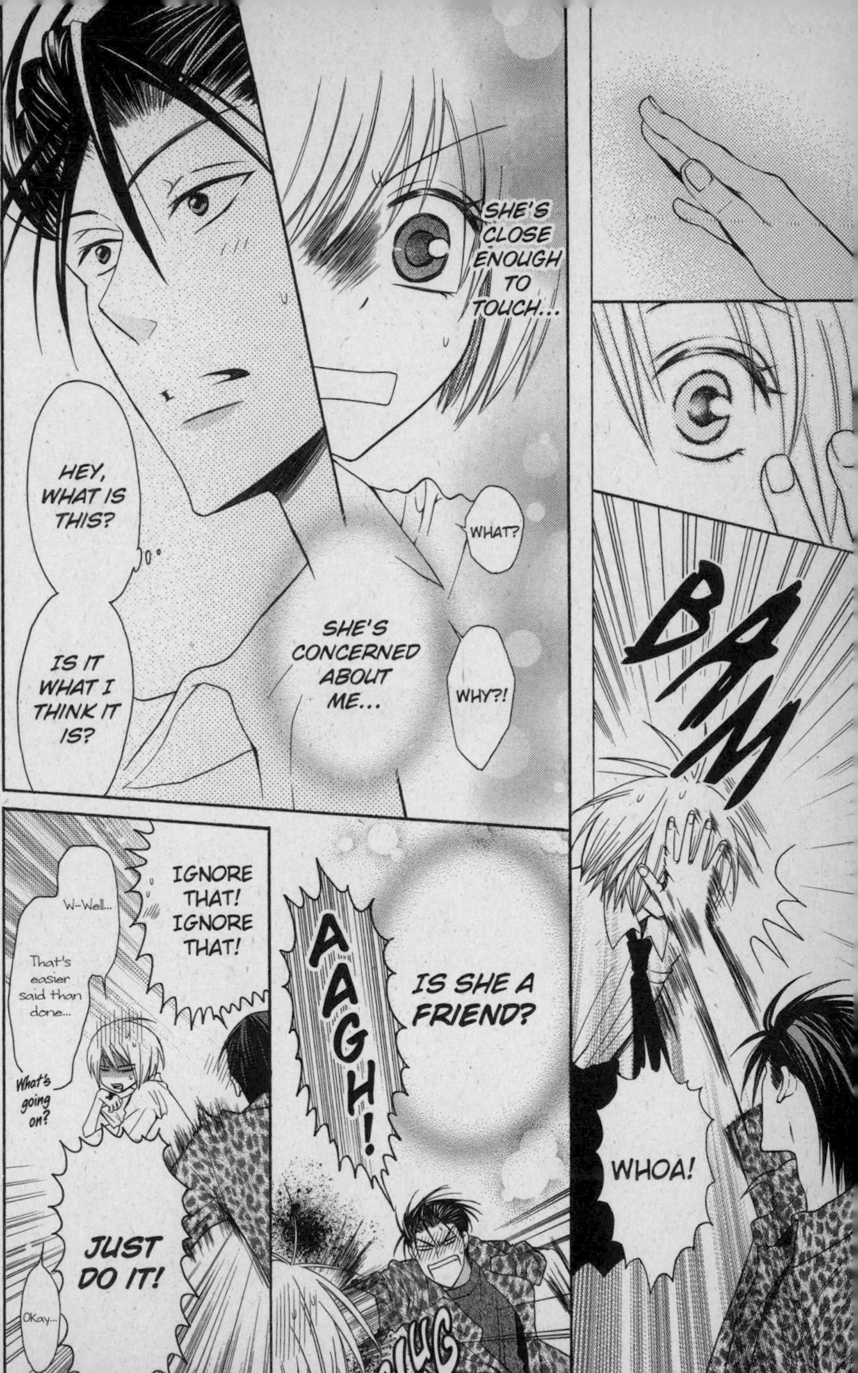
BAM
WHOA!
SHE'S CLOSE ENOUGH TO TOUCH...
WHAT?
HEY, WHAT IS THIS?
SHE'S CONCERNED ABOUT ME...
WHY?!
IS IT WHAT I THINK IT IS?
IS SHE A FRIEND?
AAGH!
SLUG
IGNORE THAT! IGNORE THAT!
W-Well...
That's easier said than done...
What's going on?
JUST DO IT!
Okay...

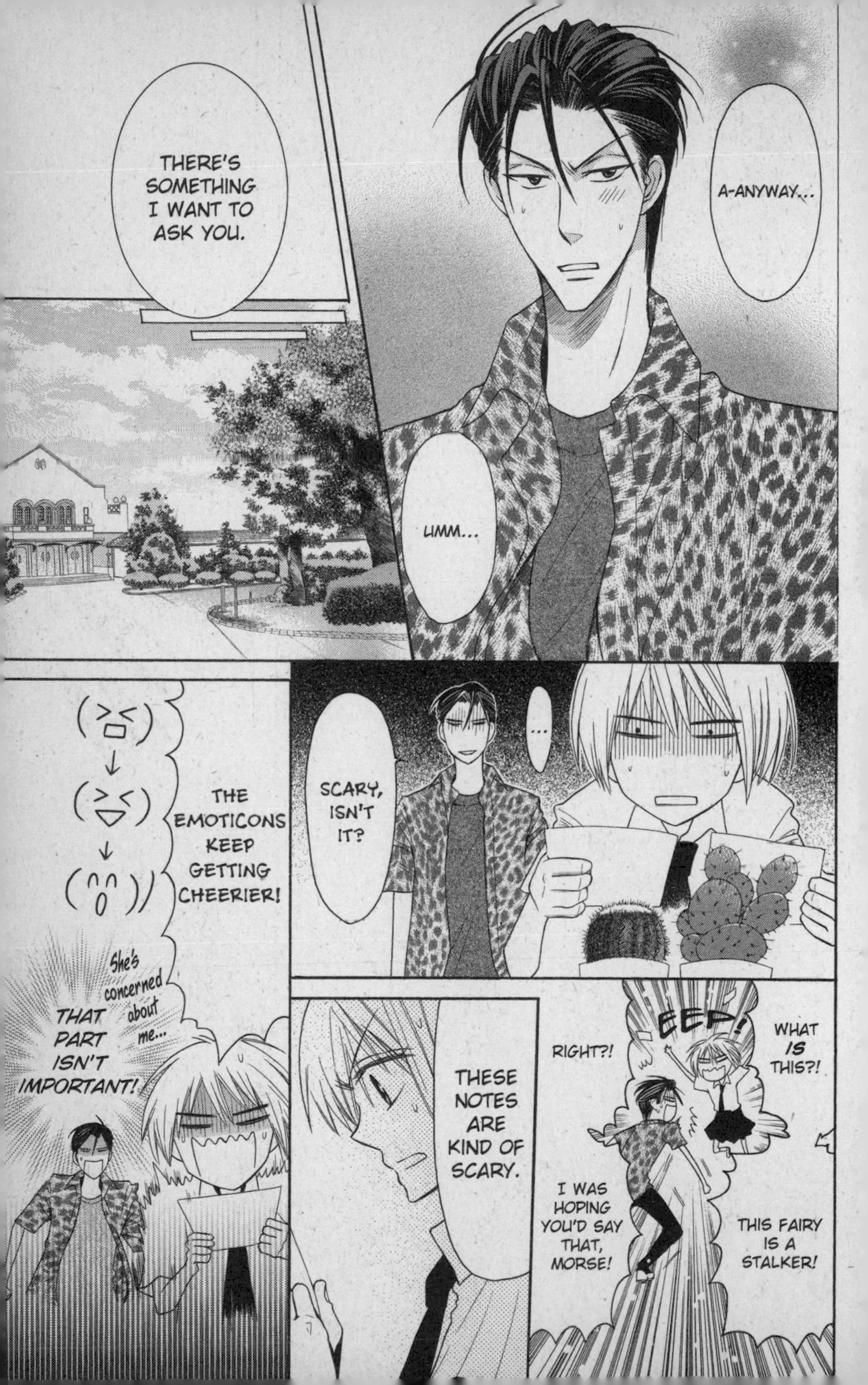
A-ANYWAY...
UMM...
THERE'S SOMETHING I WANT TO ASK YOU.
...
SCARY, ISN'T IT?
EEP!
WHAT IS THIS?!
RIGHT?!
THIS FAIRY IS A STALKER!
I WAS HOPING YOU'D SAY THAT, MORSE!
THESE NOTES ARE KIND OF SCARY.
(><) → (><) → (^^)
THE EMOTICONS KEEP GETTING CHEERIER!
She's concerned about me...
THAT PART ISN'T IMPORTANT!

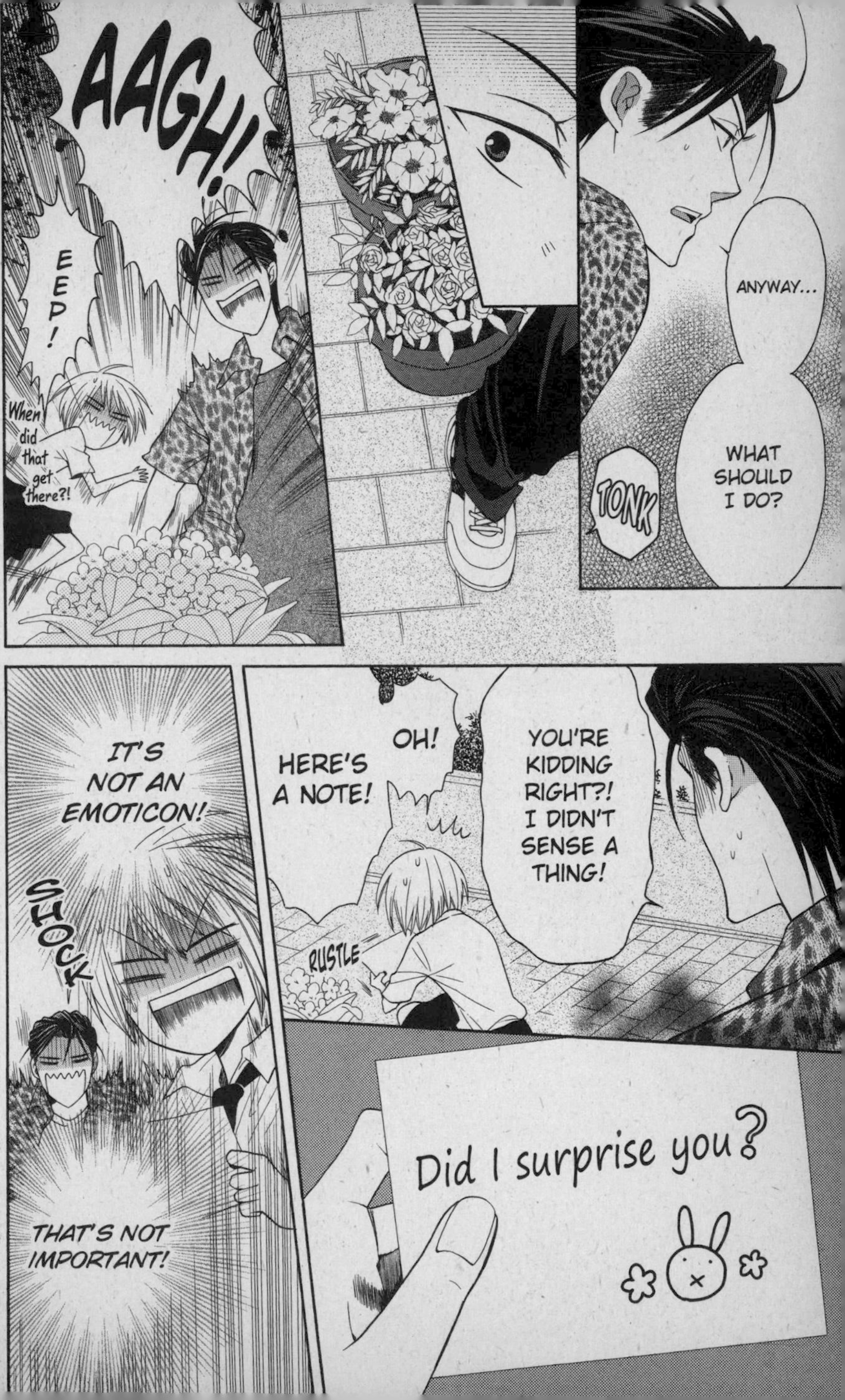
ANYWAY...
WHAT SHOULD I DO?
TONK
AAGH!!
EEP!
When did that get there?!
YOU'RE KIDDING RIGHT?! I DIDN'T SENSE A THING!
OH!
HERE'S A NOTE!
RUSTLE
Did I surprise you?
IT'S NOT AN EMOTICON!
SHOCK
THAT'S NOT IMPORTANT!

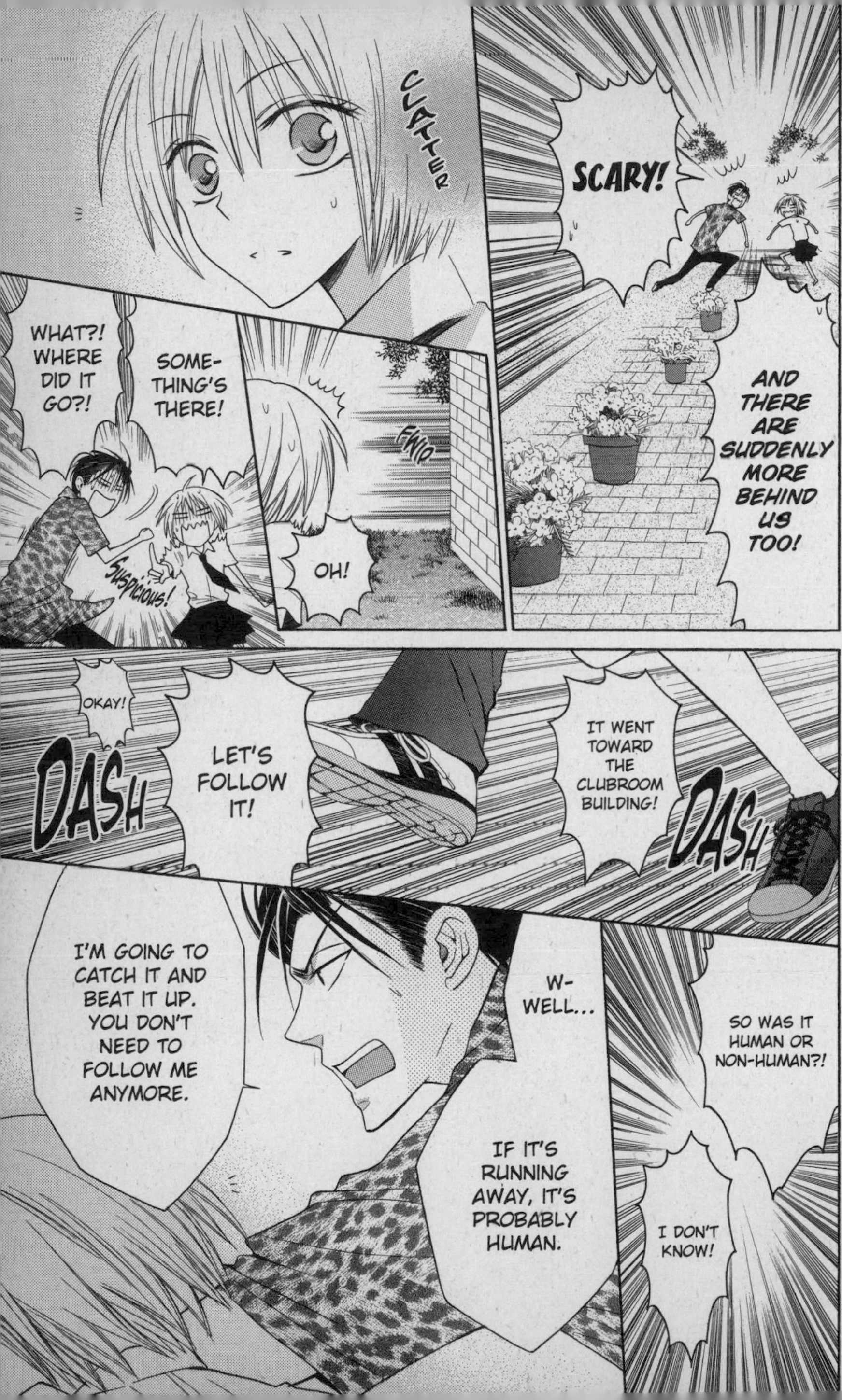
SCARY!
AND THERE ARE SUDDENLY MORE BEHIND US TOO!
CLATTER
FWIP
OH!
SOME-THING'S THERE!
WHAT?! WHERE DID IT GO?!
Suspicious!
DASH
IT WENT TOWARD THE CLUBROOM BUILDING!
LET'S FOLLOW IT!
OKAY!
DASH
SO WAS IT HUMAN OR NON-HUMAN?!
I DON'T KNOW!
W-WELL...
IF IT'S RUNNING AWAY, IT'S PROBABLY HUMAN.
I'M GOING TO CATCH IT AND BEAT IT UP. YOU DON'T NEED TO FOLLOW ME ANYMORE.

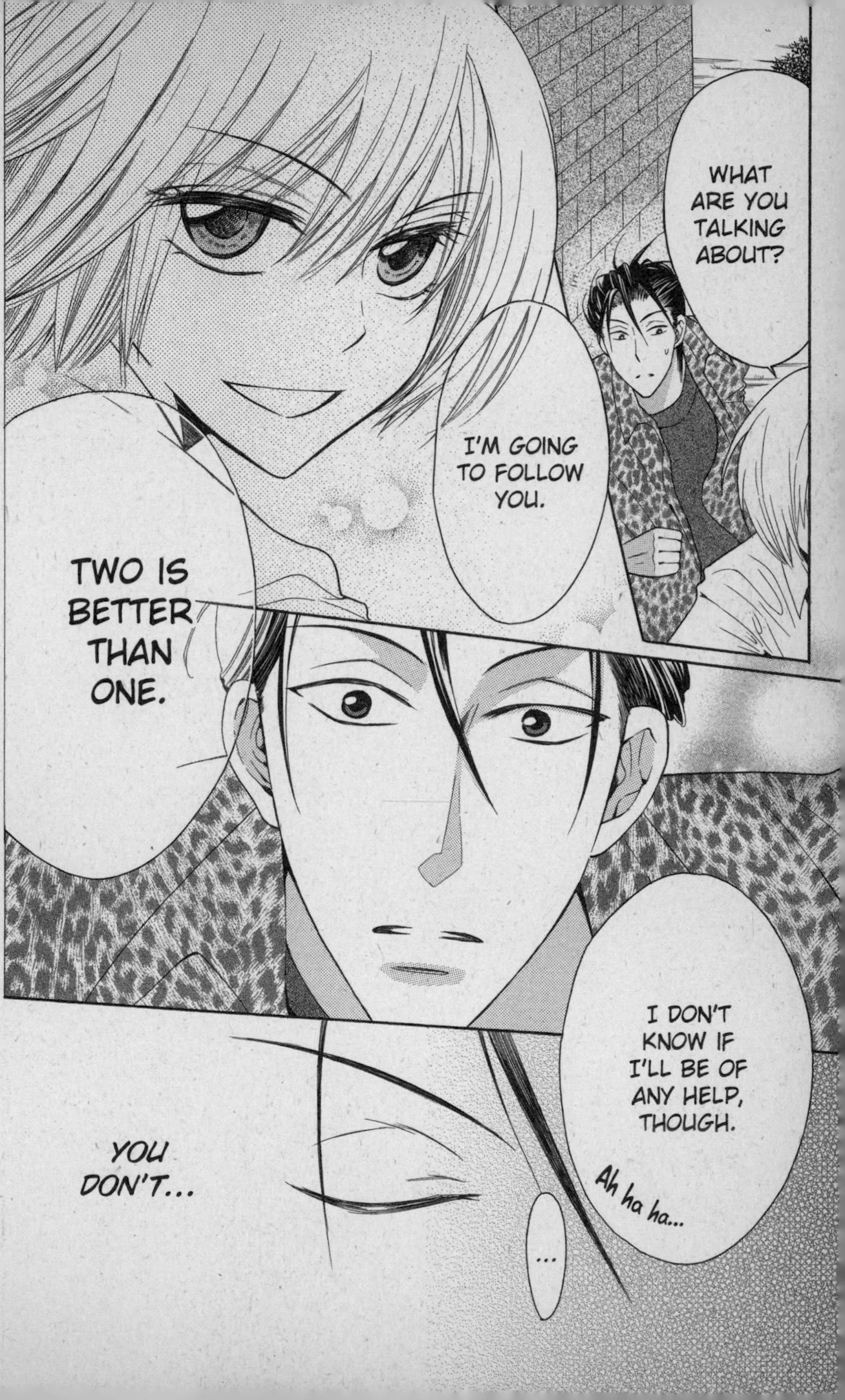
WHAT ARE YOU TALKING ABOUT?
I'M GOING TO FOLLOW YOU.
TWO IS BETTER THAN ONE.
I DON'T KNOW IF I'LL BE OF ANY HELP, THOUGH.
Ah ha ha...
...
YOU DON'T...

...NEED TO HELP.
I'M NOT GOING TO RELY ON YOU.
I WOULDN'T FORGIVE MYSELF FOR BEING SO WEAK.
BUT...
...WHEN YOU SAY THAT...
...IT MAKES ME FEEL HAPPY.

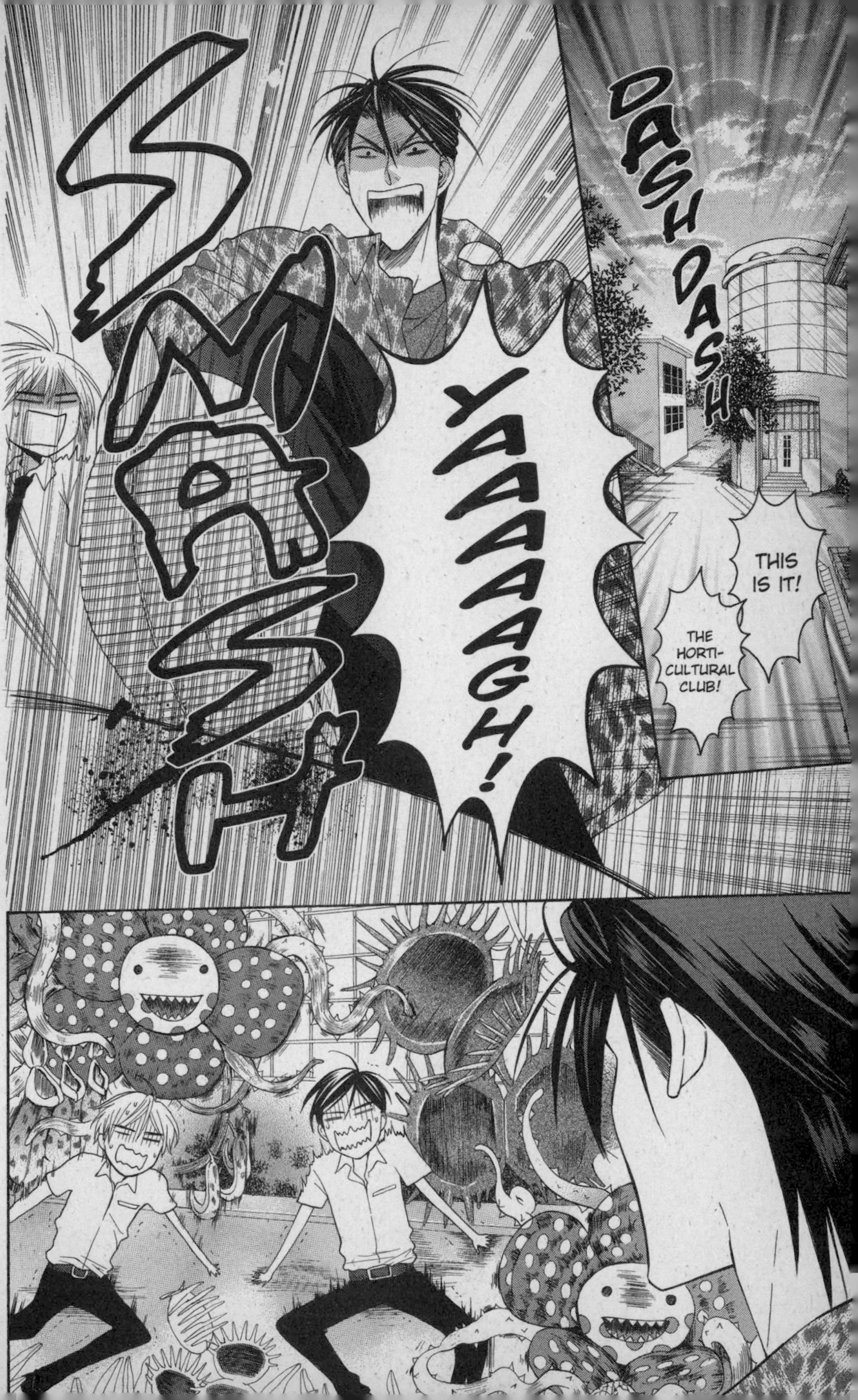
DASHDASH
THIS IS IT!
THE HORTI-CULTURAL CLUB!
YAAAAAAGH!
SMASH

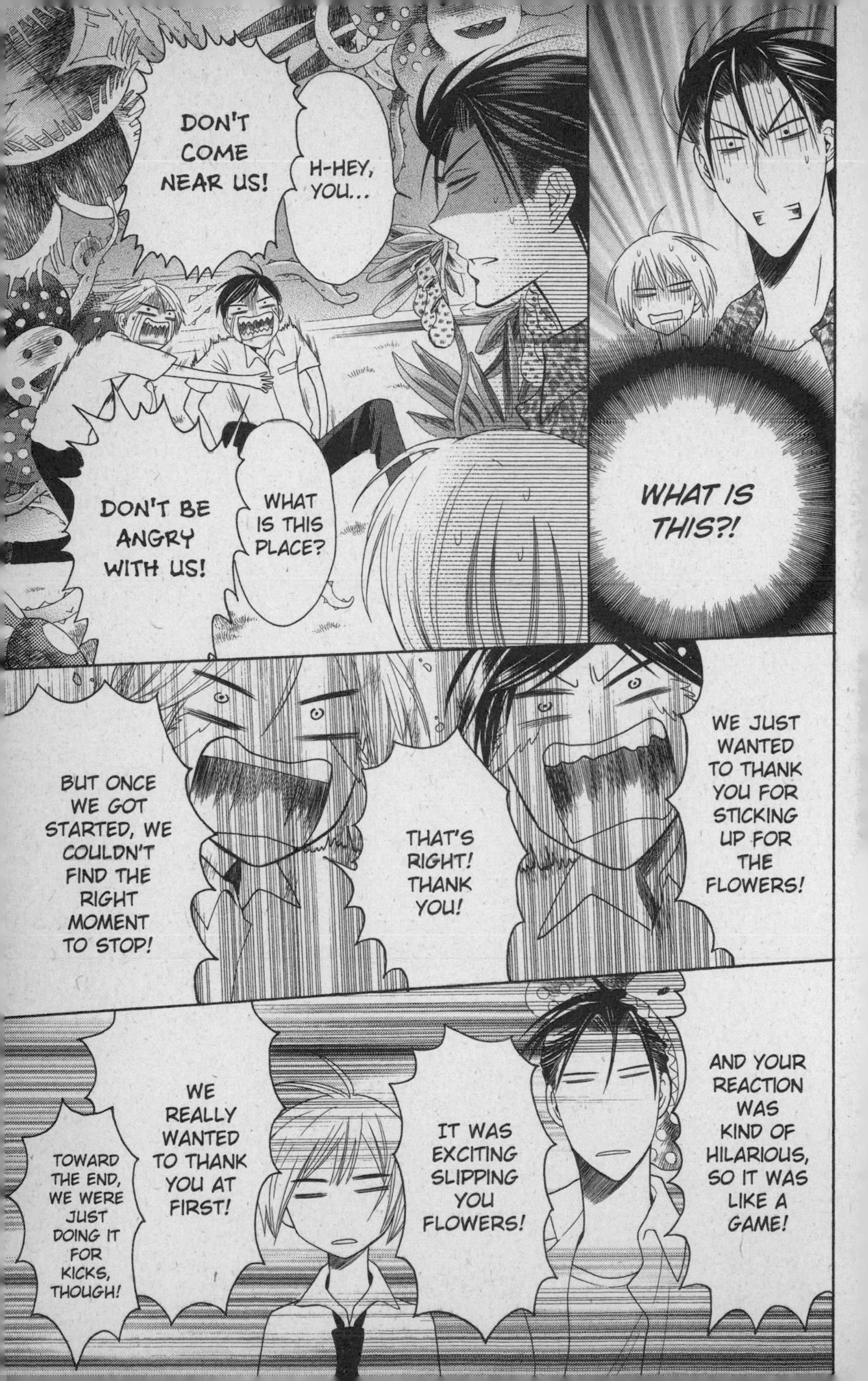
WHAT IS THIS?!
H-HEY, YOU...
DON'T COME NEAR US!
WHAT IS THIS PLACE?
DON'T BE ANGRY WITH US!
WE JUST WANTED TO THANK YOU FOR STICKING UP FOR THE FLOWERS!
THAT'S RIGHT! THANK YOU!
BUT ONCE WE GOT STARTED, WE COULDN'T FIND THE RIGHT MOMENT TO STOP!
AND YOUR REACTION WAS KIND OF HILARIOUS, SO IT WAS LIKE A GAME!
IT WAS EXCITING SLIPPING YOU FLOWERS!
WE REALLY WANTED TO THANK YOU AT FIRST!
TOWARD THE END, WE WERE JUST DOING IT FOR KICKS, THOUGH!

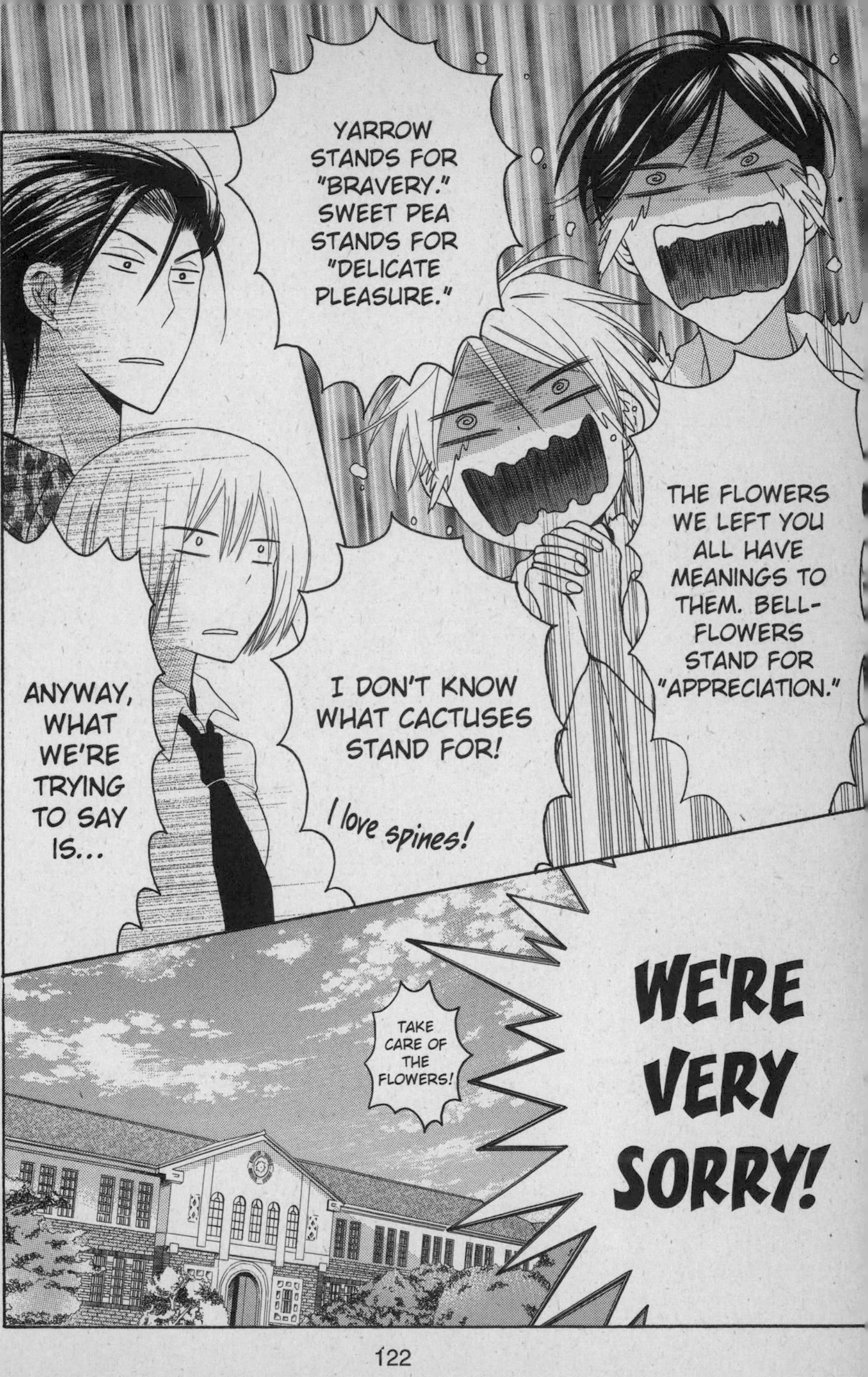
THE FLOWERS WE LEFT YOU ALL HAVE MEANINGS TO THEM. BELL-FLOWERS STAND FOR "APPRECIATION."
YARROW STANDS FOR "BRAVERY." SWEET PEA STANDS FOR "DELICATE PLEASURE."
I DON'T KNOW WHAT CACTUSES STAND FOR!
I love spines!
ANYWAY, WHAT WE'RE TRYING TO SAY IS...
WE'RE VERY SORRY!
TAKE CARE OF THE FLOWERS!

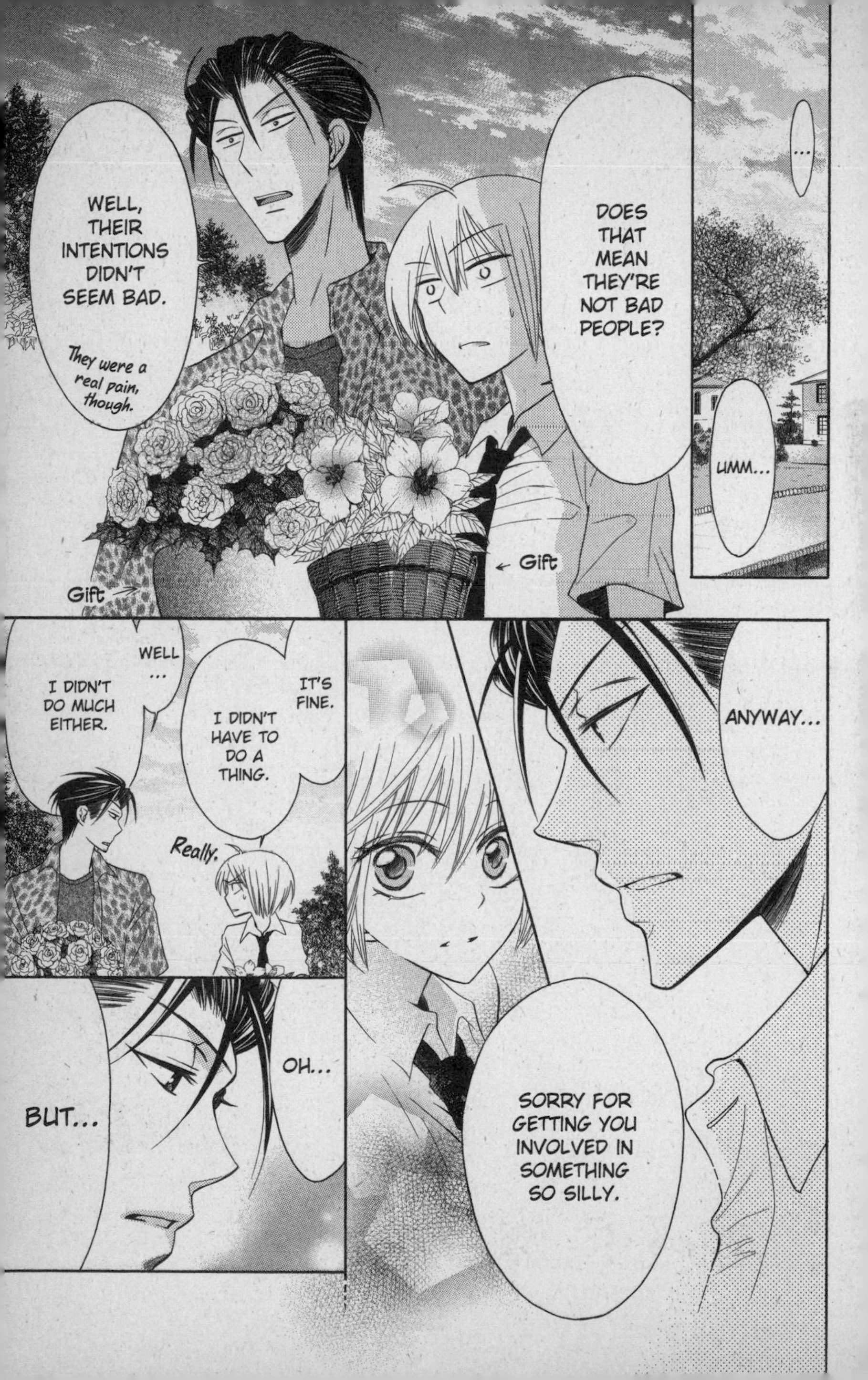
...
UMM...
DOES THAT MEAN THEY'RE NOT BAD PEOPLE?
Gift
WELL, THEIR INTENTIONS DIDN'T SEEM BAD.
They were a real pain, though.
Gift
ANYWAY...
SORRY FOR GETTING YOU INVOLVED IN SOMETHING SO SILLY.
IT'S FINE.
I DIDN'T HAVE TO DO A THING.
Really.
WELL...
I DIDN'T DO MUCH EITHER.
OH...
BUT...

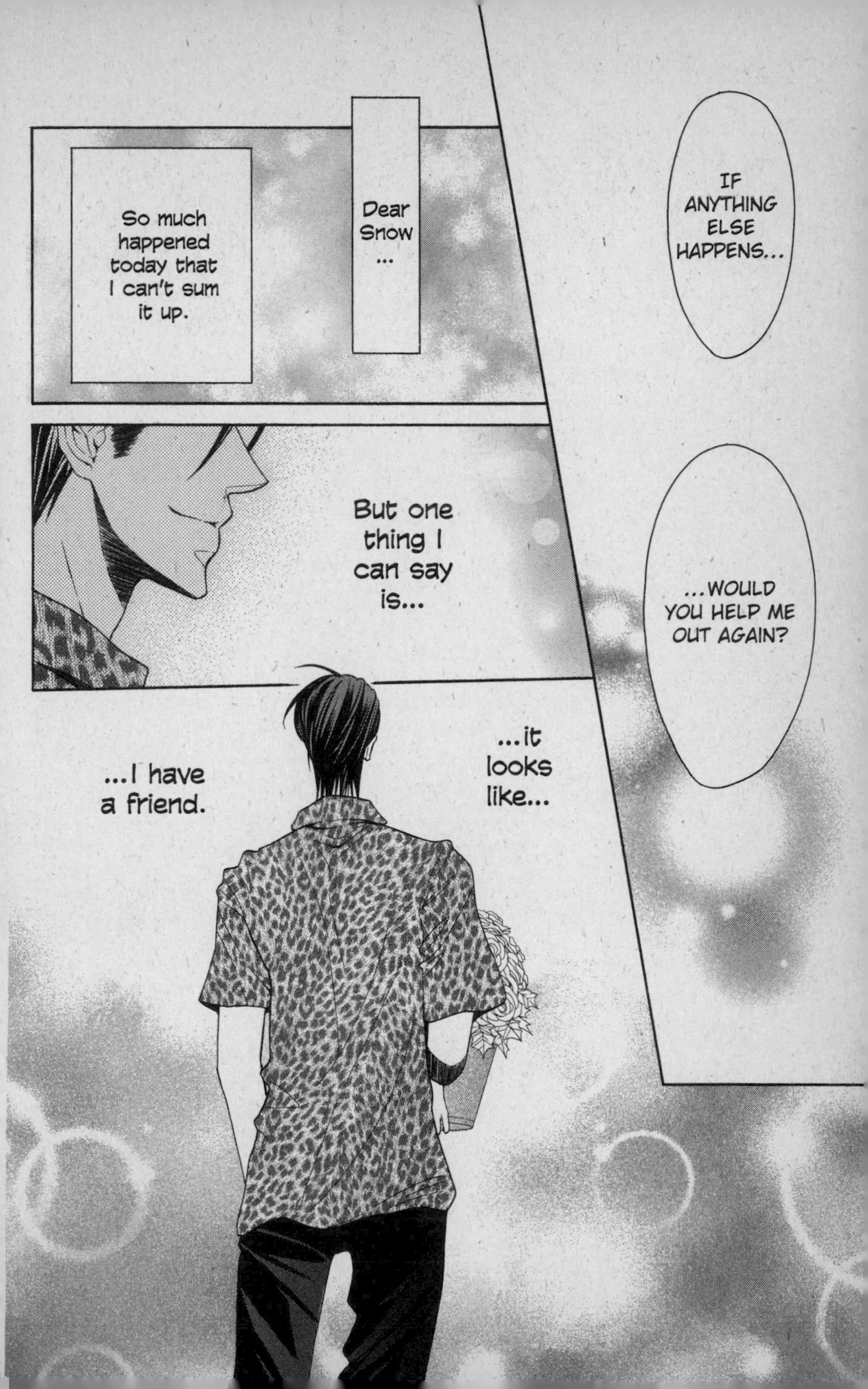
IF ANYTHING ELSE HAPPENS...
...WOULD YOU HELP ME OUT AGAIN?
Dear Snow ...
So much happened today that I can't sum it up.
But one thing I can say is...
...it looks like...
...I have a friend.

Chapter 28

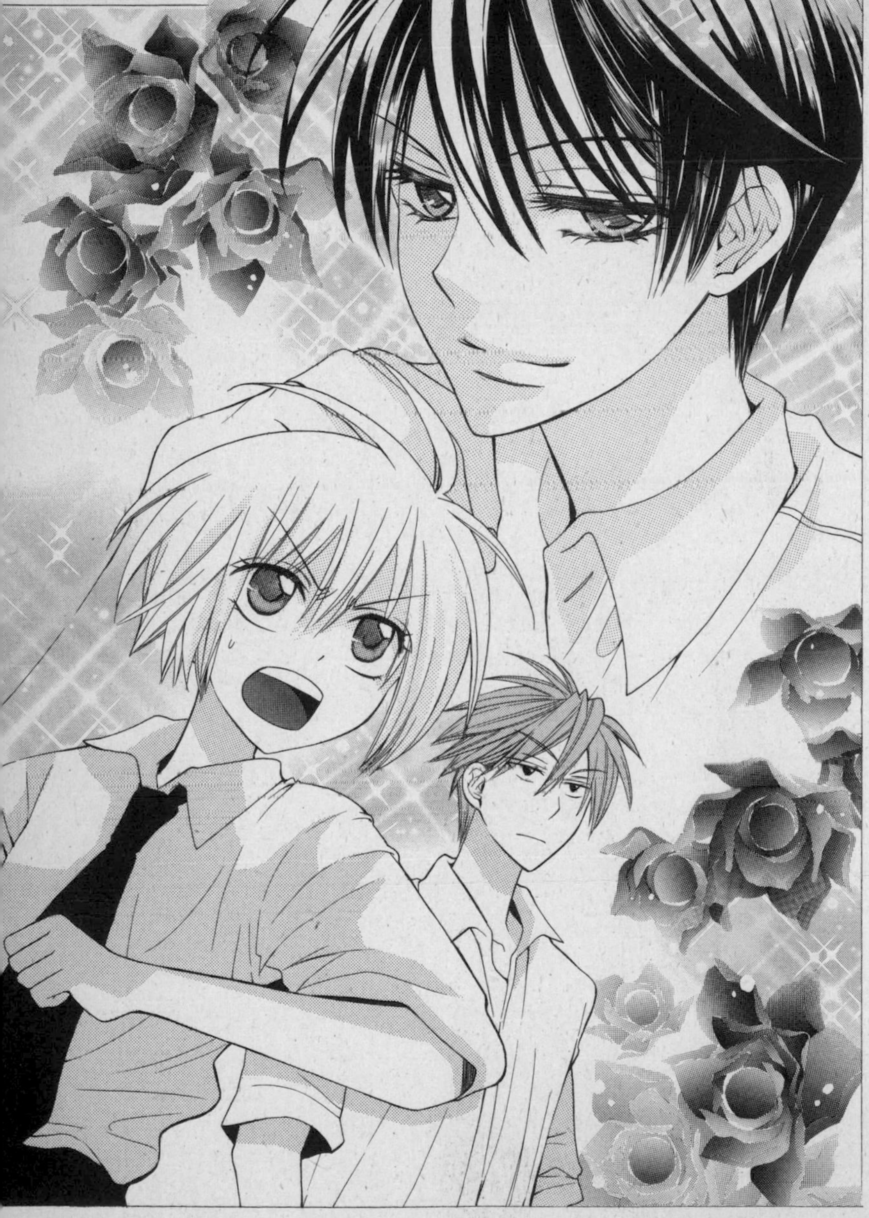

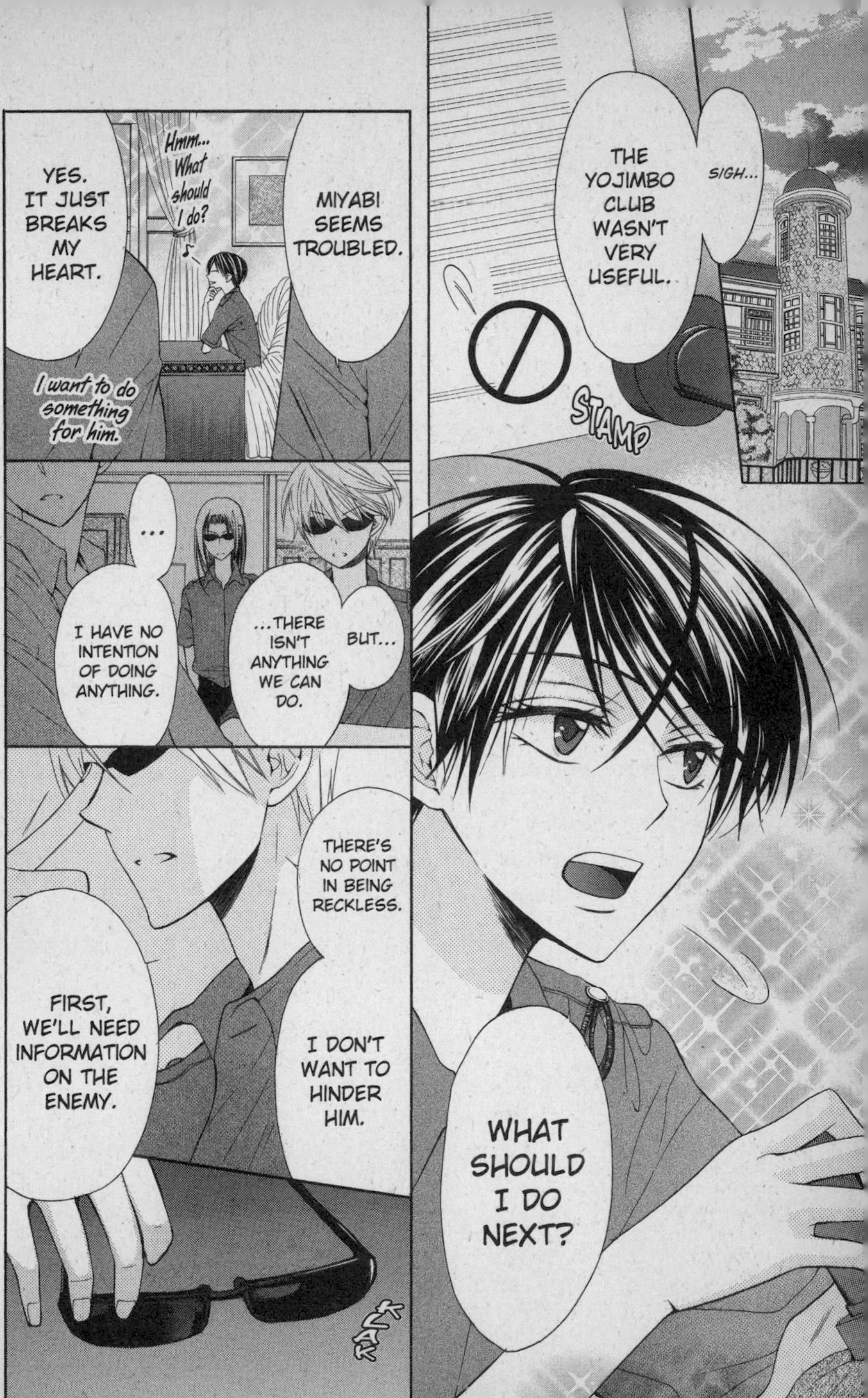
THE YOJIMBO CLUB WASN'T VERY USEFUL.
SIGH...
STAMP
WHAT SHOULD I DO NEXT?
MIYABI SEEMS TROUBLED.
Hmm... What should I do?
YES. IT JUST BREAKS MY HEART.
I want to do something for him.
BUT...
...THERE ISN'T ANYTHING WE CAN DO.
...
I HAVE NO INTENTION OF DOING ANYTHING.
THERE'S NO POINT IN BEING RECKLESS.
I DON'T WANT TO HINDER HIM.
FIRST, WE'LL NEED INFORMATION ON THE ENEMY.
KLAK KLAK

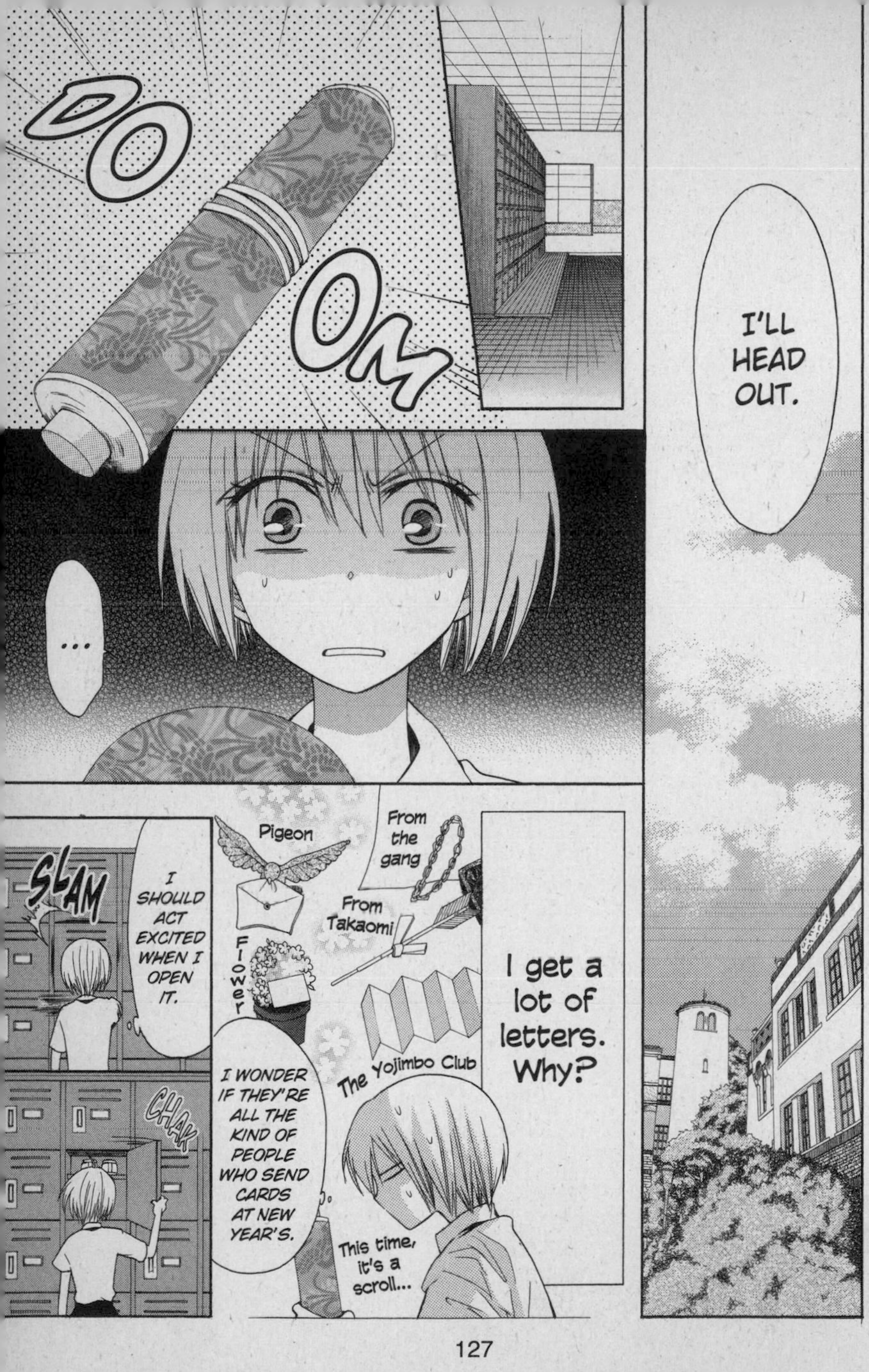

I'LL HEAD OUT.
DOOM
...
I get a lot of letters. Why?
From the gang
Pigeon
From Takaomi
Flower
The Yojimbo Club
I WONDER IF THEY'RE ALL THE KIND OF PEOPLE WHO SEND CARDS AT NEW YEAR'S.
This time, it's a scroll...
I SHOULD ACT EXCITED WHEN I OPEN IT.
SLAM
CHAK

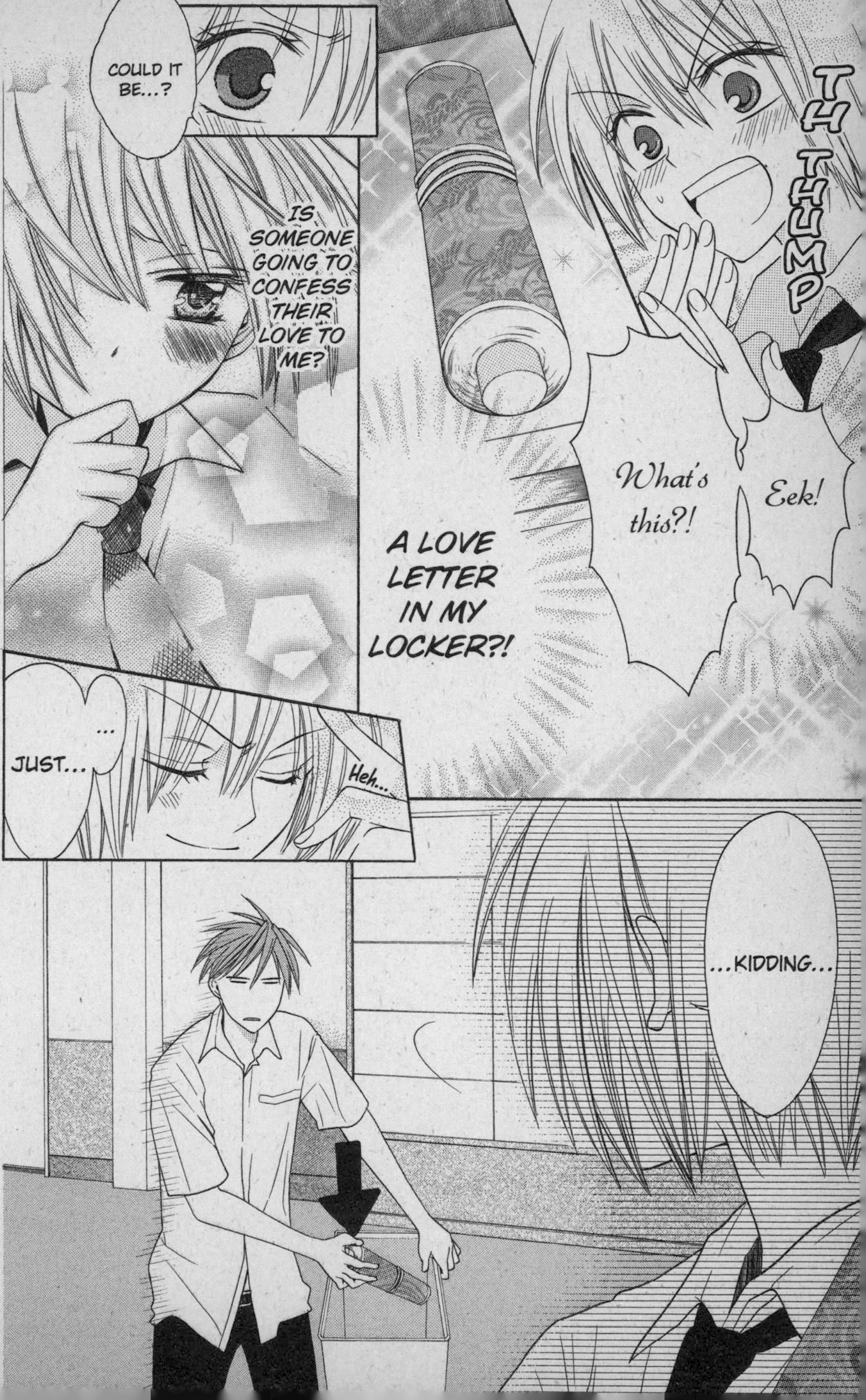
Eek!
What's this?!
TH THUMP
A LOVE LETTER IN MY LOCKER?!
COULD IT BE...?
IS SOMEONE GOING TO CONFESS THEIR LOVE TO ME?
...
JUST...
Heh...
...KIDDING...

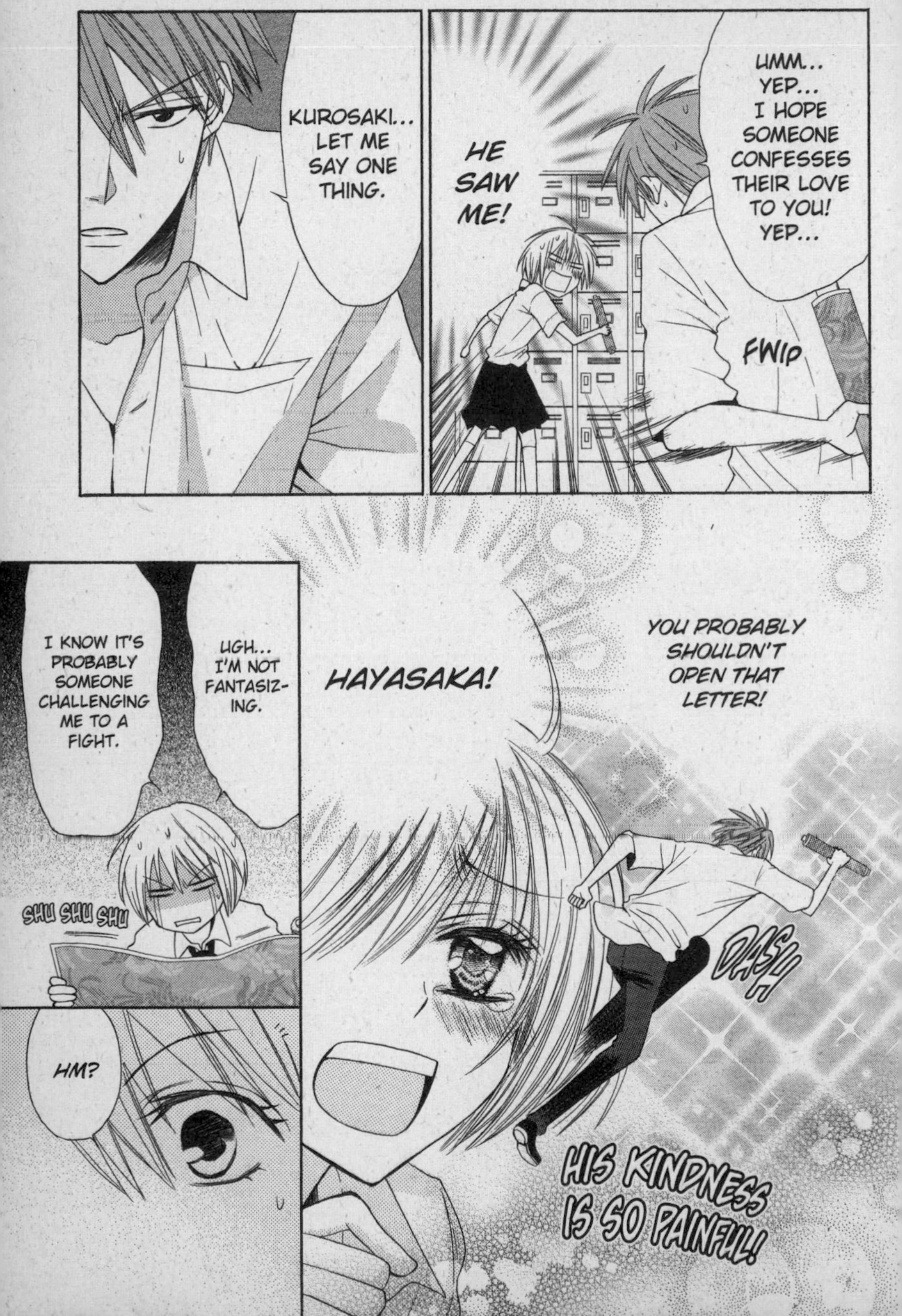
UMM... YEP... I HOPE SOMEONE CONFESSES THEIR LOVE TO YOU! YEP...
HE SAW ME!
FWIP
KUROSAKI... LET ME SAY ONE THING.
YOU PROBABLY SHOULDN'T OPEN THAT LETTER!
HAYASAKA!
DASH
HIS KINDNESS IS SO PAINFUL!
UGH... I'M NOT FANTASIZ-ING.
I KNOW IT'S PROBABLY SOMEONE CHALLENGING ME TO A FIGHT.
SHU SHU SHU
HM?

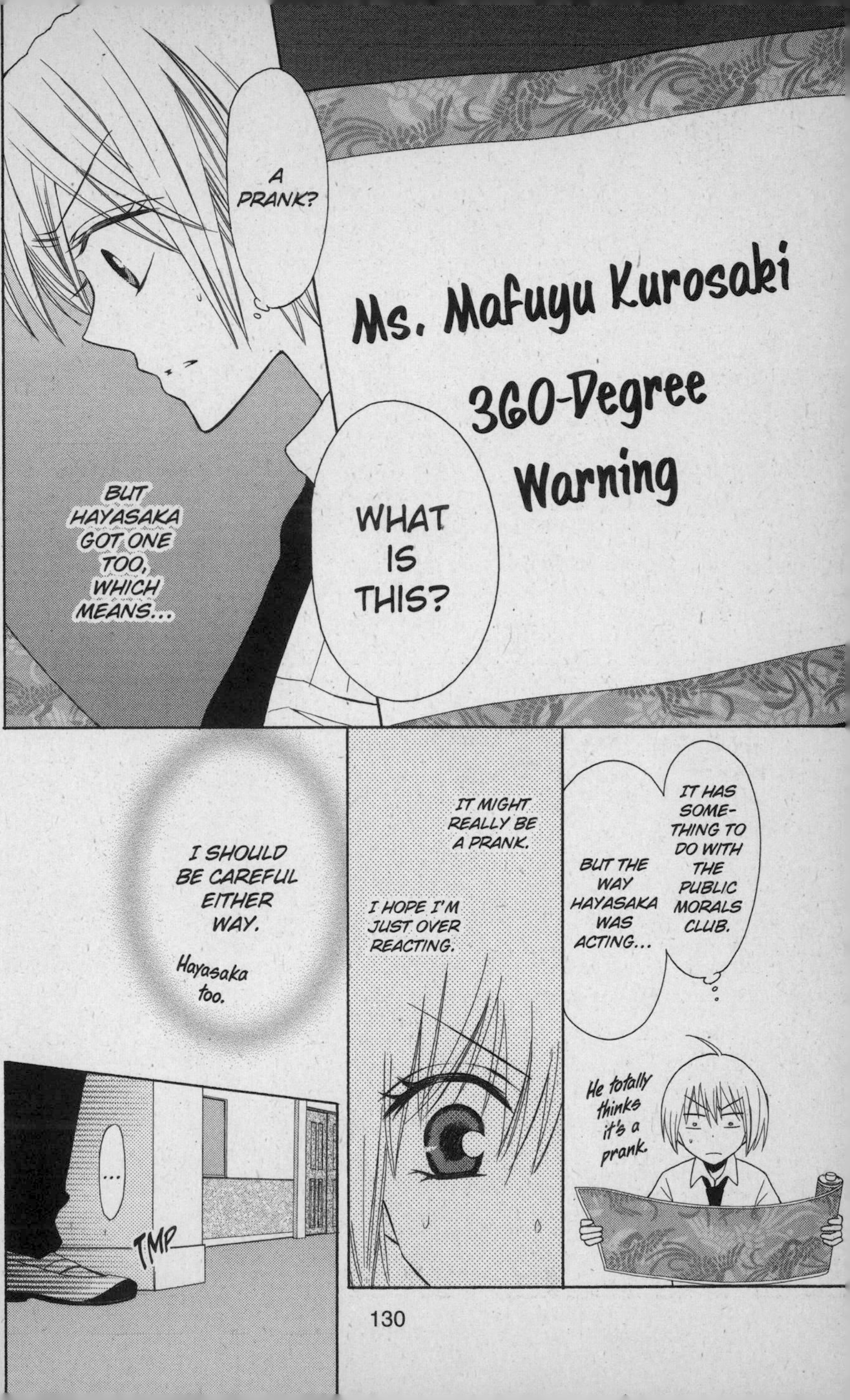
Ms. Mafuyu Kurosaki
360-Degree
Warning
WHAT IS THIS?
A PRANK?
BUT HAYASAKA GOT ONE TOO, WHICH MEANS...
IT HAS SOMETHING TO DO WITH THE PUBLIC MORALS CLUB.
BUT THE WAY HAYASAKA WAS ACTING...
He totally thinks it's a prank.
IT MIGHT REALLY BE A PRANK.
I HOPE I'M JUST OVER REACTING.
I SHOULD BE CAREFUL EITHER WAY.
Hayasaka too.
...
TMP

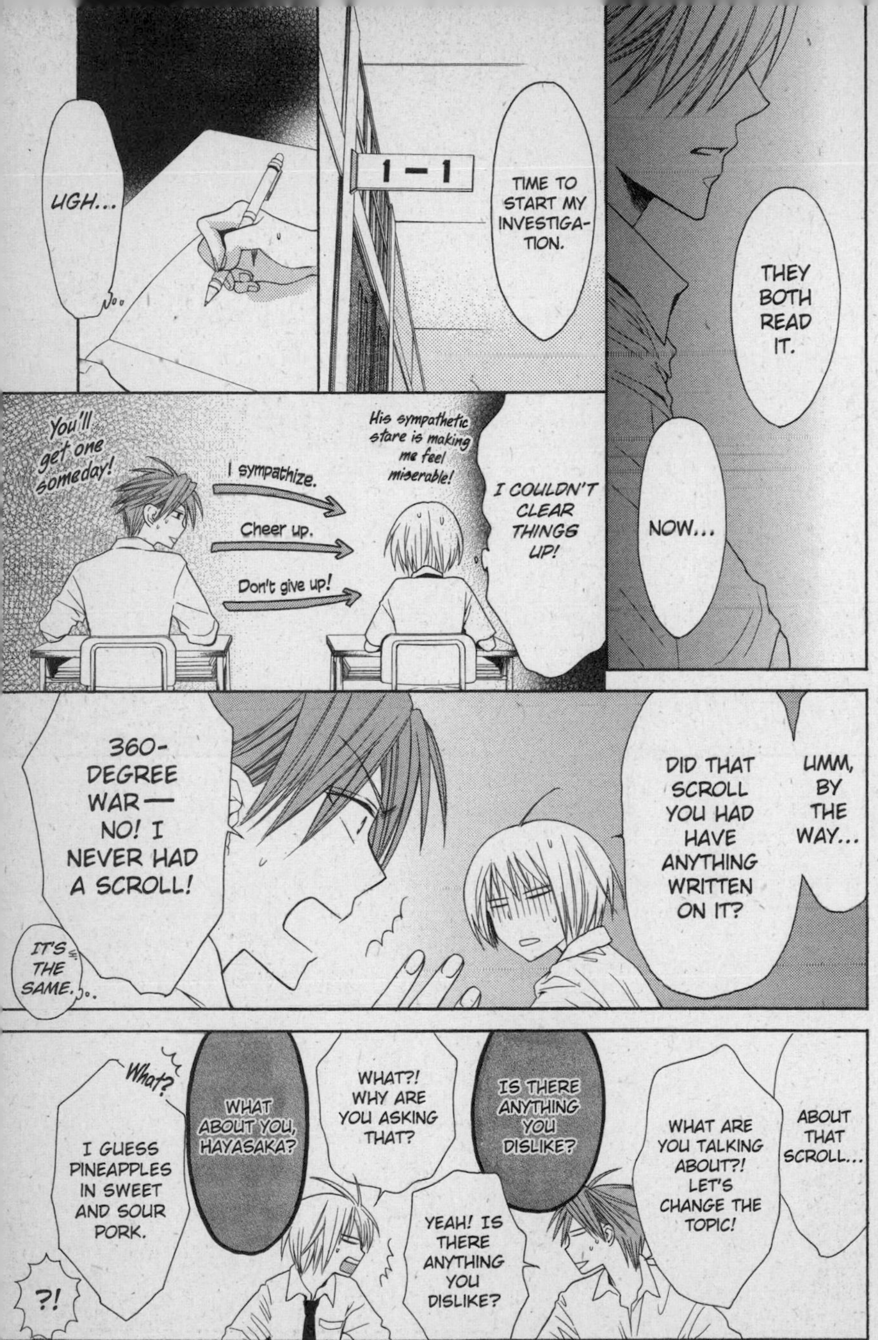
THEY BOTH READ IT.
NOW...
TIME TO START MY INVESTIGATION.
UGH...
I COULDN'T CLEAR THINGS UP!
His sympathetic stare is making me feel miserable!
I sympathize.
Cheer up.
Don't give up!
You'll get one someday!
UMM, BY THE WAY...
DID THAT SCROLL YOU HAD HAVE ANYTHING WRITTEN ON IT?
360-DEGREE WAR— NO! I NEVER HAD A SCROLL!
IT'S THE SAME.
ABOUT THAT SCROLL...
WHAT ARE YOU TALKING ABOUT?! LET'S CHANGE THE TOPIC!
IS THERE ANYTHING YOU DISLIKE?
YEAH! IS THERE ANYTHING YOU DISLIKE?
WHAT?! WHY ARE YOU ASKING THAT?
WHAT ABOUT YOU, HAYASAKA?
What?
I GUESS PINEAPPLES IN SWEET AND SOUR PORK.
?!

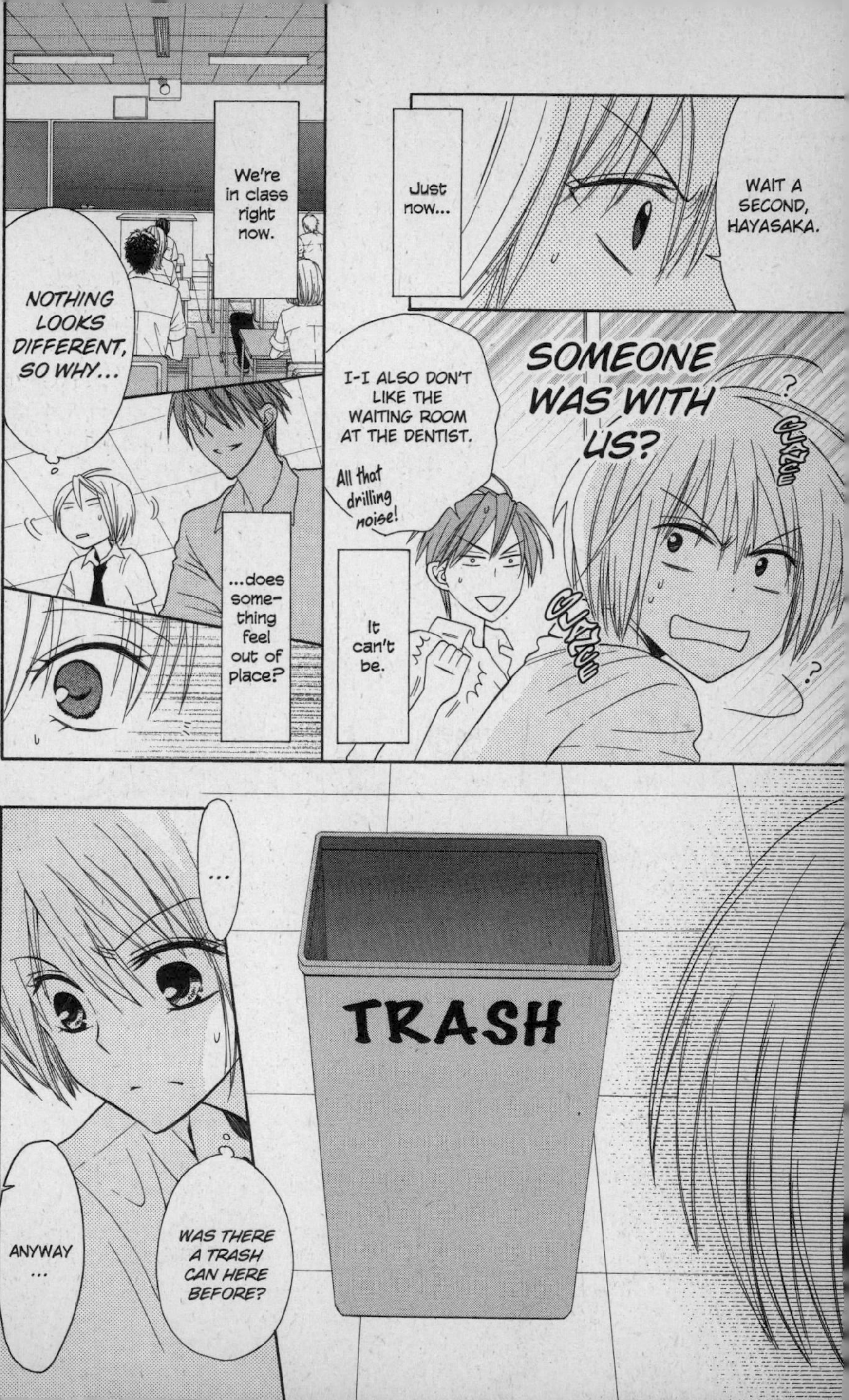
WAIT A SECOND, HAYASAKA.
Just now...
SOMEONE WAS WITH US?
I-I ALSO DON'T LIKE THE WAITING ROOM AT THE DENTIST.
All that drilling noise!
It can't be.
We're in class right now.
NOTHING LOOKS DIFFERENT, SO WHY...
...does something feel out of place?
...
TRASH
WAS THERE A TRASH CAN HERE BEFORE?
ANYWAY ...

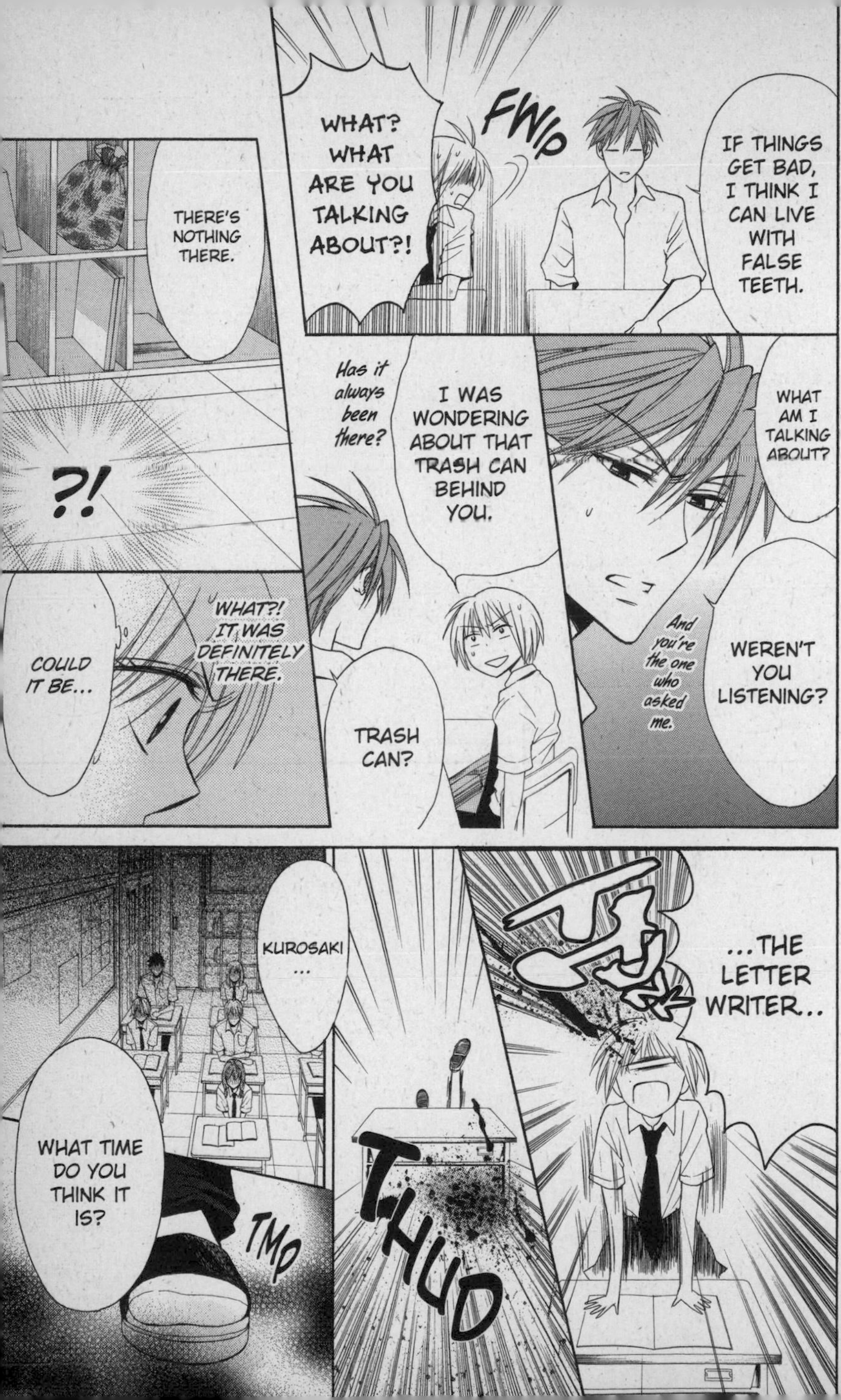
IF THINGS GET BAD, I THINK I CAN LIVE WITH FALSE TEETH.
FWIP
WHAT? WHAT ARE YOU TALKING ABOUT?!
WHAT AM I TALKING ABOUT?
WEREN'T YOU LISTENING?
And you're the one who asked me.
I WAS WONDERING ABOUT THAT TRASH CAN BEHIND YOU.
Has it always been there?
TRASH CAN?
THERE'S NOTHING THERE.
?!
WHAT?! IT WAS DEFINITELY THERE.
COULD IT BE...
...THE LETTER WRITER...
THUD
KUROSAKI ...
WHAT TIME DO YOU THINK IT IS?
TMP

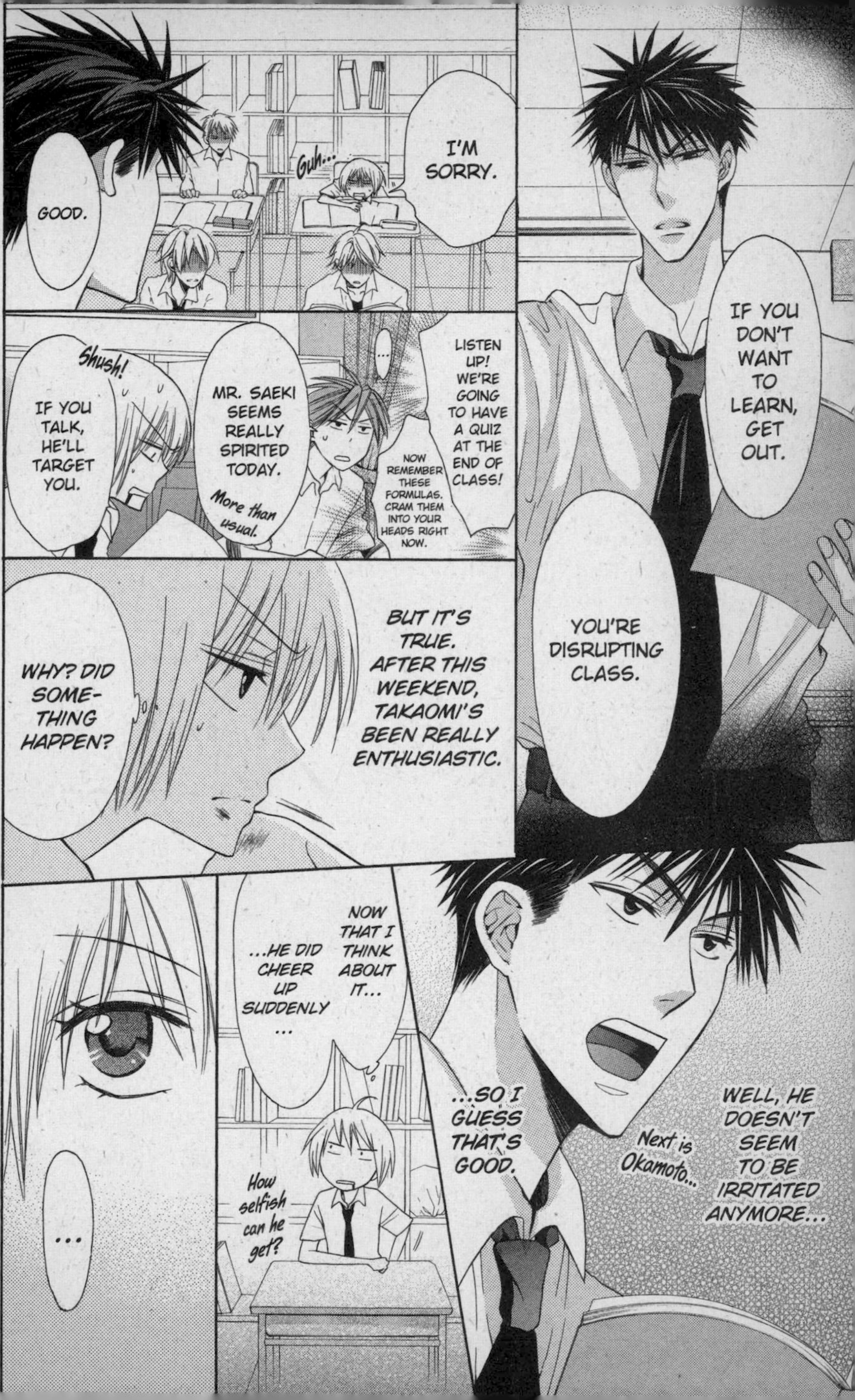
IF YOU DON'T WANT TO LEARN, GET OUT.
YOU'RE DISRUPTING CLASS.
I'M SORRY.
Guh...
GOOD.
LISTEN UP! WE'RE GOING TO HAVE A QUIZ AT THE END OF CLASS!
NOW REMEMBER THESE FORMULAS. CRAM THEM INTO YOUR HEADS RIGHT NOW.
...
MR. SAEKI SEEMS REALLY SPIRITED TODAY.
More than usual.
Shush!
IF YOU TALK, HE'LL TARGET YOU.
BUT IT'S TRUE. AFTER THIS WEEKEND, TAKAOMI'S BEEN REALLY ENTHUSIASTIC.
WHY? DID SOMETHING HAPPEN?
WELL, HE DOESN'T SEEM TO BE IRRITATED ANYMORE...
Next is Okamoto...
...SO I GUESS THAT'S GOOD.
NOW THAT I THINK ABOUT IT...
...HE DID CHEER UP SUDDENLY...
How selfish can he get?
...

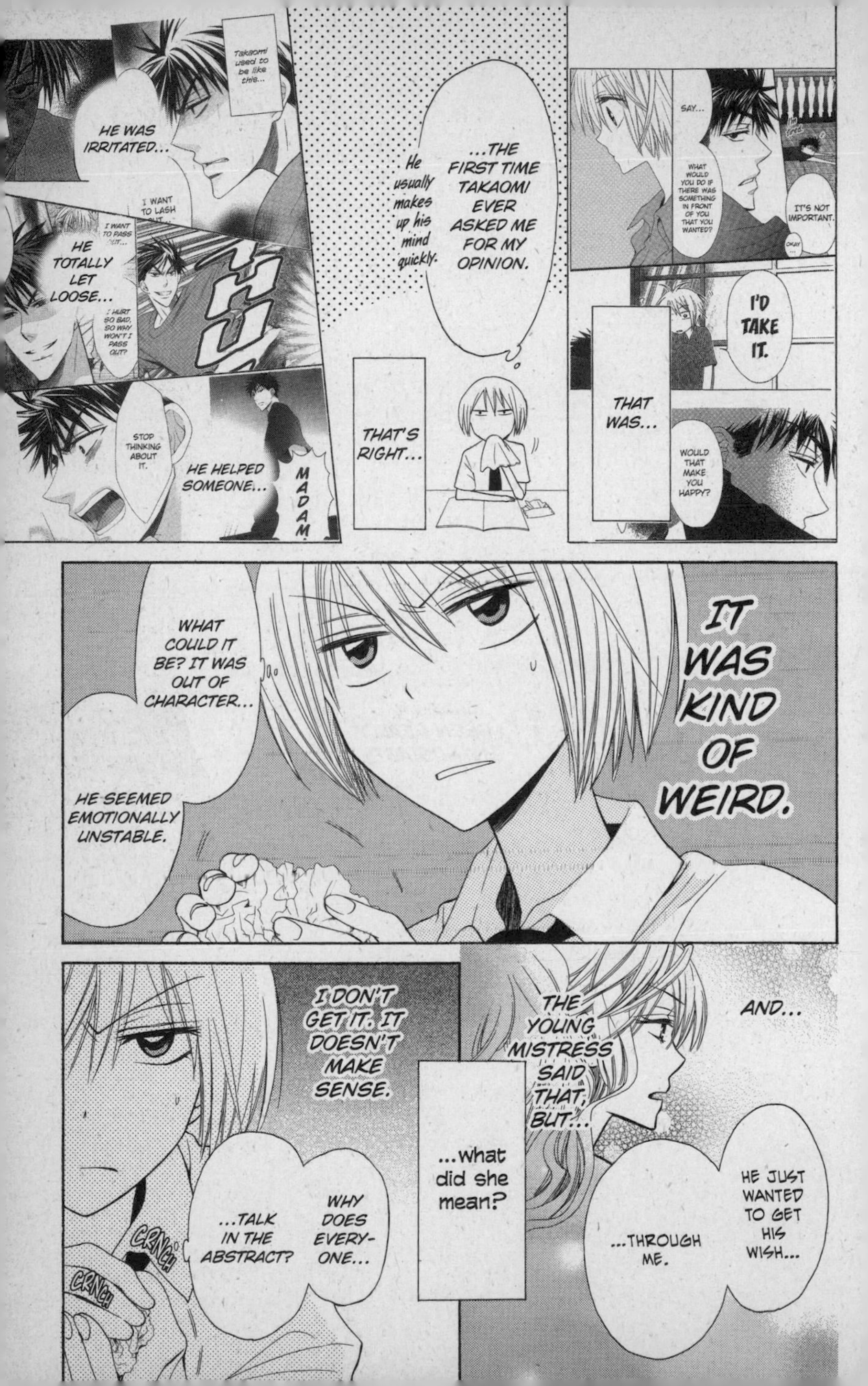
SAY...
WHAT WOULD YOU DO IF THERE WAS SOMETHING IN FRONT OF YOU THAT YOU WANTED?
I'm tired.
IT'S NOT IMPORTANT.
OKAY...
I'D TAKE IT.
THAT WAS...
WOULD THAT MAKE YOU HAPPY?
...THE FIRST TIME TAKAOMI EVER ASKED ME FOR MY OPINION.
He usually makes up his mind quickly.
THAT'S RIGHT...
Takaomi used to be like this...
HE WAS IRRITATED...
I WANT TO LASH
I WANT TO PASS OUT...
HE TOTALLY LET LOOSE...
I HURT SO BAD, SO WHY WON'T I PASS OUT?
MADAM!
HE HELPED SOMEONE...
STOP THINKING ABOUT IT.
IT WAS KIND OF WEIRD.
WHAT COULD IT BE? IT WAS OUT OF CHARACTER...
HE SEEMED EMOTIONALLY UNSTABLE.
AND...
THE YOUNG MISTRESS SAID THAT, BUT...
HE JUST WANTED TO GET HIS WISH...
...THROUGH ME.
...what did she mean?
I DON'T GET IT. IT DOESN'T MAKE SENSE.
WHY DOES EVERY-ONE...
...TALK IN THE ABSTRACT?
CRNCH
CRNCH

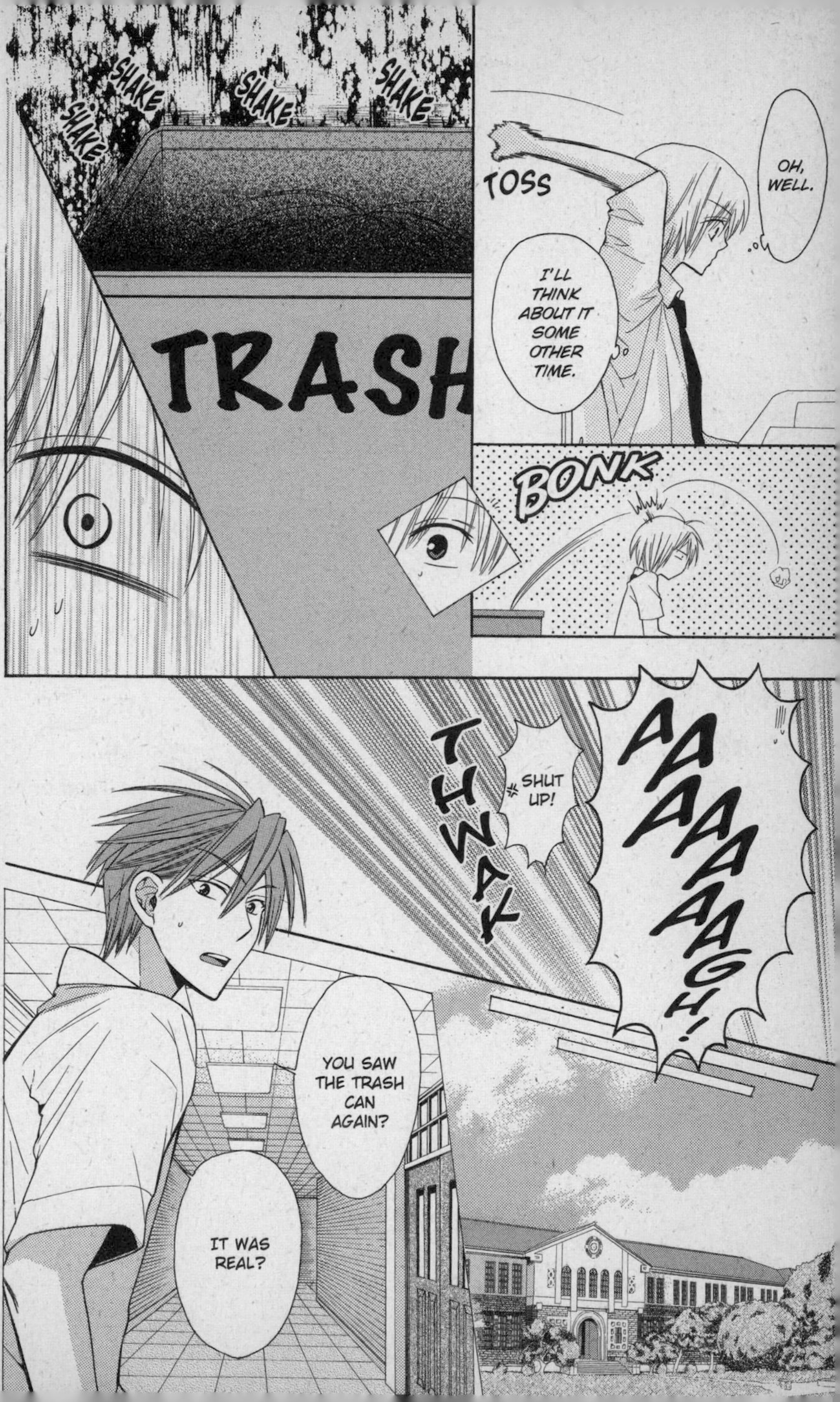
OH, WELL.
TOSS
I'LL THINK ABOUT IT SOME OTHER TIME.
BONK
SHAKE
SHAKE
SHAKE
SHAKE
TRASH
AAAAAAAAGH!
SHUT UP!
THWAK
YOU SAW THE TRASH CAN AGAIN?
IT WAS REAL?

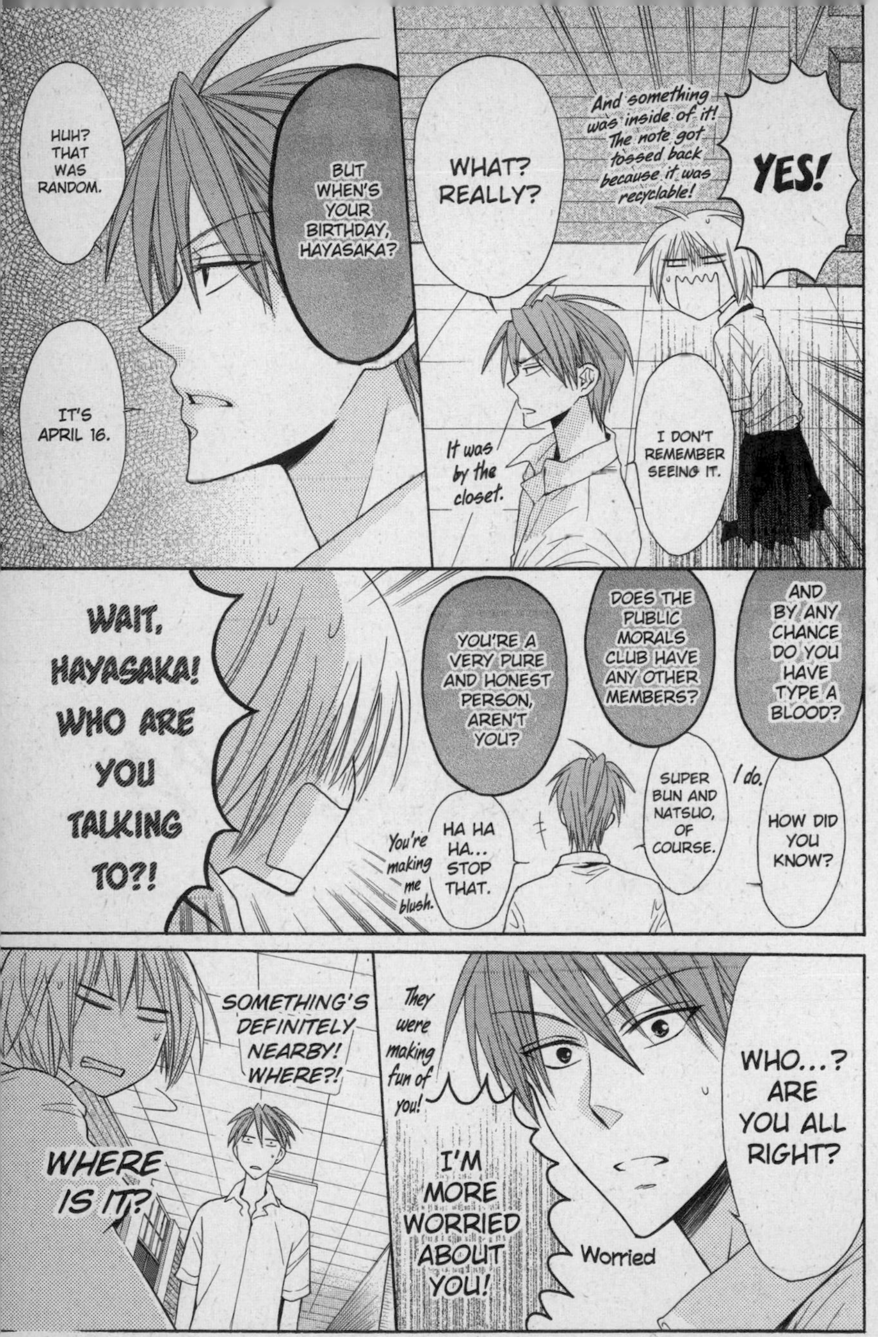
YES!
And something was inside of it! The note got tossed back because it was recyclable!
WHAT? REALLY?
I DON'T REMEMBER SEEING IT.
It was by the closet.
BUT WHEN'S YOUR BIRTHDAY, HAYASAKA?
HUH? THAT WAS RANDOM.
IT'S APRIL 16.
AND BY ANY CHANCE DO YOU HAVE TYPE A BLOOD?
I do.
HOW DID YOU KNOW?
DOES THE PUBLIC MORALS CLUB HAVE ANY OTHER MEMBERS?
SUPER BUN AND NATSUO, OF COURSE.
YOU'RE A VERY PURE AND HONEST PERSON, AREN'T YOU?
HA HA HA... STOP THAT.
You're making me blush.
WAIT, HAYASAKA! WHO ARE YOU TALKING TO?!
WHO...? ARE YOU ALL RIGHT?
Worried
They were making fun of you!
I'M MORE WORRIED ABOUT YOU!
SOMETHING'S DEFINITELY NEARBY! WHERE?!
WHERE IS IT?

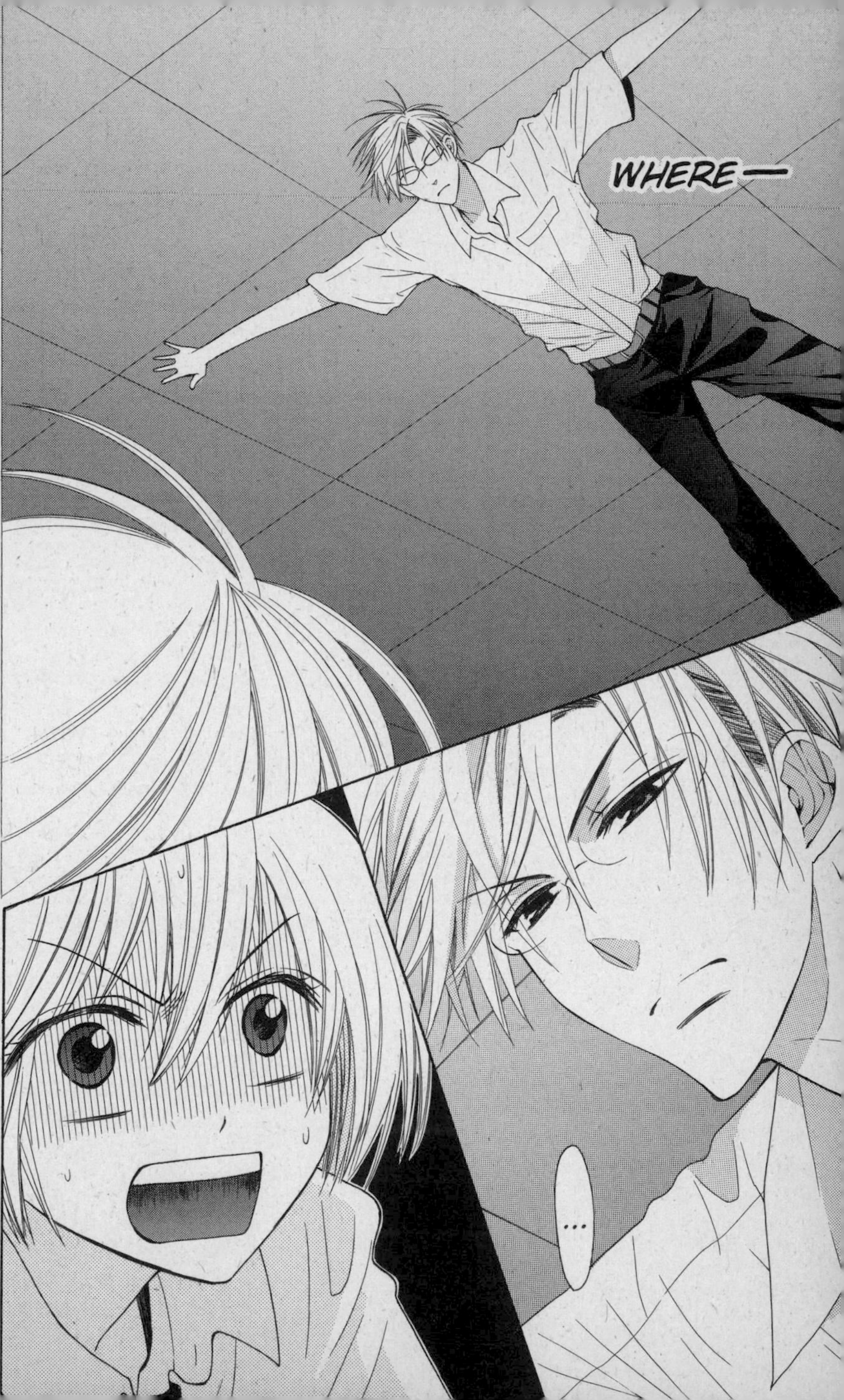
WHERE—
...

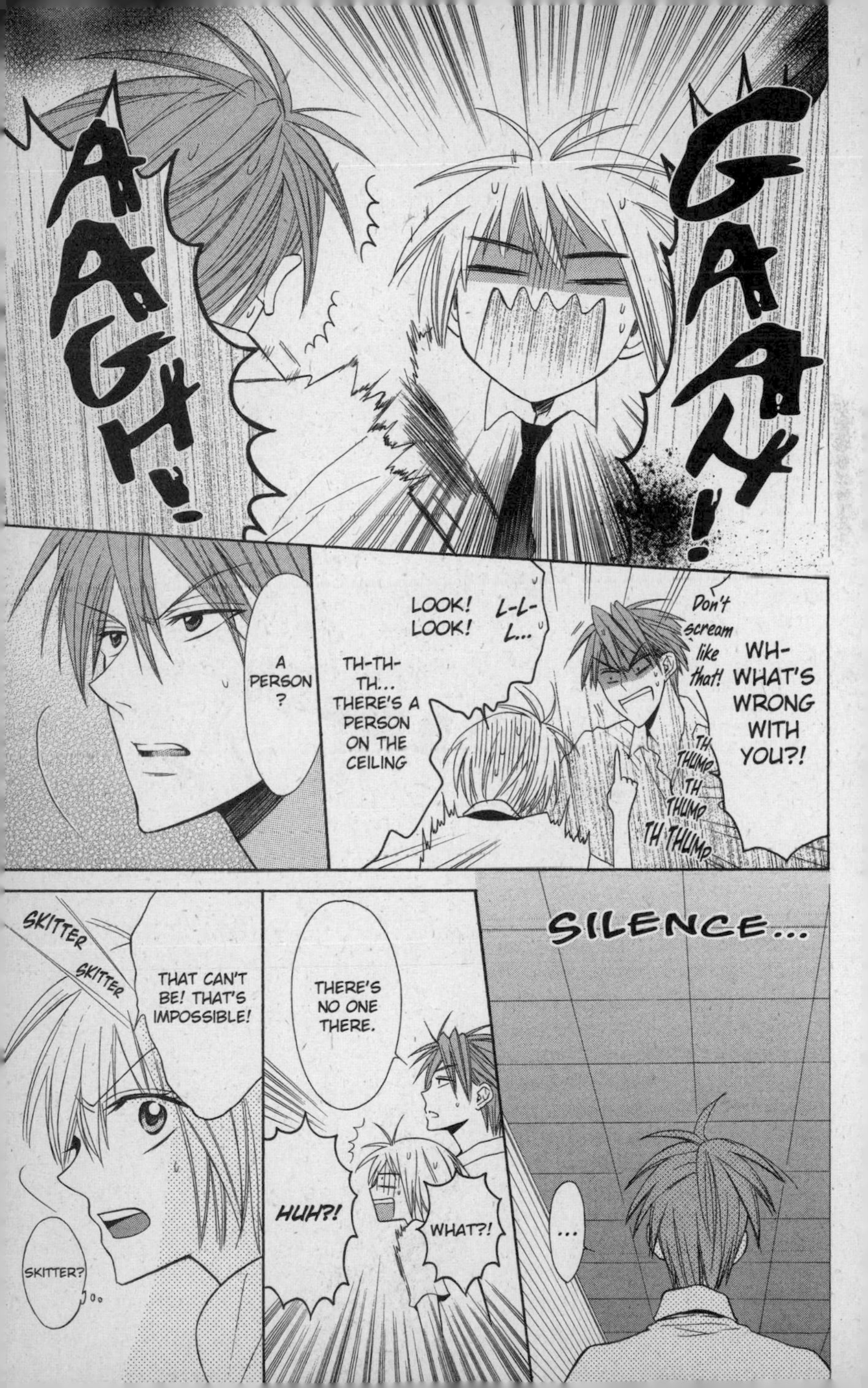
GAAH!
AAGH!
Don't scream like that!
WH-WHAT'S WRONG WITH YOU?!
TH THUMP TH THUMP TH THUMP
L-L-L...
LOOK! LOOK!
TH-TH-TH... THERE'S A PERSON ON THE CEILING
A PERSON?
SILENCE...
...
THERE'S NO ONE THERE.
WHAT?!
HUH?!
SKITTER SKITTER
THAT CAN'T BE! THAT'S IMPOSSIBLE!
SKITTER?

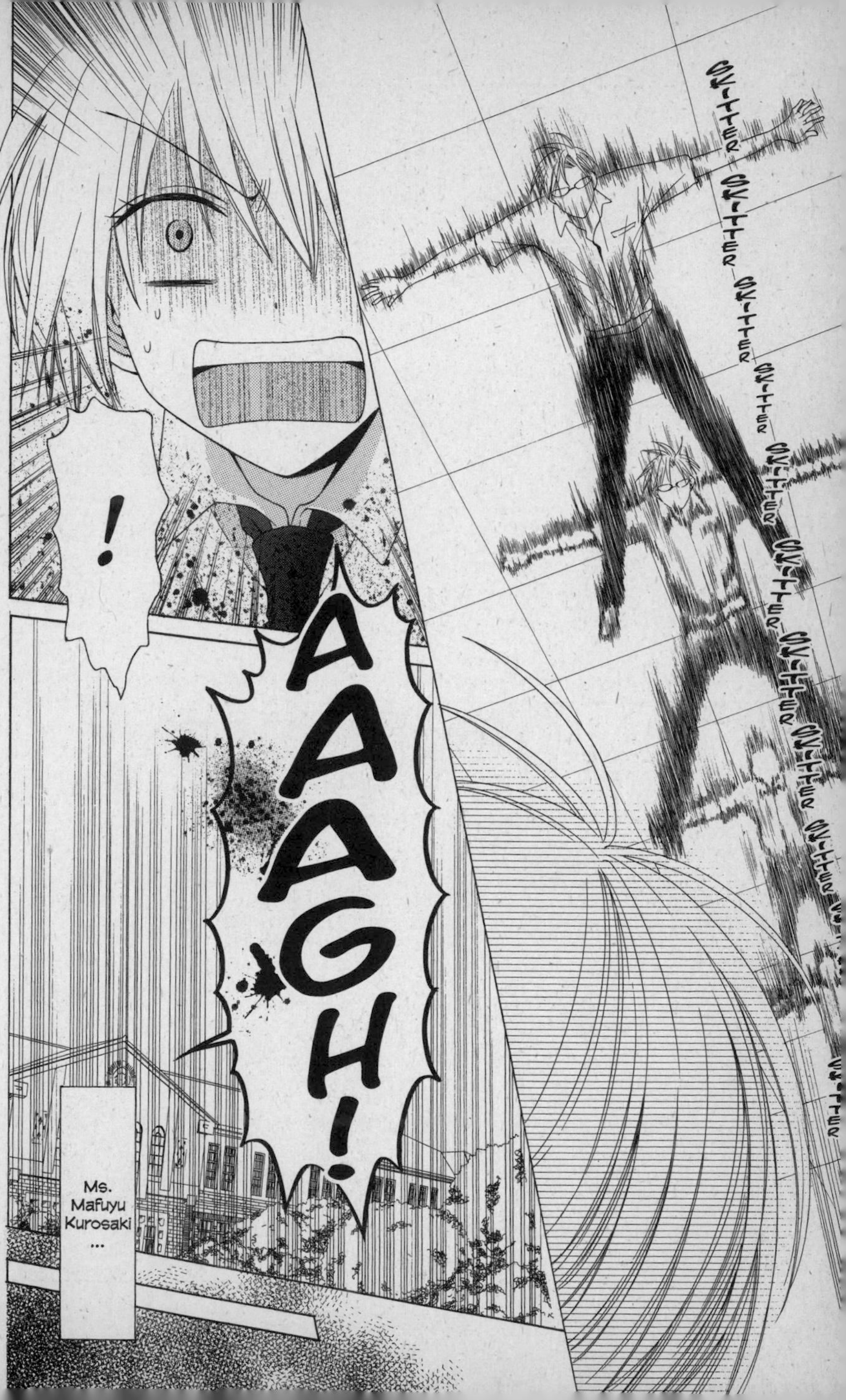
SKITTER SKITTER SKITTER SKITTER SKITTER SKITTER SKITTER SKITTER SKITTER SKITTER
!
AAAGH!
Ms. Mafuyu Kurosaki ...

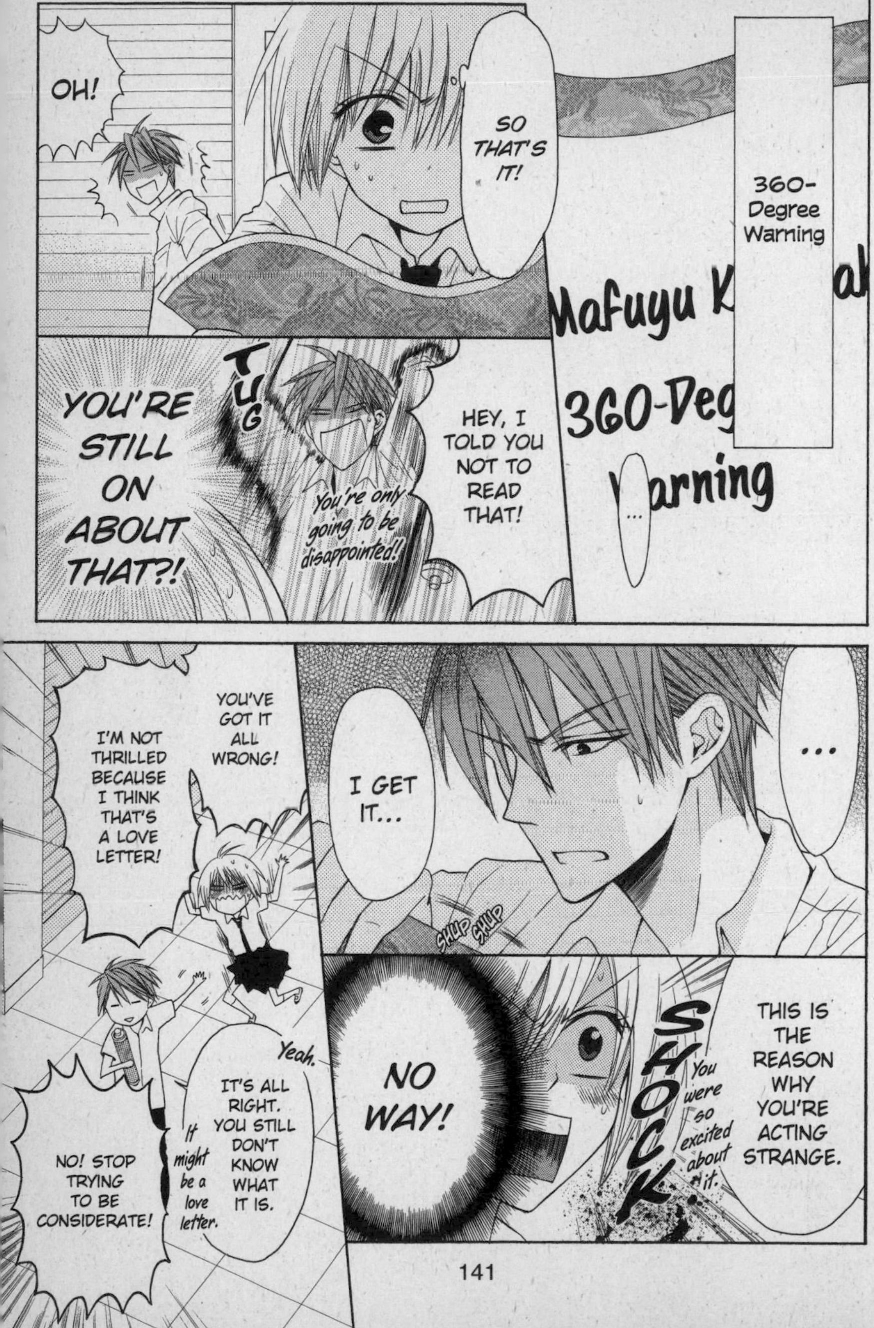
360-Degree Warning
SO THAT'S IT!
OH!
...
HEY, I TOLD YOU NOT TO READ THAT!
You're only going to be disappointed!!
TUG
YOU'RE STILL ON ABOUT THAT?!
...
I GET IT...
SHUP SHUP
THIS IS THE REASON WHY YOU'RE ACTING STRANGE.
You were so excited about it.
SHOCK
NO WAY!
YOU'VE GOT IT ALL WRONG!
I'M NOT THRILLED BECAUSE I THINK THAT'S A LOVE LETTER!
Yeah.
IT'S ALL RIGHT. YOU STILL DON'T KNOW WHAT IT IS.
It might be a love letter.
NO! STOP TRYING TO BE CONSIDERATE!

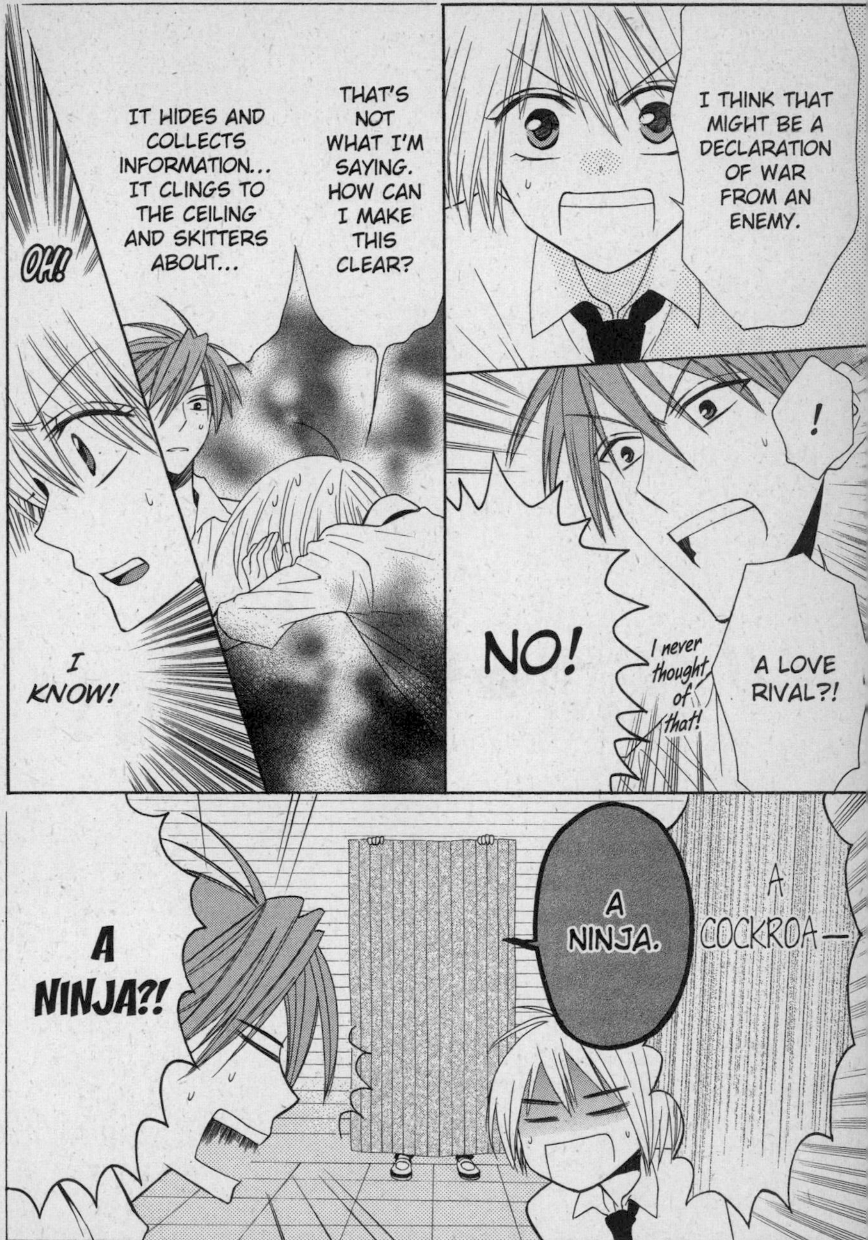
I THINK THAT MIGHT BE A DECLARATION OF WAR FROM AN ENEMY.
!
A LOVE RIVAL?!
I never thought of that!
NO!
THAT'S NOT WHAT I'M SAYING. HOW CAN I MAKE THIS CLEAR?
IT HIDES AND COLLECTS INFORMATION... IT CLINGS TO THE CEILING AND SKITTERS ABOUT...
OH!
I KNOW!
A COCKROA—
A NINJA.
A NINJA?!

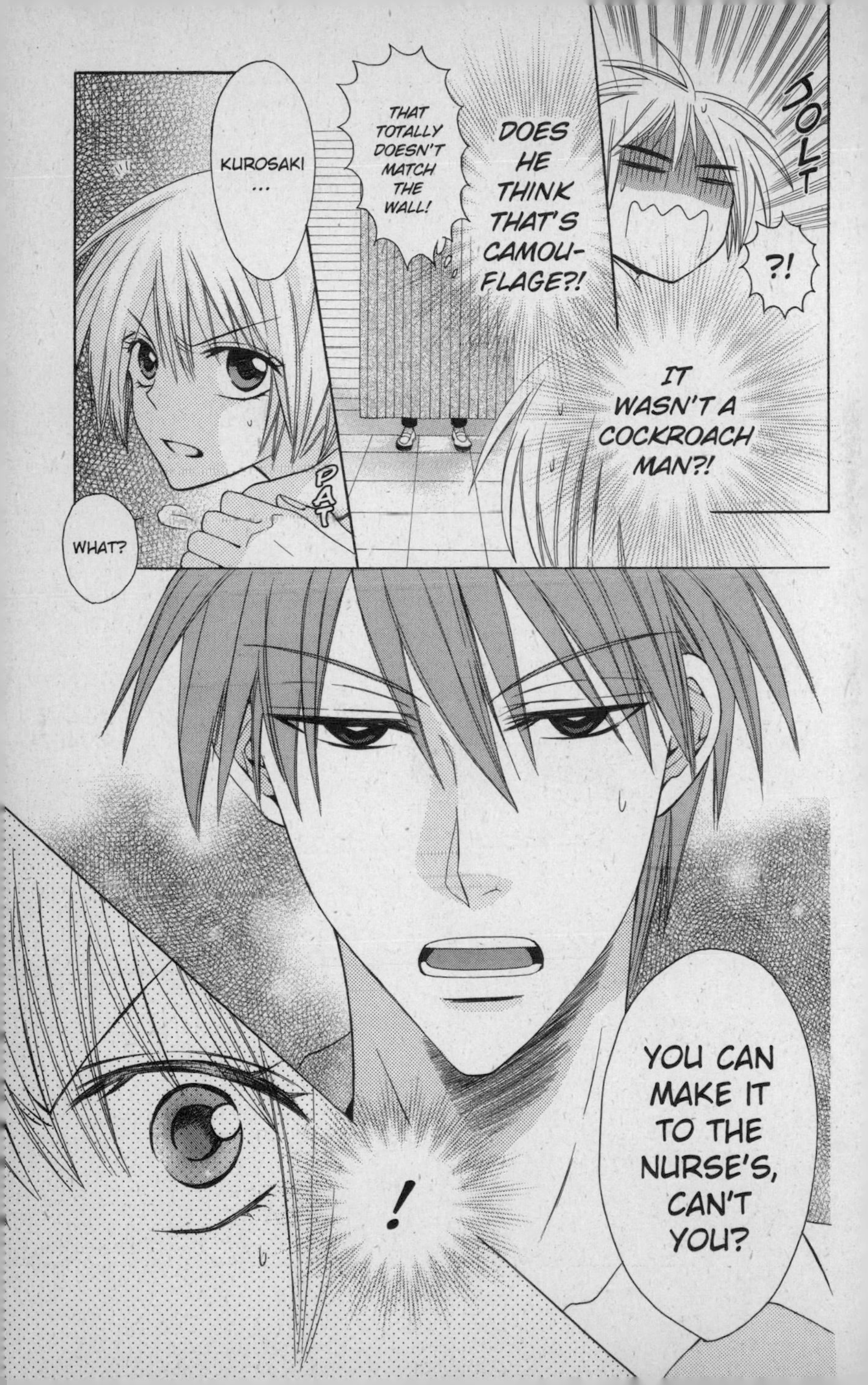
JOLT
?!
IT WASN'T A COCKROACH MAN?!
DOES HE THINK THAT'S CAMOUFLAGE?!
THAT TOTALLY DOESN'T MATCH THE WALL!
KUROSAKI...
PAT
WHAT?
YOU CAN MAKE IT TO THE NURSE'S, CAN'T YOU?
!

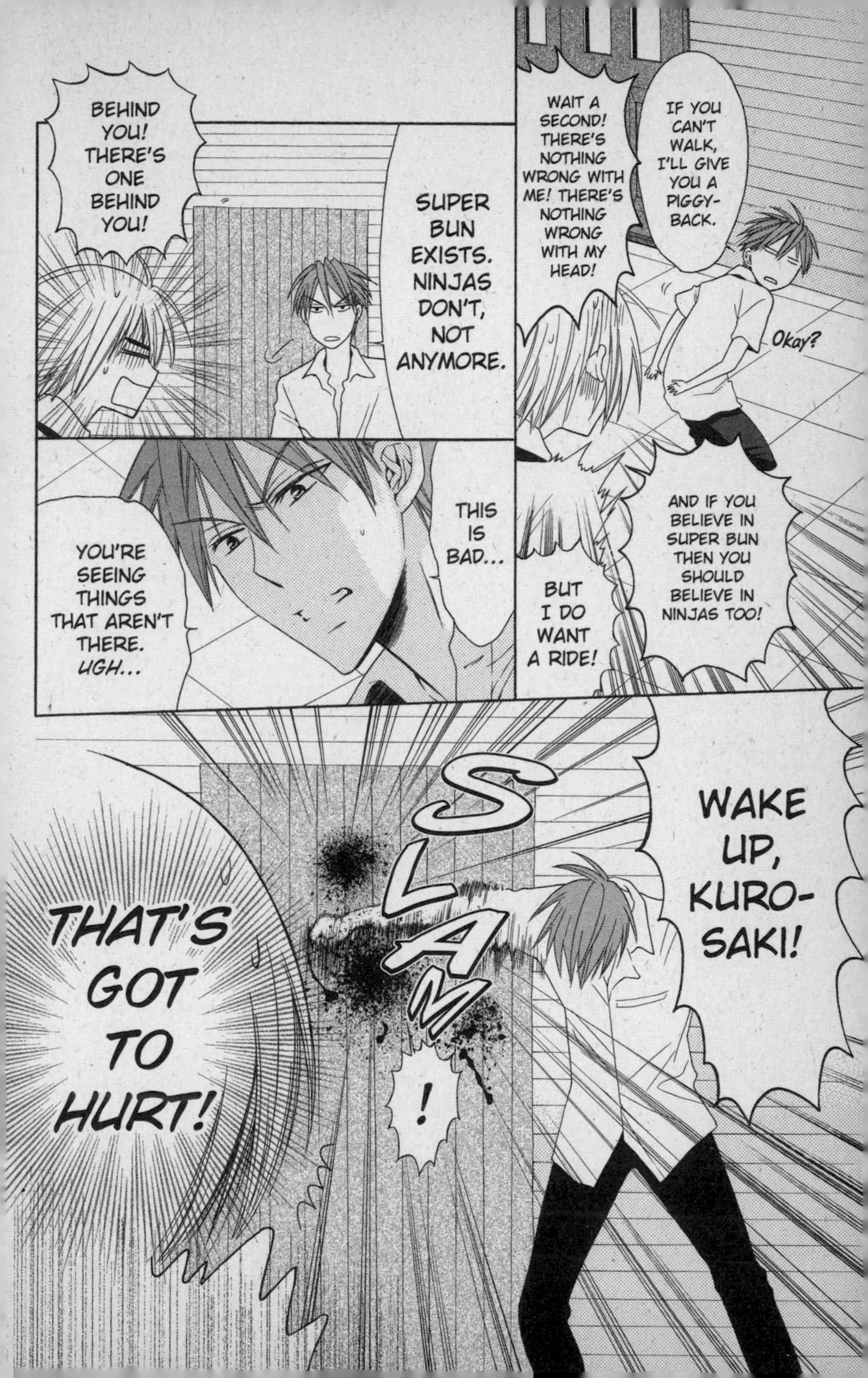

BEHIND YOU! THERE'S ONE BEHIND YOU!
SUPER BUN EXISTS. NINJAS DON'T, NOT ANYMORE.
THIS IS BAD...
YOU'RE SEEING THINGS THAT AREN'T THERE. UGH...
IF YOU CAN'T WALK, I'LL GIVE YOU A PIGGY-BACK.
WAIT A SECOND! THERE'S NOTHING WRONG WITH ME! THERE'S NOTHING WRONG WITH MY HEAD!
Okay?
AND IF YOU BELIEVE IN SUPER BUN THEN YOU SHOULD BELIEVE IN NINJAS TOO!
BUT I DO WANT A RIDE!
WAKE UP, KURO-SAKI!
SLAM
!
THAT'S GOT TO HURT!

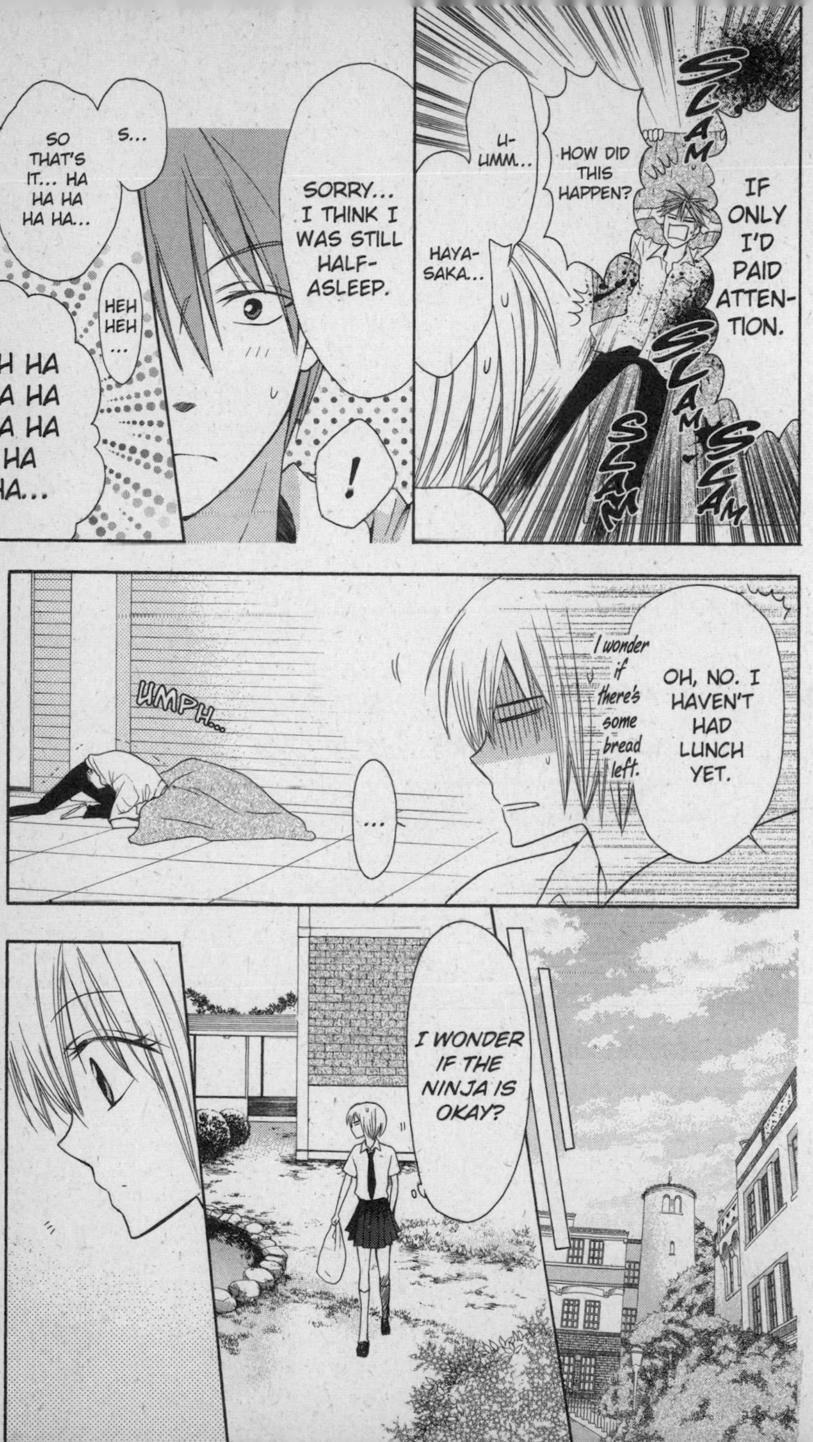
SLAM
IF ONLY I'D PAID ATTENTION.
HOW DID THIS HAPPEN?
U-UMM...
HAYA-SAKA...
SLAM
SLAM
SLAM
SORRY... I THINK I WAS STILL HALF-ASLEEP.
!
S...
SO THAT'S IT... HA HA HA HA HA...
HEH HEH ...
AH HA HA HA HA HA HA HA...
OH, NO. I HAVEN'T HAD LUNCH YET.
I wonder if there's some bread left.
...
UMPH...
I WONDER IF THE NINJA IS OKAY?

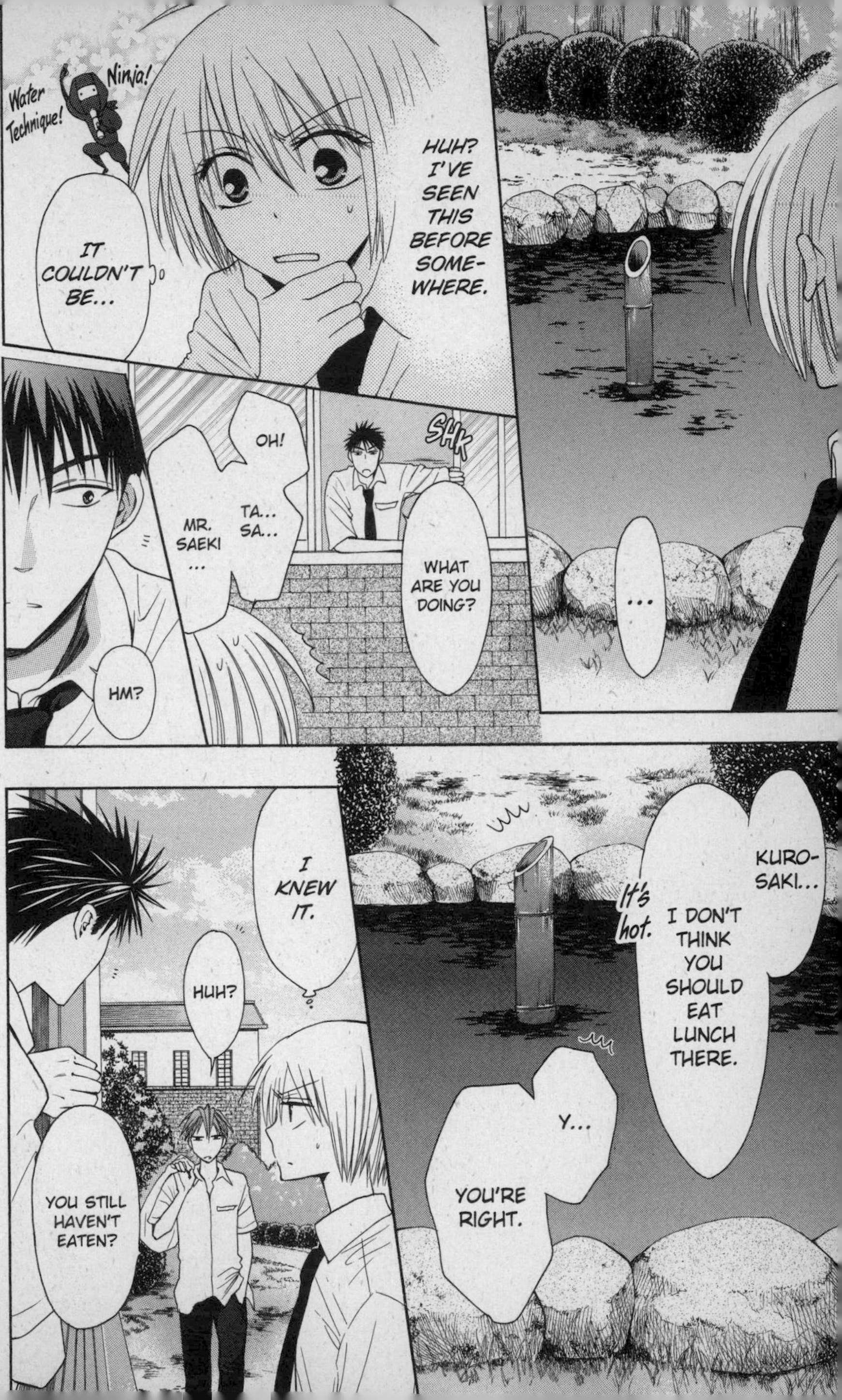
...
HUH? I'VE SEEN THIS BEFORE SOME-WHERE.
Ninja!
Water Technique!
IT COULDN'T BE...
SHK
OH!
WHAT ARE YOU DOING?
TA... SA...
MR. SAEKI...
HM?
KURO-SAKI...
I DON'T THINK YOU SHOULD EAT LUNCH THERE.
It's hot.
Y...
YOU'RE RIGHT.
I KNEW IT.
HUH?
YOU STILL HAVEN'T EATEN?

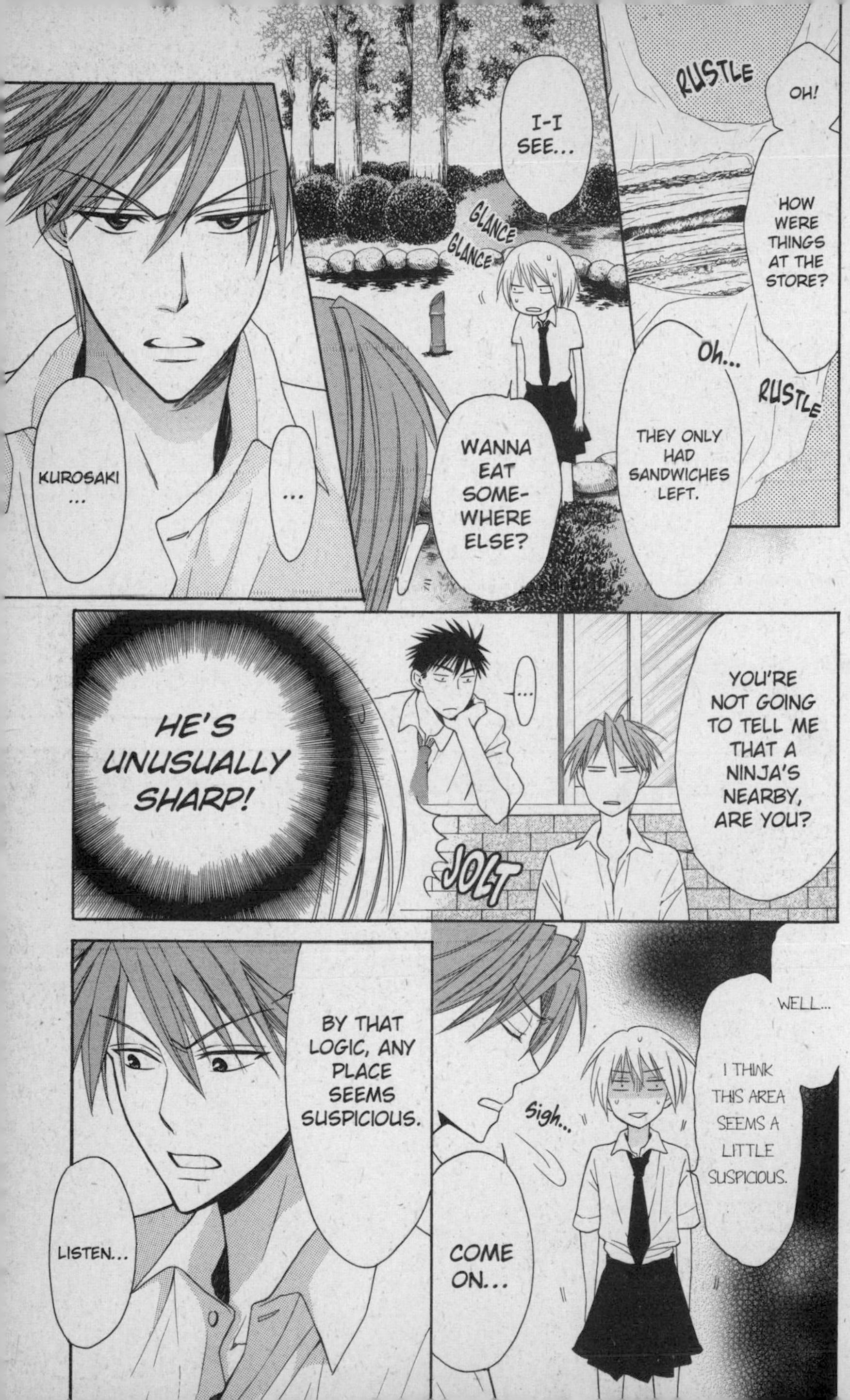
RUSTLE
OH!
HOW WERE THINGS AT THE STORE?
Oh...
RUSTLE
THEY ONLY HAD SANDWICHES LEFT.
I-I SEE...
GLANCE
GLANCE
WANNA EAT SOME-WHERE ELSE?
...
KUROSAKI...
YOU'RE NOT GOING TO TELL ME THAT A NINJA'S NEARBY, ARE YOU?
...
JOLT
HE'S UNUSUALLY SHARP!
WELL...
I THINK THIS AREA SEEMS A LITTLE SUSPICIOUS.
Sigh...
COME ON...
BY THAT LOGIC, ANY PLACE SEEMS SUSPICIOUS.
LISTEN...

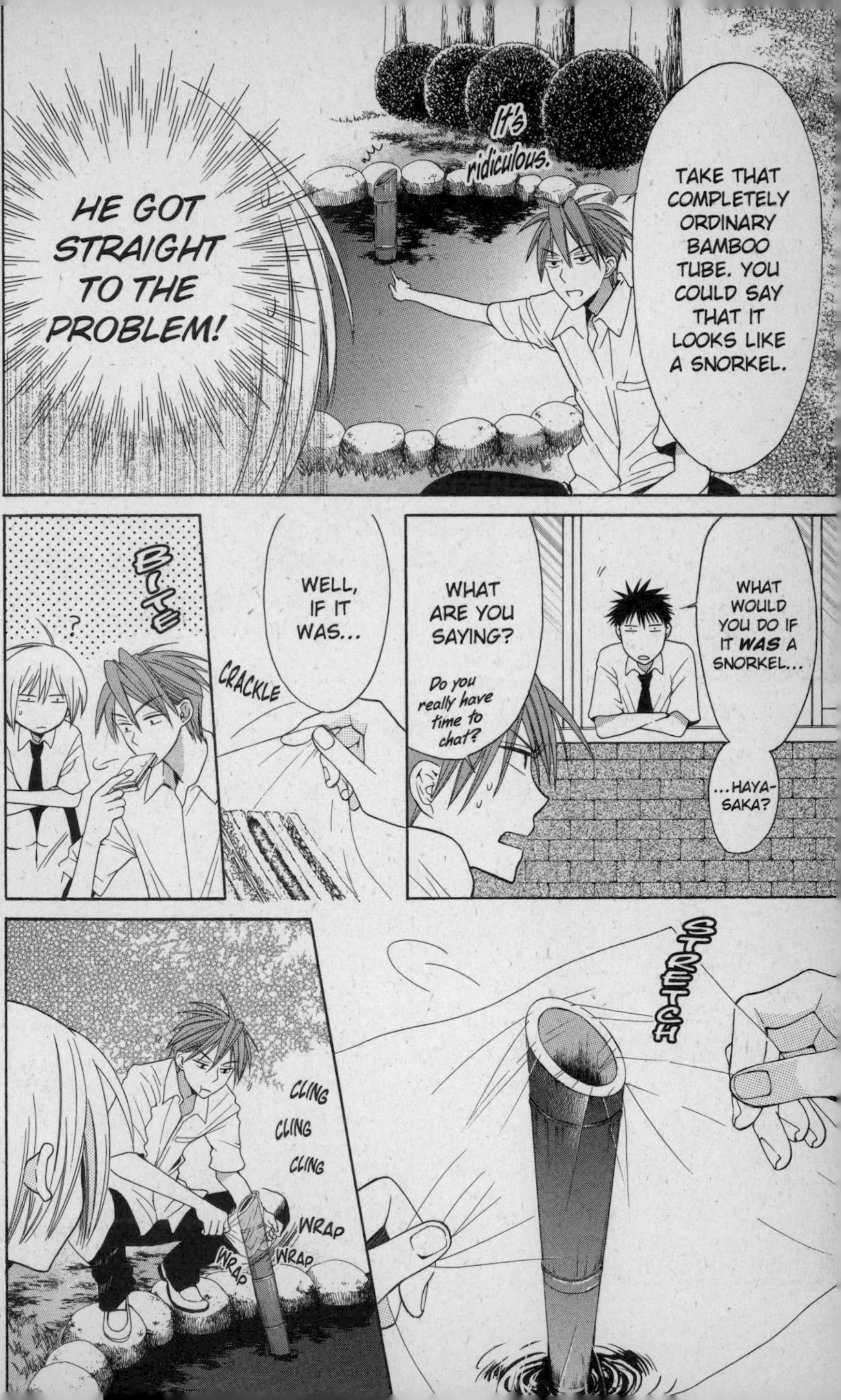
TAKE THAT COMPLETELY ORDINARY BAMBOO TUBE. YOU COULD SAY THAT IT LOOKS LIKE A SNORKEL.
It's ridiculous.
HE GOT STRAIGHT TO THE PROBLEM!
WHAT WOULD YOU DO IF IT WAS A SNORKEL...
...HAYA-SAKA?
WHAT ARE YOU SAYING?
Do you really have time to chat?
WELL, IF IT WAS...
CRACKLE
BITE
?
STRETCH
CLING
CLING
CLING
WRAP
WRAP
WRAP

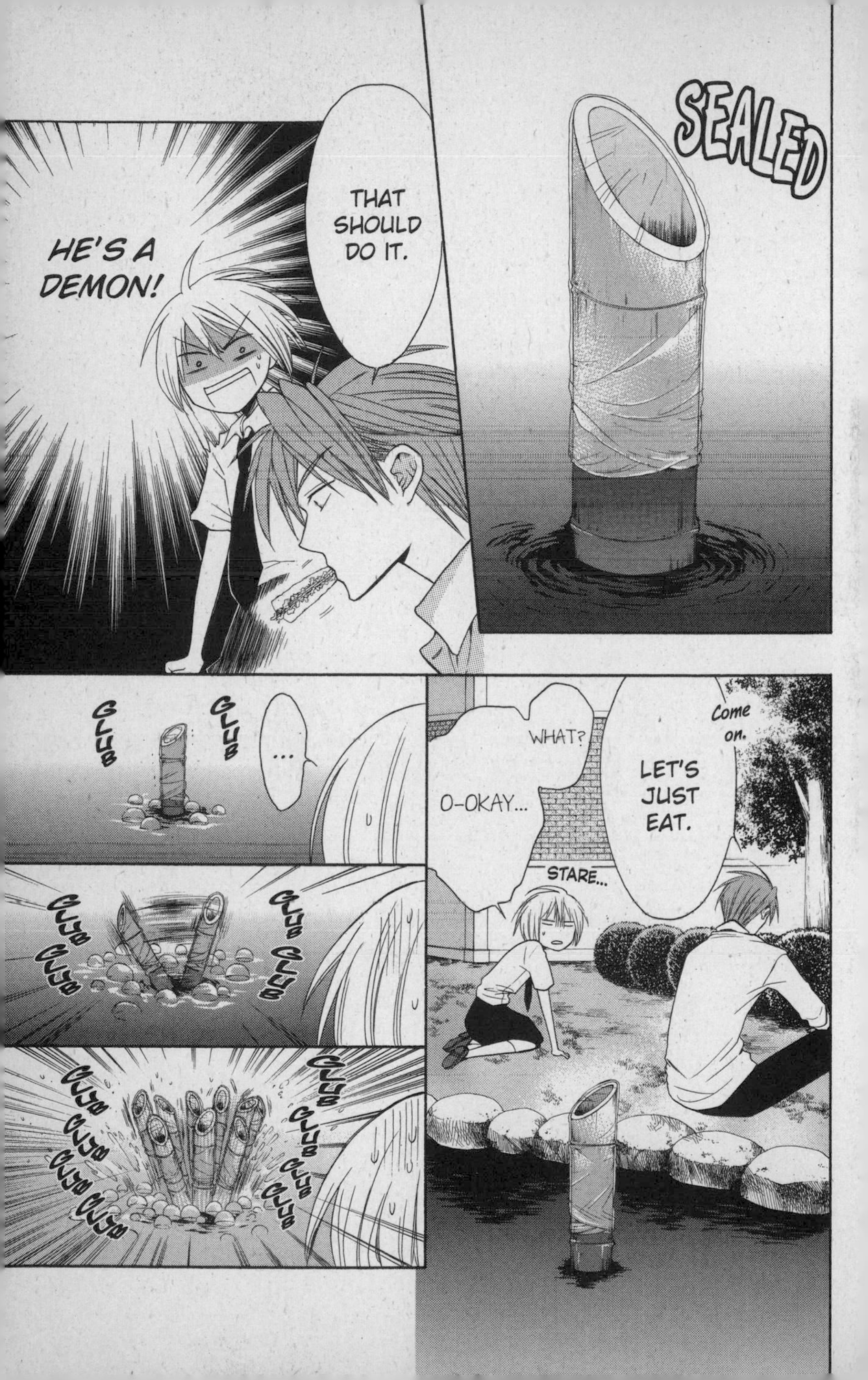
SEALED
THAT SHOULD DO IT.
HE'S A DEMON!
Come on.
LET'S JUST EAT.
WHAT?
O-OKAY...
STARE...
GLUB
GLUB
...
GLUB GLUB
GLUB GLUB
GLUB GLUB GLUB GLUB GLUB
GLUB GLUB GLUB GLUB

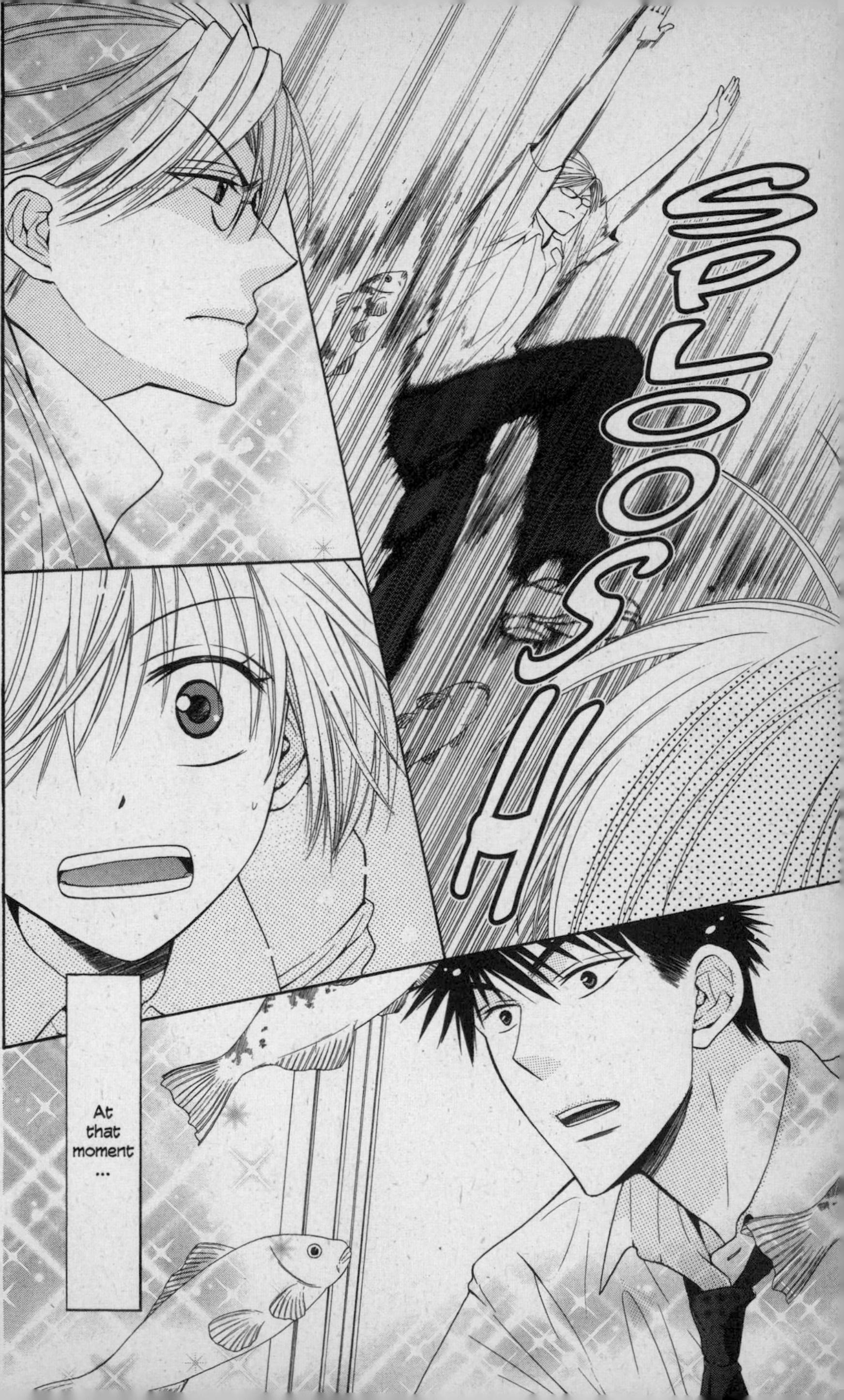
SPLOOOSH
At that moment ...

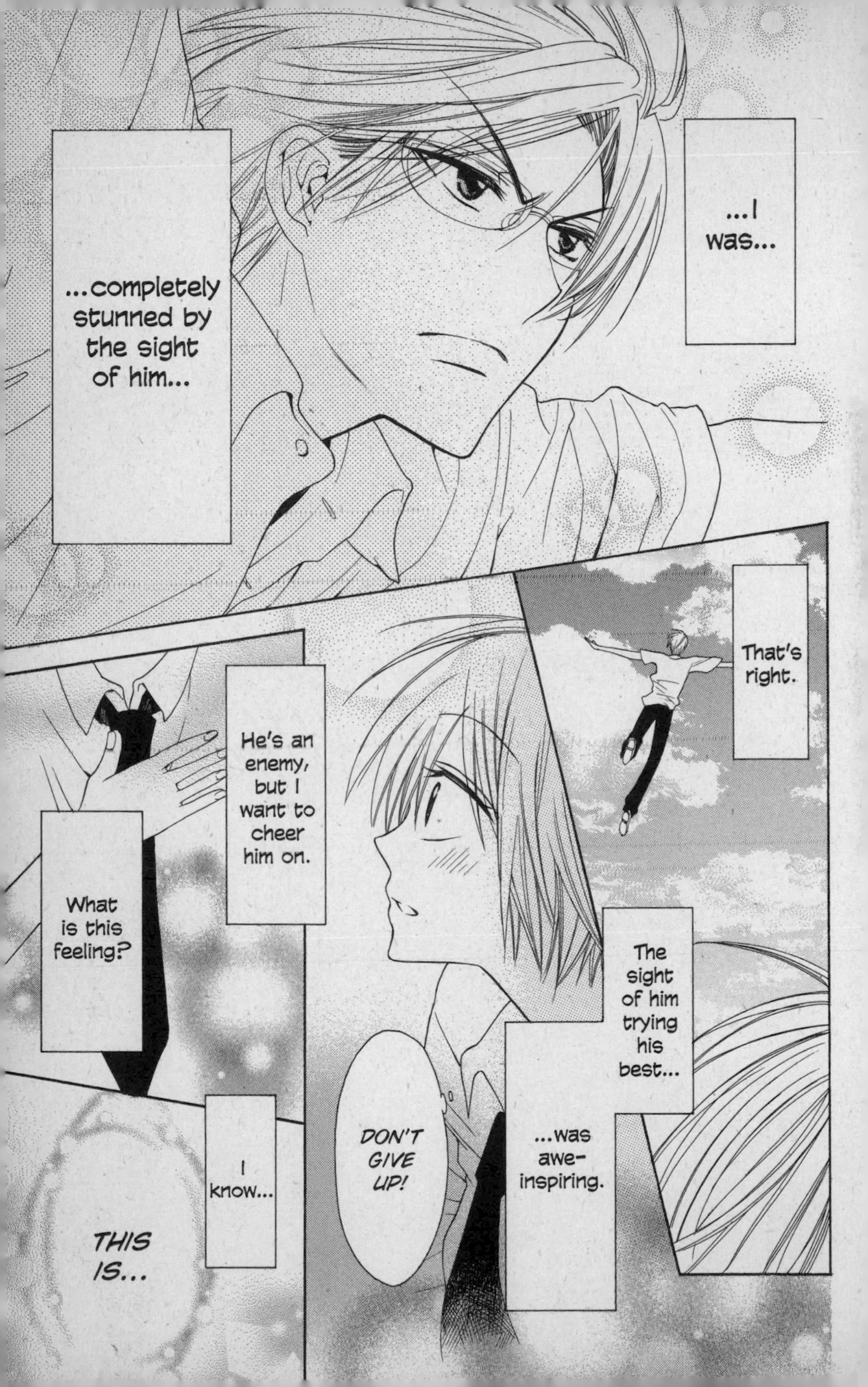
...I was...
...completely stunned by the sight of him...
That's right.
The sight of him trying his best...
...was awe-inspiring.
DON'T GIVE UP!
He's an enemy, but I want to cheer him on.
What is this feeling?
I know...
THIS IS...

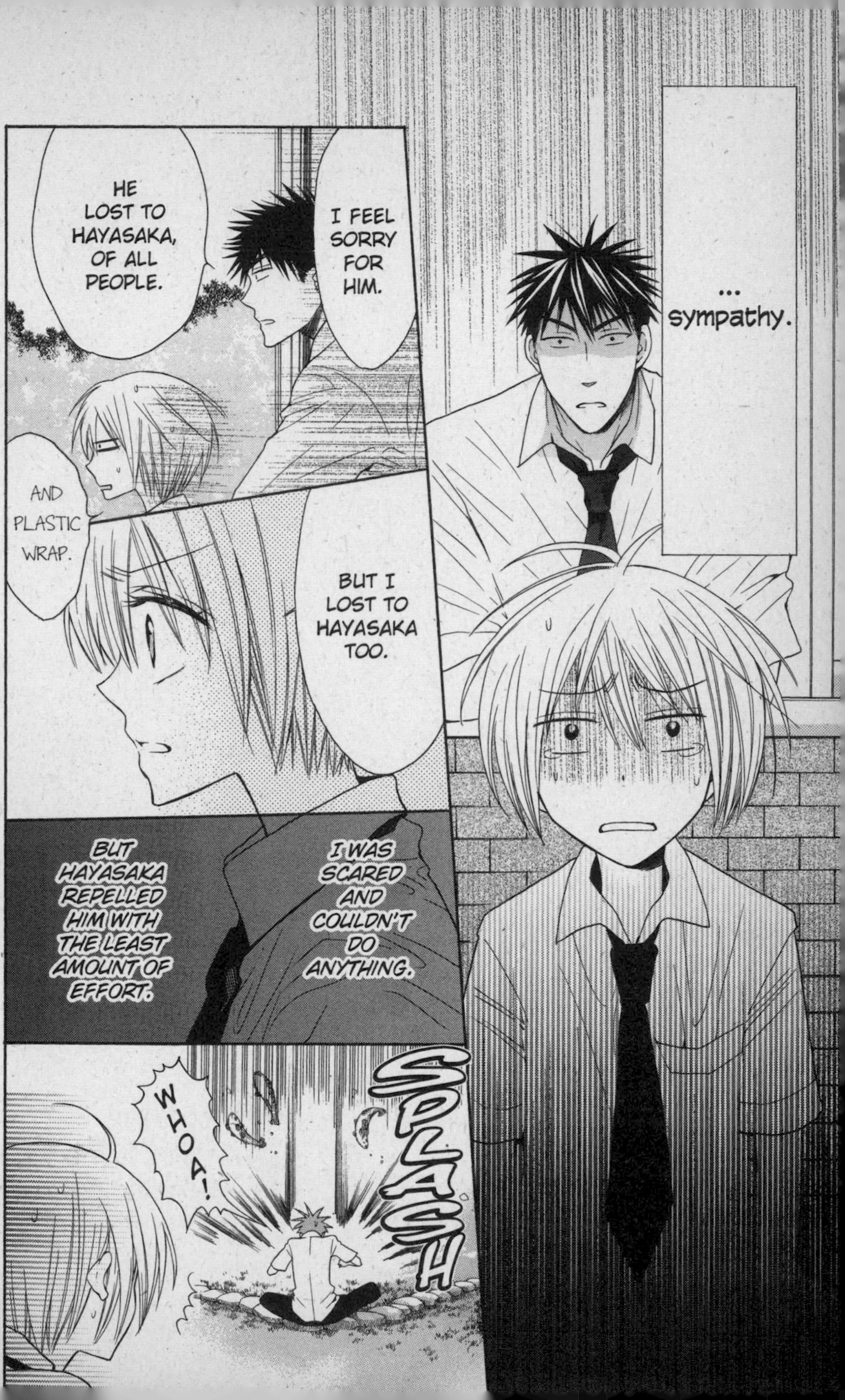
...sympathy.
I FEEL SORRY FOR HIM.
HE LOST TO HAYASAKA, OF ALL PEOPLE.
AND PLASTIC WRAP.
BUT I LOST TO HAYASAKA TOO.
I WAS SCARED AND COULDN'T DO ANYTHING.
BUT HAYASAKA REPELLED HIM WITH THE LEAST AMOUNT OF EFFORT.
SPLASH
WHOA!

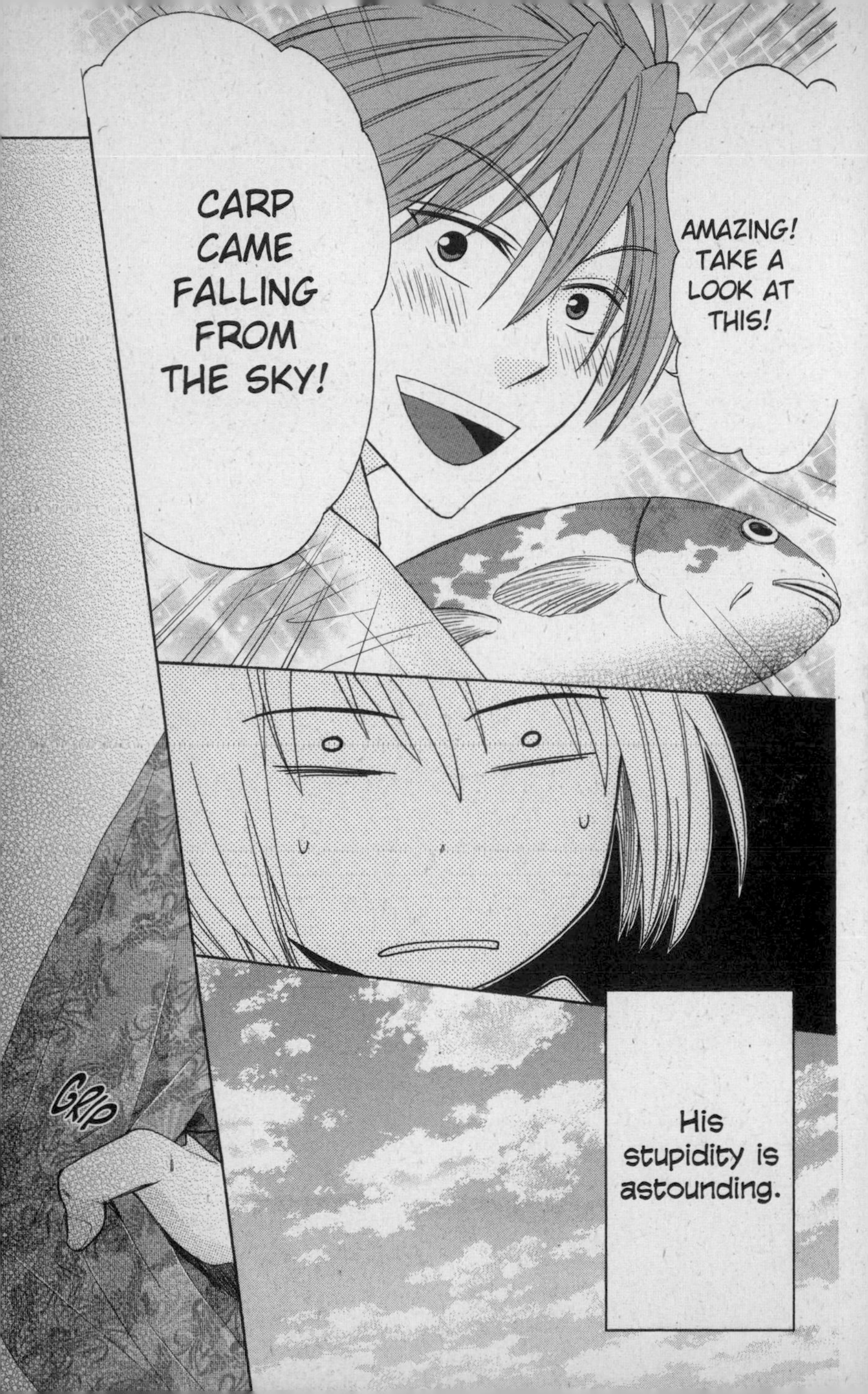
AMAZING! TAKE A LOOK AT THIS!
CARP CAME FALLING FROM THE SKY!
His stupidity is astounding.
GRIP

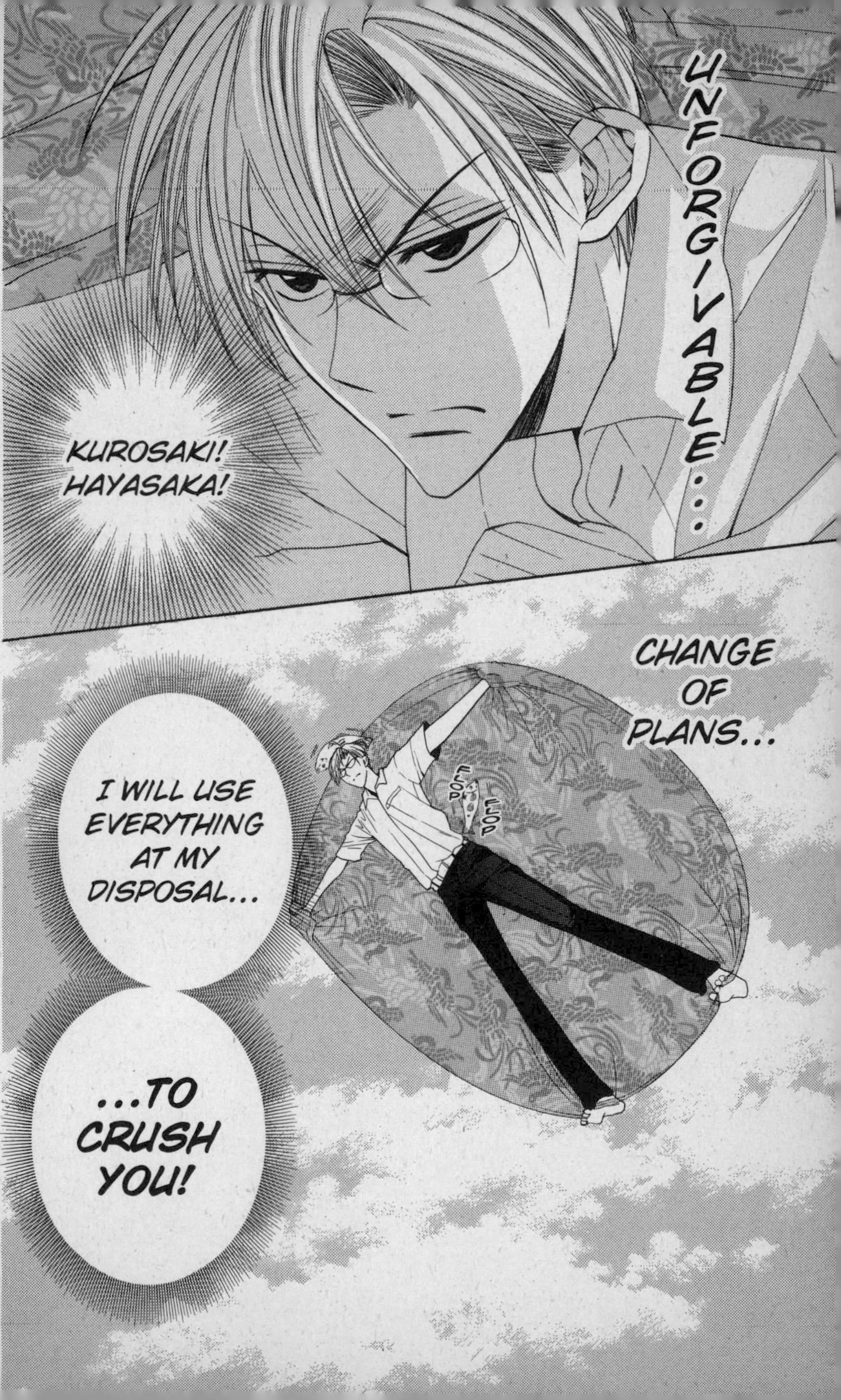UNFORGIVABLE...
KUROSAKI! HAYASAKA!
CHANGE OF PLANS...
I WILL USE EVERYTHING AT MY DISPOSAL...
FLOP FLOP
...TO CRUSH YOU!

North South East West

The time is now. The place is a town in Saitama Prefecture.

The old-fashioned delinquents who make their home here have been living peacefully, their past battles forgotten.

But with their leader, Mafuyu Kurosaki, gone...

...the balance of power has been upset.

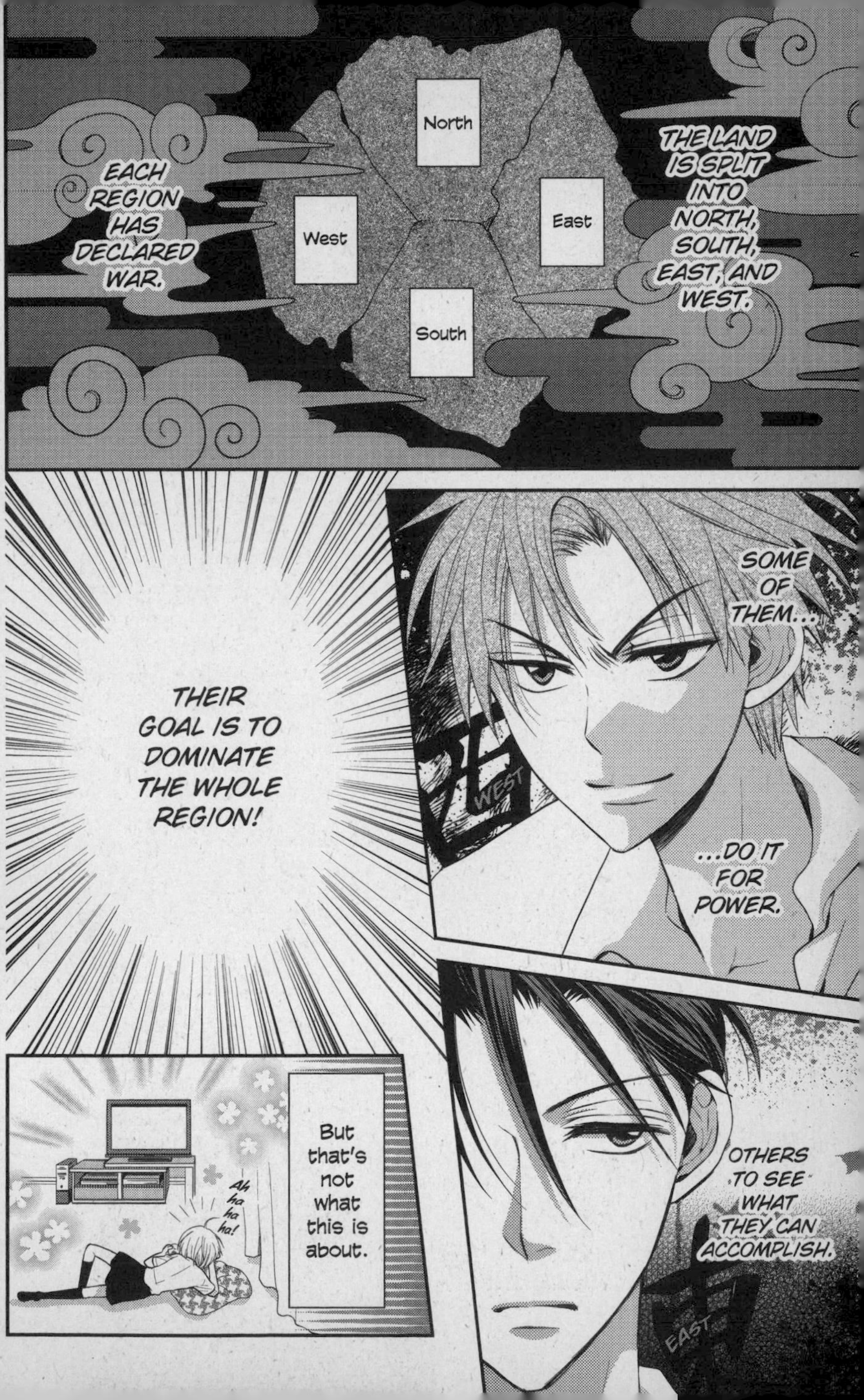
THE LAND IS SPLIT INTO NORTH, SOUTH, EAST, AND WEST.
North
East
West
South
EACH REGION HAS DECLARED WAR.
SOME OF THEM...
WEST
...DO IT FOR POWER.
OTHERS TO SEE WHAT THEY CAN ACCOMPLISH.
EAST
THEIR GOAL IS TO DOMINATE THE WHOLE REGION!
But that's not what this is about.
Ah ha ha ha!

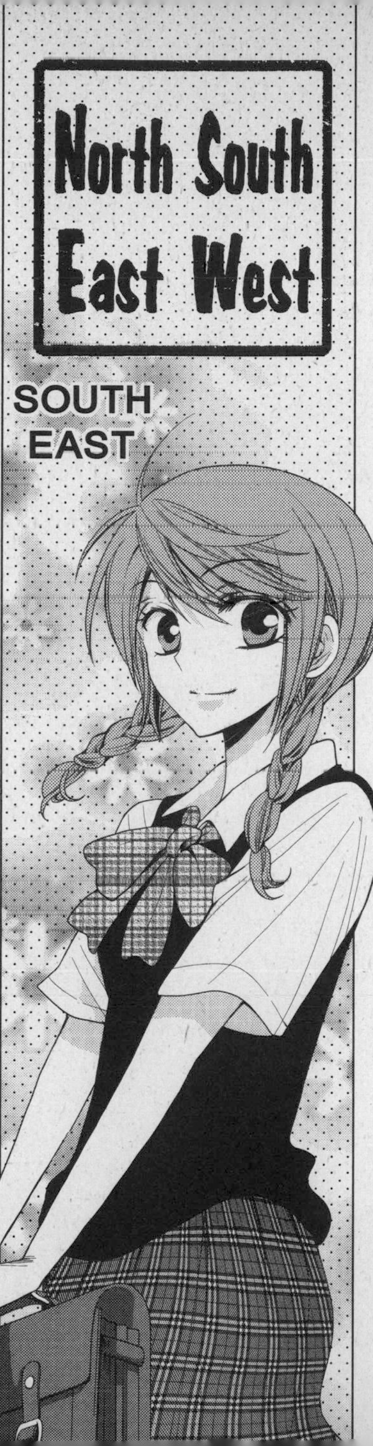
North South East West
SOUTH EAST

EAST HIGH, WEST HIGH, SOUTH HIGH, NORTH HIGH

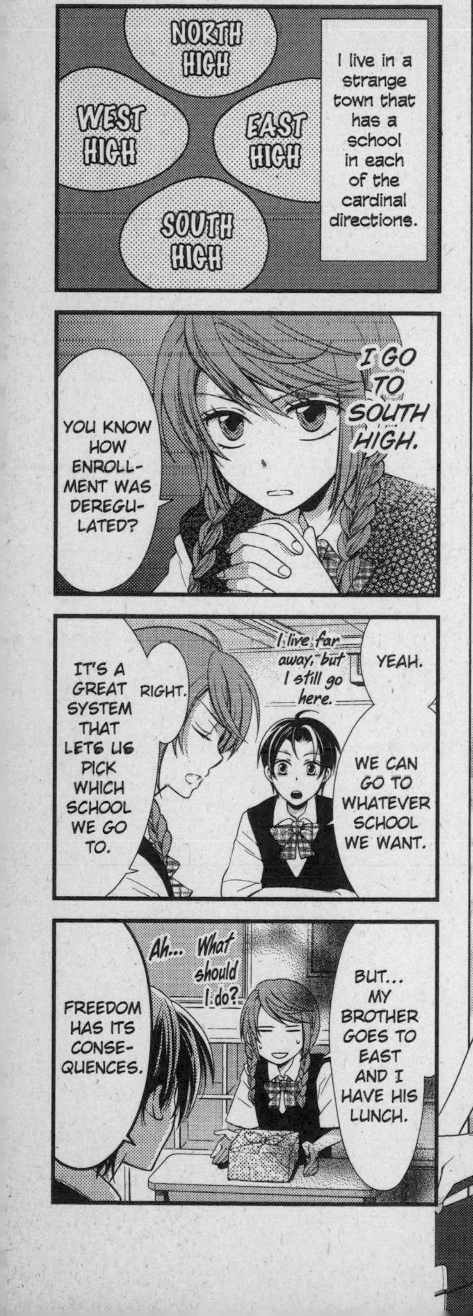
I live in a strange town that has a school in each of the cardinal directions.
NORTH HIGH
EAST HIGH
WEST HIGH
SOUTH HIGH
I GO TO SOUTH HIGH.
YOU KNOW HOW ENROLLMENT WAS DEREGULATED?
YEAH.
I live far away, but I still go here.
WE CAN GO TO WHATEVER SCHOOL WE WANT.
RIGHT.
IT'S A GREAT SYSTEM THAT LETS US PICK WHICH SCHOOL WE GO TO.
BUT... MY BROTHER GOES TO EAST AND I HAVE HIS LUNCH.
Ah... What should I do?
FREEDOM HAS ITS CONSEQUENCES.

DELIVERY

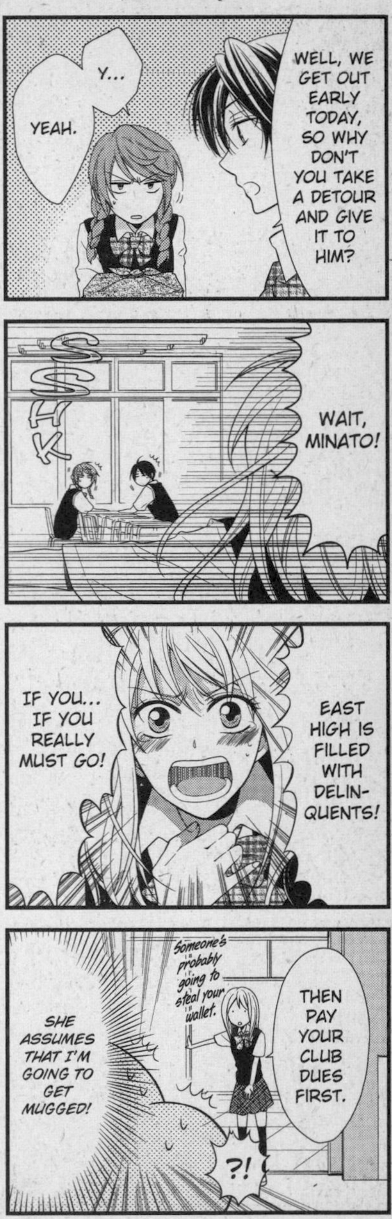
WELL, WE GET OUT EARLY TODAY, SO WHY DON'T YOU TAKE A DETOUR AND GIVE IT TO HIM?
Y...
YEAH.
SSHK
WAIT, MINATO!
EAST HIGH IS FILLED WITH DELIN-QUENTS!
IF YOU... IF YOU REALLY MUST GO!
THEN PAY YOUR CLUB DUES FIRST.
Someone's probably going to steal your wallet.
SHE ASSUMES THAT I'M GOING TO GET MUGGED!
?!

THEY WERE PROBABLY JEALOUS

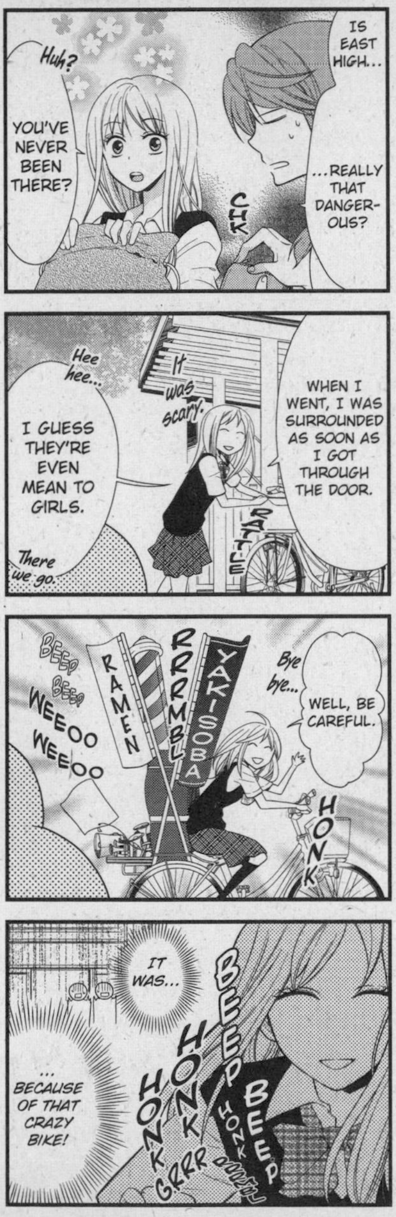
IS EAST HIGH...
...REALLY THAT DANGER-OUS?
CHK
Huh?
YOU'VE NEVER BEEN THERE?
WHEN I WENT, I WAS SURROUNDED AS SOON AS I GOT THROUGH THE DOOR.
It was scary.
RATTLE
Hee hee...
I GUESS THEY'RE EVEN MEAN TO GIRLS.
There we go.
Bye bye...
WELL, BE CAREFUL.
HONK
YAKISOBA
RRRMBL
RAMEN
BEEP BEEP
WEEOO WEEOO
BEEP
BEEP
HONK
IT WAS...
HONK HONK
GRRR
...BECAUSE OF THAT CRAZY BIKE!

DANGEROUS EAST HIGH

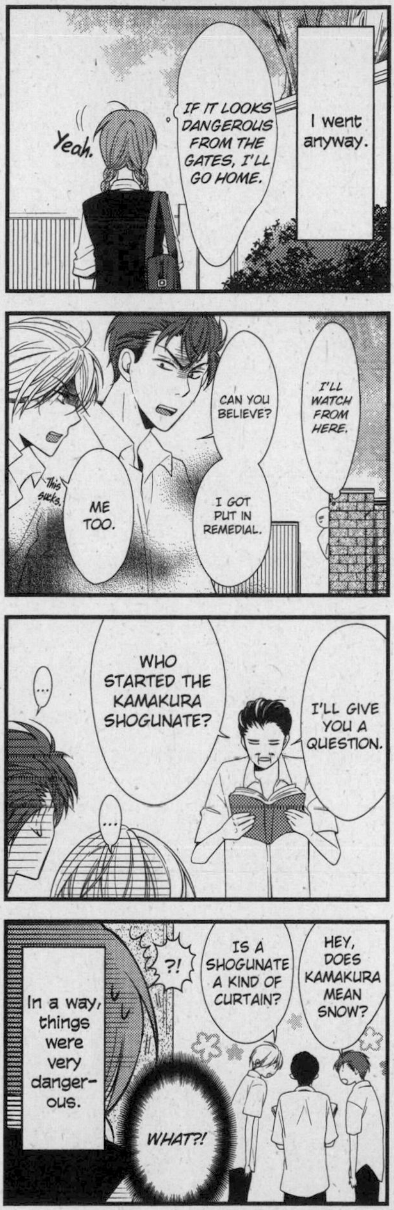
I went anyway.
IF IT LOOKS DANGEROUS FROM THE GATES, I'LL GO HOME.
Yeah.
I'LL WATCH FROM HERE.
CAN YOU BELIEVE?
I GOT PUT IN REMEDIAL.
ME TOO.
This sucks.
I'LL GIVE YOU A QUESTION.
WHO STARTED THE KAMAKURA SHOGUNATE?
...
...
HEY, DOES KAMAKURA MEAN SNOW?
IS A SHOGUNATE A KIND OF CURTAIN?
?!
In a way, things were very danger-ous.
WHAT?!

HUH?

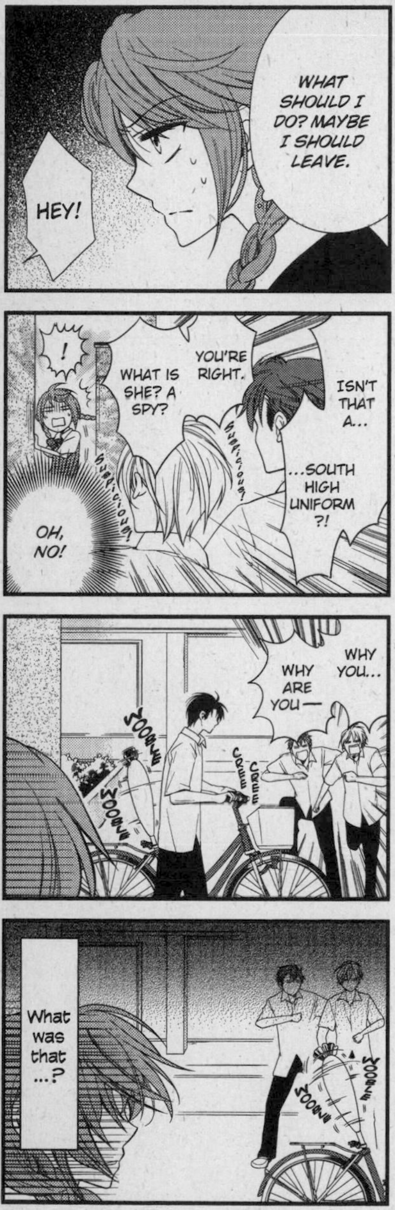
WHAT SHOULD I DO? MAYBE I SHOULD LEAVE.
HEY!
ISN'T THAT A...
...SOUTH HIGH UNIFORM?!
YOU'RE RIGHT.
WHAT IS SHE? A SPY?
!
Suspicious
Suspicious
OH, NO!
WHY YOU...
WHY ARE YOU—
CREE CREE
WOOBLE WOOBLE
What was that...?
WOOBLE WOOBLE

BY CHANCE

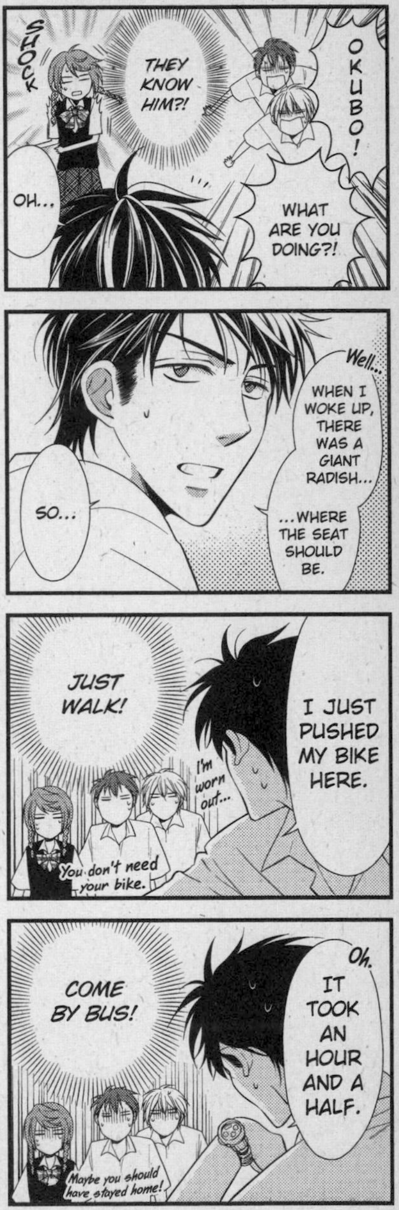
OKUBO!
THEY KNOW HIM?!
SHOCK
WHAT ARE YOU DOING?!
OH...
Well...
WHEN I WOKE UP, THERE WAS A GIANT RADISH...
...WHERE THE SEAT SHOULD BE.
SO...
I JUST PUSHED MY BIKE HERE.
I'm worn out...
JUST WALK!
You don't need your bike.
Oh.
IT TOOK AN HOUR AND A HALF.
COME BY BUS!
Maybe you should have stayed home!

THIS IS IMPORTANT

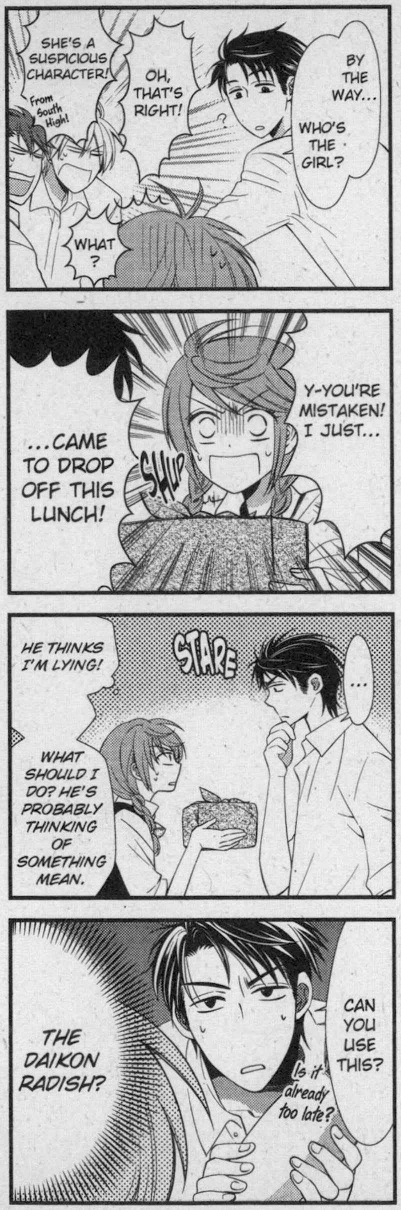
BY THE WAY...
WHO'S THE GIRL?
OH, THAT'S RIGHT!
SHE'S A SUSPICIOUS CHARACTER!
From South High!
WHAT?
Y-YOU'RE MISTAKEN! I JUST...
SHUP
...CAME TO DROP OFF THIS LUNCH!
...
STARE
HE THINKS I'M LYING!
WHAT SHOULD I DO? HE'S PROBABLY THINKING OF SOMETHING MEAN.
CAN YOU USE THIS?
Is it already too late?
THE DAIKON RADISH?

OKUBO

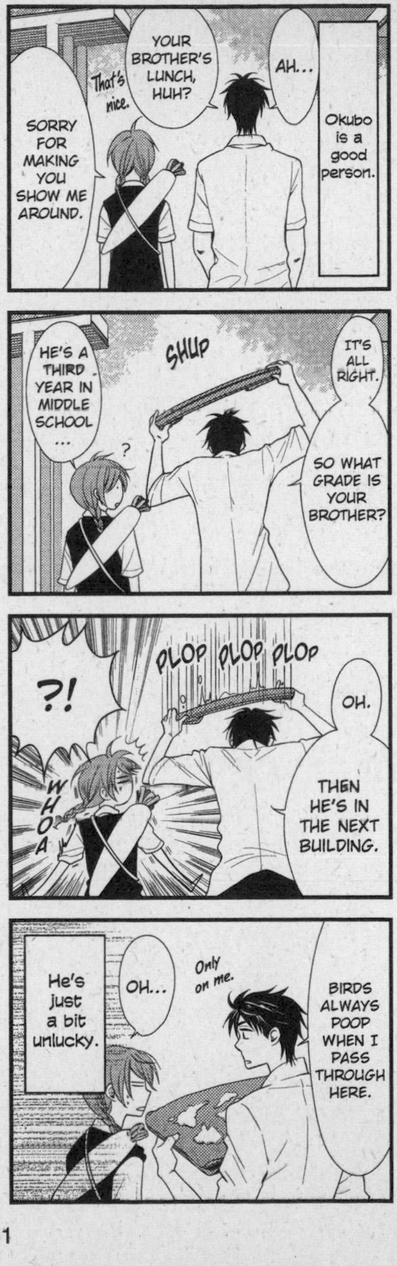

Okubo is a good person.
AH...
YOUR BROTHER'S LUNCH, HUH?
That's nice.
SORRY FOR MAKING YOU SHOW ME AROUND.
IT'S ALL RIGHT.
SO WHAT GRADE IS YOUR BROTHER?
SHUP
HE'S A THIRD YEAR IN MIDDLE SCHOOL ...
?
OH.
THEN HE'S IN THE NEXT BUILDING.
PLOP PLOP PLOP
?!
WHOA
BIRDS ALWAYS POOP WHEN I PASS THROUGH HERE.
Only on me.
OH...
He's just a bit unlucky.

UNLUCKY BOY

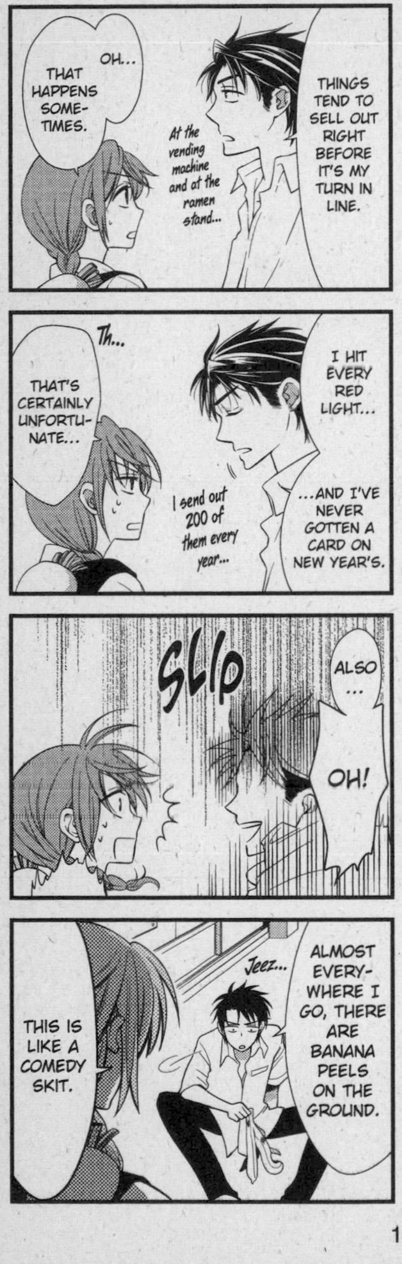

THINGS TEND TO SELL OUT RIGHT BEFORE IT'S MY TURN IN LINE.
At the vending machine and at the ramen stand...
OH... THAT HAPPENS SOMETIMES.
I HIT EVERY RED LIGHT...
...AND I'VE NEVER GOTTEN A CARD ON NEW YEAR'S.
I send out 200 of them every year...
Th...
THAT'S CERTAINLY UNFORTUNATE...
ALSO ...
OH!
SLIP
ALMOST EVERY-WHERE I GO, THERE ARE BANANA PEELS ON THE GROUND.
Jeez...
THIS IS LIKE A COMEDY SKIT.

SUBTLE

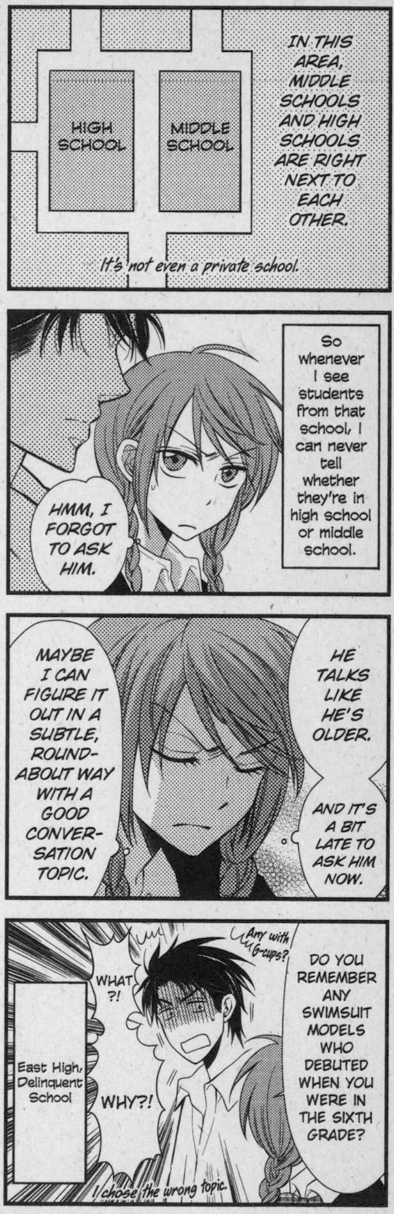
IN THIS AREA, MIDDLE SCHOOLS AND HIGH SCHOOLS ARE RIGHT NEXT TO EACH OTHER.
MIDDLE SCHOOL
HIGH SCHOOL
It's not even a private school.
So whenever I see students from that school, I can never tell whether they're in high school or middle school.
HMM, I FORGOT TO ASK HIM.
HE TALKS LIKE HE'S OLDER.
AND IT'S A BIT LATE TO ASK HIM NOW.
MAYBE I CAN FIGURE IT OUT IN A SUBTLE, ROUND-ABOUT WAY WITH A GOOD CONVER-SATION TOPIC.
DO YOU REMEMBER ANY SWIMSUIT MODELS WHO DEBUTED WHEN YOU WERE IN THE SIXTH GRADE?
Any with G-cups?
WHAT ?!
WHY?!
East High, Delinquent School
I chose the wrong topic.

EAST HIGH, DELINQUENT SCHOOL

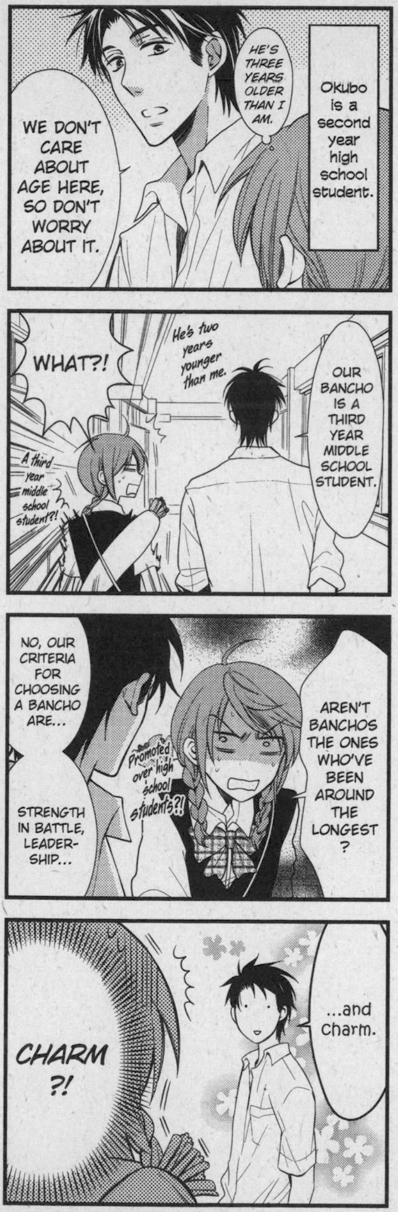
Okubo is a second year high school student.
HE'S THREE YEARS OLDER THAN I AM.
WE DON'T CARE ABOUT AGE HERE, SO DON'T WORRY ABOUT IT.
OUR BANCHO IS A THIRD YEAR MIDDLE SCHOOL STUDENT.
He's two years younger than me.
WHAT?!
A third year middle school student?!
AREN'T BANCHOS THE ONES WHO'VE BEEN AROUND THE LONGEST ?
Promoted over high school students?!
NO, OUR CRITERIA FOR CHOOSING A BANCHO ARE...
STRENGTH IN BATTLE, LEADER-SHIP...
...and charm.
CHARM ?!

FIRST ENCOUNTER

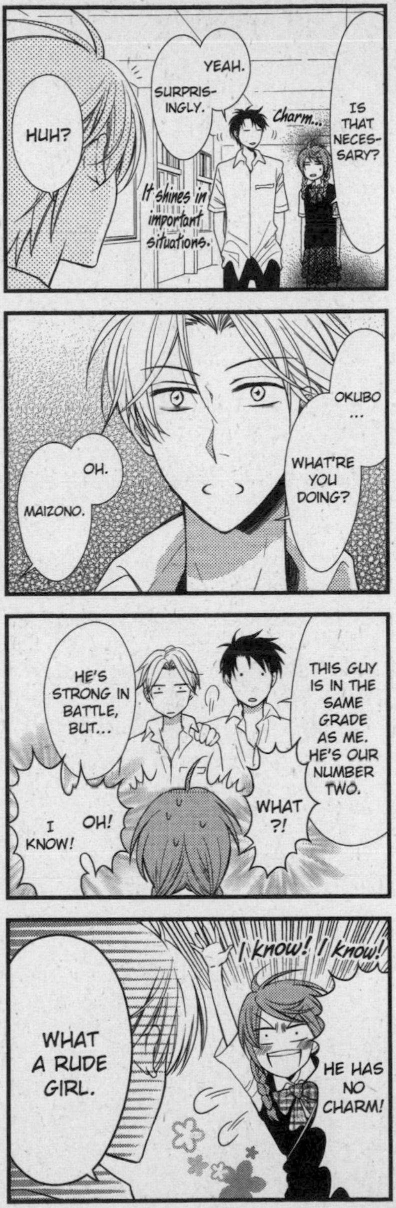
IS THAT NECES-SARY?
Charm...
YEAH.
SURPRIS-INGLY.
It shines in important situations.
HUH?
OKUBO...
WHAT'RE YOU DOING?
OH.
MAIZONO.
THIS GUY IS IN THE SAME GRADE AS ME. HE'S OUR NUMBER TWO.
WHAT?!
HE'S STRONG IN BATTLE, BUT...
OH!
I KNOW!
I know! I know!
HE HAS NO CHARM!
WHAT A RUDE GIRL.

IMPULSE

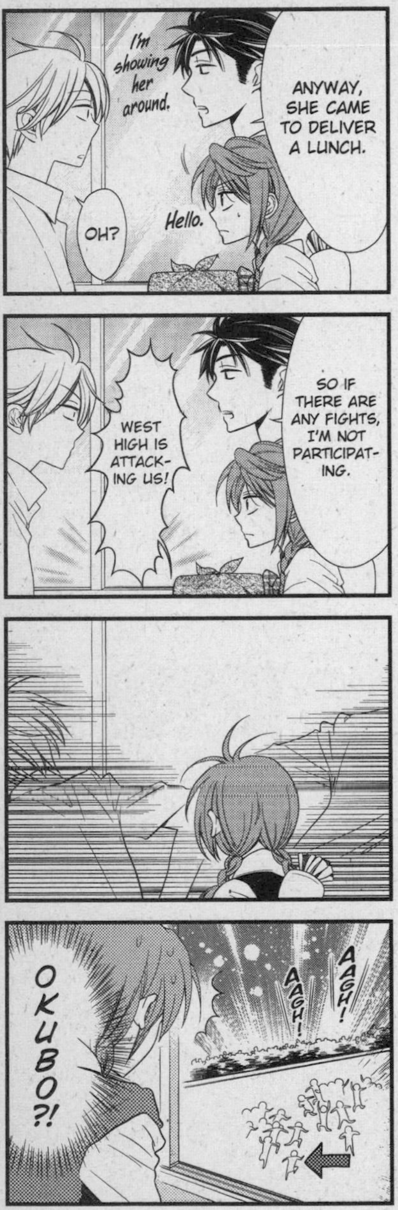
ANYWAY, SHE CAME TO DELIVER A LUNCH.
I'm showing her around.
Hello.
OH?
SO IF THERE ARE ANY FIGHTS, I'M NOT PARTICIPAT-ING.
WEST HIGH IS ATTACK-ING US!
AAGH!
AAGH!
OKUBO?!

A FIERCE BATTLE

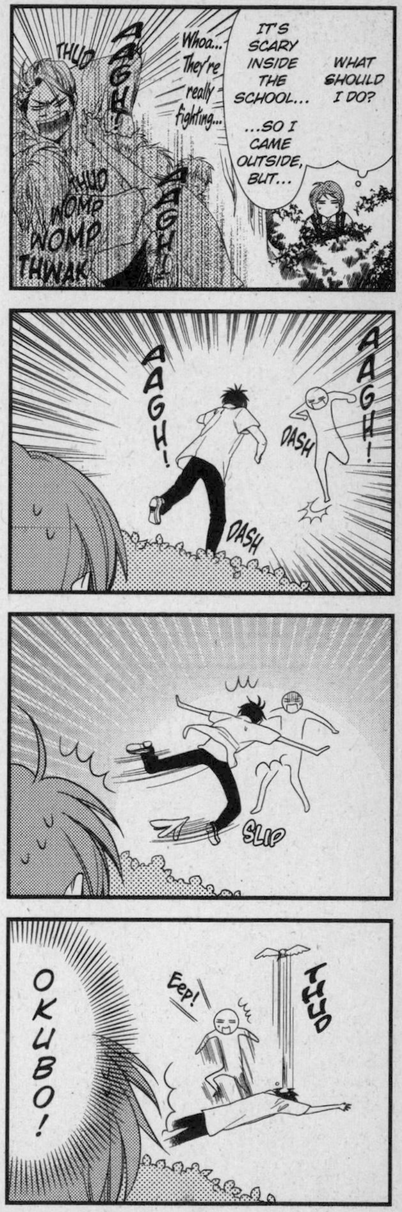

WHAT SHOULD I DO?
IT'S SCARY INSIDE THE SCHOOL...
...SO I CAME OUTSIDE, BUT...
Whoa... They're really fighting...
AAGH!
AAGH!
THUD
THUD WOMP WOMP THWAK
AAGH!
DASH
AAGH!
DASH
SLIP
THUD
Eep!
OKUBO!

YOU SHOULD HAVE REALIZED

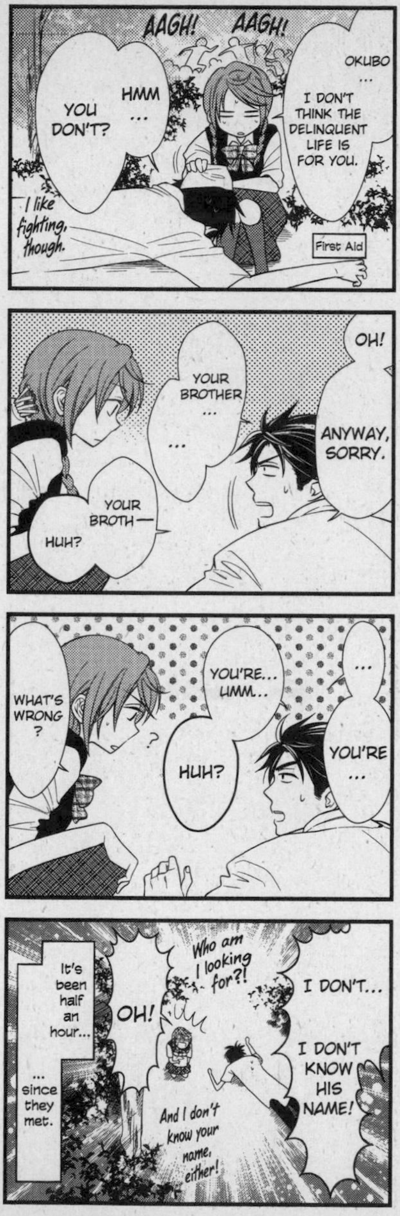

OKUBO ... I DON'T THINK THE DELINQUENT LIFE IS FOR YOU.
AAGH! AAGH!
HMM ...
YOU DON'T?
I like fighting, though.
First Aid
OH!
ANYWAY, SORRY.
YOUR BROTHER ...
...
YOUR BROTH—
HUH?
...
YOU'RE ...
YOU'RE... UMM..
HUH?
WHAT'S WRONG?
I DON'T...
I DON'T KNOW HIS NAME!
Who am I looking for?!
OH!
And I don't know your name, either!
It's been half an hour...
... since they met.

SHE'S LOOKING FOR HER BROTHER

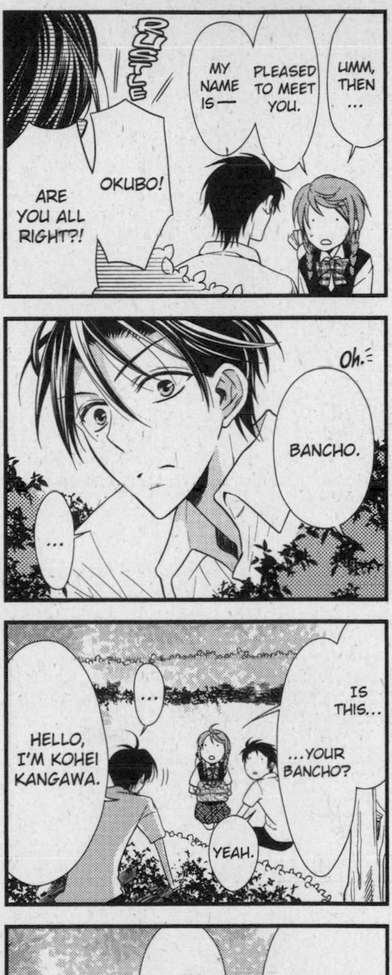

UMM, THEN...
PLEASED TO MEET YOU.
MY NAME IS—
RUSTLE
OKUBO!
ARE YOU ALL RIGHT?!
Oh.
BANCHO.
...
IS THIS...
...YOUR BANCHO?
...
YEAH.
HELLO, I'M KOHEI KANGAWA.
HELLO, I'M MINATO KANGAWA...
...BIG BROTHER.
He's her brother.

EMBARRASSING

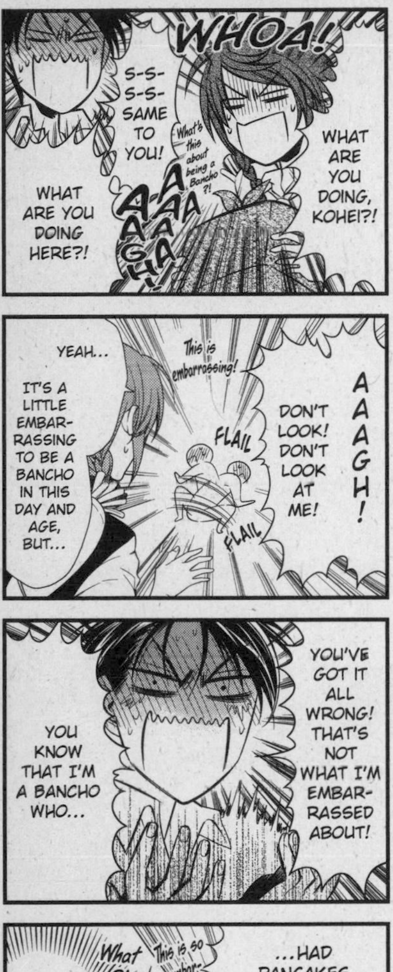

WHOA!
WHAT ARE YOU DOING, KOHEI?!
What's this about being a Bancho?!
S-S-S-S-SAME TO YOU!
AAAAAAAGH!
WHAT ARE YOU DOING HERE?!
AAAGH!
DON'T LOOK! DON'T LOOK AT ME!
FLAIL
FLAIL
This is embarrassing!
YEAH...
IT'S A LITTLE EMBARRASSING TO BE A BANCHO IN THIS DAY AND AGE, BUT...
YOU'VE GOT IT ALL WRONG! THAT'S NOT WHAT I'M EMBARRASSED ABOUT!
YOU KNOW THAT I'M A BANCHO WHO...
...HAD PANCAKES AND PUDDING FOR BREAKFAST!
This is so embarrassing!
Aagh!
What?!
THAT'S WHAT YOU'RE EMBARRASSED ABOUT?!

BANCHO REQUIREMENTS

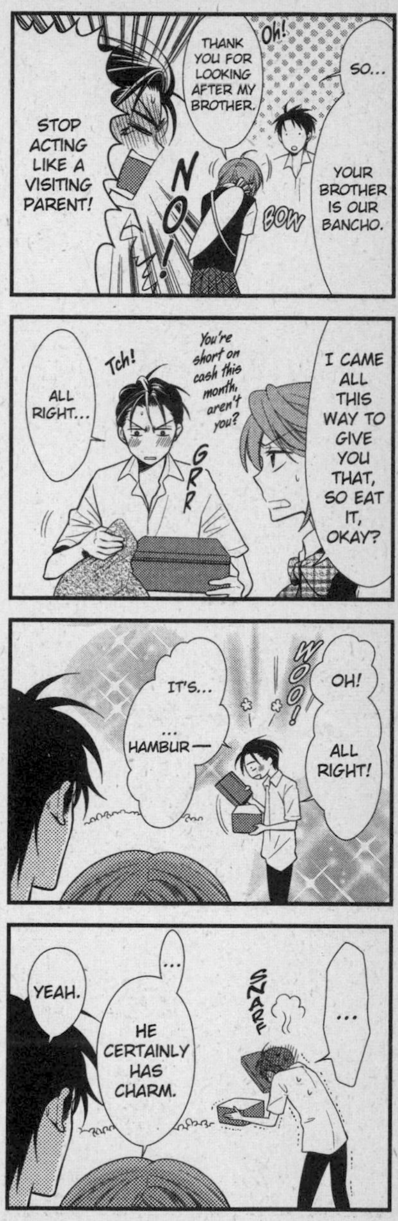
SO...
YOUR BROTHER IS OUR BANCHO.
Oh!
BOW
THANK YOU FOR LOOKING AFTER MY BROTHER.
NO!
STOP ACTING LIKE A VISITING PARENT!
I CAME ALL THIS WAY TO GIVE YOU THAT, SO EAT IT, OKAY?
You're short on cash this month, aren't you?
GRR
Tch!
ALL RIGHT...
OH!
ALL RIGHT!
WOOO!
IT'S... ...HAMBUR—
...
SNARF
...
HE CERTAINLY HAS CHARM.
YEAH.

HER BROTHER'S REASON

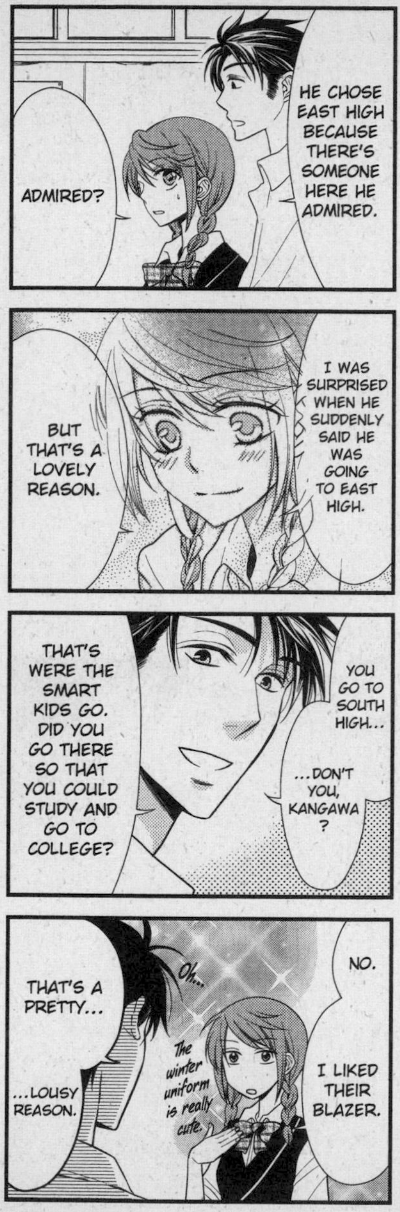
HE CHOSE EAST HIGH BECAUSE THERE'S SOMEONE HERE HE ADMIRED.
ADMIRED?
I WAS SURPRISED WHEN HE SUDDENLY SAID HE WAS GOING TO EAST HIGH.
BUT THAT'S A LOVELY REASON.
YOU GO TO SOUTH HIGH...
...DON'T YOU, KANGAWA?
THAT'S WERE THE SMART KIDS GO. DID YOU GO THERE SO THAT YOU COULD STUDY AND GO TO COLLEGE?
NO.
I LIKED THEIR BLAZER.
The winter uniform is really cute.
Oh...
THAT'S A PRETTY...
...LOUSY REASON.

NAME

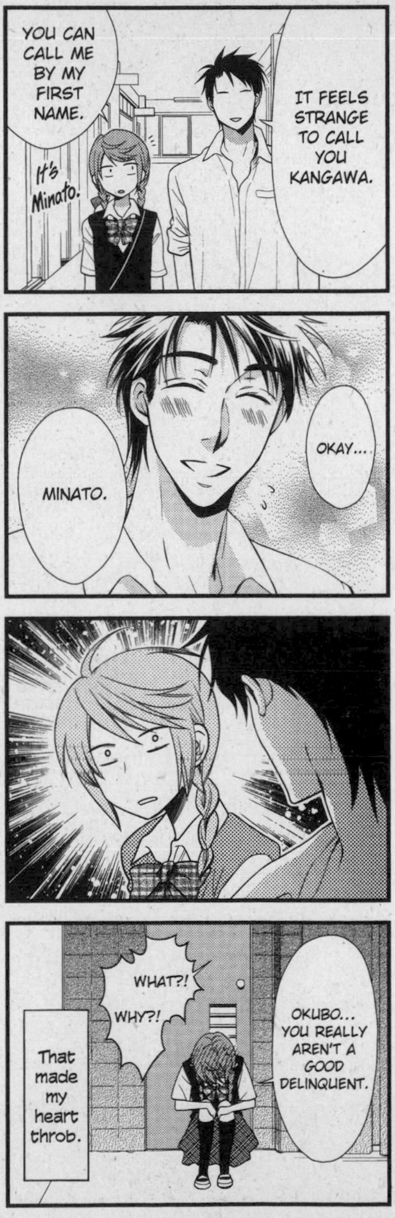
IT FEELS STRANGE TO CALL YOU KANGAWA.
YOU CAN CALL ME BY MY FIRST NAME.
It's Minato.
OKAY...
MINATO.
OKUBO... YOU REALLY AREN'T A GOOD DELINQUENT.
WHAT?!
WHY?!
That made my heart throb.

CALMED DOWN

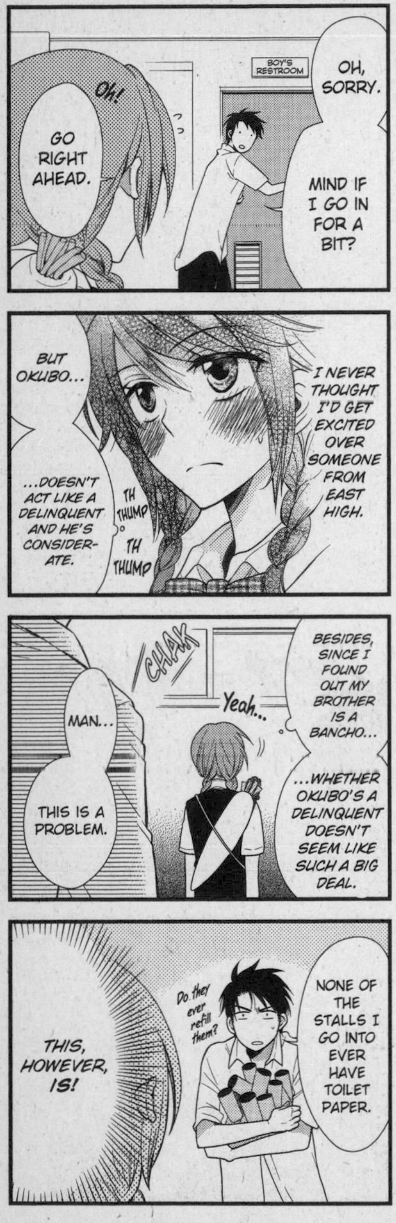
OH, SORRY.
BOY'S RESTROOM
MIND IF I GO IN FOR A BIT?
Oh!
GO RIGHT AHEAD.
I NEVER THOUGHT I'D GET EXCITED OVER SOMEONE FROM EAST HIGH.
BUT OKUBO...
...DOESN'T ACT LIKE A DELINQUENT AND HE'S CONSIDER-ATE.
TH THUMP
TH THUMP
BESIDES, SINCE I FOUND OUT MY BROTHER IS A BANCHO...
...WHETHER OKUBO'S A DELINQUENT DOESN'T SEEM LIKE SUCH A BIG DEAL.
Yeah...
CHAK
MAN...
THIS IS A PROBLEM.
NONE OF THE STALLS I GO INTO EVER HAVE TOILET PAPER.
Do they ever refill them?
THIS, HOWEVER, IS!

I'M WORRIED

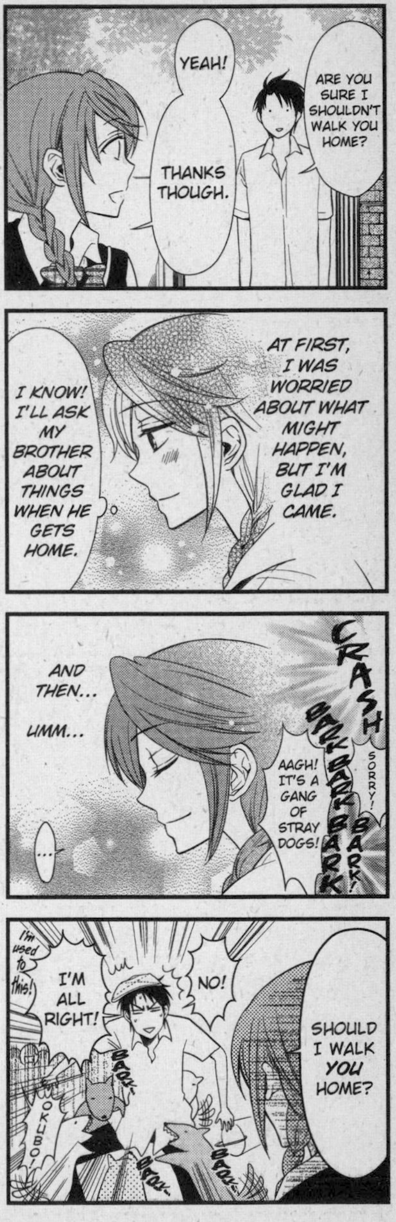
ARE YOU SURE I SHOULDN'T WALK YOU HOME?
YEAH!
THANKS THOUGH.
AT FIRST, I WAS WORRIED ABOUT WHAT MIGHT HAPPEN, BUT I'M GLAD I CAME.
I KNOW! I'LL ASK MY BROTHER ABOUT THINGS WHEN HE GETS HOME.
CRASH
SORRY!
AAGH! IT'S A GANG OF STRAY DOGS!
AND THEN...
UMM...
...
SHOULD I WALK YOU HOME?
NO!
I'M ALL RIGHT!
I'm used to this!

LATER ON

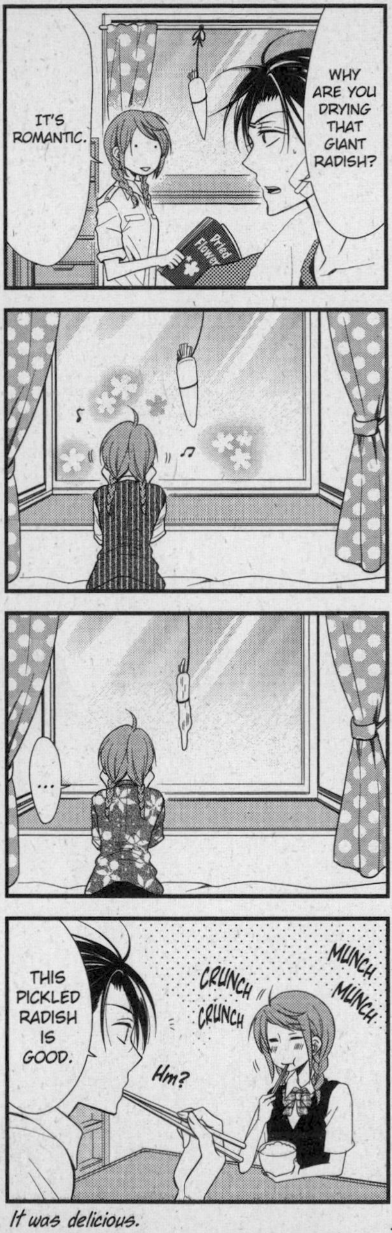
WHY ARE YOU DRYING THAT GIANT RADISH?
IT'S ROMANTIC.
Dried Flowers
...
MUNCH MUNCH
CRUNCH CRUNCH
Hm?
THIS PICKLED RADISH IS GOOD.

It was delicious.

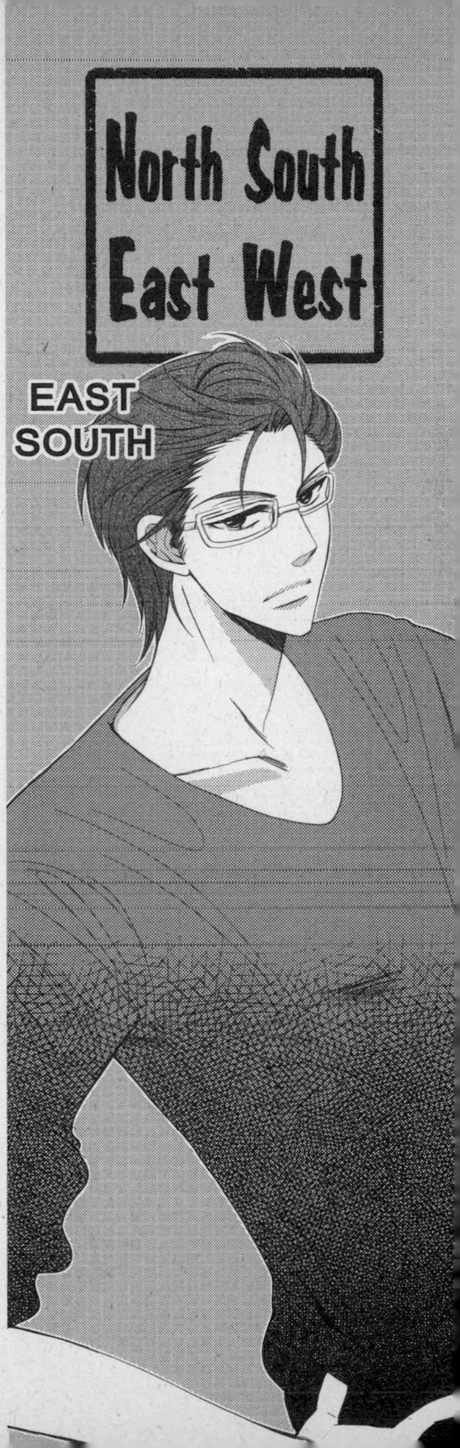
North South East West
EAST SOUTH

HE'S FROM ANOTHER SCHOOL

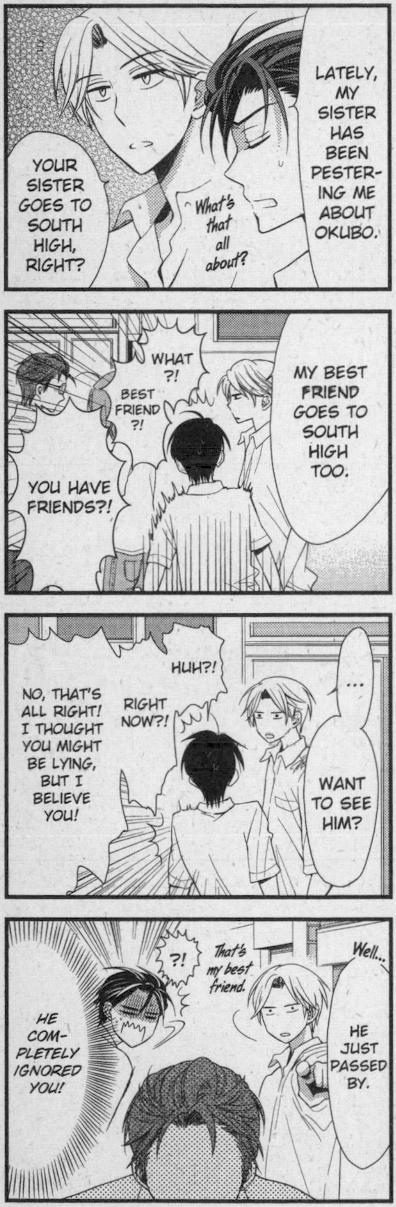
LATELY, MY SISTER HAS BEEN PESTERING ME ABOUT OKUBO.
What's that all about?
YOUR SISTER GOES TO SOUTH HIGH, RIGHT?
MY BEST FRIEND GOES TO SOUTH HIGH TOO.
WHAT?!
BEST FRIEND?!
YOU HAVE FRIENDS?!
...
WANT TO SEE HIM?
HUH?!
RIGHT NOW?!
NO, THAT'S ALL RIGHT! I THOUGHT YOU MIGHT BE LYING, BUT I BELIEVE YOU!
Well...
HE JUST PASSED BY.
That's my best friend.
?!
HE COMPLETELY IGNORED YOU!

HE'S MY BEST FRIEND

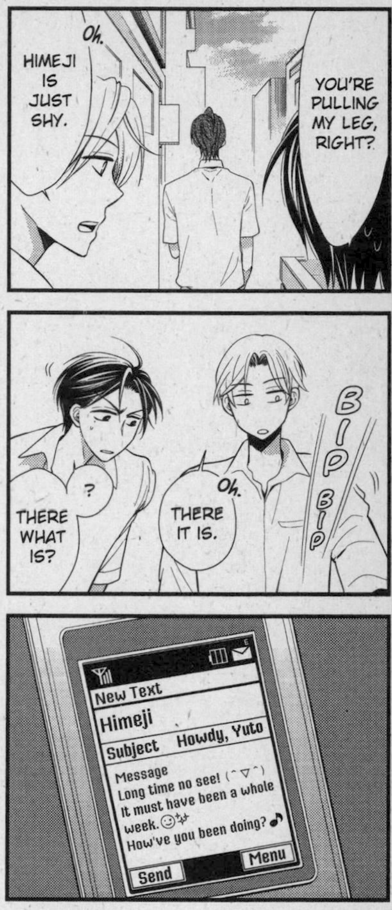
YOU'RE PULLING MY LEG, RIGHT?
Oh.
HIMEJI IS JUST SHY.
BIP BIP
Oh.
THERE IT IS.
?
THERE WHAT IS?
New Text
Himeji
Subject Howdy, Yuto
Message
Long time no see! (^▽^)
It must have been a whole week.
How've you been doing?
Send
Menu
HEY...
...IT HAS BEEN QUITE A WHILE...
Yep.
Yep.
WHAT?!
CLIK CLIK CLIK CLIK

HIMEJI

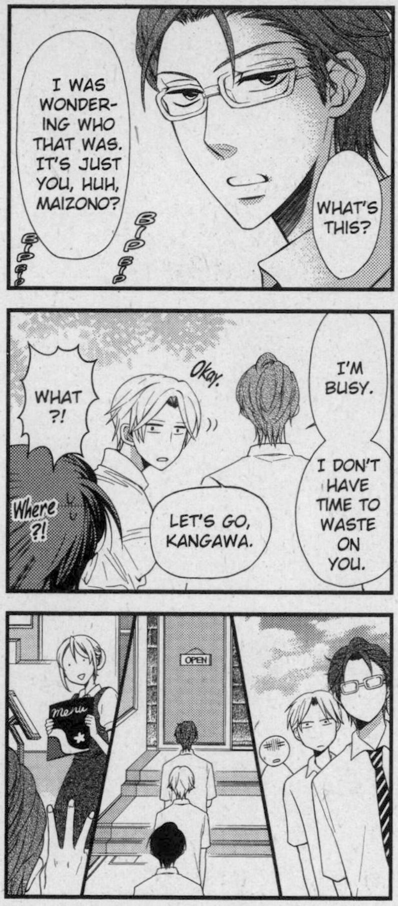
WHAT'S THIS?
I WAS WONDERING WHO THAT WAS. IT'S JUST YOU, HUH, MAIZONO?
BIP BIP
BIP BIP
I'M BUSY.
I DON'T HAVE TIME TO WASTE ON YOU.
Okay.
LET'S GO, KANGAWA.
WHAT?!
Where?!
OPEN
Menu
THANKS FOR INVITING US TO TEA.
WHAT?!
THAT WAS AN INVITATION?!
I don't understand!

HEARTWARMING PART 1

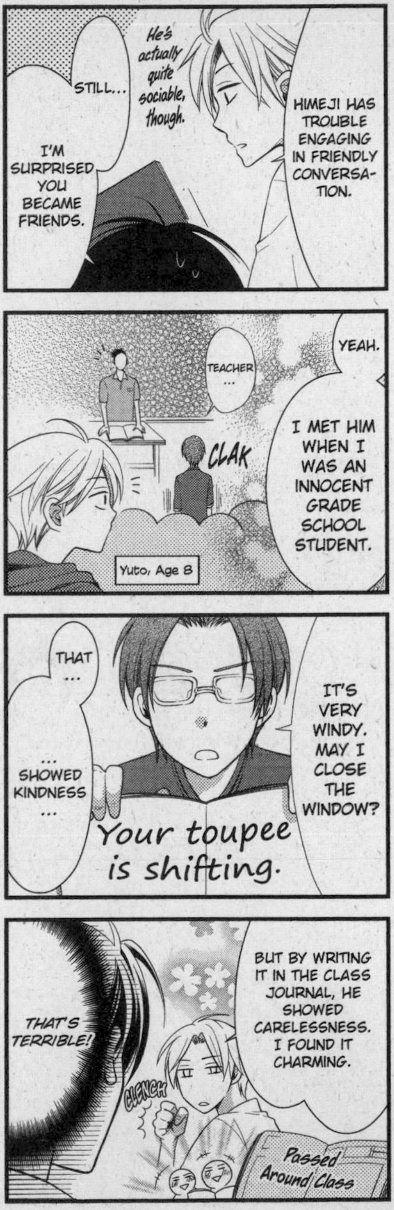
HIMEJI HAS TROUBLE ENGAGING IN FRIENDLY CONVERSA-TION.
He's actually quite sociable, though.
STILL...
I'M SURPRISED YOU BECAME FRIENDS.
YEAH.
I MET HIM WHEN I WAS AN INNOCENT GRADE SCHOOL STUDENT.
TEACHER...
CLAK
Yuto, Age 8
IT'S VERY WINDY. MAY I CLOSE THE WINDOW?
Your toupee is shifting.
THAT...
...SHOWED KINDNESS...
BUT BY WRITING IT IN THE CLASS JOURNAL, HE SHOWED CARELESSNESS. I FOUND IT CHARMING.
Passed Around Class
CLENCH
THAT'S TERRIBLE!

HEARTWARMING PART 2

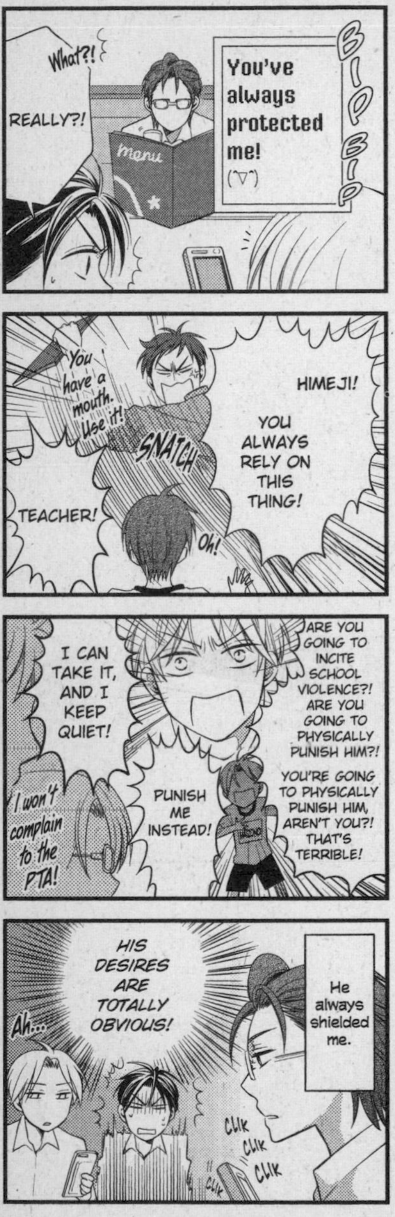
BIP BIP
You've always protected me! (^▽^)
menu
What?!
REALLY?!
HIMEJI!
YOU ALWAYS RELY ON THIS THING!
You have a mouth. Use it!
SNATCH
Oh!
TEACHER!
ARE YOU GOING TO INCITE SCHOOL VIOLENCE?! ARE YOU GOING TO PHYSICALLY PUNISH HIM?!
YOU'RE GOING TO PHYSICALLY PUNISH HIM, AREN'T YOU?! THAT'S TERRIBLE!
I CAN TAKE IT, AND I KEEP QUIET!
PUNISH ME INSTEAD!
I won't complain to the PTA!
He always shielded me.
HIS DESIRES ARE TOTALLY OBVIOUS!
CLIK CLIK CLIK
CLIK
Ah...

ON THE SIDE: FAMILY RESTAURANT

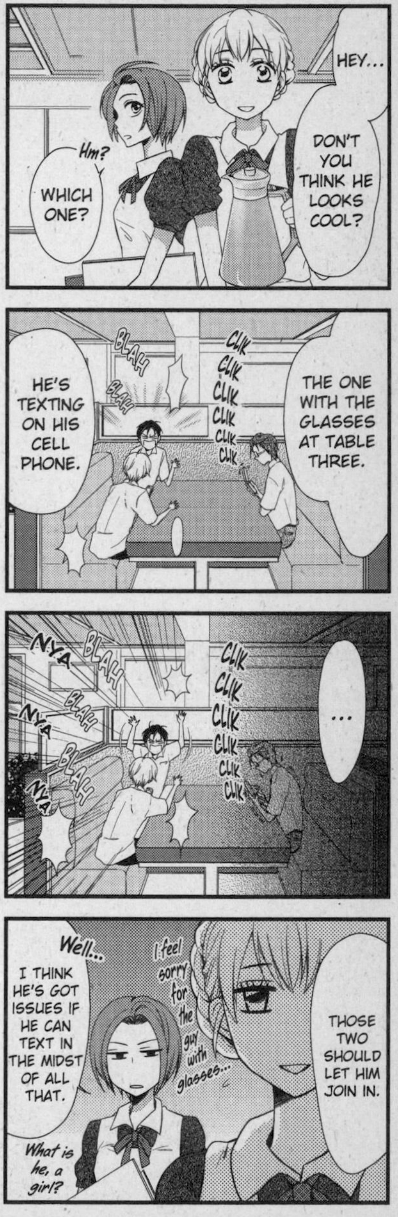
HEY...
DON'T YOU THINK HE LOOKS COOL?
Hm?
WHICH ONE?
CLIK CLIK CLIK CLIK CLIK CLIK
THE ONE WITH THE GLASSES AT TABLE THREE.
BLAH BLAH
HE'S TEXTING ON HIS CELL PHONE.
...
CLIK CLIK CLIK CLIK CLIK CLIK
BLAH BLAH BLAH
NYA NYA NYA
THOSE TWO SHOULD LET HIM JOIN IN.
I feel sorry for the guy with glasses...
Well...
I THINK HE'S GOT ISSUES IF HE CAN TEXT IN THE MIDST OF ALL THAT.
What is he, a girl?

ORDER UP

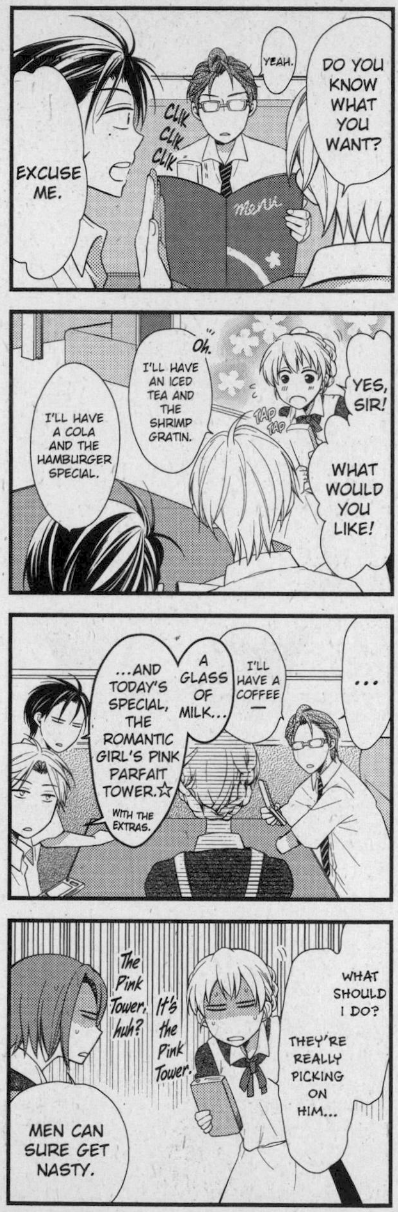
DO YOU KNOW WHAT YOU WANT?
YEAH.
CLIK CLIK CLIK
EXCUSE ME.
YES, SIR!
WHAT WOULD YOU LIKE!
TAP TAP
Oh.
I'LL HAVE AN ICED TEA AND THE SHRIMP GRATIN.
I'LL HAVE A COLA AND THE HAMBURGER SPECIAL.
...
I'LL HAVE A COFFEE —
A GLASS OF MILK...
...AND TODAY'S SPECIAL, THE ROMANTIC GIRL'S PINK PARFAIT TOWER.☆
WITH THE EXTRAS.
WHAT SHOULD I DO?
THEY'RE REALLY PICKING ON HIM...
It's the Pink Tower.
The Pink Tower, huh?
MEN CAN SURE GET NASTY.

HE'S DOING WELL FOR SOME REASON

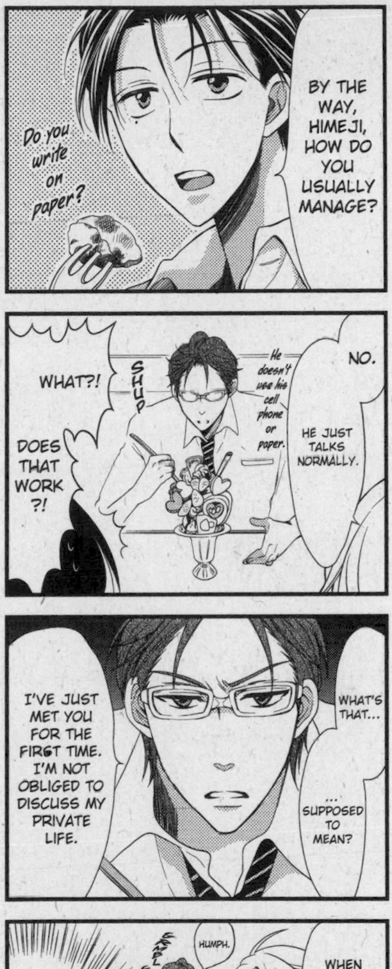
BY THE WAY, HIMEJI, HOW DO YOU USUALLY MANAGE?
Do you write on paper?
NO.
He doesn't use his cell phone or paper.
HE JUST TALKS NORMALLY.
SHUP
WHAT?!
DOES THAT WORK?!
WHAT'S THAT...
...SUPPOSED TO MEAN?
I'VE JUST MET YOU FOR THE FIRST TIME. I'M NOT OBLIGED TO DISCUSS MY PRIVATE LIFE.
WHEN HIMEJI DOESN'T HAVE HIS CELL PHONE, HE JUST LOOKS LIKE AN INTELLIGENT, RATIONAL PERSON.
HUMPH.
GRMBL GRMBL
HEY! THAT'S NOT FAIR!

THE MECHANICS OF A TSUNDERE

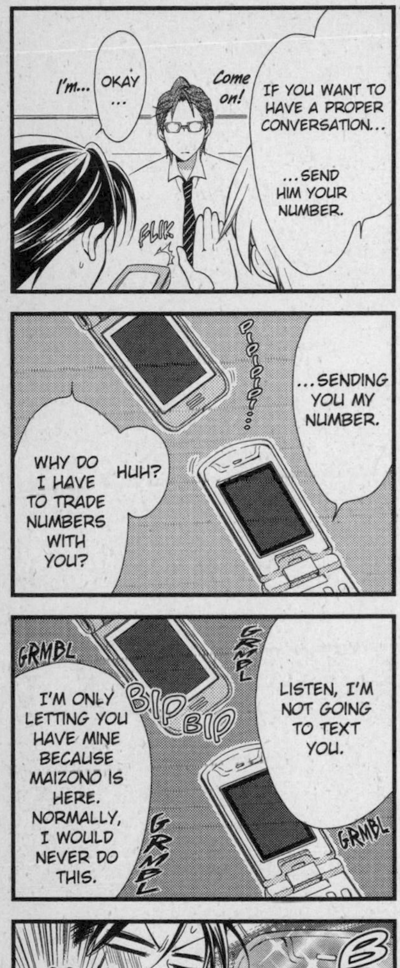
IF YOU WANT TO HAVE A PROPER CONVERSATION...
...SEND HIM YOUR NUMBER.
Come on!
OKAY...
I'm...
FLIK
...SENDING YOU MY NUMBER.
PIPIPIPIPI...
HUH?
WHY DO I HAVE TO TRADE NUMBERS WITH YOU?
LISTEN, I'M NOT GOING TO TEXT YOU.
GRMBL
BIP BIP
GRMBL
I'M ONLY LETTING YOU HAVE MINE BECAUSE MAIZONO IS HERE. NORMALLY, I WOULD NEVER DO THIS.
GRMBL
BIPBIP♪
New Text
Himeji
Subject Thanks You!
Message
I'm sorry for saying mean things to you earlier. Those aren't my true feelings! Hope to see you around!
Send
Menu
THUMP THUMP
MUSHY!

THE CHOSEN ONES

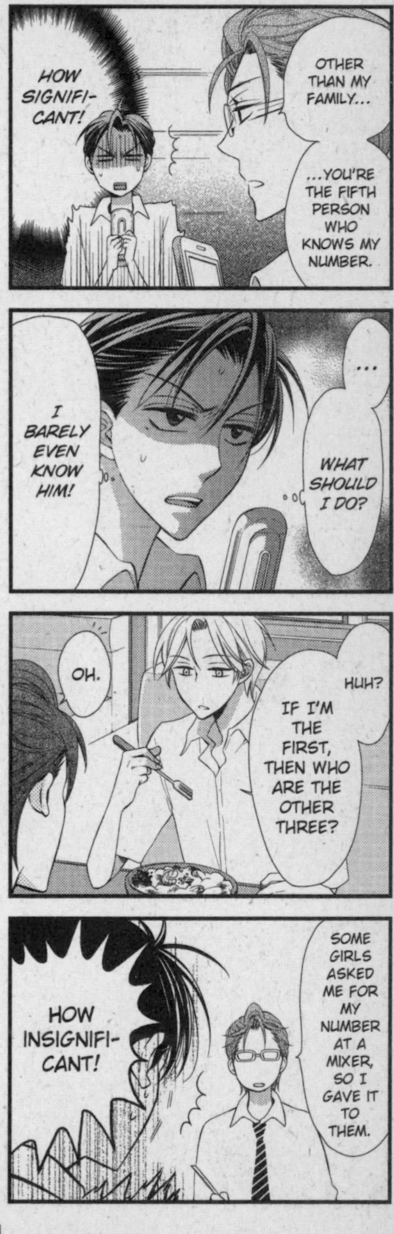
OTHER THAN MY FAMILY...
...YOU'RE THE FIFTH PERSON WHO KNOWS MY NUMBER.
HOW SIGNIFICANT!
...
WHAT SHOULD I DO?
I BARELY EVEN KNOW HIM!
HUH?
IF I'M THE FIRST, THEN WHO ARE THE OTHER THREE?
OH.
SOME GIRLS ASKED ME FOR MY NUMBER AT A MIXER, SO I GAVE IT TO THEM.
HOW INSIGNIFICANT!

A MAN'S PERSONALITY GAP

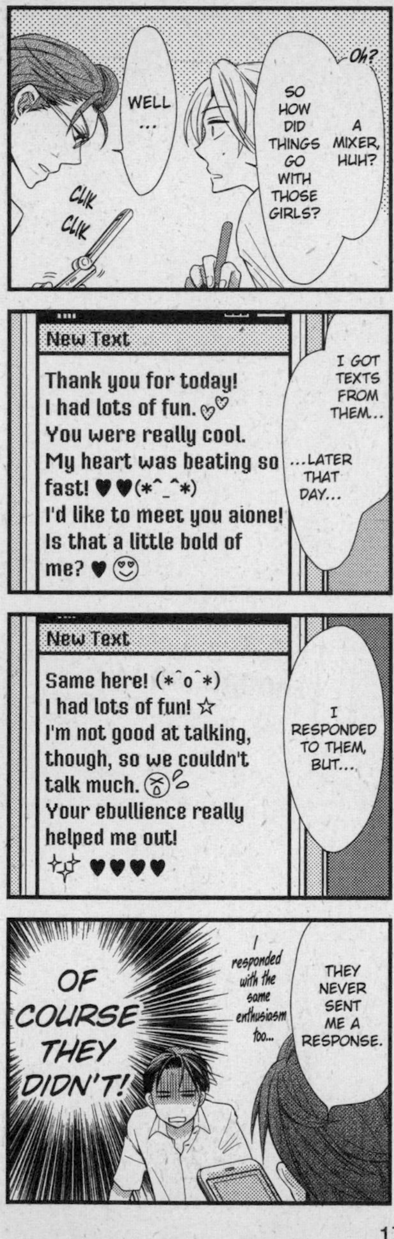
Oh?
A MIXER, HUH?
SO HOW DID THINGS GO WITH THOSE GIRLS?
WELL...
CLIK CLIK
I GOT TEXTS FROM THEM...
...LATER THAT DAY...
New Text
Thank you for today! I had lots of fun. ♡♡ You were really cool. My heart was beating so fast! ♥♥(*^_^*) I'd like to meet you aione! Is that a little bold of me? ♥
I RESPONDED TO THEM, BUT...
New Text
Same here! (*^o^*) I had lots of fun! ☆ I'm not good at talking, though, so we couldn't talk much. Your ebullience really helped me out! ♥♥♥♥
THEY NEVER SENT ME A RESPONSE.
I responded with the same enthusiasm too...
OF COURSE THEY DIDN'T!

SOMEONE TEACH ME

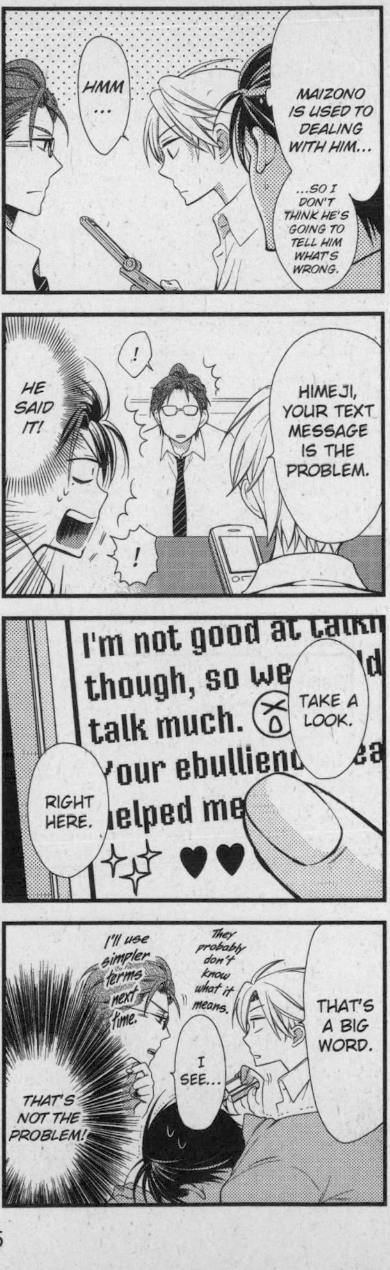
MAIZONO IS USED TO DEALING WITH HIM...
...SO I DON'T THINK HE'S GOING TO TELL HIM WHAT'S WRONG.
HMM ...
HIMEJI, YOUR TEXT MESSAGE IS THE PROBLEM.
!
HE SAID IT!
!
TAKE A LOOK.
I'm not good at talk
though, so we
talk much.
Your ebullien
helped me
RIGHT HERE.
THAT'S A BIG WORD.
They probably don't know what it means.
I'll use simpler terms next time.
I SEE...
THAT'S NOT THE PROBLEM!

KANGAWA IS A NICE GUY

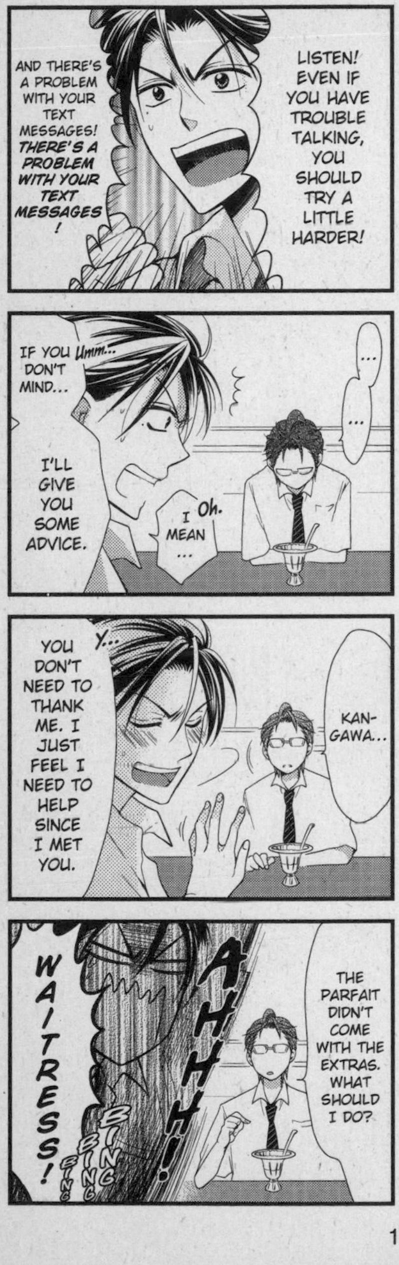
LISTEN! EVEN IF YOU HAVE TROUBLE TALKING, YOU SHOULD TRY A LITTLE HARDER!
AND THERE'S A PROBLEM WITH YOUR TEXT MESSAGES! THERE'S A PROBLEM WITH YOUR TEXT MESSAGES!
... ...
Umm...
IF YOU DON'T MIND...
Oh.
I MEAN ...
I'LL GIVE YOU SOME ADVICE.
KAN-GAWA...
Y...
YOU DON'T NEED TO THANK ME. I JUST FEEL I NEED TO HELP SINCE I MET YOU.
THE PARFAIT DIDN'T COME WITH THE EXTRAS. WHAT SHOULD I DO?
AHHH!
BING BING BING
WAITRESS!

WE'RE FRIENDS, AFTER ALL

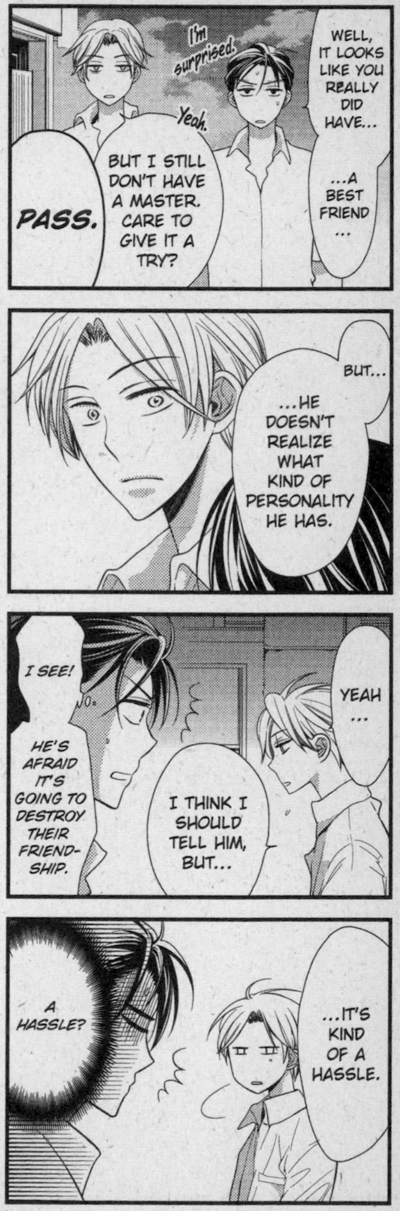
WELL, IT LOOKS LIKE YOU REALLY DID HAVE...
...A BEST FRIEND...
I'm surprised.
Yeah.
BUT I STILL DON'T HAVE A MASTER. CARE TO GIVE IT A TRY?
PASS.
BUT...
...HE DOESN'T REALIZE WHAT KIND OF PERSONALITY HE HAS.
YEAH...
I THINK I SHOULD TELL HIM, BUT...
I SEE!
HE'S AFRAID IT'S GOING TO DESTROY THEIR FRIEND-SHIP.
...IT'S KIND OF A HASSLE.
A HASSLE?

LEGENDARY POPULARITY

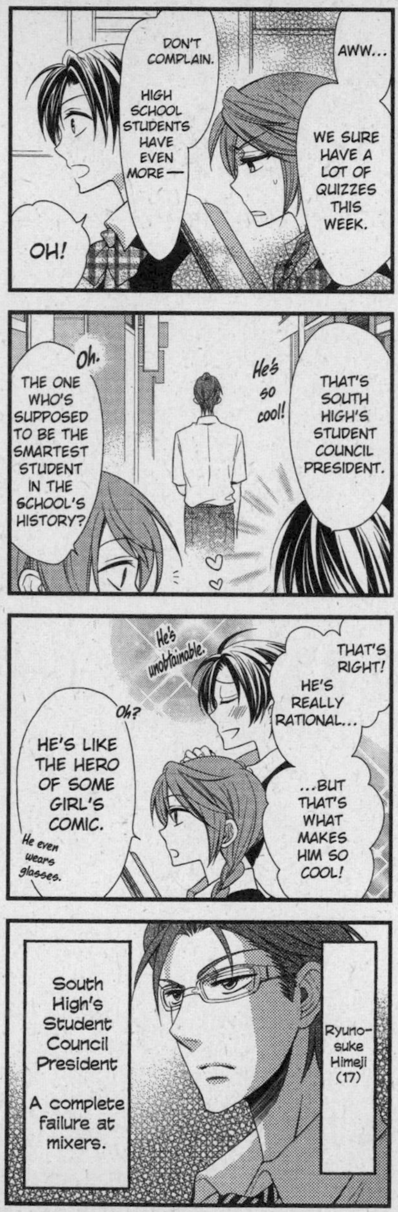
AWW...
WE SURE HAVE A LOT OF QUIZZES THIS WEEK.
DON'T COMPLAIN.
HIGH SCHOOL STUDENTS HAVE EVEN MORE—
OH!
THAT'S SOUTH HIGH'S STUDENT COUNCIL PRESIDENT.
He's so cool!
Oh.
THE ONE WHO'S SUPPOSED TO BE THE SMARTEST STUDENT IN THE SCHOOL'S HISTORY?
THAT'S RIGHT! HE'S REALLY RATIONAL...
He's unobtainable.
...BUT THAT'S WHAT MAKES HIM SO COOL!
Oh?
HE'S LIKE THE HERO OF SOME GIRL'S COMIC.
He even wears glasses.
Ryuno-suke Himeji (17)
South High's Student Council President
A complete failure at mixers.

North South East West

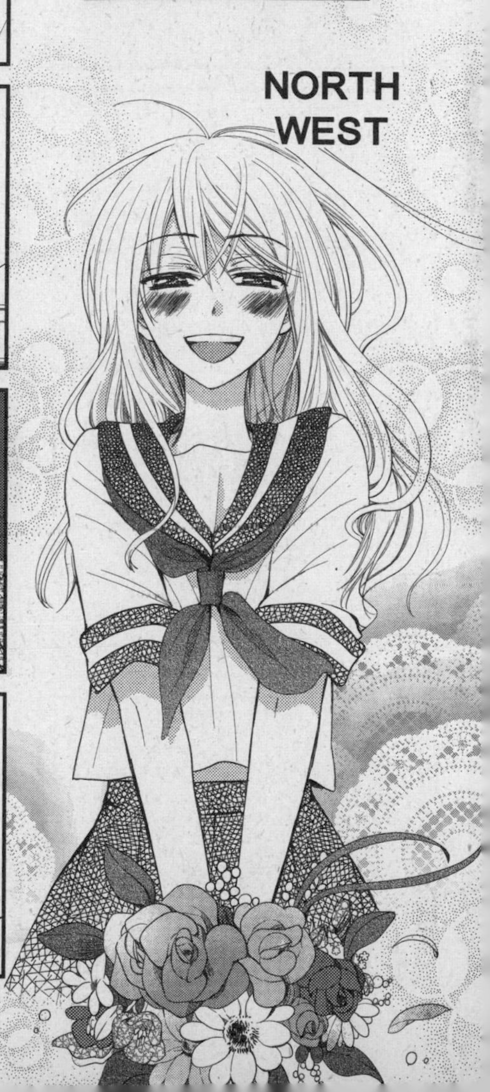
NORTH WEST

THE PEOPLE OF WEST HIGH

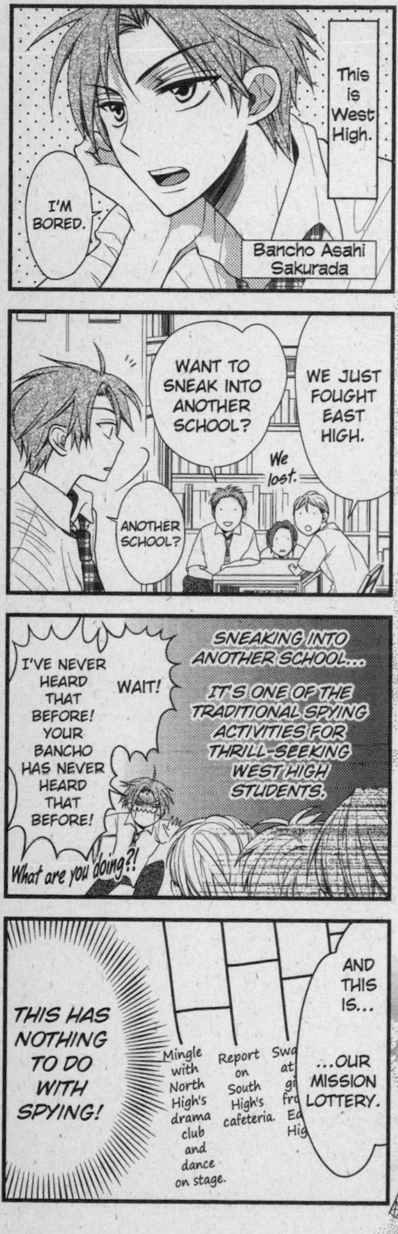
This is West High.
Bancho Asahi Sakurada
I'M BORED.
WE JUST FOUGHT EAST HIGH.
We lost.
WANT TO SNEAK INTO ANOTHER SCHOOL?
ANOTHER SCHOOL?
SNEAKING INTO ANOTHER SCHOOL...
IT'S ONE OF THE TRADITIONAL SPYING ACTIVITIES FOR THRILL-SEEKING WEST HIGH STUDENTS.
WAIT!
I'VE NEVER HEARD THAT BEFORE! YOUR BANCHO HAS NEVER HEARD THAT BEFORE!
What are you doing?!
AND THIS IS...
...OUR MISSION LOTTERY.
Report on South High's cafeteria.
Mingle with North High's drama club and dance on stage.
THIS HAS NOTHING TO DO WITH SPYING!

SPY ACTIVITIES

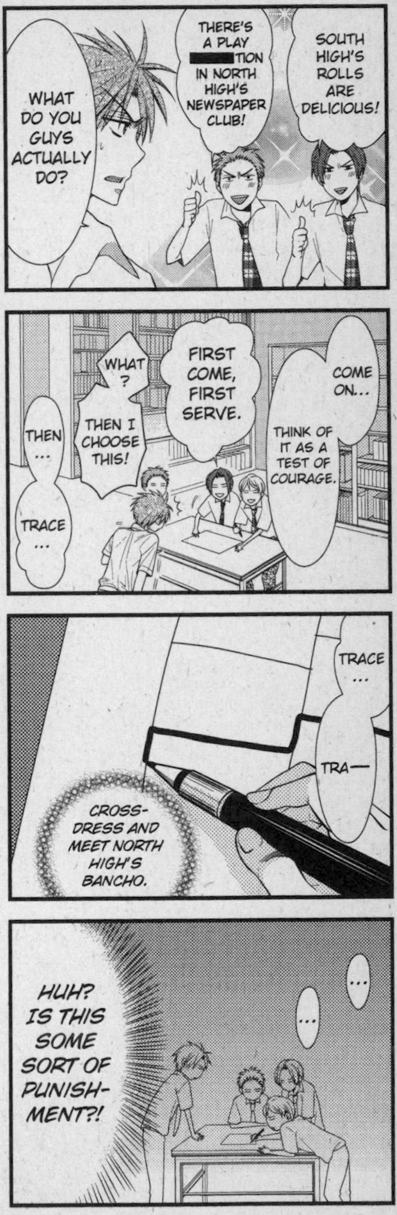
SOUTH HIGH'S ROLLS ARE DELICIOUS!
THERE'S A PLAY [redacted]TION IN NORTH HIGH'S NEWSPAPER CLUB!
WHAT DO YOU GUYS ACTUALLY DO?
COME ON...
THINK OF IT AS A TEST OF COURAGE.
FIRST COME, FIRST SERVE.
WHAT?
THEN I CHOOSE THIS!
THEN...
TRACE...
TRACE...
TRA—
CROSS-DRESS AND MEET NORTH HIGH'S BANCHO.
...
...
HUH? IS THIS SOME SORT OF PUNISHMENT?!

100% SUCCESS RATE

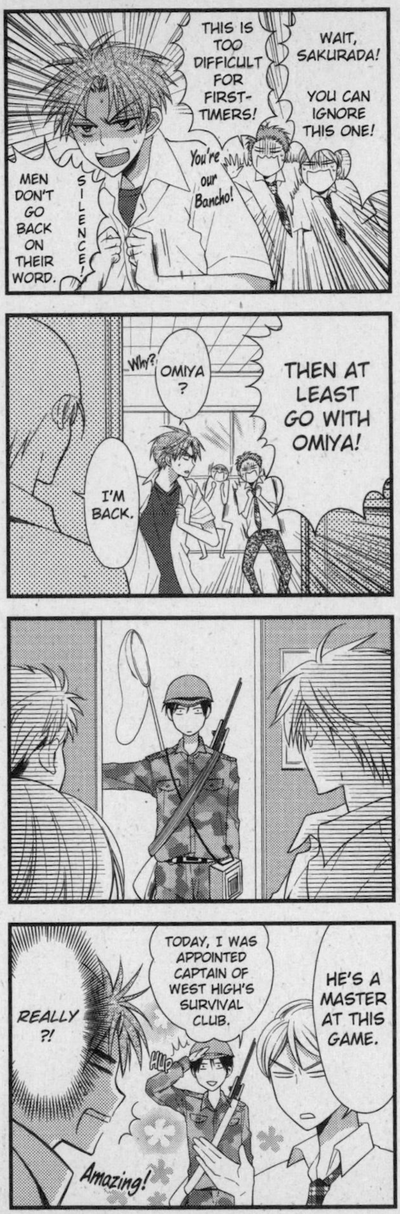
WAIT, SAKURADA!
YOU CAN IGNORE THIS ONE!
THIS IS TOO DIFFICULT FOR FIRST-TIMERS!
You're our Bancho!
SILENCE!
MEN DON'T GO BACK ON THEIR WORD.
THEN AT LEAST GO WITH OMIYA!
OMIYA?
Why?
I'M BACK.
HE'S A MASTER AT THIS GAME.
TODAY, I WAS APPOINTED CAPTAIN OF WEST HIGH'S SURVIVAL CLUB.
HUP
REALLY?!
Amazing!

OMIYA

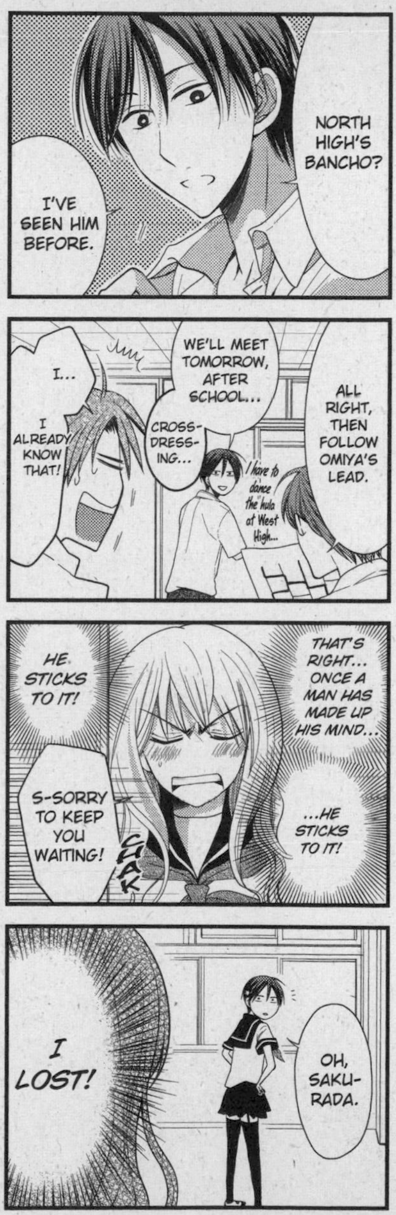
NORTH HIGH'S BANCHO?
I'VE SEEN HIM BEFORE.
ALL RIGHT, THEN FOLLOW OMIYA'S LEAD.
WE'LL MEET TOMORROW, AFTER SCHOOL...
CROSS-DRESSING...
I have to dance the "hula" at West High...
I...
I ALREADY KNOW THAT!
THAT'S RIGHT... ONCE A MAN HAS MADE UP HIS MIND...
HE STICKS TO IT!
...HE STICKS TO IT!
S-SORRY TO KEEP YOU WAITING!
CHAK
OH, SAKURADA.
I LOST!

A MAN'S PRIDE

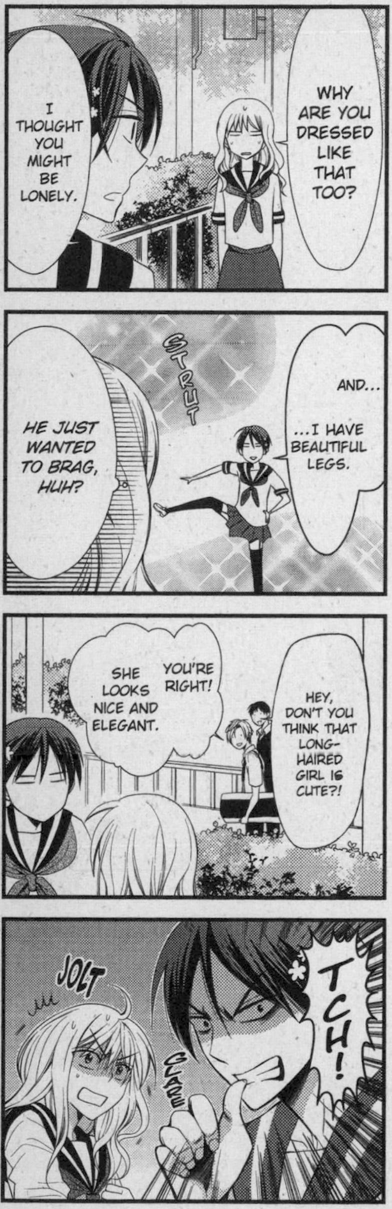
WHY ARE YOU DRESSED LIKE THAT TOO?
I THOUGHT YOU MIGHT BE LONELY.
AND...
...I HAVE BEAUTIFUL LEGS.
STRUT
HE JUST WANTED TO BRAG, HUH?
HEY, DON'T YOU THINK THAT LONG-HAIRED GIRL IS CUTE?!
YOU'RE RIGHT!
SHE LOOKS NICE AND ELEGANT.
TCH!
JOLT
GLARE

THE LEGEND OF NORTH HIGH

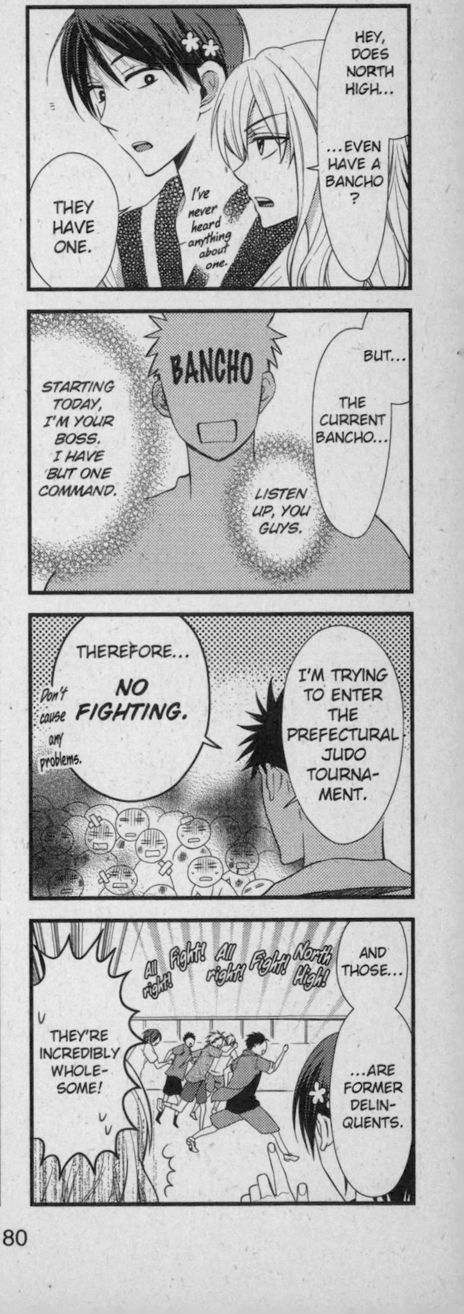
HEY, DOES NORTH HIGH...
...EVEN HAVE A BANCHO?
I've never heard anything about one.
THEY HAVE ONE.
BUT...
THE CURRENT BANCHO...
BANCHO
LISTEN UP, YOU GUYS.
STARTING TODAY, I'M YOUR BOSS. I HAVE BUT ONE COMMAND.
I'M TRYING TO ENTER THE PREFECTURAL JUDO TOURNA-MENT.
THEREFORE... NO FIGHTING.
Don't cause any problems.
AND THOSE...
...ARE FORMER DELIN-QUENTS.
North High! Fight! All right! Fight! All right!
THEY'RE INCREDIBLY WHOLE-SOME!

DRY RUN

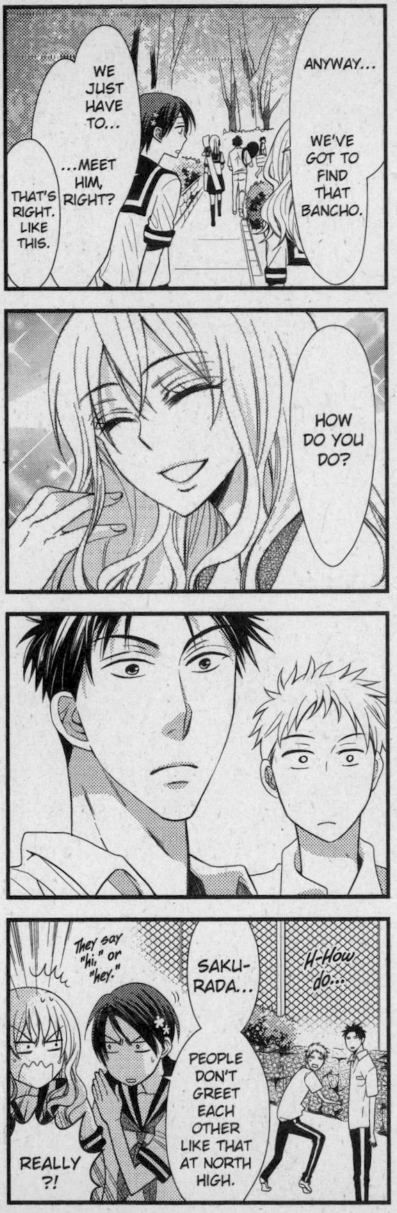
ANYWAY...
WE'VE GOT TO FIND THAT BANCHO.
WE JUST HAVE TO...
...MEET HIM, RIGHT?
THAT'S RIGHT. LIKE THIS.
HOW DO YOU DO?
H-How do...
SAKU-RADA...
PEOPLE DON'T GREET EACH OTHER LIKE THAT AT NORTH HIGH.
They say "hi," or "hey."
REALLY ?!

A REGULAR GIRL

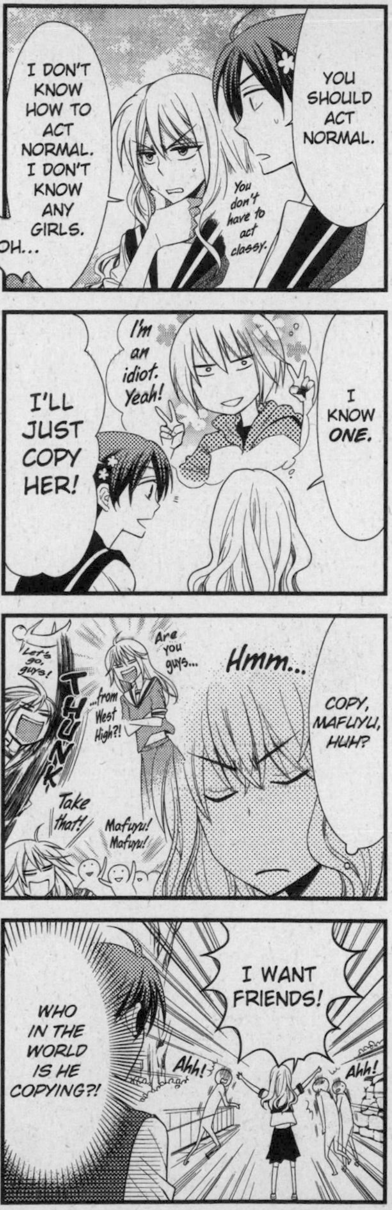
YOU SHOULD ACT NORMAL.
You don't have to act classy.
I DON'T KNOW HOW TO ACT NORMAL. I DON'T KNOW ANY GIRLS.
OH...
I KNOW ONE.
I'm an idiot. Yeah!
I'LL JUST COPY HER!
COPY, MAFUYU, HUH?
Hmm...
Are you guys...
...from West High?!
Let's go, guys!
THUNK
Take that!
Mafuyu! Mafuyu!
I WANT FRIENDS!
Ahh!
Ahh!
WHO IN THE WORLD IS HE COPYING?!

SPORTSMANSHIP

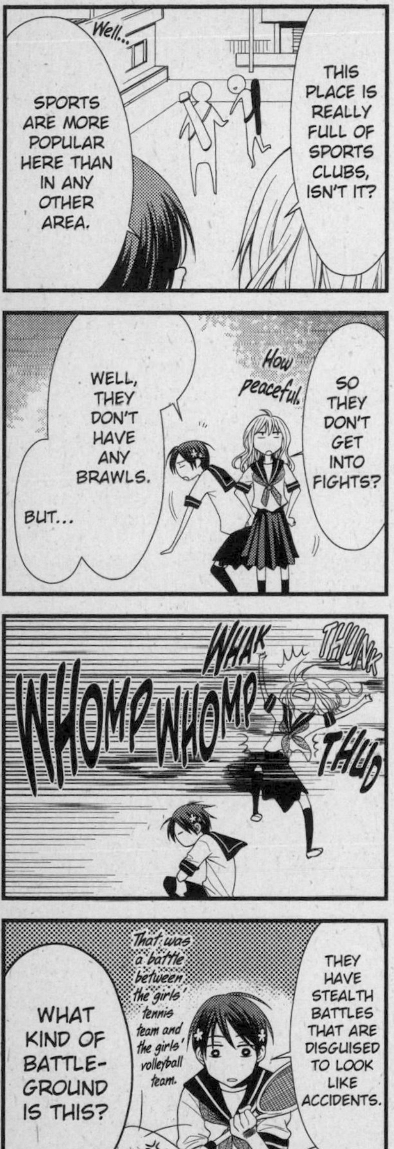
THIS PLACE IS REALLY FULL OF SPORTS CLUBS, ISN'T IT?
Well...
SPORTS ARE MORE POPULAR HERE THAN IN ANY OTHER AREA.
SO THEY DON'T GET INTO FIGHTS?
How peaceful.
WELL, THEY DON'T HAVE ANY BRAWLS.
BUT...
THUNK
WHAK
WHOMP WHOMP
THUD
THEY HAVE STEALTH BATTLES THAT ARE DISGUISED TO LOOK LIKE ACCIDENTS.
That was a battle between the girls' tennis team and the girls' volleyball team.
WHAT KIND OF BATTLE-GROUND IS THIS?

SAKURADA-ISM

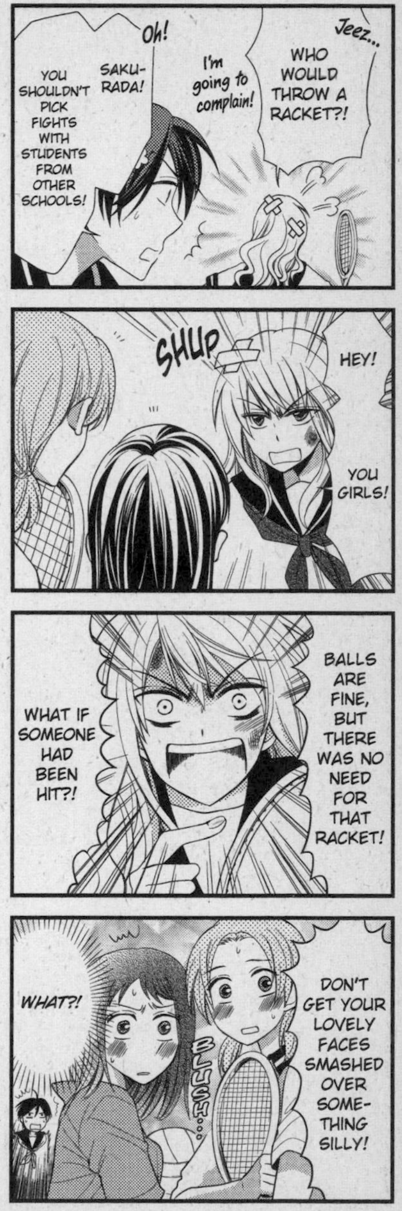
Jeez...
WHO WOULD THROW A RACKET?!
I'm going to complain!
Oh!
SAKURADA!
YOU SHOULDN'T PICK FIGHTS WITH STUDENTS FROM OTHER SCHOOLS!
HEY!
SHUP
YOU GIRLS!
BALLS ARE FINE, BUT THERE WAS NO NEED FOR THAT RACKET!
WHAT IF SOMEONE HAD BEEN HIT?!
DON'T GET YOUR LOVELY FACES SMASHED OVER SOMETHING SILLY!
BLUSH...
WHAT?!

STILL CROSS-DRESSING

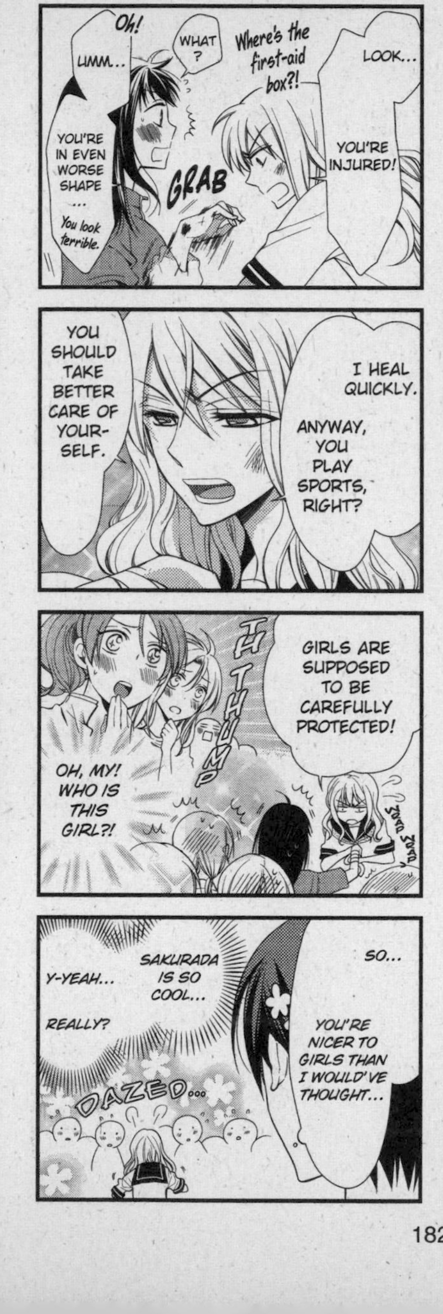
LOOK...
YOU'RE INJURED!
Where's the first-aid box?!
WHAT?
Oh!
UMM...
GRAB
YOU'RE IN EVEN WORSE SHAPE...
You look terrible.
I HEAL QUICKLY.
ANYWAY, YOU PLAY SPORTS, RIGHT?
YOU SHOULD TAKE BETTER CARE OF YOURSELF.
GIRLS ARE SUPPOSED TO BE CAREFULLY PROTECTED!
THTHUMP
WRAP WRAP
OH, MY! WHO IS THIS GIRL?!
SO...
YOU'RE NICER TO GIRLS THAN I WOULD'VE THOUGHT...
SAKURADA IS SO COOL...
Y-YEAH...
REALLY?
DAZED...

NICE TO GIRLS

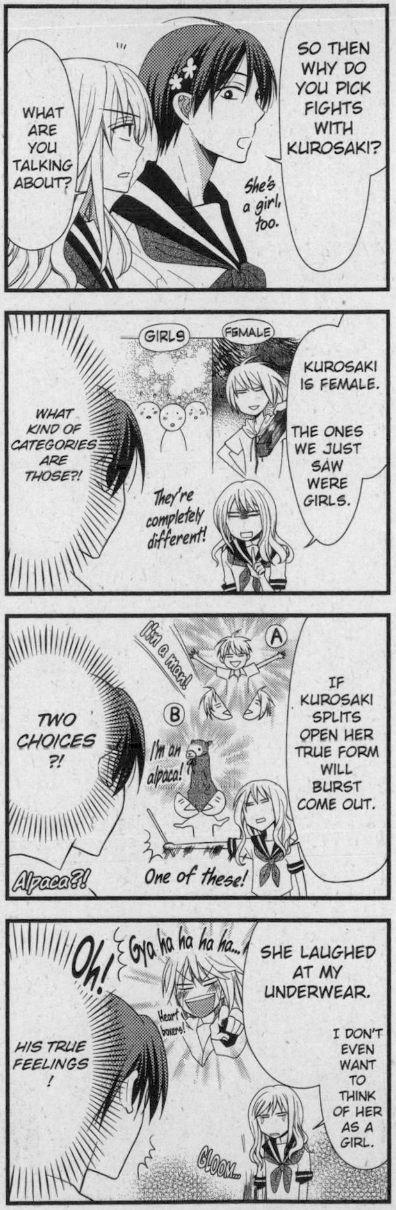
SO THEN WHY DO YOU PICK FIGHTS WITH KUROSAKI?
She's a girl, too.
WHAT ARE YOU TALKING ABOUT?
KUROSAKI IS FEMALE.
THE ONES WE JUST SAW WERE GIRLS.
FEMALE
GIRLS
They're completely different!
WHAT KIND OF CATEGORIES ARE THOSE?!
IF KUROSAKI SPLITS OPEN HER TRUE FORM WILL BURST COME OUT.
A
I'm a man!
B
I'm an alpaca!
TWO CHOICES ?!
One of these!
Alpaca?!
SHE LAUGHED AT MY UNDERWEAR.
Gya ha ha ha ha...
Oh!
Heart boxers!
I DON'T EVEN WANT TO THINK OF HER AS A GIRL.
HIS TRUE FEELINGS !
GLOOM...

AN ACTIVE ROLE

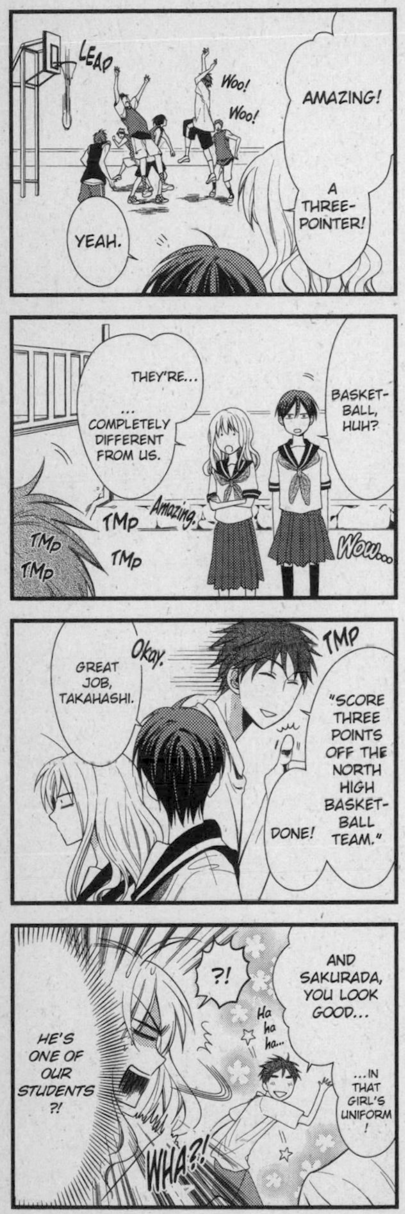
AMAZING!
A THREE-POINTER!
Woo!
Woo!
LEAP
YEAH.
BASKET-BALL, HUH?
THEY'RE...
...COMPLETELY DIFFERENT FROM US.
Wow...
Amazing.
TMP
TMP
TMP
TMP
TMP
"SCORE THREE POINTS OFF THE NORTH HIGH BASKET-BALL TEAM."
DONE!
Okay.
GREAT JOB, TAKAHASHI.
AND SAKURADA, YOU LOOK GOOD...
...IN THAT GIRL'S UNIFORM!
Ha ha ha...
?!
HE'S ONE OF OUR STUDENTS ?!
WHA?!

MISSION COMPLETE

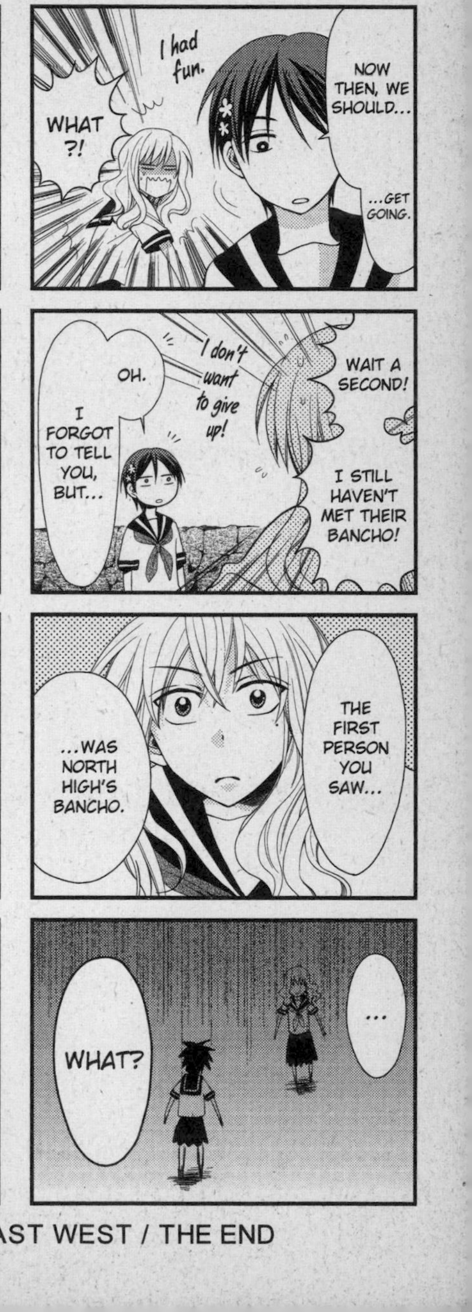
NOW THEN, WE SHOULD...
...GET GOING.
I had fun.
WHAT ?!
WAIT A SECOND!
I STILL HAVEN'T MET THEIR BANCHO!
I don't want to give up!
OH.
I FORGOT TO TELL YOU, BUT...
THE FIRST PERSON YOU SAW...
...WAS NORTH HIGH'S BANCHO.
...
WHAT?

THAT WON'T WORK

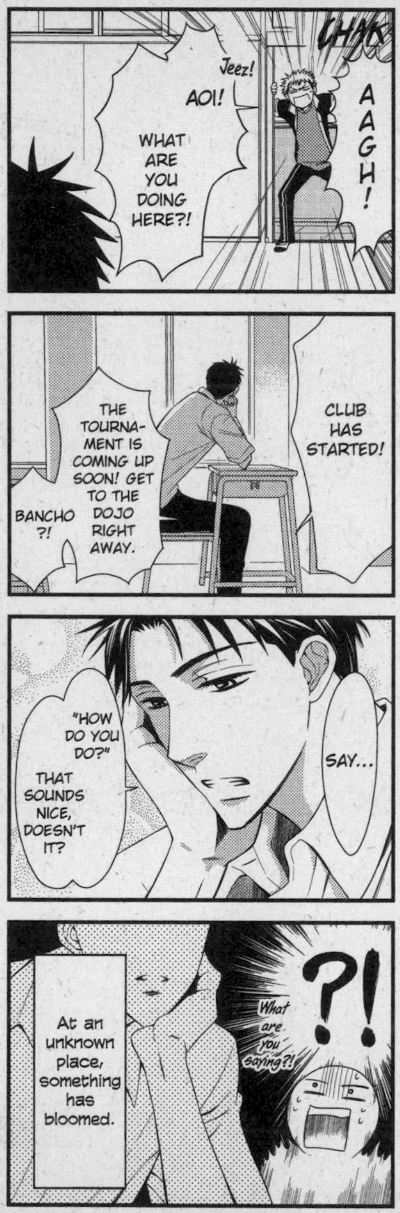
AAGH!
CHAK
Jeez!
AOI!
WHAT ARE YOU DOING HERE?!
CLUB HAS STARTED!
THE TOURNAMENT IS COMING UP SOON! GET TO THE DOJO RIGHT AWAY.
BANCHO ?!
SAY...
"HOW DO YOU DO?" THAT SOUNDS NICE, DOESN'T IT?
?!
What are you saying?!
At an unknown place, something has bloomed.

NORTH SOUTH EAST WEST / THE END

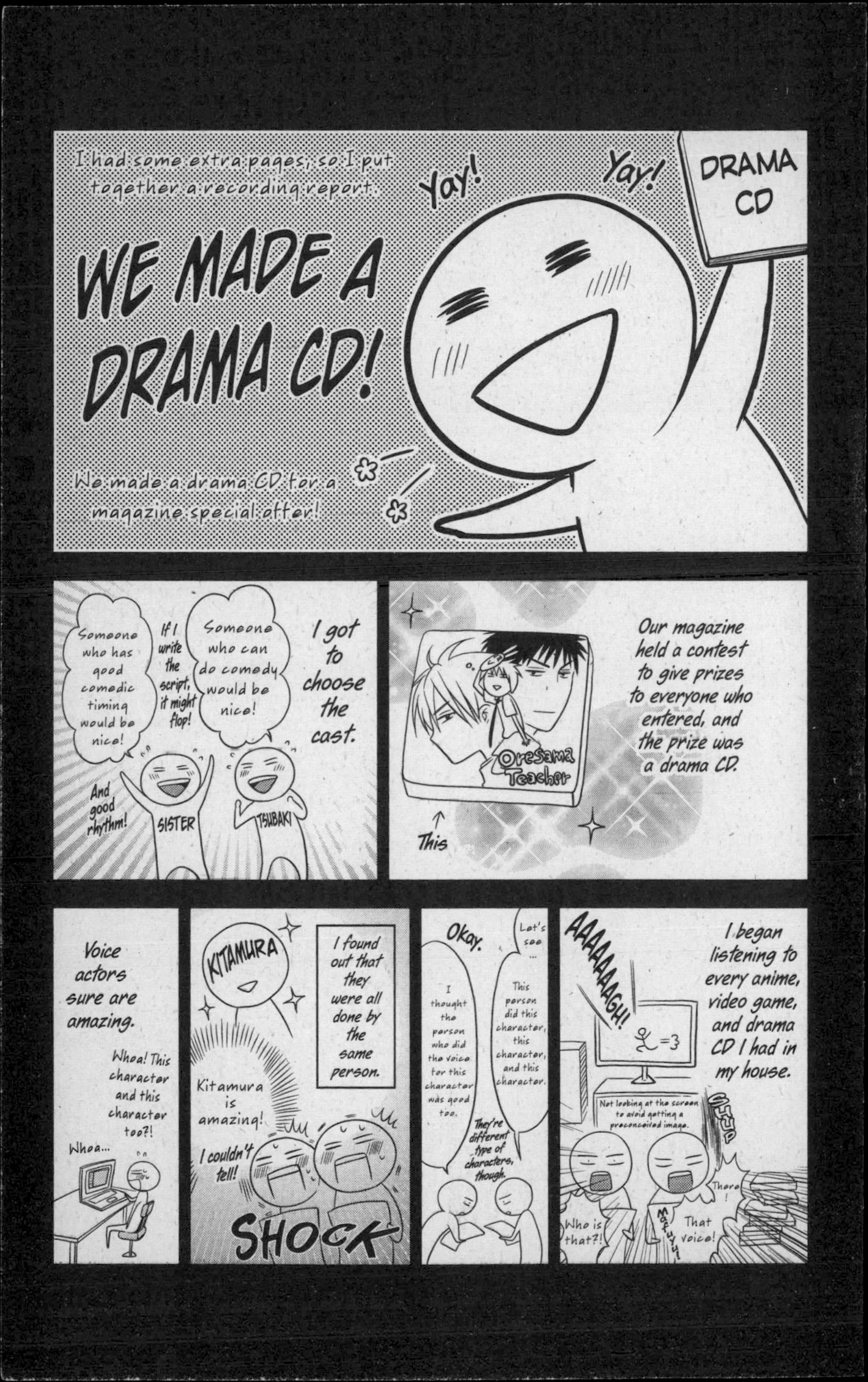
DRAMA CD
Yay!
Yay!
I had some extra pages, so I put together a recording report.
WE MADE A DRAMA CD!
We made a drama CD for a magazine special offer!
Our magazine held a contest to give prizes to everyone who entered, and the prize was a drama CD.
Oresama Teacher
This
I got to choose the cast.
Someone who can do comedy would be nice!
If I write the script, it might flop!
Someone who has good comedic timing would be nice!
TSUBAKI
SISTER
And good rhythm!
I began listening to every anime, video game, and drama CD I had in my house.
AAAAAAGH!
=3
Not looking at the screen to avoid getting a preconceived image.
There!
That voice!
Mafuyu!
Who is that?!
Let's see...
Okay.
This person did this character, this character, and this character.
I thought the person who did the voice for this character was good too.
They're different type of characters, though.
I found out that they were all done by the same person.
KITAMURA
Kitamura is amazing!
I couldn't tell!
SHOCK
Voice actors sure are amazing.
Whoa! This character and this character too?!
Whoa...

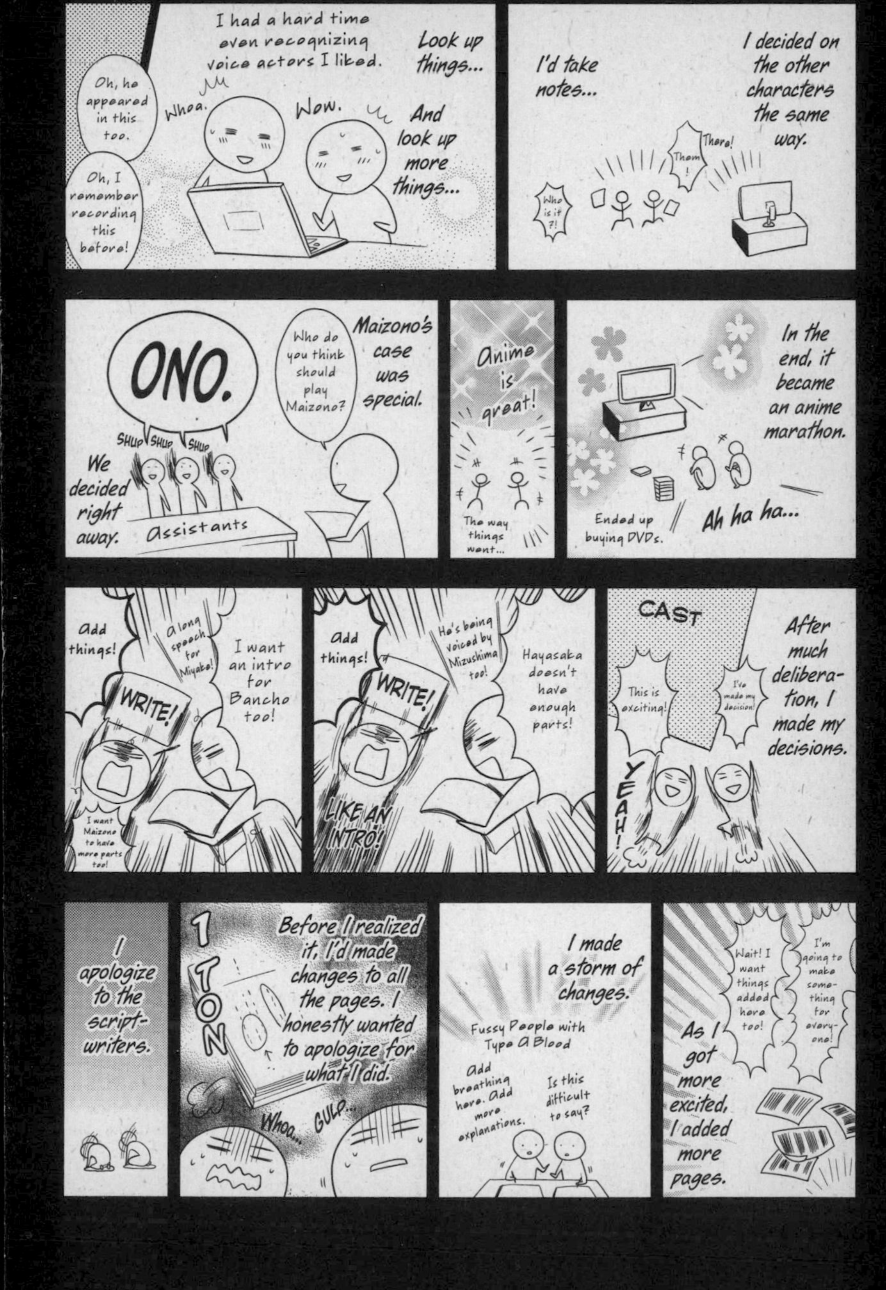
I decided on the other characters the same way.
There!
Them!
Who is it?!
I'd take notes...
Look up things...
I had a hard time even recognizing voice actors I liked.
Wow.
Whoa.
And look up more things...
Oh, he appeared in this too.
Oh, I remember recording this before!
In the end, it became an anime marathon.
Ah ha ha...
Ended up buying DVDs.
Anime is great!
The way things went...
Maizono's case was special.
Who do you think should play Maizono?
ONO.
SHUP SHUP SHUP
We decided right away.
Assistants
After much deliberation, I made my decisions.
CAST
I've made my decision!
This is exciting!
YEAH!
Hayasaka doesn't have enough parts!
He's being voiced by Mizushima too!
Add things!
WRITE!
LIKE AN INTRO!
I want an intro for Bancho too!
A long speech for Miyako!
Add things!
WRITE!
I want Maizono to have more parts too!
I'm going to make something for everyone!
Wait! I want things added here too!
As I got more excited, I added more pages.
I made a storm of changes.
Fussy People with Type A Blood
Is this difficult to say?
Add breathing here. Add more explanations.
Before I realized it, I'd made changes to all the pages. I honestly wanted to apologize for what I did.
1 TON
Whoa...
GULP...
I apologize to the script-writers.

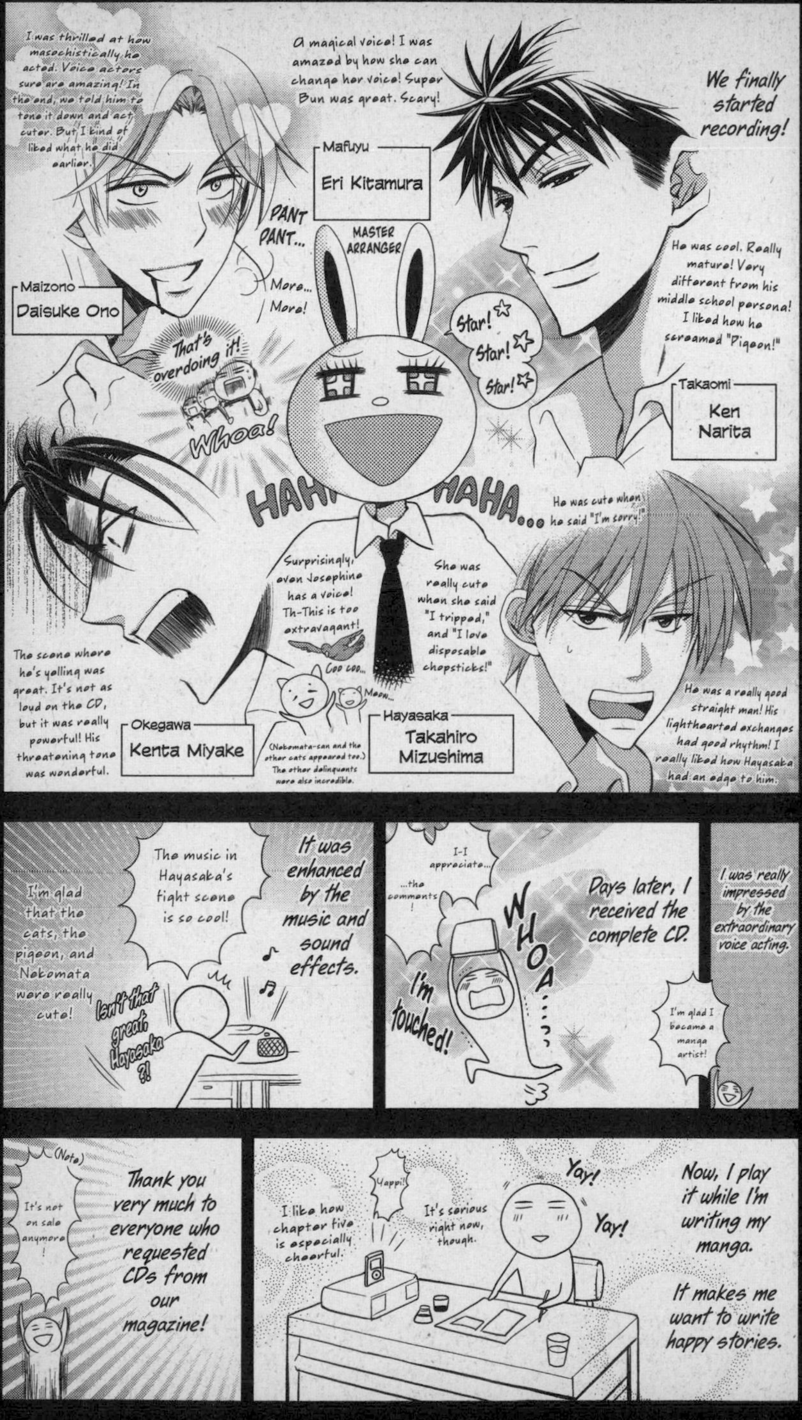
We finally started recording!
Takaomi
Ken Narita
He was cool. Really mature! Very different from his middle school persona! I liked how he screamed "Pigeon!"
Mafuyu
Eri Kitamura
A magical voice! I was amazed by how she can change her voice! Super Bun was great. Scary!
MASTER ARRANGER
Star!
Star!
Star!
PANT PANT...
More... More!
Maizono
Daisuke Ono
I was thrilled at how masochistically he acted. Voice actors sure are amazing! In the end, we told him to tone it down and act cuter. But I kind of liked what he did earlier.
That's overdoing it!
Whoa!
HAHA...
He was cute when he said "I'm sorry!"
Hayasaka
Takahiro Mizushima
He was a really good straight man! His lighthearted exchanges had good rhythm! I really liked how Hayasaka had an edge to him.
She was really cute when she said "I tripped," and "I love disposable chopsticks!"
Surprisingly, even Josephine has a voice! Th-This is too extravagant!
Coo coo...
Meow...
(Nekomata-san and the other cats appeared too.) The other delinquents were also incredible.
Okegawa
Kenta Miyake
The scene where he's yelling was great. It's not as loud on the CD, but it was really powerful! His threatening tone was wonderful.
I was really impressed by the extraordinary voice acting.
I'm glad I became a manga artist!
Days later, I received the complete CD.
I-I appreciate...
...the comments!
WHOA...
I'm touched!
It was enhanced by the music and sound effects.
The music in Hayasaka's fight scene is so cool!
I'm glad that the cats, the pigeon, and Nekomata were really cute!
Isn't that great, Hayasaka?!
Now, I play it while I'm writing my manga.
It makes me want to write happy stories.
Yay!
Yay!
It's serious right now, though.
Yappi!
I like how chapter five is especially cheerful.
Thank you very much to everyone who requested CDs from our magazine!
(Note)
It's not on sale anymore!

Special Thanks!

Big thanks to my sister, my family, Toya-san, Shiina-san, Pochi-san, and all you readers!

Now then, this is the final page, but thanks very much for purchasing volume five! This time, Kangawa and Maizono were on the cover, so I tried to have them show up a lot in the comic strips in the back. I got a lot of page space, so I have twenty-four pages of extras. I'll be very happy if you enjoy it!

KLAKKA
CHAKKA
KLAKKA
CHAKKA
KLAKKA
CHAKKA
ZZZ...

The chapters that take place at the ocean are set two prefectures away. They probably didn't sit next to each other on the train home. (They are student and teacher, after all.)

End Notes

Page 54, panel 2: Hikaru Genji
The protagonist of *The Tale of Genji*, the first known novel. In the story, Genji raises a young girl to eventually be his wife.

Page 54, panel 5: Tsundere
A popular stereotype of someone (usually a woman) who is cold or prickly, but can show a kind and loving side.

Page 56, panel 3: 10,000 yen
About $122 U.S.

Page 72, panel 1: Ladybug Samba
"Tentoumushi no Samba." A popular song sung at weddings.

Page 98, panel 1: Gold angel
A small number of boxes of Choco Ball candies have tabs with gold or silver angels printed on them, which can be traded in for prizes.

Page 98, panel 3: Family altar
Homes in Japan often include small altars where the family can make offerings, display pictures of the deceased, and place good luck charms.

Page 106, panel 1: Slit-mouth Woman
Kuchisake-onna is a Japanese urban legend about a woman whose mouth is slit from ear to ear. She is said to walk around with a surgical mask and ask people if she is pretty. If they answer "yes," she'll remove the mask and ask "Am I pretty now?" If they answer "no," she'll slit their mouth to look like hers.

Izumi Tsubaki began drawing manga in her first year of high school. She was soon selected to be in the top ten of *Hana to Yume's* HMC (*Hana to Yume* Mangaka Course), and subsequently won *Hana to Yume's* Big Challenge contest. Her debut title, *Chijimete Distance* (Shrink the Distance), ran in 2002 in *Hana to Yume* magazine, issue 17. Her other works include *The Magic Touch* (*Oyayubi kara Romance*) and *Oresama Teacher*, which she is currently working on.

ORESAMA TEACHER
Vol. 5
Shojo Beat Edition

STORY AND ART BY
Izumi Tsubaki

English Translation & Adaptation/JN Productions
Touch-up Art & Lettering/Eric Erbes
Design/Yukiko Whitley
Editor/Pancha Diaz

ORESAMA TEACHER by Izumi Tsubaki © Izumi Tsubaki 2009
All rights reserved. First published in Japan in 2009 by HAKUSENSHA, Inc., Tokyo.
English language translation rights arranged with HAKUSENSHA, Inc., Tokyo.

Printed in Canada

Published by VIZ Media, LLC
P.O. Box 77010
San Francisco, CA 94107

10 9 8 7 6 5 4 3 2 1
First printing, November 2011

www.viz.com   www.shojobeat.com

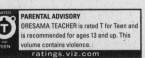